D1336959

05346251

Across the Moscow River

Across the Moscow River

The World Turned Upside Down

Rodric Braithwaite

Yale University Press
New Haven and London

For information about this and other Yale University Press Publications, please contact:
U.S. Office: sales.press@yale.edu   yalebooks.com
Europe Office: sales@yaleup.co.uk   www.yaleup.co.uk

Set in Minion by Northern Phototypesetting Co. Ltd, Bolton, Lancs
Printed in Great Britain by St Edmundsbury Press, Suffolk

Library of Congress Cataloging-in-Publication Data

Braithwaite, Rodric, 1932–
   Across the Moscow River / Rodric Braithwaite.
      p. cm.
Includes bibliographical reference and index.
   ISBN 0-300-09496-5 (cloth : alk.paper)
   1. Russia (Federation)—Politics and goverment—1991–2.
   Post-communism—Russia (Federation) I. Title.
   DK510.763 .B73 2002
   947.086–dc21   2001007277

A catalogue record for this book is available from the British Library.

10 9 8 7 6 5 4 3 2 1

Without Jill's enthusiasm, energy and boundless curiosity, without her knowledge of Russia's language, history, culture and people, my life in Moscow would have been quite different and this book could not have been written. It is dedicated to her with all my love and affection.

Contents

Prologue

Our last day in Petrograd! – and yet, in spite of all that we have gone through, we are sad at the thought. Why is it that Russia casts over all who know her such an indefinable mystic spell that, even when her wayward children have turned their capital into a pandemonium, we are sorry to leave it?

George Buchanan, British ambassador to Russia, 1910–18.

George Buchanan, my immediate predecessor as ambassador to Russia (those who came between were ambassadors to the Soviet Union merely), left Petrograd in January 1918, broken down by eight grinding years of war and revolution. Like so many foreigners before and since, he found it hard to understand why he had become so attached to this immense, shambling, muddy, disorganised, and ferocious country.

Russians, of course, do not expect foreigners to understand them. They quote with approval Pushkin's friend Prince Vyazemsky, who once remarked that if you want a foreigner to make a fool of himself, just ask him to make a judgement about Russia. Today, as in the past, Russians regard their country as almost infinitely mysterious, not to be judged by the normal yardstick of analysis, not to be grasped by the ordinary processes of the mind. They agree with the nineteenth-century poet Tyuchev that Russia can only be judged by the light of faith. That is not a proposition to which someone brought up in the tradition of Western rationalism can easily assent.

I spent four exhilarating years in Moscow during what has – inaccurately – come to be called 'The Second Russian Revolution',[1] the revolution initiated by Gorbachev and consolidated by Yeltsin, the years in which Russia re-emerged from under the carapace of the Soviet Union. On 17 May 1992, my sixtieth birthday, my own last day in the Russian capital, I too attempted to answer the conundrum posed by George Buchanan. I have not devised better words since.

'It is not at first sight', I then wrote, 'the physical look of the place, a boundless plain on which even the oldest cities sit precariously like nomadic encampments. Nor is it the art, the literature and the music, which are among the glories of European culture. Nor is it even the marvellous Russian language, in the view of one of our friends the only thing the Russians have produced whose value is beyond all doubt. All these exercise a fascination which is easier to experience than to explain. But in the end it is the people themselves who constitute the riches of the country. This judgement is none the less true for being wholly unoriginal. Political oppression, the atomisation of society, and generations of poverty have forced the Russian people back on one another. Only in small groups have they been able to muster enough trust to guard against the informer. Only in their kitchens have they felt free to talk – endlessly, ineffectively, and beguilingly – about the problems of life and the universe which their political system has never allowed them to tackle direct. Because they are so vulnerable, human relationships in Russia have an intensity which they lack in the more orderly West. Foreigners can be admitted at least in part to these relationships: Russians are embarrassingly generous with their time and their few possessions, in a way which is wholly uncharacteristic in the West. We would not dream of sharing our last piece of sausage with a guest, not least because either of us could just slip down to the supermarket for another. It is the lack of these things which all Russians notice as soon as they go abroad, and which makes exile so hard for them to bear.

'Above all, Russia is an epic country, not only in its size but in its moral quality. Because it is a land where the lie has been erected into a principle of conduct, concepts such as Truth, Honour, Loyalty, Courage have a real meaning for the most ordinary of people, who are continually having to make the kind of choices which Englishmen have not had to make since our Civil War three hundred years ago. To us these big words are an embarrassment. For Russians they are an inescapable part of everyday life. Because Russia has always been a land of villains, it is also a land of heroes and saints. Without Stalin, there could have been no Solzhenitsyn and no Sakharov.'

It was not all that easy to be confident of Russia's future as Jill and I left Moscow for the last time. The capital's public buildings were collapsing, the roads were full of potholes, the shops were quite literally empty, ancient ladies sold their family treasures on the pavements, and refugees from the Caucasus and Central Asia camped in the metro. The battered Aeroflot Ilyushin in which we flew to Peking was crowded with equally dilapidated Russians loaded with petty consumer goods to sell in the Peking markets: a profitable undertaking because Aeroflot had still not learned to charge a commercial rate for its tickets.

And yet we left convinced that Russia retained its greatness and that it could, and with any luck would, rise to the unprecedented challenges it faced. Over the next decade, despite the traumas and the setbacks, Russia did indeed continue to stumble away from its authoritarian and imperial past towards its own version of a workable market democracy. Perhaps even the rational Westerner has to conclude that it does after all help to judge Russia by the light of faith as well as reason.

Faith, a dash of hope, and some of that charitable understanding which Russians have not often enjoyed from those who look in on them from outside.

1

The View across the River

... Moscow, with her stonework white
And ancient cupolas, all blazing
With golden crosses fiery-bright.

Pushkin, *Eugene Onegin*

On that first night in September 1988, Jill and I went fearfully to bed in Pavel Kharitonenko's great mansion on the Moscow River. Dark, cavernous, menacing, it seemed a lonely and uneasy place to begin nearly four years of life in Moscow during the Second Russian Revolution. But the house, with its magnificent view of the Kremlin, came to symbolise for both of us the Russia that had existed before the First Revolution in October 1917, the Russia of brash and increasingly self-confident entrepreneurs, men like Pavel's father Ivan, the ex-serf who had become rich in the sugar business, the Russia that might perhaps eventually rise like a Phoenix from the reforms of Gorbachev and his successors.

Despite that first impression, we were of course never alone in the building. We had no front door of our own. A Gothic staircase led down to the front hall, bearing carved on its banister a perched eagle, a crouching dragon, and the date of 1893 when the house was built. By day the hall was like Piccadilly Circus as people streamed into the embassy offices, an overcrowded warren of partitioned spaces on the ground floor. By night it fell silent, and was inhabited by the two security guards, endlessly prowling to prevent the ingenious KGB from slinking in through the cellars or through the doors, part of the endless battle to secure a building which was by nature as leaky as the Jumblies' sieve. We lived in a goldfish bowl which resembled not at all the Englishman's traditional castle. The ambassador's private residence on the first floor consisted of two main rooms only: a large sitting room, and a rather smaller bedroom. The two were connected by a small room, divided by a partition reaching halfway up to the ceiling. On the other side of the partition were a bath, a washbasin, and a lavatory. Here the ambassador and his wife performed their ablutions almost as publicly as Louis XIV, the Sun King: usually without the entourage of courtiers, though on one occasion one of my staff penetrated into the 'bathroom' on an urgent official matter, apparently without noticing that Jill was standing beside me with almost no clothes on. The sitting room was littered with books and newspapers, and piled high with medical supplies and wheel-chairs for the various charities in which Jill was involved, since there was nowhere else for them to be stored.

The public rooms of the 'Residence' were designed in an exuberantly eclectic variety of styles by Fyodor (Franz) Shekhtel (1859–1926), the fashionable Art Nouveau architect, associated with Charles Rennie Mackintosh of Glasgow. On the first floor, at the top of the staircase, was the great dining room, in the style of the Second Empire with massive portraits of Victoria, her son Edward VII and her grandson George V, and their two wives. George looked so like his cousin that Soviet guests used to fall silent before plucking up the courage to ask why we had a picture of the last Tsar Nicholas II on our wall.

The rococo 'White and Gold' ballroom overlooked the river and the Kremlin. It still contained the First Empire furniture, in the mock-Egyptian style known as 'Retour de l'Egypte', which had once belonged to Kharitonenko himself. Dominated by an unconvincing reproduction of Annigoni's portrait of the young Elizabeth II, this room was ideal for parties and concerts. The Borodin Quartet played for us there twice, and Stephen Isserlis once. It provided the perfect setting for two performances of Mozart's *Figaro* by Pavilion Opera. Students from the Conservatoire practised their chamber music, enjoyed some decent cooking for once, and occasionally allowed me to join in on my viola.

The Renaissance room, heavily panelled, contained a collection of English marine paintings from the eighteenth century, much appreciated by General Leonov, the first cosmonaut to walk in space, and himself a competent amateur painter. From this room you could walk out onto the terrace overlooking the river, or on into the sitting room. This was even more heavily panelled, with its huge fireplace carved with medieval hunting scenes, and the grotesque garden gnomes on the ceiling, but still intimate enough for everyday life. Finally came an even more ornate bathroom, leading into a guest room in which the traces of Art Nouveau decoration could still be dimly discerned. On the second floor were further guest rooms, carved out of the attics, accessible only through the kitchen, and at first without a lavatory between them.

The magnificence did not extend to the ground floor. In Kharitonenko's day there had been, to the left of the entrance hall, a dining room and a panelled library with a cast iron spiral staircase leading to an upper range of bookshelves. To the right were more panelled reception rooms. All had suffered grievously at the hands of generations of British bureaucrats packed into the grand rooms like sardines, who had erected shelves, drilled holes, run wiring, and pinned up their Christmas cards on such of the elegantly carved panelling as survived. The rest, so rumour had it, was burned by one of the postwar ambassadors because it took up too much storage space in the attic.

At the end of the entrance hall a short corridor led into another large room giving out onto the garden. This was the ambassador's study. It had suffered in a different way. In the 1970s it was refurnished by the Ministry of Works in what they fondly believed was the height of modern British design. The furniture was rosewood, stainless steel, and black leather. Apart from a pastel portrait of Queen Victoria in an oval frame and a marble bust of William Cobbett, the pictures were modern and British, in colours variously garish and drab. They attracted admiring comments from knowledgeable visitors, but did nothing for the room. The overall effect was one of muddled and amateurish bad taste. Over the next two years, under pressure from Jill, it was transformed to look like one of the grander nineteenth-century offices in Whitehall, with furniture to match and portraits of Charles II and other British worthies to keep Victoria company.

The outside of the house was pleasant enough, though the architect Vasili Zalessky (born 1847) was no innovator like Shekhtel. Two separate wings abutted onto the Sofiiskaya Naberezhnaya, the embankment on which the mansion was built. One contained the defence attachés, the other the Russian administration, and both shared party walls with the neighbouring buildings, a great convenience for the KGB's eavesdroppers. The main body of the house, painted in a pale yellow wash with the architectural details picked out in white, was set back in a courtyard, with a raised *porte-cochère* and a terrace above. At the back was a garden, with a battered tennis court on which a lethal game of broomball – a primitive form of ice hockey – was played during the winter months, and a collection of low buildings which had formerly been the stable block.

When we arrived in Moscow in September 1988 the building was under sentence, at least in its function as an embassy. At the end of the Second World War, Stalin decided that it was inconvenient and probably insecure to have the embassies of his former allies so close to the Kremlin. After a brief tussle the American embassy was decanted from its building facing Red Square and removed to a ramshackle multistorey building several miles distant. Either because they were better negotiators or worse administrators the British remained where they were. Negotiations about an alternative site continued on and off for the next four decades. But by 1988 the unholy alliance between the KGB (who thought the British were eavesdropping on the Kremlin), the British Security Service (who thought the KGB were eavesdropping on us), and the British Treasury (who thought the whole thing was a gross extravagance) appeared to have won the day. The British ambassador would go to live on a landlocked site in the shadow of his American colleague's imposing residence – a satisfactory metaphor for the Special Relationship. A new office would be built further up the river.

An architectural competition for the new residence was already in full swing. The Duke of Gloucester was chairman of the panel of judges. Three weeks after our arrival the short list of designs was displayed in the embassy. Most were wholly unsuitable, either for their function as a working building, or as an addition to the cityscape of Moscow. The architects on the panel favoured a design that looked like a Zeppelin hangar from the 1930s. When we protested, we were told that we were not qualified to judge. We favoured a neo-classical design by Julian Bicknell, which had been carefully planned to fit the Moscow style and to function flexibly as luxury hotel and restaurant, concert house, and conference centre: which is what an ambassadorial residence is for. Jill spent a whole night writing a memorandum for the Duke explaining the practical advantages of Julian Bicknell's design. The two architects voted against, but the Duke exercised his decisive casting vote in favour. The architectural press universally condemned the choice because it 'failed to make a statement about British architecture in the centre of Moscow'. One commentator admitted sourly that the winning design might provide a workable base from which the ambassador and his wife could do their job. But he seemed to regard that as an additional criticism.

We were not alone in the battle to keep the house. Leonid Zamyatin, the Soviet ambassador in London, wanted to keep his large official residence in Kensington Palace Gardens, and believed that there was a deal to be done. Professor Arbatov, the wily old director of the Institute for the USA and Canada, argued that the KGB's fears were absurd. For one thing, he used to tell them, with modern technology the British could listen to what was going on in the Kremlin from anywhere in the city; and for another, nothing that went on in the Kremlin was worth listening to anyway.

Mrs Thatcher won the final victory. 'One of the few points on which the Foreign Office and I agreed', she later admitted, 'was the need for British embassies to be architecturally imposing and provided with fine pictures and furniture'; or as she remarked to me, 'Prestige has no price!' She brushed aside the attempts of the Whitehall bureaucrats to demonstrate that there was no money available. She badgered Gorbachev incessantly. At lunch in Moscow in June 1990 she had a final go. Gorbachev turned to Shevardnadze, his Foreign Minister, who reluctantly admitted that he could see no real objection. The Soviet Foreign Ministry officials clustering outside protested when I told them what had happened. Did they think, I asked them, that the President of the Soviet Union and the Prime Minister of Great Britain had just made a mistake? No, no, of course not, they chorused. They tried to claw the thing back later. But the deal was done.

There was a price to pay. In 1931 the Kharitonenko house had been more than large enough to accommodate the ambassador, his family, and his small staff. By 1988 the embassy consisted of an ambassador, his deputy, six counsellors, nine service attachés, and other British staff to a total of seventy. The pressure on space was almost more than the building or its inhabitants could bear. The British Council, the embassy doctor, the embassy shop, and the visa section fought for space in the stable block at the back. The political section, the communications, and the archives were crowded three and four to a room on the ground floor of the main building.

It was not only inefficient: it was insecure and demoralising for the people who had to live and work there. For all its grandeur the house was barely equal to its function as a small but busy office-block-cum-hotel. Perestroika was fashionable. No self-respecting Cabinet Minister could afford to go to a London dinner party unless he had just been to Moscow or was just about to go there. By the time we left Moscow we had been visited by Margaret Thatcher three times, John Major twice, the Foreign Secretary six times, and by nine other Cabinet ministers, four junior ministers, three members of the royal family, the Governor of the Bank of England, the Chief of the Defence Staff, the Chief of the General Staff, the First Sea Lord, the American Commander in Chief of NATO, and a host of only slightly more junior officials. The hotels in Moscow were dire: the rooms were dreadful; the food was worse; the telephones did not work; there was no fax. So we supplied the deficiency of food, accommodation, transport, and communications. Our domestic arrangements were under constant strain. Shopping, cooking, drawing up guest lists, ensuring that invitations were delivered, tracking down acceptances – all was like wading through treacle.

Slowly Jill put together a ramshackle organisation, advised and supported by Noel Marshall, my deputy, who was an indispensable prop in our first faltering weeks. She shopped in the Moscow markets and supervised the cooking. The maids, the cooks and the laundrywoman referred to themselves as 'the girls', and addressed one another with raucous nicknames – 'Nin', 'Liud', 'Marin'. They belied their lethargic appearance at ordinary times by their hardworking efficiency when we entertained. Of course they kept an eye on us as well for the benefit of 'the organs'. I did not mind if they borrowed my address book or my bank statements in order to photocopy them for the KGB. It seemed to be a matter of supreme unimportance whether the KGB knew who my friends in Britain were, or whether they knew that I had on the whole a fairly healthy bank balance. I did however get very angry with the maids on one occasion when I thought they had taken some undeveloped films. I called them in, told them I knew perfectly well what they were up to, and asked them to return the films immediately. They scattered around in a panic of apprehension mixed with irritation that I had broken the convention that one does not talk about these things, even if one knows perfectly well that they happen. The films were not found. But they eventually turned up under our bed, where I knew perfectly well they had never been.

Jill revived the post of 'Social Secretary', and we had in succession three admirable Russian speakers to fill it: Carmel Power, Alison Watt, and Ann Brown, all with boundless energy, enthusiasm and common sense. Lena, the Russian cook, rapidly learned Jill's recipes. Stephen Baldwin, whose only relevant experience was working in an Australian men's club, joined to do the shopping, help in the kitchen, and act as pastrycook. He was immediately adopted as a mascot by 'the girls'. It was a flimsy arrangement. But it worked. By the time we left Moscow the entertainment machine was functioning surprisingly smoothly.

Two other people inevitably became very close: my drivers Konstantin Demakhin and Sasha Motov. They acted as a Greek chorus commenting on the passing scene; or more precisely, like the low-life characters who figure in so many Russian operas – Varlaam and Missail in *Boris Godunov*, Grisha in *The Invisible City of Kitezh*, Skula and Yeroshka in *Prince Igor* – drunk, irreverent, the voice of the people; except that for professional reasons neither Sasha nor Konstantin were ever (I am glad to say) drunk, at least in my presence. Our discussions about politics became increasingly lively as we got to know one another better. Their judgements were often superior to my own. I would sometimes have done better to listen to them more carefully. I naturally assumed that they both reported our conversations to the KGB. But I was reasonably sure that, like Lady Pettigrue, I corrupted them more than they ever corrupted me.[1]

Konstantin was the senior of the two: he had been with the embassy for seventeen years, for many of them as the ambassador's driver. He was quite different from the prudent, orderly, and deferential Sasha, and the two men disliked one another intensely. With his long black sideburns and gypsy looks, Konstantin had a swashbuckling manner, and a conspiratorial way of speaking as though everything he told you verged on the politically improper. His life history was erratic. His grandparents were kulaks from Orel, south of Moscow. They had been denounced to the authorities by one of his uncles: something he claimed to have discovered only in the later years of Perestroika. He had worked on the cosmodrome in Kazakhstan, been a champion rally driver, held the prize for motorcycling on ice, and was still active among the stunt-drivers at the Moscow film studios. He boasted of his connections with the underworld which clung to the fringes of Soviet sport. As our conversations became more intimate, he revealed more and more about the darker side of his life. His father had been an officer in the NKVD. Konstantin remembered him returning from work at five and six in the morning during the purge year of 1937: hotfoot from rounding up fodder for the Gulag. It was only towards the end of our association that he gave a reasonably accurate account of his own involvement with 'the organs'.

Konstantin's professional skills as a stunt-driver were not necessarily those required by the chauffeur of an ambassadorial Rolls-Royce. He loved to show off by speeding over potholes and through snowdrifts in the most scarifying manner. Shortly after we arrived in Moscow we went to see Gorbachev and his wife off on the trip that was to take him to the United Nations and to Britain. The huge marble terminal at Vnukovo airport was empty except for Gorbachev and his entourage; and the cloud of colleagues, sycophants, and officials who had come to pay their respects. We foreigners hung around on one side of the reception hall while Gorbachev held an informal meeting of the Politburo on the other. Then in a spattering of kisses and waving hands he departed, while the rest of us stood in a line on the tarmac, in rough protocol order, trying to look as if we were enjoying ourselves. It was a ritual tediously repeated on many later occasions. This time we were in a hurry to get back for a lunch date, and foolishly asked Konstantin to make his best speed home. Inexorably he pursued the procession of black limousines taking Prime Minister Ryzhkov and his colleagues back to Moscow. Mud and slush spattered the leaders of the second most powerful country in the world as we started to overtake them. It was only when the escort cars began to weave menacingly ahead of us that Jill and I, who had been deep in conversation, began to notice what was going on. I made Konstantin slow down, thinking ruefully that I had never met the Soviet Prime Minister, and now I probably never would.

Sasha Motov was a complete contrast. Flashily handsome, dapper and fleshy, with jet black hair and eyes, his main ambition was to please. He had an ailing wife, and two daughters of whom he was immensely proud. Like so many Russians seeking an explanation of a world that was falling about their ears, he was a passionate believer in extrasensory perception, flying saucers, and Kashpirovsky, the fashionable faith-healer who exercised his healing powers on a gullible public through the television, and later became a supporter of the exhibitionist nationalist Zhirinovsky. Kashpirovsky's influence was almost universal. The Deputy Director of the prestigious Institute of the World Economy and International Relations (IMEMO) believed that Kashpirovsky had done wonders for his gout. A woman I met in church asked me to intercede with Kashpirovsky on behalf of her sick daughter: a touching faith in the powers of ambassadors as well as faith-healers. The belief in flying saucers was even more widespread. Sasha's mother once saw a flying saucer out of her bedroom window at night. It was hovering over the Yaroslavl Highway and looked like an upturned bath. Unfortunately Sasha was unable to find his camera in time to photograph it. In October 1989 TASS, the Soviet news agency, reported that a flying saucer had landed in the Park of Culture and Rest in Voronezh. The crew of aliens walked around the park for a while, then flew away, no one knew whither. Afterwards, so TASS said, the imprints of the alien machine's landing gear were clearly visible in the flowerbeds.

My predecessor Bryan Cartledge had warned me that Sasha would bore me to distraction by repeating the latest Party line as dictated to him by his bosses in UPDK, the agency attached to the Foreign Ministry which supplied our Russian staff and was the KGB's instrument of control over them. I was pleasantly surprised. Ordinary Russians, lamenting the state of their country, would tell you time and again: 'What can we do about it? We are only little people, slaves. All we can do is suffer, as the Russian people have always suffered.' Only rarely did they consider the possibility that a people gets the government it deserves. Sasha started in the same vein. But in the course of our many conversations he became steadily less orthodox. He canvassed for the opposition during the elections in March 1989, handed in his Party card with fear and trepidation a year before the Communist Party was banned, stood his term on the barricades in August 1991, and thereafter worked to ensure that his daughters learned the commercial skills which he thought they would most require in the New Russia. His Russian patriotism grew more articulate as Yeltsin's Russia began to emerge from the shadow of the Soviet Union. He returned from a family trip on the Volga during the summer holiday of 1990 furious with indignation at the decay which the ancient cities had suffered during the years of Communist rule. In our first weekend in Moscow he surprised me by saying, in a car which had presumably been wired for sound, that 'it was a pity that Gorbachev had been given two terms of office at the 19th Party Conference. One would have been enough, then we could have got rid of him and had someone competent instead.' No official driver would have dared to speak like that in earlier years. It was a vivid illustration of the underlying irony of Gorbachev's position. The very people to whom he had given freedom of expression already felt confident about using it to attack him.

Pavel Ivanovich Kharitonenko (1853–1914), the man who built the great mansion and whose name is still carved into the gateways which flank the two entrances, was a member of Moscow's powerful merchant class. The mansion itself was a symbol of the transformation which was taking place in Russian social, political, economic, and cultural life at the end of the nineteenth century.

The Moscow merchants of his day were the descendants of a class which had been carefully defined and regulated under the Tsarist system since the seventeenth century. They represented the continuity of a style of life that had begun in the Middle Ages and had, until the last thirty or forty years of the Tsarist regime, changed surprisingly little. The Russian merchants of the seventeenth, eighteenth, and the first part of the nineteenth century bore little resemblance to the bankers, industrialists, innovators, agents, and adventurers of contemporary Western Europe. They traded in furs, foodstuffs, textiles, and simple handicraft products. Their word in a bargain was not always to be relied upon, and they preferred a quick and if necessary illicit profit to the fostering of a long-term relationship with their customers. They were ignorant men, brutal patriarchs in their domestic life, pious after a stiff-necked fashion. They resented the attempts of Peter the Great to make them shave their beards and to force them into Western dress. They were organised by the state into rigid guilds for purposes of tax collection and local administration. But these guilds never acquired the political weight of their opposite numbers in the bustling commercial cities of Western Europe. Progress from the Third to the First Guilds, and perhaps to the title of Honoured Citizen, represented the extent of these men's social ambition. They were relentlessly despised by the gentry and the intelligentsia above them, and resented by the peasantry below. They were ruthlessly satirised in the works of Russia's first great playwright, Aleksandr Ostrovsky (1823–1886).

Despite the inbred conservatism of these men, the more energetic and enterprising among them had been carving out industrial and commercial empires for themselves from the sixteenth century onwards. Some got rich through tax farming and the vodka monopoly. Some, like the Demidov and Stroganov families, developed the mineral wealth of the Urals with the active encouragement of the Tsars. And towards the end of the eighteenth and the beginning of the nineteenth centuries another striking phenomenon appeared. The old merchant class, especially in Moscow, began to find that they were being outperformed by competitors from the peasantry. At a remarkable rate enterprising peasants began to buy themselves free from their masters and seek work in the towns. In 1826 alone well over half a million serfs managed to get the necessary papers to leave the land. Their former owners usually insisted on taking a substantial part of whatever profits they might make. But the movement continued to grow until it peaked on the eve of the emancipation of the serfs in 1861. Many of these people worked as hired labourers. But a significant minority went into business and industry on their own account in the cities of the Volga and in Moscow itself, trading, manufacturing cheap consumer goods and textiles, and money-lending. It was a remarkable display of social mobility, of a kind which one does not easily associate with the rigidities of the Tsarist regime. And from these people sprang many of the great commercial dynasties of the last decades of the Tsarist empire.

Many of them came also from the Old Belief, the schismatics who had broken away from the official Orthodox Church in the seventeenth century in protest against reforms introduced by Tsar Aleksei and his Patriarch Nikon. Fiercely independent, deeply pious, these men were willing to die for their belief if necessary. But in the meanwhile, they – like the dissenters in England at about the same time – saw nothing against engaging, more energetically than their fellows, in the business of trade and commerce.

The first generation of these new men – the men who flourished in the middle of the nineteenth century – were nationalistic, anti-Semitic, fearful of competition from the Jewish, German, and Polish periphery. They were deeply conservative and respectful of the authority of the Tsar and the bureaucracy. Not only foreigners, but also Tsarist officials commented that they still hung onto the shifty business standards of their forefathers. One British merchant remarked: 'A dexterous theft in the way of overreaching is regarded by them as the very triumph of their genius.'

But their sons had greater social, commercial, and even political ambitions. They abandoned the old dress and many of the old ways. It was they, rather than the gentry who had earlier made the running, who were in the lead as Russia began to move towards something like a capitalist system in the last thirty years of the Tsarist regime. They moved out of the traditional merchant activities of textile production, vodka, timber and sugar into banking and industry, railways, newspapers, publishing and foreign trade. They adopted modern methods of business, and encouraged commercial and professional training. Many of them had a European education and they were more broad-minded than their fathers. But they too were Russian nationalists. Like many other Russians – of their day, and even a century later – they believed that Russia could find a 'Third Way' which would enable the country to prosper without going through the painful social disruption that had accompanied industrialisation in Western Europe. They patronised new movements in Russian art, literature, the theatre. They supported Diaghilev and his ballet, and encouraged the brilliant school of Russian painting of the 1890s and the first decades of the twentieth century. The Tretyakov brothers founded Moscow's Museum of Russian Art. The Morozovs and the Mamontovs founded the Moscow Art Theatre where many of Chekhov's plays were first performed. As a symbol of their emancipation, many of them moved from the Zamoskvorechie, the area south of the river where the Old Believers had traditionally lived, and built themselves spectacular Art Nouveau and Russian revivalist mansions in more fashionable parts of Moscow – several to the design of Franz Shekhtel.

The rise to wealth and position of the Kharitonenko family followed the pattern. Ivan Gerasimovich Kharitonenko (1820–1891) came from near Sumy in the Northern Ukraine. Contemporaries always remarked that Ivan 'came from the people'. His family were state serfs, and he too may have been a freed serf. He was entirely self-made and owed his success to his intelligence, his capacity for work, his moral character, his outstanding enterprise, and his remarkable energy. 'They say', his admiring and loquacious obituarist remarks, 'that colossal fortunes cannot be created out of nothing: they are always based on some dark deal.' But Ivan apparently disproved this rule, and even his enemies never attempted to argue the contrary. Beginning as a young assistant to a local merchant, he had already amassed a little capital by the time of the emancipation of the serfs. That event unleashed his energies and launched him on an independent commercial career in the sugar business. The Ukrainian sugar industry had not flourished in the hands of the unenterprising local landowners who had previously dominated it. New men like Ivan Kharitonenko turned it into one of the most dynamic and heavily mechanised industrial sectors in the Russian empire. Thanks partly to their skill in securing concessions from the government, by the middle of the nineteenth century the Ukrainians were producing four-fifths of the empire's granulated sugar, and by 1914 Ukrainian production was second only to that in Germany.

Ivan prospered too. By 1913 'Kharitonenko I.G. and Son', the company Ivan had founded in 1884 in Sumy, owned about 65,000 hectares of arable land in Ukraine, a sugar refinery, and eight sugar factories. In the early 1880s Ivan built a country house, which he named 'Natalevka' after his grand-daughter, on an estate which he carved out of unpromising sandy territory north of Kharkov. In 1915 a fashionable magazine – still publishing despite the war – inaccurately described the house as 'a cross between a Swiss chalet and English cottage'.[2] Ivan's cattle- and horse-breeding establishments attracted favourable attention from as far away as Germany, and his horses regularly won in the Moscow races. He founded a student hostel in Kiev, a church in his home village, civil and military academies, charitable hostels, a hospital, and a cathedral and orphanage in Sumy itself. For these public benefactions the authorities awarded him the official title of Actual Civil Counsellor (equating to a major general in the army) which brought with it formal hereditary membership of the gentry. There is a photograph of him at this stage in his career: bald, with a humorous twinkle in his eye, a man of obvious force and will. Fifteen thousand people attended his funeral. The grateful townspeople of Sumy erected a statue to him in their main square, for which his son provided half of the finance. It was torn down after the October Revolution to make way for a statue of Lenin.

As the Ukrainian sugar industry expanded, it began to compete with the established industry in Moscow and the Russian heartland. This was of course by no means to the taste of the Moscow merchants, who by the middle of the nineteenth century were already complaining about unfair compe-tition. Ivan Kharitonenko followed the trend. In 1879 he bought a house on the Moscow River where the present mansion now stands. At first he used the yard of the old house to store sugar. But in 1891 he died, and his son Pavel Ivanovich began work on a new building which was completed in 1893.

Pavel continued his father's progress up the social ladder. His wife, Vera Andreyevna Bakeyeva, came from a family of gentry with estates near Kursk, towards the border with Ukraine. Their daughter Natalia married Prince Gorchakov, the grandson of one of Russia's longest serving foreign ministers. The other daughter married a fashionable guards officer. The Kharitonenko family had thus moved far since the days of their serfdom. They do not, however, appear to have followed the more prominent Moscow merchants into municipal and national politics, nor into new kinds of commercial activity. They did not diversify out of the sugar industry. Nor, when Pavel built his fashionable new mansion, did he take the opportunity to follow the Morozovs and the Riabushinskis and others out of the Zamoskvorechie, with its old-fashioned atmosphere, into the more fashionable areas north of the river. The family seems, perhaps, to have remained of a somewhat conservative bent.

In addition to expanding the family business – the refinery in Sumy became the largest in the country – Pavel too had a strong sense of his civic duties. He was an elder of his local church of St Sofia just along the Moscow River from his new mansion, and he paid for its restoration. He paid the fees for twenty students at the Moscow Conservatoire of which he was a director. He built schools and medical clinics at all his factories. And on the eve of the war he made a substantial financial contribution to the expansion of the Russian air force, which at that stage was probably the most advanced in the world. His photograph shows a typical member of the prosperous European middle class of the turn of the century: bearded, self-satisfied, indistinguishable from his peers in Edwardian England. But his portrait as painted by Valentin Serov (1865–1911), one of Russia's greatest painters, seems to show a different side of him: a rather weak face, the face of one of Chekhov's ineffective intellectuals. Those who knew him in his prime describe a man solid but emotional, haunting art exhibitions, buying pictures, and patronising artists, entertaining lavishly and extravagantly, hobnobbing with the aristocracy, a passionate huntsman, perhaps a bit of a snob and a playboy. Kharitonenko was not one of the great innovative collectors, men like Sergei Shchukin who were among the first to appreciate and to buy the early works of Picasso and Matisse. He did not help to launch the Russian avant-garde, like his fellow Muscovite Savva Morozov. But he had the largest collection of pictures by the well-known painter Nesterov (1862–1942), who painted the icons for the little church that Pavel built at Natalevka to a design by the architect Shchusev. And the gallery in what is now the Second Empire dining room contained the arrogant *Portrait of an Unknown Woman* by Ivan Kramskoi (1837–1887), a picture known to most Russians, and indeed to many people in Britain as well, since it figures on the front cover of the Penguin edition of *Anna Karenina*.

One suspects that Vera, a reserved and pinched-faced woman, was the driving force in the family's social life. Chaliapin is supposed to have sung in the White and Gold room, and Prokofiev to have played the piano there. Nesterov describes a Christmas party in the house in 1912 which was attended by over three hundred guests, aristocracy and merchants alike. Nesterov's two small children were given presents off the tree worth a hundred roubles each. Next came a 'spectacle' produced by a distinguished actor from the Moscow Art Theatre, in which the participants were the gilded youth of Moscow led by Pavel's son Ivan, whom Vera used to refer to gloomily as 'the only one we've got'. Although the show went on until very late, Nesterov and his wife were unable to escape the dinner that followed, elegant service and tables covered with flowers. Not until four o'clock in the morning were they able to get away, sent home by their hosts in a newfangled motor car.

Robert Bruce Lockhart, in his *Memoirs of a British Agent*, gives a similar glimpse of the style in which the Kharitonenkos entertained. In January 1912, as a newly appointed Vice Consul in Moscow, he accompanied a British parliamentary delegation to a reception there. The delegation, eighty strong, was led by the Speaker, and included four bishops and the notorious Admiral Sir Charles Beresford. By the time the delegates arrived in Moscow from St Petersburg their number had been depleted by the rigours of the hospitality they had already experienced. The Kharitonenkos invited all Moscow to meet them. The house was bursting with flowers despite the season, orchestras played in every room, and the main staircase was packed with guests struggling to get in, as it was to be eight decades later. Endless drinks and endless hors d'oeuvres were followed by dinner, dancing, and in the small hours a ride by troika out to the famous (or notorious) gypsy restaurant Strelna on the outskirts of the city.

Bruce Lockhart's neighbour at dinner had been Commander Kakhovsky, the Russian officer acting as naval aide to Beresford. Next morning Lockhart heard that the young man had shot himself by the telephone after hearing from St Petersburg that his mistress had deserted him. Generations of British diplomats have assumed that the tragedy must have occurred at the height of the festivities and in the Kharitonenko house itself, though this is not supported either by contemporary evidence or the laws of probability.[3]

Scholars disagree violently about how far the Tsarist economy had advanced by 1914, about whether it could have produced the kind of economic growth, and the kind of social and political change, that would have brought Russia to prosperity and liberal democracy. One school of thought holds that, if you look at the figures properly, the Russian economy was growing in the last thirty years before the First World War at rates comparable or even superior to those of Western Europe. A genuine capitalist class was emerging, with an increasing sense that its prosperity could best be assured by adopting standards of professionalism and probity comparable with those in the West. Russia had become part of the world economy. Foreigners were willing to invest very substantially in the country and Russian stock was traded in London, Paris and Amsterdam as well as in Moscow and St Petersburg. Even agriculture was beginning to do well, though massive grain exports were still punctuated from time to time by devastating famines. Russian scientists made major contributions to knowledge, and received two of the earliest Nobel Prizes. Russian military technologists produced the first four-engined bomber in history, the *Ilya Muromets*.[4] Political turmoil apart, these people say, the likelihood was that by the end of the twentieth century Russia would have become a world economic power capable of offering living standards to its citizens comparable with those prevailing in Western Europe. The most optimistic amongst them believe that even the politics was beginning to settle down in the decade after the revolution of 1905.

There are plenty who argue the opposite case. They admit that two of Russia's prime ministers – Witte (1849–1915) and Stolypin (1862–1911) – had a clear vision of what was needed to modernise the Russian economy. They recognise that the economy was indeed growing on the eve of the war. But they argue that the ponderous and self-serving Tsarist bureaucracy had no conception of the needs of business. Even the most progressive bureaucrats believed that ever more elaborate government regulation was the best way to guide the country towards prosperity – a philosophy which had the added advantage of preserving their own power. Although there were indeed the glimmerings of a capitalist class, the new men were still hamstrung by their origins, and by the deference they continued to pay towards their betters in the aristocracy and around the court. Some structural changes had taken place in the economy by the time the First World War began. But they were fragile and half-baked. The chances that these achievements would have survived in the febrile political atmosphere of Tsarist Russia were slim. They were scuppered by the combination of the incompetent and reactionary Tsar Nicholas II, the ruthless, narrow-minded, and in his way equally incompetent revolutionary Lenin, and the destructive tornado of the First World War.

Even a regime more enlightened than that of the last Tsar, even one that was unburdened by the accidents of war and revolution, would still have had to overcome the two factors which have always made Russia almost unmanageable: Russia's intense poverty and its almost unimaginable size. The question then was the same as it is now: Is Russia capable of change, or is it condemned by history and geography endlessly to repeat its mistakes? But even a cautious observer might conclude that far-reaching change was clearly under way in Kharitonenko's Russia. It would be stretching scepticism too far to conclude that a Russia unravaged by war and revolution could have stood wholly aside from the currents which within a century had given universal suffrage, social security, and a hitherto unimagined level of prosperity to the peoples of the West.

The Moscow merchants, and their brethren in St Petersburg, Odessa, and the other great cities of the Empire would have played a key role. They may not yet have been capitalists in the Western sense. But they were serious men, both in their businesses and in their sense of civic responsibility. They were no mere asset-strippers and profiteers, battening on a decaying state like the 'oligarchs' who followed them in the Yeltsin era nine decades later. They were never numerous: the leading merchant families numbered no more than one hundred. They were ill at ease in a society where their simple origins and their commercial pursuits were still despised by court and aristocracy. Even at the height of their influence under the energetic Riabushinsky, they were not particularly effective in national politics, which remained dominated by the gentry, the Petersburg bureaucracy, and increasingly by the left-wing revolutionary parties. Nevertheless the rise from simple beginnings to respectable and sophisticated prosperity of the Kharitonenkos, the Morozovs, the Mamontovs and others marked a revolution in Russia's social and political life, and the beginning of Russia's transformation into a bourgeois capitalist state. The two Kharitonenkos and their peers from among 'the people' amply demonstrate the capacity of Russians to adapt to the modern world.

Pavel died in 1914 and was buried in Shchusev's church at Natalevka. Vera kept the business going for a few brief years. Then came the October Revolution in 1917. The house was briefly caught in the crossfire as the Bolsheviks sought to capture the Kremlin from the Whites. Vera prudently donated her paintings to the new Revolutionary authorities, and the Kharitonenkos left, to settle in Paris, Brussels, and Canada. The mansion became a guesthouse for visiting friends of the new regime: H. G. Wells, Arthur Ransome, Armand Hammer, and Enver Pasha, the politician who led Turkey into the First World War and found an obscure death in Central Asia trying to raise the Pan-Turkic flag against the Bolsheviks. Next the mansion was used to accommodate Soviet officials from the Commissariat of Foreign Affairs, many of whom were later shot in the purges. Finally, in 1931, it became the residence and offices of the British ambassador, returning to Moscow after the hiatus in relations caused by the British police raid in 1927 on the London offices of 'Arcos', the Soviet trade delegation. While the Soviet regime preserved its grip, Russians dared to visit the house only if they had a watertight official excuse. But as the country opened up under Gorbachev, Russians with an earlier connection with the building began to reassert their interest: relatives of Kharitonenko himself, the granddaughter of Shekhtel, the Litvinovs who had lived there as children when their father was Deputy Commissar for Foreign Affairs in the new Bolshevik state; and the municipal authorities from Sumy, now planning to re-erect the statue of Ivan Gerasimovich Kharitonenko in the town he had done so much to benefit.

There used to be a tradition in the British embassy that Kharitonenko built his mansion on the river facing the Kremlin because, as an Old Believer, he wished to have a constant view of Russia's Holy Places. The grounds for this tradition are shaky, to say the least. The Old Believers regarded the Tsar, the official Church, and all their works – including no doubt the Kremlin itself – as manifestations of the Antichrist. The real reason why old Ivan Kharitonenko chose the site was because it was a convenient place to store his sugar. And the church of which his son was warden was wholly Orthodox.

But it is certainly true that the view from the terrace at the front of the house is its greatest glory. For it looks straight across the river at the Kremlin, the central point of a city like no other, half European, half Asian, an imperial city radiating power, the great red walls built by Italian engineers in the fifteenth century to resemble the walls of Verona, the cathedrals built in the next century also by Italians, but in the finest style of medieval Russian church architecture; the nineteenth-century imperial residence in the neo-classical style, quintessentially Russian whatever the nationality of the architect. And above it all, the golden domes, the golden crosses which the Bolsheviks failed to remove, the red stars and the Red Flag which they placed to proclaim their domination, the symbols of two religions, the religion of Christ subservient and coexisting uneasily with the religion of Marx. In the red sunset, in the golden autumn, on a clear white winter's day, in the rain, the slush and the fog which dominate much of the Moscow year, whatever the weather the view across the river is a perpetual feast for the eye. Senior Russian officials come to the embassy on the insistence of their wives just to see the view. Visiting ministers and journalists gasp with delight even as they meditate their next attack on idleness and high living in the British Foreign Service. That image of the Kremlin has become the cliché of Western newscasters, advertising executives, and TV audiences.

As for ourselves, the view across the river never lost its grip on our imagination and our emotions. It was from there that we saw the cheerful crowds on their way to celebrate May Day or the anniversary of the October Revolution. It was from that terrace that we saw the tanks rolling past the Kremlin on parade or moving towards a coup. And it was from that terrace, at 7.35 p.m. on the evening of Christmas Day 1991, that we saw the Red Flag flutter down from the Kremlin for the very last time.

2

The Russians are Coming

When during the last 1000 years have such enormous acquisitions been made in so brief a period by any European conqueror? ... There is no sane mind in Europe that can look with satisfaction at the immense and rapid overgrowth of Russian power.

The Times, London, 1829

Even today, shorn of its empire, Russia is a land of superlatives, the largest country in the world. It covers nearly one ninth of the land surface of the globe: eleven time zones from the far West to the far East. No other country has more neighbours. Until quite recently the size and the climate made it very difficult to move goods, or people, or ideas, from one end of the Empire to the other. It took Chekhov nearly three months at the end of the nineteenth century to travel from Moscow to Sakhalin in the Far East by a combination of train, carriage and horseback. In the 1960s it took me five days to travel by train from the Pacific seaport of Nakhodka to the Central Siberian city of Irkutsk – not even half the way to Moscow. The Russian landscape is like no other: a vast expanse of plain and forest, punctuated by the occasional small town or village separated from its neighbour by tens (and in Siberia sometimes by hundreds) of miles, connected by roads which have always been a byword for awfulness. It is an unspectacular landscape, neither pretty nor imposing. A broad flat expanse of pasture, with a straggled knot of birch trees off to the left, some tumbledown wooden cottages or the onion dome of a small church on the right, and a river in the middle distance, is bounded by a tangled and impenetrable forest of pine trees, stretching limitlessly to the horizon. The finest examples of the Russian landscape painter's art and the crude prints stuck on the walls of the most ordinary dwellings reflect one or other of these scenes. This unemphatic landscape grips the imagination of all Russians, above all in the Autumn, when they go into the woods to seek out the contorted fungi which only Slavs believe are edible, when the glorious days of Indian Summer seem to go on for ever, pale blue skies and milk-warm sunshine, silver birches turning golden, a season of particular magic.

The ancient towns and villages of Russia match the landscape. Built from the wood of the surrounding forest, a peasant cottage abandoned simply reverts to the humus from which it originally sprung. Many of the towns are very old. Novgorod was founded over a thousand years ago, Moscow in the twelfth century. Many Siberian cities are three or four hundred years old: Cossack adventurers reached the Pacific Ocean at about the time that the Pilgrim Fathers reached Massachusetts. Even today one can find – especially in the more remote parts of European Russia to which the invading Tatars, Poles, Swedes, French, or Germans never penetrated – unspoiled towns with their ancient Kremlin, their churches – gold in azure, their neo-classical buildings of nineteenth-century bureaucrats and merchants, their fringe of wooden cottages; and beyond them the fortified monasteries and the country estates of gentlefolk from before the Flood, an urban landscape and an architectural style uniquely Russian.

Yet despite their antiquity, Russian cities have a nomadic quality about them. Even the regular facades of the neo-classical buildings are often no more than stucco on wood, a transient medium. It is as if the inhabitants fear that at any moment they will be swept onward by a new natural catastrophe, by another invasion, or simply by the whim of their own government. Chaadaev was a dissident guards officer who returned from Paris after the Napoleonic Wars with such subversive views about Russia's future that the Tsar had him declared insane. His works were barely available inside Russia until Gorbachev freed the printing presses in the late 1980s. He wrote in his first *Lettre philosophique* of 1829: 'In our houses we live as in a camp; in our families we seem like newcomers; in our towns we resemble nomads, worse than nomads, because they are more closely bound to their flocks than we are to our cities.'

Chaadaev's judgement is not a trivial conceit. Time and again the settlements in Russia were destroyed by invaders, or by fire and other catastrophes. The Soviet period was a disaster both for the landscape and for the architecture. Churches, monasteries, and country houses were allowed to fall into ruin. Many were deliberately destroyed in the atheistic campaigns under Stalin and Khrushchev. New buildings and factories were run up at top speed to fulfil the plan, regardless of aesthetic or environmental considerations. Even today, even in the rural areas, Russia is possibly the untidiest, least kempt country in the world. Near the industrial cities of the Soviet era the countryside is polluted to a degree not to be imagined in the West. The approach to almost any Russian city is intensely depressing. The tree-lined road gives way to a straggle of jerry-built grey brick apartment blocks, run up in a hurry to cope with the acute housing shortage of the 1950s and

1960s, a petrol station with empty pumps, ancient wooden houses leaning drunkenly on their rotten foundations; and construction rubbish everywhere, piles of broken paving stones, huge concrete pipes left higgledy-piggledy on the side of the road, their original purpose and ownership long forgotten. If the town contains a major industry, it will be overhung by a polluted cloud. Outrage at what the Soviet system had done to Russia's towns and villages and to the Russian countryside helped turn millions of ordinary people against it at the end.

By its history, its culture, and its religion, Russia is European. It is the addition of Siberia which turns Russia into something unique. Like Canada, Siberia entered history as an Eldorado for trappers and prospectors and adventurers. As in North America, the trappers were followed by soldiers who paid scant regard to interests of the native inhabitants. For four centuries thereafter Siberia was a haven for runaways and a dumping ground for those who offended the government in Moscow. It is Siberia which has created the image of Russia as a land of infinite wealth, of furs and timber, of vast mineral resources – almost uniquely rich in oil and gas, and precious and rare metals.

This wealth was not the blessing it seemed. It allowed Russia's rulers to exploit, usually by the most brutal and wasteful means, their country's natural resources and exchange them for the goods, and especially the sophisticated weapons, produced by more complex economies elsewhere. But the Russian people remained poor. The government too remained poor, unable to pay for the efficient and comparatively honest bureaucratic mechanisms growing up further to the West. Stalin's policy of forced industrialisation, the wartime evacuation of industry from Western Russia, and the renewed drive to develop Siberia under Khrushchev and Brezhnev further distorted the economic geography of the country. Where a Western company would have built a mining camp, huge cities were constructed, often with forced labour, to exploit the mineral riches of the inaccessible North and the empty expanses of Central Asia. Few people went to live of their own accord in the forbidding Siberian taiga. Once slave labour was no longer available, the government had to pay immense subsidies to heat these new cities, to transport their products, and to persuade people to live there. When the Soviet Union collapsed, the subsidies began to dry up, the people began to leave, and the economy of Siberia ran into increasing trouble.

Russia a thousand years ago was not so different from other states on the periphery of Europe. Like most of Germany, much of the Balkans, and the whole of Scandinavia, Russia was never part of the Western Roman

Empire, and did not share in the linguistic, religious, and legal traditions which that empire bequeathed to its former subjects. But Russia's conversion to Byzantine Christianity in 988 brought the country decisively into an alternative European tradition. The tensions between the Eastern and the Western variants of Christianity were no more bloody that those between its Catholic and Protestant variants. In terms of scholarship – especially Classical scholarship – Byzantium had the edge over the Rome of the Dark Ages until it too fell to the conqueror in 1452. Kievan Russia was an equal partner in the European world, a state whose princes made more than one dynastic marriage with the daughters of English and French monarchs. Political scientists who argue that the division between Orthodoxy and Western Christendom is doomed to remain a watershed between two civilisations skate on thin ice. In those early days Russia was not, of course, a democracy. Neither were the other countries of Europe. The political, cultural, and religious institutions of the first Russian state, founded in Kiev in the ninth century, were not much different from those of those of its contemporaries in Western Europe.

The Tatar destruction of Kiev in 1242 broke many of these links, severed Russia from the ferment of ideas which accompanied the European Renaissance, and set it off on a somewhat different path. The Russians had to accommodate to their powerful Tatar neighbours, and adopted several of their less attractive habits. But contrary to what later became a popular perception in Russia as well as the West, the country was never wholly submerged under the 'Tatar yoke'. Up in the forests of the North, the Russians remained resolutely Christian. The republican city-state of Novgorod the Great maintained a flourishing trade with the rest of Europe. The Grand Duchy of Moscow went another way, towards introversion and autocratic rule. This was less attractive than the experiment in Novgorod. But it too had its contemporary parallels in the West.

A clash between Novgorod and Moscow was inevitable, and it was Moscow that prevailed. In the sixteenth century Muscovy began to impinge more forcefully on its East European neighbours. Cautiously and suspiciously it opened the Northern sea routes to trade with Western Europe. Western visitors – whose own countries were by no means models of liberal democracy, a concept not yet invented – were genuinely shocked by the Russian system of government in which arbitrary power was unchecked by law. They criticised the Russians – women as well as men – for their dirtiness, their laziness, their brutality, their drunkenness, their mendacity, and their lewdness. Sigmund von Herberstein, the sixteenth-century German diplomat, wondered whether it was the brutality of the Russian people that made their prince a tyrant, or whether the people themselves had become brutal and cruel through the tyranny of their prince.[1] George Turbervile, a homesick young member of the first English mission in Moscow, wrote in dubious verse to his friend Parker back in London that Russia was

> ... a savage soile, where lawes do bear no sway,
> Where all is at the king his wille, to save or els to slay,

though he did note with approval that

> The common game is chess, almost the simplest will
> Both give a check and eke a mate, by practise comes their skill. [2]

The political system which the Russians created to manage their vast, vulnerable, and poverty-stricken country was indeed unpleasant. But it was neither irrational nor accidental. To hold their huge country together, to sustain the burden of defending it, and to keep order among an ignorant and unruly population, was a daunting task. Catherine the Great was not the only Russian sovereign, nor the only political scientist, to argue that

> The sovereign must be autocratic, for no other form of government but that which concentrates all power in his person is compatible with the dimensions of a State as great as ours. Only swiftness of decision in matters sent from distant realms can compensate for the slowness caused by great distances. Any other form of government would be not only harmful, but utterly ruinous for Russia.[3]

For the other side of the coin was the thing that Russia's rulers – and most ordinary Russians – have always feared: what Pushkin called 'The Russian *bunt*, bloody and mindless'.[4] Time and again the Russian people have rebelled against oppression, even where there was no hope of success, if only to burn and destroy the lives and property of their masters until their rebellion was put down with equal or greater brutality.

And so Russia's rulers relied on political institutions of almost military severity. The Tsars claimed a mandate from heaven. The Communists claimed a mandate from history. The principle that the rule of law was superior to that of the sovereign – the principle that divided the two sides in the English Civil War – was never accepted either by the Tsars or by their successors. Count Benkendorf, Chief of Police in the 1830s, a gallant and honourable officer of limited understanding, argued that 'laws are made for underlings, not for their bosses',[5] a sentiment that prevails widely in Russia today. The Old Bolshevik Kaganovich, responsible under Stalin for the ruthless collectivisation of agriculture and the destruction of many of Moscow's finest churches, argued that the rule of law, the *Rechtsstaat* to which Gorbachev was later to attach so much importance, was contrary to Marxism-Leninism. The proposition that law is subordinate to the requirements of the Party was the organising principle of Stalin's 'democratic' constitution of 1936 and of Brezhnev's new constitution of 1977.

Disdain for the rule of law was not confined to the bosses. The intellectuals were equally contemptuous. Dostoevsky and Tolstoy believed that the Russian passion for 'Justice' was superior, more human and more moral than the formalistic and cold-blooded Western regard for 'Law'. They ridiculed the attempts of Russian liberals to introduce a more humane legal system. They failed to explain why the abstract Russian passion for justice appeared to produce so much crying injustice in the real world.

To bolster their power the Tsars deliberately and systematically cultivated the use of terror. The Tsar was above the law. So were his political police. Ivan the Terrible created the *oprichniki*, who rode through the countryside on black horses like the Dark Riders in *The Lord of the Rings*, wearing black cloaks and carrying dogs' heads, with a licence to torture, rob, and kill. Peter the Great took a personal hand in the torture and execution of his real or suspected opponents, including his own son. During his reign the population of Russia declined by a quarter as a consequence of war, forced labour, famine and revolt, a larger proportion than died under Stalin. Nicholas I formed the Third Department to keep suspects under surveillance, to track foreigners, to supervise places of political exile and imprisonment, and to provide 'information and reports on all events without exception'. Even in the comparatively liberal 1860s Aleksei Tolstoy wrote a grimly comic poem about Popov, an unfortunate official who dreams he has been caught by his minister improperly dressed at an official function. He is arrested, tortured, and forced to denounce his accomplices. The image of the political prisoner, walking for hundreds or thousands of miles to his place of imprisonment and exile in Siberia, pervades Russian art, literature, and poetry.

The theory behind the use of terror was rational enough, even under Ivan the Terrible, whose sanity is certainly open to question. Ivan aimed to atomise society, and so prevent the emergence of organisations capable of challenging his power. Successive Russian governments also exploited the size and remoteness of their country to isolate their people from subversive influences. Russians were not allowed to travel abroad, or to meet the few foreigners who visited their country. This was a matter of deliberate policy. The monk Kzhizhanich told a seventeenth-century Tsar that 'Next to autocracy itself the most valuable of our traditions is the closing of the frontiers, i.e. the prohibition to foreigners of facile access to our country, and the prohibition to our people of wandering outside the borders of the realm without important reason.'[6] The control over the physical movement of people was matched by the control over the movement of ideas: by censorship. Religious heresy was ferociously hunted down in Muscovy. Catherine the Great imprisoned dissident writers. Her grandson Nicholas I had them declared insane and put Pushkin and his writings under Benkendorf's personal control.

The number of policemen and their agents continued to grow. They penetrated and manipulated revolutionary organisations, set up their own trade unions, provoked political assassination and racial violence. But time and again their intrigues collapsed in scandal. Yevno Azef, who worked as an undercover agent in the terrorist organisation of the Socialist Revolutionary Party, betrayed his comrades to the police, organised the assassination of senior Tsarist officials, and escaped the vengeance of both to die in his bed in 1918. By 1917 the roots of revolution were far too deep to be eradicated by even the most brutal and ingenious police force.

The autocrat had one more instrument of rule: the manipulation of privilege and favour. Peter the Great's predecessors imposed a rigid system of hierarchy to strengthen their political control over their subordinates. Peter rationalised these arrangements into a military system of ranks and privileges, the so-called 'Table of Ranks', under which all were expected to serve the state and to make their careers by advancing up the ladder until they reached the level at which they became members of the hereditary aristocracy. The Communist system of *nomenklatura* was an almost exact parallel. Under both, promotion and privilege were in the gift of the autocrat. Private property – estates and great houses under Peter, cars and dachas under the Communists – could be withdrawn as soon as the autocrat was displeased. The denial of any source of independent wealth or income was a deliberate measure of social and political control. These arrangements reinforced the arrogance of the powerful and the sycophancy of subordinates. The principle of management was simple. 'I'm the boss,' as later Russians said, 'and you're an idiot.' It was the state of affairs satirised in *The Government Inspector* by Gogol, an author who always seemed a far better guide to Soviet reality than the theories spun by Kremlinologists during the Cold War. The results were inevitable: fear of responsibility, bullying of inferiors, and the taking of bribes. There were dedicated and honourable servants of the state in Communist as in Tsarist times. But the system itself was an obstacle to the exercise of initiative both in government and in business. In the end both the Tsarist and the Communist regimes were destroyed by their inability to employ the talents of the people effectively.

The power of the autocratic state rested not only on force – the police and the army – unconstrained by the law. The Russian political system contained two other major institutions: the Orthodox Church and the intelligentsia. The Church played an ambiguous role – sometimes a pillar of the state, often a consolation for the people, and from time to time a source of opposition in a system where opposition was always forbidden.

The central myth of Russia is the idea of Holy Russia, the citadel of purity amidst a hostile sea of schismatics and infidels. Rimsky-Korsakov's opera *The Legend of the Invisible City of Kitezh* is a mystical hymn to the holy city which miraculously sank beneath the waves to save it from the Tatar invader, only to emerge in unblemished glory after years or centuries, when the evil men had finally and inevitably departed. Russia's sacrifice, so the myth goes, saved Europe from the Horde, and Europe has been ungrateful ever since.

The Russian Orthodox Church, like the Catholic Church in Poland, preserved the spirit of the nation in adversity over the centuries. It profoundly shaped the Russians' idea of themselves and their country. During the Tatar invasions the Church was the rallying point for Russians whose secular rulers were dead, dispersed, or collaborating with the enemy. For the Russians the fall of Constantinople to the Turks in 1453 was the just punishment of a Church and state which – unlike their own – had tried in its last extremity to form a desperate and disgraceful alliance with the heretical Church of Rome. Thereafter Russians were convinced that they alone possessed the truth, and increasingly that it was their historic task to convey that truth to the infidels of East and West. As Dostoevsky put it, 'The whole significance of Russia is contained in Orthodoxy, in the light from the East, which will flow to blind mankind in the West, which has lost Christ.' Russians called themselves 'Orthodox' because they firmly believed that other faiths were to a greater or lesser extent false: Catholics and Protestants are barely Christians at all. In his opera *Boris Godunov* Mussorgsky contrasts not only the dramatic roles, but even the musical language, of the warm-hearted Russian characters (the villains as well) with those of the cold, formalistic, Catholic, Western, Jesuitical Poles. The music of Dmitri the Pretender degenerates when he changes sides to join the Polish attack on Russia. Western critics regard the Polish scenes of the opera as musically inferior to the others. But what else, a Russian might reply, would you expect from a bunch of Poles?

The Russian Orthodox Church has no strong theological tradition. The deliberately anti-intellectual strand in its thinking emerges in the novels of Dostoevsky, and in the respect paid to 'Holy Fools', the simpletons to be found in Orthodox monasteries even today, people whose incapacity for normal life is taken as a sign that they are touched by God. The Simpleton in *Boris Godunov* foretells the misery of Russia and dares to tell the truth even to the Tsar in two of the most affecting moments of the opera. The Russian Orthodox Church carries the worship of holy relics to oppressive lengths: a visit to the catacombs in the monasteries of Kiev and Pechory, populated by the desiccated remains of hundreds of long dead but deeply revered churchmen, repels the non-believer – bewitched though he may be by the splendour of the churches, the magnificence of the liturgy, and the dedication of the congregation.

Many foreigners, and many Russian liberals and revolutionaries, saw the Russian Church as a mere instrument of despotism, an arm of the Russian state, corrupt, superstitious, dirty and uninteresting. But even the apparent subservience of the Church to the state was far from a simple phenomenon. English critics, whose monarch is the head of the English Church, should be particularly circumspect. The Russian Orthodox Church was never an independent secular power like the Roman Catholic Church: pious Russians regarded the worldliness of the Church of Rome as a sin. But the leaders of the Russian Church did not always lack moral courage or independence of mind. They were ready to die if they thought that their faith or their duty required it. Ivan the Terrible murdered Metropolitan Philip. Tsar Fyodor burned the dissident priest Avvakum alive. Peter the Great systematically humiliated the Church and broke its independence. In 1918 Patriarch Tikhon warned the Bolsheviks that 'all the righteous blood you shed will cry out against you.'[7] Over three hundred bishops and priests were executed between 1917 and 1920. Thousands more died in the Great Terror of the 1930s. A wholly servile Church has no martyrs.

But apart from a few lonely and heroic figures, those who survived collaborated with the regime, like millions of Russians in other walks of life. The churchmen who emerged into the public eye under Perestroika represented the whole gamut of the Russian people: Patriarch Aleksi II, born Von Rüdiger of a Baltic German family in Tallinn in 1929, a statesman of the Church; Metropolitan Pitirim, handsome and elegant, deeply reactionary; Pavel, Abbot of Pechory, young, ambitious, and highly intel-ligent; Elefthery, Abbot of the Monastery of Kiev, subtly anti-Communist;

the tough nuns of the convent of Tolga on the Volga near Yaroslavl; Father Gleb Yakunin and Father Georgi of Kostroma, dissidents at odds with their superiors; the Head of the Theological Academy at the Monastery of St Sergius, who told me in 1989 that the Soviet regime 'began with civil war and it will end with civil war: they lived by the sword and they will perish by the sword'; two ingratiating priests in Volgograd, sycophants of the regime, straight out of a nineteenth-century anti-clerical cartoon; Nafanial of Pechory, an elderly and simple-minded Holy Fool; Mother Magdalena, the middle-class Englishwoman who had taken the Orthodox veil; Father Men, the half-Jewish religious philosopher who was murdered by an axeman in Autumn 1990.

The myths and the practice of autocracy and Orthodoxy allowed no room in Russia for ideas of pluralism, dissent or loyal opposition. The gap thus left in the Russian body politic was filled by the Russian intelligentsia. 'Intelligentsia' is a Russian word, and the Russian intelligentsia bore little resemblance to the 'intelligentsia' elsewhere. In Western or even in Central Europe the 'intelligentsia' is a collection of more or less well-educated individuals, mostly involved with the liberal arts. They may from time to time set an intellectual or even a political fashion. But their political significance as a group is negligible. Not so the Russian intelligentsia, which became a political phenomenon, almost a political class, a reaction – perhaps the only possible reaction – to a political system in which organised opposition was always severely discouraged and usually banned outright.

The Russian intelligentsia took shape at the end of the eighteenth century in opposition to serfdom and the increasingly oppressive rule of Catherine the Great. Its first members were drawn from the aristocracy. But with the spread of education and the liberation of the serfs, more and more members of the intelligentsia came from the ranks of the lesser bureaucracy, the professional classes, and the peasantry. Despite their weakness, the regime took the political pretensions of the intelligentsia seriously. Both the KGB and the Okhrana subjected them to the closest surveillance and often to violent repression. They reciprocated in kind. Denied a legitimate means of expressing opposition to the prevailing order, they turned increasingly to conspiracy, terrorism, and revolutionary agitation among the proletariat. The Decembrists, the assassins of Tsar Alexander II, the terrorists of the Social Revolutionary Party, and Lenin's Bolsheviks were drawn primarily from the intelligentsia. The Russian populist revolutionaries of the nineteenth century and their Social Democratic rivals fought, murdered, and died for the revolution, overthrew the old regime, and attempted to set up utopia in its place.

But until the middle of the twentieth century the vast majority of Russians were peasants, impoverished workers, ruthlessly exploited and recruited to fulfil the state's military ambitions. Both the Tsars and the Communists claimed their love and demanded their support. Neither offered them a share of power. So they devised a variety of ways to evade and survive the impact of arbitrary power. Occasionally they rioted. In more peaceful times they combined together in small groups – village communities, bands of roving artisans, groups of friends – who could trust one another and whose solidarity was some defence against the climate of brutality, suspicion, and betrayal which autocracy encouraged. Before the October Revolution the symbol of this solidarity was the village commune, the *mir*. Russian socialists romanticised the *mir*, which they believed could become the core of a peculiarly Russian form of social democracy. Russian nationalists and churchmen romanticised it as a symbol of *sobornost*, the spirit of communal solidarity which (as many Russians still believe) set them on a higher moral plane than the selfish bourgeois of the West. Neither seemed to notice that the *mir* served another useful purpose as well: as a convenient device through which the authorities could collect taxes and recruits, and on which they could impose a collective punishment at the first sign of indiscipline.

Needless to say, few Russians felt any compunction about ignoring or subverting – whenever they safely could – the requirements of their superiors. As the liberal Herzen pointed out in the middle of the nineteenth century:

> The crying injustice of one half of its laws has taught the Russian people to hate the other as well: the Russian submits to the law from force alone. Complete inequality before the courts has killed in him all respect for legality. A Russian, whatever his calling, evades or violates the law whenever he can do so with impunity, and the government does exactly the same.

This ingrained, and in the circumstances perfectly rational, contempt for a formal system of law was as powerful in post-Communist Russia as it was when Herzen was writing more than a century earlier.

In most societies people navigate the difficulties of everyday life by culti-vating the powerful, peddling influence, exchanging favours, and giving bribes, which they prefer to call presents – activities not always illegal, but rarely entirely proper. The French used to call it 'le système D'. It has always been well developed in Russia. They too have a special name for it: *Blat. Blat* flourished in Tsarist Russia. It helped to make life bearable under Stalin. And it remains an essential lubricant of Russian society today.

Russians also had resort to another weapon of self-defence: the disconcerting phenomenon of *vranyo*, the Great Russian Lie. Originally, the lie in Russia was an essential instrument of self-preservation. To tell the truth under Ivan the Terrible or Peter the Great or Stalin was as likely as not to be fatal, in the most literal sense. The nineteenth-century historian Kostomarov, who was deported by the Tsarist authorities because of his Ukrainian nationalism, once wrote:

> Ivan [the Terrible] set the Russian people against one another, showed them that the way to favour or to salvation lay in the destruction of their fellows … In moments of personal danger every man naturally thinks only of himself. But for the Russian people such moments lasted for decades at a time. A generation inevitably arose of self-seeking and cruel-hearted egoists, whose every thought, every striving, was directed only to their own security, a generation for whom no inner truth remained, however much they preserved the common external forms of piety, legality and morality.[8]

Kostomarov was writing about Russia in the seventeenth century. But the parallel with his own time surely did not escape him. And as so often, what was written about the Tsarist past could also have been applied to the Soviet present.

And so *vranyo* became an integral part of the conduct of public business. Junior officials lied to their seniors, the government lied to the public and to foreigners. In 1557 the 'Company of the Merchant Adventurers to Moscow' warned their agent there that the Russian ambassador in London

> is verie mistrustfull, and thinketh everie man will beguile him. Therefore you had neede to take heede howe you have to do with him or with any such, and to make your bargaines plaine, and to set them downe in writing. For they bee subtill people, and do not alwaies speake the trueth, and think other men to be like themselves.[9]

More than three centuries later, Teddy Roosevelt complained that the Russian diplomats with whom he had to negotiate lied with 'brazen and contemptuous effrontery'.[10] The Russian naval authorities who lied in explanation of the disaster to the submarine *Kursk* in the summer of 2000 were operating in an old tradition.

Vranyo still permeates even the most trivial aspects of everyday life and goes much beyond the mere requirements of self-preservation and careerism. In May 1992 we stayed in the surprisingly good Soviet-style hotel in the provincial town of Kostroma. On the lavatory seat in the bedroom was a seal in four different languages: 'Disinfected for your comfort and safety.' Every Russian would know that this could not be true. Only the most naive of foreigners would think differently. Yet in a great country, you disinfect the lavatory seats. So the notice has to go up. *Vranyo* is something the Russians can usually forgive in themselves and others. Dostoevsky argued that it was through lying that one might arrive at the truth. But from time to time Russians are overwhelmed by guilt at their acts of commission and omission. Confession helps to purge the sense of shame. And so the Great Russian Confession – in Dostoevsky's novels, and in many midnight conversations in Gorbachev's Russia – became the reverse side of the Great Russian Lie.

And yet the Tsarist regime did change and begin to modernise itself during the nineteenth century. It ended serfdom a couple of years before slavery was abolished in America. Alexander II (1818–1881) made a real though limited attempt to introduce local democracy and the rule of law. Under Nicholas II (1868–1918) far-sighted ministers launched a radical transformation of the Russian economy.

It was under these men that Russian music, literature, painting, dance exploded. European culture was permanently transformed: it is now inconceivable without the great Russian novelists, above all Tolstoy and Dostoevsky; without Russia's greatest playwright, Chekhov; without Tchaikovsky, Mussorgsky, Stravinsky, Prokofiev, and Shostakovich; and without the great artists of the first decades of the twentieth century. The argument about whether Russia is European or Asian will no doubt rage on. The Russians themselves cannot decide. But Russia is part of Christendom, an integral part of European history, and the great Russian novelists are read by all educated English people, most of whom have never read a page of Goethe, Dante, or Racine; and have no idea whether or not there is such a thing as the great Indian, Japanese, or Chinese novel. Russia is a problem to the rest of us, not because it is insufficiently European, but because it is insufficiently small. The larger part of its territory – though a minority of its people – looks to the Pacific and Asia. This affects attitudes and politics, but does not affect the essentially European nature of Russian civilisation.

For the Russians themselves it is Pushkin who defines not only their culture but their image of who they are. For them Pushkin is more than a poet. He is the sum of wisdom and a consolation in time of trouble. They took him with them into the concentration camps. And as the Soviet Union staggered towards collapse he became a symbol for ultra-nationalists. One critic said on television in January 1990: 'Pushkin is one of the last saints to remain to our people in this spiritually tragic time'.[11]

Seventy-five miles to the south of Pskov, an ancient and beautiful city on the Western marches of Russia, there is an unspoilt stretch of nineteenth-century Russian countryside – the River Sorota, broad pastureland, woods, a windmill, three manor houses in the old style, and not a single factory chimney or electricity pylon in sight. This is Mikhailovskoe, where Pushkin lived in exile and where he wrote much of his best work. What one can see today is an illusion. Mikhailovskoe was burned down more than once over the years by angry peasants and by warring civil bands, and it was fought over during the Second World War. It looks the way it does today because it was recreated by the formidable Semyon Geichenko, the son of a sergeant-major in the imperial horse guards. Before the war Geichenko was a museum curator and a scholar. He was arrested during the purges, released to serve in a penal battalion during the war, and lost an arm. He lived close to Pushkin's own home in a wooden house filled with samovars, church bells, and innumerable portraits of himself. It was he who had fought the vandals who wanted to disfigure the countryside with modern industry, and he had won. The landscape was his creation, and so were the buildings, perfect replicas of three country houses of the late eighteenth century all risen from the ashes of war: Pushkin's own Mikhailovskoe; Petrovskoe, where his Ethiopian grandfather lived; and Trigorskoe, the home of Tatiana and her family, the heroines of Pushkin's *Eugene Onegin*. Splendidly vain, magnificently handsome despite his eighty-odd years, Geichenko was another of the real heroes of Russia, the men and – more often – the women who slaved and scraped, often for the most miserable of salaries, to preserve the physical traces of their culture. I said as much to his wife Ludmila Jalalovna, whom he had met and married in a military hospital in Dagestan. 'You needn't think he did it all on his own,' she said with a flash of bitter spirit.

Whatever prospects for liberal change lay before the Russian state at the beginning of the twentieth century were destroyed by war and revolution. The victorious Bolsheviks absorbed and turned the institutions of the autocratic state to their own purposes. The system they set up was a brutal satire on what had gone before. But there was nothing remotely comic about it. This time the new policemen – the Cheka [12] – were determined not to fail. Actively encouraged by Lenin, their operations were based on the explicit use of terror from the very beginning. Stalin carried the Bolshevik logic to its limit. His regime was almost uniquely horrible. Stalin, like Ivan the Terrible, set out to atomise society in order to guarantee his personal rule. His political practice placed a positive premium on brutality – as a way of showing revolutionary fervour; as a way of showing zeal in the hope that others, not you, would attract the lightning; as the only way to get things done in a system where the normal motivations had been destroyed. He deliberately suppressed all natural human links, whether at the level of the family or of the nation. Soviet children were exhorted to admire the example of Pavlik Morozov, who denounced his family to the secret police. In his personal copy of *The Prince*, Stalin underlined the passage where Machiavelli concludes that it is better to be feared than loved. Stalin managed to persuade most of his subjects to love him almost as much as they feared him. But then Stalin was a political genius.

Almost everyone in Russia lost a close relative as a result of Stalin's repressions and his brutal economic policies. Gorbachev's family was nearly wiped out in 1933 in the artificial famine which accompanied Stalin's collectivisation of agriculture. Both his peasant grandfathers were arrested during the purges. His wife's grandfather was shot: he was not finally 'rehabilitated' until 1988, three years after her husband had come to power.

Vladimir Lukin – a leading champion of reform in the late Gorbachev years, and subsequently ambassador to Washington – was born in 1937, at the height of the great purge. Shortly after his birth, his father was arrested. His mother went to the local Party and NKVD offices to protest her husband's innocence. One of the local NKVD officers, at considerable risk to himself, warned her that if she went on making trouble she too would be arrested. She ignored his advice to go into hiding with her baby and was arrested shortly afterwards. A neighbour, the wife of an NKVD officer and a nursing mother, suckled the young Lukin until his grandmother came from Moscow to take him.

The author Lev Razgon was eighty years old when we first met him in 1989, still very lively, with a fine-drawn face, a quick and subtle intelligence, a serene and lively manner which belied his sad Jewish eyes and the memories which lay behind them. He remembered the elections to the Constituent Assembly in 1917. He was an observer at the XVIIth Congress of the Soviet Communist Party in 1934: over half of the delegates were later shot. One night in 1937 they came for his parents-in-law. In 1938 they took Razgon himself; and a week later his young wife as well. In 1947 Razgon was let out of the camp, and allowed to live in exile near Stavropol in the South,

Gorbachev's home territory. There he was told that his father-in-law had been shot, and that his mother-in law and his wife had subsequently died in the camps. His daughter, one year old at the time of his arrest, was in an orphanage. In 1950 he was rearrested and sent back to the camps.

Razgon was not finally released until 1955. In 1988, when Gorbachev had made it possible, he published a slim account of his experiences in the camps, balanced and humane, like Primo Levi's book about his time in Auschwitz. But in 1991 he was allowed to look at the KGB's files on his case. They contained almost nothing: no denunciations, no interrogation reports, only the order for the arrest, a brief protocol of the investigation, and the sentence. But from these meagre documents Razgon was able to piece together some horrifying facts. Yezhov himself, the head of the NKVD, whom his mother-in-law had comforted when he was no more than a lonely young Communist official from the provinces, had scribbled on the order for her husband's arrest: 'Take the wife as well.' She had died, not of heart failure in the camp as Razgon had been told when she was 'rehabilitated' in the 1950s, but butchered like an animal in a Moscow cellar within days of her arrest. Razgon's wife, a diabetic, soon died in the camp for lack of insulin.

Faced with these revelations, Razgon was no longer able to preserve his philosophical detachment: the article he wrote for the press was a ferocious denunciation of the KGB past and present.

Much as they disliked Russia's internal arrangements, foreign observers would not have been particularly concerned had they not also seen Russia as a threat to their own interests. In the early modern period the Russians were of course regularly at war with their neighbours. They were victims as often as they were aggressors. In this they did not noticeably distinguish themselves from the other European states of the day. They were invaded from time to time by Poles, Swedes, Tatars, and Turks. From time to time they returned the compliment.

The perception of Russia as a unique threat to the outside world was a more recent phenomenon. It can perhaps be dated from the appearance of Peter the Great, determined to modernise his country and to force Russia onto the attention of the established states of Europe. 'We have come out of the darkness into the light,' he said, 'and people who did not know us now do us honour.'[13] It was not only Russia's immediate neighbours who were dismayed. Peter and his successors compelled the Great Powers of Europe to treat Russia as an equal. Russian troops fought all over the continent in Europe's complex wars – in Germany, France, Italy, Holland, Switzerland. Russian ambitions in Asia seemed to threaten the empires that the British and others were already constructing there. By the nineteenth century, Western armchair strategists were thoroughly unnerved. Foreshadowing the language of the Cold War, General Mitchell wrote in 1838 that 'The most important political question on which modern times have to decide, is the policy that must now be pursued, in order to maintain the security of Western Europe against the overgrown power of Russia.'[14] By the end of the century the Victorians were fearing that at any moment the Russians would pour over the Himalayas into India. One wonders if these people ever looked at a map.

This British Russophobia was a particularly odd phenomenon. The only serious armed clashes that have ever occurred between the two countries were fought out on Russian territory during the Crimean War, followed by some minor scuffles, also on Russian territory, when the British intervened in the Russian civil war after the October Revolution. There were measured voices as well. The Whig newspaper *The Chronicle* warned: 'Do not let a great nation ... make itself ridiculous by an insane Russo-Phobia' – possibly the first use of the word. Lord Durham, the British ambassador in St Petersburg, wrote in 1838 that

> The power of Russia has been greatly exaggerated. There is not one element of strength which is not directly counterbalanced by a corresponding ... weakness. In fact her power is solely of the defensive kind. Leaning on and covered by the impregnable fortresses with which nature has endowed her – her climate and her deserts – she is invincible, as Napoleon discovered to his cost.

In 1854 the *Edinburgh Review* wrote that the Russian government had deliberately interposed 'a thick veil between [Russia] and the rest of Europe, leaving the latter to ruminate over her vast but unknown resources, till at length everybody is affected by a panic fear, for which there is absolutely no reason whatsoever'.[15] These disputes were echoed a century later when analysts began to debate the extent and reality of the Soviet threat.

The Russians did indeed show themselves capable of ruthless imperial aggression within Europe and beyond. So did the English, the French, the Spaniards, the Dutch, the Portuguese, the Belgians, and the Germans. The Russians did indeed maintain the largest standing army in Europe right up to the outbreak of the First World War. But the Russian steamroller which filled the nightmares of Victorian defence analysts proved to be a sham. The imperial armies did well against the minor Muslim states of Central Asia, and against the declining power of the Turk. But except in wars of national survival the Russians were regularly defeated whenever they came up against more modern states – the British and French in the Crimea, the Japanese in the Far East, and the Germans in the First World War. Even in the Second World War – the most extreme of all Russia's wars of national survival – the Red Army at first performed badly, despite the vast numbers, the modern equipment, and the aggressive military doctrine with which it faced the German onslaught in the summer of 1941.

Thus even before the Bolsheviks arrived, with their claim that Russia was destined to lead world revolution, Russophobia was already deeply rooted in the Western way of thought. It reached dangerous levels during the Cold War, to which the nuclear confrontation gave a unique character. There was much loose and boastful talk throughout the Cold War on the American side, magnified by the usual mechanisms of democracy and a free press. In 1953 *Collins Magazine* published a detailed account of how the West ('the United Nations') would win a nuclear war against the Soviet Union. Reagan's arms build-up and his generously leaked musings on Armageddon – the ultimate battle between good and evil – reduced the Soviet leadership to a state of near panic. In the mid-1980s Gordievsky, the KGB officer who worked for many years for the British, rendered great service to all by conveying some sense of this panic to Western leaders, who began to address their Soviet opposite numbers with more soothing language.

Once they were both sufficiently armed, each superpower adopted – explicitly or implicitly – the strategy of Mutual Assured Destruction, known by its acronym 'MAD', the threat to unleash a nuclear holocaust of incalculable scope if the other pushed it too far.[16] There were those on the Western side who argued that it was better to be Dead than Red, even at the price of nuclear war. Others believed, apparently sincerely, that the Soviet leadership would be willing to unleash nuclear war to achieve its global ambitions even at the price of losing millions of its own citizens. Still others thought that the problem could best be solved if the West itself launched a quick preventive nuclear war against the Soviets. From time to time senior US generals came close to arguing as much. After the Cuba missile crisis Robert Kennedy remarked on 'the many times that I had heard the military take positions which, if wrong, had the advantage that no one would be around at the end to know.'[17] Most assumed that similar ideas were debated in Moscow.

The intellectual challenges posed by the existence and the possible use of nuclear weapons are amongst the most demanding that statesmen have ever had to face. Extreme propositions were adopted by rational and decent people on both sides. They were implausible at the time, and almost incomprehensible with the benefit of hindsight. Individuals, even groups, have always been willing to die for their freedom or for an ideal. That is their right. But it is not evident that any group of people has the right to condemn the whole species, or a large part of it, to nuclear catastrophe for the sake of an idea. The strategy of 'Mutually Assured Destruction' was a huge gamble. It may also have been a bluff: as Geoffrey Hosking says, 'to threaten with weapons which could not be deployed without bringing about one's own destruction always contained an element of unhinged fantasy.'[18] But Vice President Nixon publicly acknowledged, as early as 1958, that Americans would hardly risk sacrificing Philadelphia by retaliating against a Soviet nuclear strike on Paris. A Whitehall paper of the day, commenting on Nixon's views, said that we were approaching

> a situation in which the nuclear stalemate would be complete. One side or the other may have a temporary or lasting superiority in some field, but by definition this superiority would be limited; each side would know that, even if it got in the first blow, the other would still have, to all practical purposes, an unlimited destructive capacity.

We serving officials managed to persuade ourselves that mutual terror would ensure mutual restraint. So indeed it did. The West's policy paid off. Its willingness to cross the nuclear threshold was never tested, because the Soviets eventually blinked. But future historians will marvel that our generation was prepared to take such a horrendous risk.[19]

For years the received wisdom in the West was that the Cold War was the fault of Stalin and the world Communist conspiracy. Like *The Times* of 1829, people argued that the Russian state – now the Soviet state – was determined to extend its boundaries at all costs. Partly in reaction, a school of revisionists emerged, both at the time and later, to argue that the Cold War happened because of America's drive for military and economic hegemony, and its unwillingness to take account of the legitimate interests of the Soviet Union. Both interpretations attributed an improbable degree of cunning and competence to politicians, generals, arms manufacturers, and spies. Both were crude oversimplifications.

Stalin was an unusually villainous dictator. The Soviet political and economic system was both vicious and incompetent. Conflict with capitalism was embedded in its state ideology. By contrast America was not a dictatorship and its economy boomed almost continuously from 1945 onwards, despite Communist predictions of its imminent collapse. Both the Soviet Union and America operated a form of imperial control over their associates during the Cold War. But association with the Soviet Union was never voluntary, and the Soviet empire was maintained by force. At least in Western Europe, association with America was voluntary, and the Americans were never tempted to use force there. Both sides in the Cold War committed atrocities and stupidities. This does not mean that there was nothing to choose between them. Everyone is better off because it was American power and American will which prevailed, though that is not of course a proposition which Russians find it easy to share.

The Cold War was crucially shaped by the position the victors found themselves in when the guns fell silent. In 1943 the Soviets demonstrated at the battle of Kursk, the largest tank battle in history, that they could now beat the Germans at their own game of armoured warfare. At that time their Western allies had still not landed on the continent of Europe. As the Western armies were invading Normandy, the Soviets were beginning the breakthrough which ten months later would bring them to Berlin. Not surprisingly, the Russians believe that they won the war, with very little help from their allies. Even a less ruthless leader than Stalin would have followed the ancient motto – 'To the Victor the Spoils'. After 1945 it was inevitable that the Soviet Union would dominate Eastern and Central Europe. There was nothing that the West could do about it, unless it went to war, or unless the Soviet Union changed profoundly. The West was unwilling to do the first. The second was beyond its control.

Stalin had four objectives after the war: to rebuild his country, to consolidate his wartime gains, to match American nuclear power, and to see how far he could safely exploit the fruits of victory. Wherever he held the ground he imposed satellite regimes. He adventured into Persian Azerbaijan. He encouraged the North Koreans to attack the South. He hoped the massive Communist Parties in France and Italy would give him decisive influence in Western Europe. At each point he came up against American power and prudently withdrew. Only once did he risk a direct confrontation with the Americans. It led to humiliation at the hands of the American air force in Berlin. He never attempted such a confrontation again.

Stalin's successors kept an iron grip on their Eastern European backyard. The West observed the rules, and made only the most timid attempts to interfere. Khrushchev genuinely believed in the eventual victory of Communism worldwide. He was not content to rest on the defensive. In 1961 and 1962 he provoked confrontation with America over Berlin and Cuba: the seventeen most dangerous months in the whole of the Cold War. He too backed down in the face of American power.

These humiliations contributed to Khrushchev's downfall in 1964. His successor Brezhnev was very different: less ebullient, more cautious, and until his last years a competent though workaday politician. He chose to deal with the domestic crisis by pretending it didn't exist. He stopped the debate on economic reform, and cracked down on dissidence. Unlike his predecessor, he was not prepared to risk direct confrontation with the Americans. His search for détente in Europe was, according to his collaborators, perfectly genuine. But in the Third World it was America's turn to be comprehensively humiliated. Defeat in Vietnam and a high oil price sapped Western morale. Brezhnev seized the opportunity to spread Soviet influence in Asia, Latin America, and Africa – areas of no direct interest to the Soviet Union. He continued with a massive arms build-up in the hope of achieving 'strategic parity' with the Americans. But in the end he, too, overreached himself. He was bamboozled by his colleagues into invading Afghanistan, which became the Soviet Union's very own Vietnam. Brezhnev's foreign policy, like his domestic policy, condemned the Soviet system to collapse. He got away with it for as long as he did because the Soviet economy was kept afloat on high oil prices.

On balance therefore – apart of course from the special case of Eastern Europe – the record of Soviet external adventure in the postwar period is a record of consistent failure and humiliation. The 'Soviet threat' was not of course a total myth. Optimistic British diplomats, who had hoped during the war that even Stalin's Russia was capable of changing for the better, were doomed to be disappointed for the next four decades. By the 1980s Soviet weapons were very sophisticated, and there was a very large number of them. The Communist ideology was universalist and Messianic. The Soviet Union was aggressively extending itself – overextending itself – into parts of the world which had little to do with the country's real interests. Western analysts and policymakers were right to take these things seriously. But they made three basic errors. They assumed that it was possible for a universalist political philosophy to achieve world domination. They consistently overestimated the effectiveness of the Soviet armed forces and their weapons. And they consistently underestimated Soviet political, economic, and social weakness.

The first assumption was wrong *in principle*. The overestimation of the Soviet armed forces and of the Soviet capacity to assert subversive influence abroad may have been understandable. But it was fraught with the worst kind of danger. And it ignored the fact that what Clausewitz called 'friction' – the cussedness of reality – will always ensure that no bid for world domination can succeed.

Less excusable was the underestimation of Soviet weakness. The failure of Western analysts to produce a balanced picture was evident at the time, and not only with the benefit of hindsight. By 1945 the Red Army was exhausted, its equipment worn out. The one desire of the victorious soldiers was to get back to what was left of their families and to rebuild their shattered country, where people were once again beginning to die of starvation. Primo Levi's memoirs of Eastern Europe after the war paint an unforgettable picture of the Soviet army going home: men, women, and children in rags, broken-down vehicles pulled by oxen and laden with loot; a nomad horde on the move. There was no possibility – political, military, or psychological – that this army could resume any kind of serious offensive action for years to come.

The Soviets rebuilt their country after a fashion, but with amazing speed. Soviet military science and industry forged ahead. Soviet scientists and engineers mastered thermonuclear fusion, built formidable bombs and rockets and catapulted a dog, and then a man, into space. The Soviet leaders and the Soviet people felt – for the first time in their history – that they were beating the West at its own game of technical excellence. The Party Programme of 1961 predicted that within twenty years the Soviet consumer would be provided with an abundance of material and cultural goods.

But the Soviet Union was already in deep domestic crisis. Its political and economic system was muscle-bound and sclerotic. Agriculture was a mess. Capital construction was grossly wasteful. The consumer was ignored, and social services were underfunded. Above all, despite its successes in space and defence, Soviet technology was lagging increasingly behind the West. By the 1960s some courageous and clear-sighted Soviet citizens were already pointing out the bitter truth. Most prominent was Sakharov, the nuclear physicist. He told the Soviet leadership in 1970 that 'the more novel and revolutionary the aspect of the economy, the wider becomes the rift between the USA and ourselves.' The Soviet Union, he said, could 'gradually revert to the status of a second-rate provincial power'.

Khrushchev, who was First Secretary of the Soviet Communist Party from 1953 to 1964, was not a fool. He knew he had a serious problem on his hands. He started with short-term measures – importing Western technology and Western grain. He then went further. He launched a far-reaching debate on economic reform. Soviet economists toyed with complex and heretical ideas. They wondered whether central planning should be modified or even replaced by market mechanisms. They talked of introducing interest payments on capital. These were concepts which could have earned their authors prison or worse under Stalin.

The intellectual ferment of the Khrushchev years did not long survive; 1968 and the suppression of the liberal regime in Prague brought all that to an end. Public discourse was again dominated by tired slogans from the old ideology. The slogans were important because they provided emotional comfort to the gerontocrats in the Kremlin, for whom they were the justi-fication for the Soviet Union's pointless and provocative lurches into Africa and Latin America. The intelligentsia no longer believed them. Many slipped into a weary cynicism, wickedly satirised by Yeltsin's biographer Leon Aron:

> These gentle, smart, likeable and utterly cynical idlers ... spent days chatting, trading rumours and anti-Soviet political jokes, reading and passing along the underground *samizdat* manuscripts, flirting, talking on the telephone, taking hourly smoking breaks, and raiding nearby stores on hot tips about new shipments of Japanese umbrellas, Finnish boots or Turkish leather coats. These were veterans of evasion, grand masters of bamboozling and window dressing, aces at avoiding work — much of it, to be fair, senseless and invented by the despised *oni*, 'them', the Party and state bureaucrats, whom these safely and very privately indignant anti-Communist radicals, most of them Party members in good standing, hated with a passion.[20]

But not everyone gave up. Some courageous souls – Solzhenitsyn, Sakharov, Amalrik, Shcharansky, and others – spoke out in public and were publicly punished with imprisonment or exile. And there were others, whose role was in the end no less significant. It is a mistake to believe that the servants of an authoritarian state are incapable of thinking for themselves. The Tsarist censor Alexander Nikitenko (1804–1877) wrote in his diary: 'Our qualities as responsible citizens have not yet been formed because we do not yet have the essential elements ... namely public spirit-edness, a sense of legality, and honour.' Men and women with a similar understanding of their country's ills continued their intellectual enquiry throughout the Brezhnev era in the nooks and crannies of the estab-lishment, the professional journals, in the elite institutes of economic and political studies, in the apparatus of the Central Committee of the Communist Party itself, banding together, as Russians have always banded together, in small protective groups against the pressures of authority. In the nature of things these people were little noticed by the outside world, and when they appeared in public, and especially abroad, they were neces-sarily cautious in what they said. But they knew, as Khrushchev had dimly perceived, that things could not go on as they were. Building on the new thinking of the Khrushchev years, they created a body of political and economic theory, a climate of intellectual opinion, and a critical mass of reform-minded advisers, which were to provide the essential support for the breakthrough which Gorbachev was to make a decade later.

These complex realities were not widely appreciated in the West. Hard-headed Western analysts continued to insist that what you had to measure was Soviet *capabilities*, the facts of military power, so many missiles, so many tanks, so many divisions. You couldn't measure Soviet *intentions*, and so there was no point in basing your own policy on what you feared or hoped might be the driving force behind Soviet policies.

In practice, of course, Western governments had to make a continuous judgement about Soviet political objectives. In this, as in many other spheres of domestic and foreign policy, they had little special knowledge on which to base their conclusions. In 1969, for example, the British Joint Intelligence Committee admitted that its paper about 'the fundamental factors influencing the formulation of Soviet foreign policy and the principles which now appear to underlie it' drew on no relevant secret intelligence, and was, in effect, based on nothing which was not available to the intelligent outside observer.[21] Despite their apparent determination to draw a logical distinction between capabilities and intentions, Western analysts regularly failed to draw the equally important connection between the outward appearance of Soviet military power and the everyday realities of the Soviet economic and political system, which was clearly incapable of matching the broad economic, technological, political, and social advances being made by the developed countries of the West. As late as 1988 one distinguished American strategic analyst returned from her first visit shocked to the core by the sorry state of the shops in Moscow's smartest street: 'What sort of a superpower is that?'

Thus for much of the Cold War the West misinterpreted and overesti-mated the Soviet threat. It failed to draw an adequate conclusion from the widespread evidence of Soviet domestic and imperial weakness. Western analysts seemed unable or unwilling to make the imaginative effort of putting themselves in their opponents' shoes. The task of military planning which the Soviet General Staff faced for most of the Cold War was daunting in the extreme. On their Western flank they confronted an increasingly prosperous and coherent group of European countries united under American leadership. To the North lay the threat of nuclear annihilation from the Strategic Air Command. To the East they faced over a billion potentially or actively hostile Chinese. And unlike their American opponents, the Soviets had no allies, only satellites who showed from time to time a distressing tendency to rebel. Like their

Western counterparts, their inevitable reaction was to overinsure against the worst case.

The failure of interpretation often reflected the ebb and flow of domestic political fortunes in the West, and especially in America, rather than significant changes either in the reality of Soviet power or in the ability of Western agencies to collect information about the Soviet Union and analyse it properly. President Eisenhower called the gross overestimates by US intelligence of Soviet bomber and missile strength – the bomber and missile gaps of the 1950s – 'nothing more than imaginative creations of irresponsibility'. Sober men in London thought that the Russians wanted the fruits of the war without its risks. But there were those who concentrated on the most unlikely case of all: the possibility that the Soviets would launch a bolt from the blue, a surprise attack in Europe or elsewhere designed to achieve – what? No one ever quite said.

The more sophisticated claimed, then or later, that they never really believed in the bolt from the blue. The more insidious danger, they considered, was political blackmail backed by the implicit threat of overwhelming military power. This may have been a reasonable argument in the decade after the war. Western Europe lay in ruins, and one might at a pinch turn a blind eye to the fact that the Soviet Union lay in ruins as well. The argument became less plausible as the West European democracies recovered their political and economic equilibrium, and as a series of risings in Eastern Europe showed how shallow were the roots of the Soviet empire there.

By the beginning of the 1970s CIA analysts and others had begun to recognise the Soviet Union's weaknesses, and to factor them into their estimates. But in the second half of the decade American enthusiasm for détente waned. The American Right accused the CIA of complacent overoptimism. One of President Ford's most outspoken intelligence advisers argued that the Soviet leaders, secure in their nuclear shelters, would not shrink from sacrificing a few million of their own people to gain their ideological and imperial ends.[22] As the mood in America changed, the President agreed to set up a team of independent experts to look into the matter. This 'B Team' contained a number of highly competent but very conservative analysts. They deliberately abandoned the principle that you should look only at your opponent's capabilities. At the end of 1976 the B Team reported that the Soviet Union was preparing for a Third World War. The Soviet leaders, said the B Team, believed that superior military force could be used either to fight and win, or to blackmail the West into submission.[23] The B Team produced no serious evidence to justify these claims.

As the 1970s turned into the 1980s, American rhetoric ran even further out of control. An article in the authoritative journal *Foreign Policy* argued in 1980 that 'The United States should plan to defeat the Soviet Union and to do so at a cost that would not prohibit US recovery.' Reagan's Deputy Under Secretary for Defense, T. K. Jones, thought that the American recovery from nuclear war need only take two to four years, provided that the populace observed a few simple measures of civil defence. 'If there are enough shovels to go around,' he said, 'everyone's going to make it. It's the dirt that does it.'[24] Influential analysts and politicians became obsessed with the idea that the Soviets might use their newest rockets, the super-accurate SS-19, to destroy all the American land-based missiles, the Minutemen, in a first strike. Even if such a thing had been technically possible, the US submarine and air forces would have been left intact. Nobody had a convincing explanation of why the Soviet leadership should do anything so self-evidently barmy.

Those who conducted these convoluted arguments resembled the intellectual revolutionaries of nineteenth-century Russia in their enthusiasm for pushing arguments to logical and potentially murderous extremes. Their conclusions had little to do with common sense: John Newhouse pointed out as the confrontation ground towards its end that 'Most of what passes for strategic doctrine in the nuclear age is abstraction, not reality.'[25] Ordinary Americans protested vigorously at their leaders' apparent attempt to condition them to the idea that nuclear war could be a normal instrument of policy. An organisation called Ground Zero called massive demonstrations in Washington, on lines pioneered by the Campaign for Nuclear Disarmament in Britain. Communities throughout the country protested at the prospect of a new generation of American missiles, the MX, being based near them.

Reagan himself, a remarkable if muddled politician, had a genuine moral horror of nuclear weapons.[26] With missionary zeal he promoted his impractical Strategic Defence Initiative (SDI) for an astrodome covering the whole of the United States, off which the Soviet missiles would bounce harmlessly. In Reykjavik in Autumn 1986 he reached out to Gorbachev and the nuclear confrontation began to unwind. Experts on both sides were surprised and disconcerted. But their objections were progressively overcome.

Western overestimation of Soviet power continued until the very end. In April 1989 the US Government's National Intelligence Estimate concluded that the Soviet Union would remain an adversary for the foreseeable future and would pose serious challenges to NATO unity.[27] The experts dismissed Gorbachev's UN announcement in December 1988 of massive troop cuts as one more Communist trick. The atmosphere inside the analytical community militated against more subtle interpretations. A senior CIA analyst admitted in 1988 that the Agency had never studied the possibility of political change in the Soviet Union. Had he written and circulated such a study, he said, 'people would have been calling for my head.'[28]

The American experts on the Soviet Union, in particular, were professional, knowledgeable, and covered the full gamut of opinion. It is easy enough to mock their failures with the benefit of hindsight. But there are a number of reasons why these failures were perhaps inevitable. Above all, the Cold War was a real war, even though Russians and Americans never got to shoot at one another directly. It was also a religious war for both sides. And in wartime – especially if it is a religious or ideological war – each side demonises the other. Second, the military and those who assess intelligence and advise governments always look at the worst case. Nobody ever got into trouble for predicting a crisis that didn't happen. But if you fail to let your bosses know a crisis is coming, you risk losing your job or worse. This was as true of the Soviet military and intelligence agencies as it was of the American. The consequence was an inevitable process of threat inflation on both sides. Third, however much these warnings may have lacked plausibility, they had one pleasing consequence for the American military-industrial complex: they encouraged Congress to vote the funds for ever more powerful, exotic, and lucrative weapons. In 1979 the Chief of US Air Force Intelligence threw out an assessment that the Soviet Union would not attack Western Europe. It would, he said, make it harder to persuade the US Congress to vote funds. Reagan's Defense Secretary, Cap Weinberger, had no doubt of the rightness of this approach: 'Yes, of course we used worst case analysis. You should always use a worst-case analysis in this business. You can't afford to be wrong. If we won by too much, if it was overkill, so be it.'[29]

On 4 May 1979 Mrs Thatcher came to power in Britain. She saw – or thought she saw – an increasingly self-confident Soviet Union 'expanding its power and influence in Afghanistan, southern Africa and Central America by subversion and outright military invasion ... planting offensive missiles in its eastern satellites, building its conventional forces far in excess of NATO equivalents'.[30] The West, she thought, was neither psychologically, nor militarily, nor economically in a shape to resist. President Reagan came to power a year later on a crest of even more overblown rhetoric.

Not only the Soviet government was terrified. The British historian Timothy Garton Ash wrote in his diary for 1980 that he expected a nuclear war before the end of the decade. The stage appeared to be set for a new – and as it turned out, the last – confrontation between the Forces of Light and the 'Evil Empire'.

And yet it was Mrs Thatcher, the Iron Lady, who first scented the wind of change. She did not believe that the Soviet system could survive for ever. If it did not throw away its advantages, she rightly argued, the West would triumph because it 'rested on the unique, almost limitless, creativity and vitality of individuals'. Given the closed nature of the Soviet political system, she believed, it could only be challenged by an insider, a man who had made his career within it. She was the first Western leader to spot Gorbachev, she claimed, because she was looking for someone like him. She devoted a substantial part of her formidable energies to trying to understand the essence of the system. She became something of an expert in her own right, though she did admit, when visiting a Moscow housing estate in 1987, that the people living there 'knew the system even better than I did'. [31]

My professional involvement in these matters began in 1959, when I was sent to the embassy in Warsaw (Jill came out to Warsaw a year later, and for a brief while we constituted the embassy's political section). The country was still basking in the aftermath of Poland's 'Spring in October' of 1956, when Polish workers, Polish students, and even the Polish Communist Party had successfully faced down Khrushchev and brought Gomulka to power. For five years Poland was unique – the only Communist country in the world where ordinary people could express their political views without harassment, where modern art, avant-garde music, and political theatre flourished. Foreigners were actually popular – an unusual phenomenon in any country. Our Polish friends were absurdly outspoken, even in front of the microphones which we all assumed were still buried in the walls of our apartments. The secret police began to get more uppity towards the end of our stay. The Poles were not deterred. One knowledgeable insider – a Communist journalist on the government newspaper – took it upon himself to warn me that the policemen were hoping to trap me. He advised me to keep clear of Polish girls for the next month.

The Poles feared but admired the Germans. They feared and despised the Russians. A few hopeful Communists – hard to find in Poland even then – still believed in the eventual victory of Communism worldwide. They included Mieczyslaw Rakowski, the brilliant editor of the liberal *Polityka*, who later became Poland's last Communist prime minister. But for most the ideology was wholly discredited. So was the gallantry that had led to so many forlorn risings against Russian and German occupation in the past. Now realism prevailed. The realists were thoroughly aware how lucky Poland was compared with Russia's other satellites, and how fragile their relative freedom remained as long as the Soviet Union retained the will and capacity to preserve its empire. Much though they disliked the thought, they knew that Poland would never be able to assert its full independence until the process of change had begun in Russia itself. History was to show that the realists were right. Walesa, Solidarity, and many others in Eastern Europe chipped away at the empire courageously and relentlessly. But their gallantry was frustrated time and again by an imperial system that still appeared to enjoy commanding power and will. The avalanche did not begin until the ice started to break up in the Soviet Union with the arrival of Gorbachev.

Signs that the Soviet Union was in crisis by the 1960s were evident even to the outsider. Jill and I lived in Moscow from 1963 to 1966. Moscow was a patently run-down city. Apart from one huge placard high on the Moscow skyline which exhorted the citizen to 'FLY AEROFLOT' (an unnecessary injunction in a country with huge distances and only one airline), there were no advertisements, only endless Communist slogans in white lettering on a red ground. There were few goods in the shops, and none of quality. Western popular music, dances, and dress were frowned upon. There was grinding rural poverty just outside the city, and it got worse the further you travelled across the country.

We lived on the tenth floor of one of Khrushchev's new housing blocks on the Kutuzovsky Prospect, the route along which Napoleon entered Moscow with the Grande Armée in 1812. The enormous building, precariously put together in light grey brick, was ringed by a fence guarded by 'militiamen', regular agents of the KGB lightly disguised, who phoned through to headquarters whenever we left the compound, and deterred Russians from calling on us without a cast-iron official excuse. The foreign inhabitants of the block came from a variety of continents and a variety of cultures. Their children threw bottles from the top-floor windows, and reduced the neat little playground in the courtyard to scrap iron. Almost opposite was the Ukraina Hotel, one of the eight skyscrapers built to ring the city on Stalin's orders. These dominated the skyline, huge, a bizarre mixture of neo-classical, baroque, and neo-Gothic. Most people hated them, for their association with the tyrant and for aesthetic reasons as well. I liked them. They matched the barbaric character of the city, and mirrored the ring of monasteries – the Novodevichy, the Spassky, the Andronnikov – built to defend Moscow against the Tatars, the Poles, and its other many enemies.

Across the river the old quarter of the Arbat had been knocked down to make way for another Prospect, to be named after Kalinin, Stalin's pliant President. Once built, the huge office and apartment blocks along the

Prospect, dour and shabby, looked as if they were protruding from a rotten jaw, and were immediately dubbed 'Khrushchev's teeth' by the irreverent Muscovites. Halfway along the new Prospect a crane with a ball and chain on a pole was half-heartedly knocking down an elegant little church as part of Khrushchev's campaign against religion. In the middle of town, the churches and buildings in the ancient business quarter, the Kitaigorod, were being cleared to make way for the grotesque Rossia Hotel, which still lowers, spectacularly inefficient, over Red Square. These depredations aroused fury in the minds of ordinary Russians, and they were halted and reversed immediately Khrushchev fell. The little church on the Kalinin Prospect was rebuilt. The demolitions in Kitaigorod were brought to an end. But much had gone, apparently beyond repair: a preview of the mindless architecture and shoddy construction which came to disfigure so much of Moscow in the Brezhnev years, and a vivid symbol of the magniloquent decay of Communism itself.

Even though it was a period of comparative détente, our everyday life was nevertheless quite different from what it had been in Poland. Having lost some of my nine lives in Poland, I decided that it made sense to play by the rules. We went to the theatre, stayed at home with our little children, and made no attempt – as some of our American colleagues did – to get in touch with Russian dissidents. We compensated for the lack of human contact in Moscow by travelling as much as we could: to Central Asia, to the Caucasus, along the Trans-Siberian railway, to Yakutsk near the Northern cold pole in Siberia, where winter temperatures regularly fall to –60 centigrade. On these trips we met many people who were happy to talk to us because our contact was fleeting: the musician from the Jewish Autonomous Republic of Birobidjan who had worked for an illegal construction company along the Volga, the retired intelligence officer who told us how he had helped to break the Japanese military codes, a young man with (so he told us) a huge collection of illegal recordings of Western pop music, another young man who danced the Twist with Jill in a Sochi restaurant in defiance of the grim-faced manageress, the village baker in Pasanauri on the Georgian Military Highway who cursed Khrushchev (then still in power) for ruining his business by giving the Soviet Union's grain away to all those black men in Africa.

These encounters were often very enlightening. But they were poor fare after Poland: it was doubly frustrating to think that all over Moscow people were engaged in just the kind of all-night argument, laced with vodka and music, that we had enjoyed in Warsaw. For there were clear signs of intellectual movement. Khrushchev had all the contempt of the self-made man for intellectuals. Yet he realised dimly that something had to be done about the intellectual sclerosis which Stalin had imposed, if the Soviet Union was to compete successfully in the modern world. He allowed the publication of Solzhenitsyn's short novel *One Day in the Life of Ivan Denisovich*, about the Gulag, and Tvardovsky's *Terkin in the Underworld*, a witty satire on the Stalinist system. When the Italian Communist leader Palmiro Togliatti died in Yalta in the summer of 1964, his *Testament* – highly critical of Soviet rigidities, at least by implication – was published in *Pravda*. These events were as striking to us as they were to the average sceptical Russian: but we were, alas, excluded from the debate.

At that time, though, my task in the embassy was not to follow the politics, but to report on the Soviet economy and look after the British business visitors who were coming out to Moscow in increasing numbers. British scientists were also coming to Moscow to visit their Soviet colleagues. They would return from their meetings amazed by the sophistication of Soviet science. But the businessmen would go off to tour dirty, disorganised, patently inefficient Soviet factories, and come back shaking their heads and wondering how the Russians had ever got into space.

My ability to report accurately on the state of the Soviet economy was hampered by my lack of technical knowledge, by the total inadequacy (or worse) of Soviet economic statistics, and by the unwillingness of Her Majesty's Treasury and others in London to accept that any economy could function – or rather, fail to function – in the way I was describing. Nevertheless the economic debate which Khrushchev had launched was intellectually fascinating to follow and very revealing of the state of the country. I left Moscow convinced that despite its formidable military power, the Soviet Union was a very poor country in serious economic trouble. The political system was stagnant, and a positive deterrent to the kind of innovative energy which the Soviet Union needed to generate if it was to compete successfully with the West in the long term. I did not, of course, foresee its imminent collapse. Maybe, I thought, it could be saved by reform, the 'convergence' with the West that some people detected at the time. But on the whole I felt reasonably sure that fundamental change would eventually come.

Khrushchev's reforms got nowhere. He was dislodged by a palace coup in October 1964, just as the Chinese detonated their first nuclear device. The thing was all done in hugger-mugger. In those days the Moscow rumour mill was not accessible to foreigners. Formal contacts between the Soviet and Western governments at that time were fitful and often unproductive. The Soviet authorities preferred to get information and views out to Western diplomats and journalists through informal and deniable channels. Victor Louis was an interesting and ambiguous figure who played an important role as a go-between in the 1960s and 1970s. He had been in a camp, from which his enemies in Moscow said that he had been released following a bargain with the KGB. By the 1960s he was, by Soviet standards, a rich man, living with his English wife in a large apartment in Moscow and a dacha in the fashionable writers' colony at Peredelkino. His influence in the foreign community was much reduced when he became involved in the 1970s in a KGB campaign to discredit Solzhenitsyn. It was he who first leaked the news of Khrushchev's fall to the *Evening Standard*. Next day the Central Committee announced that Mr Khrushchev had asked to be relieved of his duties 'in view of his advanced age and the deterioration of his health'.

For a while a version of the Khrushchev experiment ran on, like a chicken without its head. Prime Minister Kosygin struggled to promote a timid economic reform. Books and films still appeared which were clearly intended to mend the fracture in Russian history caused by the Revolution and its aftermath – a film about the Bolshevik coup in October 1917 which showed Trotsky playing a positive role; another which took the form of an extended and not unsympathetic interview with Shulgin, a monarchist member of the Tsarist parliament who had advised the White leaders during the civil war. But by the time we left Moscow in the middle of 1966 the debate was already subsiding, and public life began to lapse into intellectual torpor. We were glad not to be living in Moscow during the years of Brezhnev's stagnation.

I continued to deal with Russian affairs, though at one remove. At the end of 1969 I started work in the Western Organisations Department of the Foreign Office. This obscurely named body dealt with NATO, the transatlantic politico-military relationship, nuclear policy, and European security affairs including the prospects for serious military cooperation amongst the Europeans.

I had always thought that military affairs, unlike politics, were to some extent a matter of arithmetic. We knew how many tanks, guns, ships, aeroplanes and soldiers we had. We could make an informed guess at how many they had. We could work out a reasonable strategic doctrine about how all this should interact. And there you were.

Of course it was not nearly as simple as that. Only the Americans had enough intelligence resources to produce a comprehensive view of Soviet capacities, and the rest of us had little choice but to take their estimates on trust. The real rows took place over how big our own armed forces were. Some NATO governments wanted to make a big show without spending more money. The Germans wanted to play down the extent of their military effort in order not to arouse memories of the past. The Americans wanted to quell fears that isolationist pressures would force them to cut their troops in Europe, and chose to demonstrate their resolve by piling up vast stocks of equipment and ammunition on the continent.

One of the Department's chief preoccupations at this time was the problem of what to do with the seven thousand tactical nuclear weapons stored in Europe. There was no policy for directing or controlling their use: one American commander on the Central Front in Germany told my colleague that he would blast off his weapons if the Reds started coming over the hill. While British, German, and American officials struggled to resolve this unsatisfactory state of affairs, I myself dealt mainly with the move towards a European security conference, and the proposal to negotiate conventional arms reductions with the Warsaw Pact, the so-called Mutual and Balanced Force Reductions (MBFR). NATO's ability to put together a sensible negotiating position on both these matters was severely undermined by the fear that if we entered into negotiation on either, the devilishly cunning Soviets would take us to the cleaners. They would split NATO and at last secure formal Western recognition of their empire in Eastern Europe. The Americans would go home in disgust, and Europe would once again be at the mercy of its own follies and of the Russian steamroller.

I believed that this assessment grossly overestimated Soviet negotiating skills and the underlying strength of the Soviet position both domestically and in their empire. I was not at all sure that the negotiations would yield much advantage to the West. Nor, however, could I see that they would present much danger if we handled ourselves properly. But it was not easy to get such ideas across. When I gave a seminar on MBFR at the National Defence College in 1973, I was attacked by an RAF officer for failing to understand the disastrous weakness of NATO's military position in Europe. 'The Russians', he expostulated, 'could use their new air-portable division to seize Frankfurt airport by surprise, and we would not have the strength to dislodge them.' 'But they're not going to do that,' I said. 'How do you know?' he asked. This kind of reasoning underlay much of the West's analysis of the Soviet threat throughout the Cold War.

In the event it was the Soviets who were taken to the cleaners, both in the negotiations on European security which culminated in Helsinki in 1975, and in the conventional arms agreement which was signed in Vienna in 1990 after many frustrating years. Both results were beyond what I could have imagined in 1970.

On the eve of Mrs Thatcher's election victory in 1979 I was head of the Policy Planning Staff in the Foreign Office. As part of the preparations which all Whitehall departments make during an election campaign, I wrote a paper on East–West relations for the new Foreign Secretary – whoever he or she might turn out to be. I described the Soviet Union as 'a military giant, but a political, social, and economic pigmy'. In this and subsequent papers I argued that the West's fear of the Soviet Union was exaggerated. The Soviets were overreaching themselves in Africa, Asia, and Latin America. The economic system was faltering. The immense and ubiquitous secret police was a sign of weakness, not of strength. The Soviet government feared the Soviet people. In 1962 they had put down food riots in Novocherkassk with much bloodshed. They could never be sure, as Victor Louis remarked to me, that next time the soldiers would shoot. By contrast the Western Alliance was in adequate shape. A reasonably self-confident West, I thought, should be able to handle the Soviet threat well enough. My colleagues found these judgements complacent. They never had any noticeable effect on official thinking and they did not look like prospering in the Thatcher era.

I had underestimated her. Early in 1980 her Private Secretary, Michael Alexander, persuaded her to take part in a discussion on Russia with a group of Foreign Office experts. At first she balked ('Foreign Office? Foreign Office? What do *they* know about Russia?'). But she relented. On 7 February 1980, for the first and perhaps the only time, she crossed Downing Street to Lord Carrington's ornate room in the Foreign Office building.

The home team consisted of myself and Christopher Mallaby, who had recently returned from a stint as head of the Political Section in the embassy in Moscow. Before Mrs Thatcher arrived in his office, Lord Carrington gave us some firm advice. We should let her know if we disagreed with her; and we should shout her down if she did not let us get a word in edgeways. Almost from the moment she entered the room, Mrs Thatcher launched into a monologue about the Soviet threat. But she switched into the listening mode which she adopted when she was genuinely interested (you could almost hear the change of gear) when Christopher embarked on a brilliantly informed analysis of the current state of the Union. After he had run through a list of the economic, techno-logical, social, and political difficulties the Soviet Union was facing, she remarked that, if the Soviet Union was really in such a parlous state, the system was bound to collapse before long. 'No, no,' we hastily replied, 'it's not like that at all. The germs of change are at work inside Soviet society. The system may eventually become more democratic and less expansionist.

But it will not easily happen while the Soviet Communist Party and its apparatus of repression are still intact.'

This meeting was followed by two others, including an all-day session at Chequers, in which Mrs Thatcher set a small Foreign Office team to compete against three academics, Michael Howard, Elie Kedourie, and Hugh Thomas. It was at Chequers that I first heard her develop her views on nuclear weapons as a force for peace. She remarked to me afterwards that she was not at all sure that, in the event, she could press the button: 'I want grandchildren too' – an endearing flash of humanity.

These meetings, and a subsequent seminar with academics in Chequers in 1983, demonstrated Mrs Thatcher's intellectual curiosity and a more sophisticated understanding of the problem than she was usually given credit for. She changed the nature of the debate by her announcement in December 1984 that Gorbachev was a man with whom she could do business – a historic insight for which Gorbachev always remained grateful. And during her trip to Moscow in the spring of 1987 she won the enduring admiration of Soviet television viewers, when she trounced three Soviet journalists in a television debate about the Soviet Union's aggressive military posture. For the first time the Soviet people learned the truth about the way their tax roubles were being wasted on useless military hardware. She remained a legend in Russia for many years.

Even as Mrs Thatcher came to power, the Russians were falling behind in the area to which they had attached the greatest importance of all. Strategic parity with the Americans was no sooner achieved than it proved to be an unsustainable burden. President Reagan's Strategic Defense Initiative was the final straw. The SDI program stimulated a qualitative leap in American military – and civilian – technology: an area in which the Soviet Union could no longer hope to compete. The SDI program was not the cause of the Soviet collapse, as some Americans have argued. But by the beginning of the 1980s the best of the Soviet generals, among them General Ogarkov, the Chief of Staff, and the less hidebound of the Soviet leadership had understood that the Soviet Union could afford to stagnate no longer. As the ailing gerontocrats – Brezhnev, Andropov, Chernenko – followed one another into the grave, it was clear to all that a new approach was needed: a process of reform that would get the economy going again. Otherwise the country would be unable to retain its status as the other superpower, or fulfil its Messianic role as the opposite pole of attraction from the United States for people throughout the world. When Chernenko finally died the Politburo turned to Mikhail Gorbachev, the youngest man among them. They believed him to be imaginative and energetic, but reliable and orthodox as well. On 11 March 1985 Gorbachev became the seventh, and as it turned out the last, General Secretary of the Communist Party of the Soviet Union, the heir to the ruthless totalitarian traditions of Lenin and Stalin, and to the brutal authoritarianism of the Tsars.

Gorbachev knew that the Soviet Union could not continue on its previous path. He had seen the system staggering in his home province of Stavropol. He had observed corruption, incompetence, and financial irresponsibility at the highest levels. Intellectually curious, unusually open-minded for a Party official, he listened carefully to the economists and political scientists who were still developing the new line of thinking about the Soviet Union's real needs, and the place it should properly occupy in the world, the line on which they had embarked two decades earlier in the Khrushchev years. Many of them became his close advisers in the early period of his rule. But for years he too had been thinking about the steps that must be taken if the Soviet Union was to overcome its crisis. The economy would never work properly as long as it remained in the grip of the central planners and a prey to the apparently unlimited demands of the military. Nor would it work if ordinary people were not allowed to develop their own initiative, and if they were not trusted, informed, and consulted by the government. These thoughts were reflected in the slogans – *Demokratizatsia, Perestroika, Glasnost*[32] – which Gorbachev adopted when he came to power. The slogans were not new. They figured during the brief period of reform under Khrushchev, and indeed under the liberalising Tsars of the nineteenth century. That was one of the numerous reasons why many Russians, and many foreign observers, refused to believe that Gorbachev was doing something totally unprecedented in Russian history, something which would lead to the demise of the Soviet Union, and which would cost Gorbachev his own job.

On the eve of his election as General Secretary in March 1985 Gorbachev told his wife, Raisa Maximovna, 'We can't go on living like this.' Few doubted that the country was ripe for change. But four questions exercised observers, both inside and outside the country. Was it possible to reform the Soviet Union at all, or was the thing beyond redemption? Was Gorbachev, a man who had clambered up the greasy pole to the top of a dying system, plausible in the role of reformer? Did he have any kind of strategic vision, or was he merely stumbling forward? Would his numerous opponents inside the Party apparatus, the military and the police – the traditional bulwarks of autocracy – allow him to get away with it?

Inside the Soviet Union there were many who believed that nothing good would come as long as the country was led by Communists. With charac-

teristic Russian extremism these people wanted nothing less than uncondi-
tional surrender from the Party, however unlikely such an outcome might
seem. In the West many of those who were used to the simplicities of the
Cold War assumed that Gorbachev's reforms were a blind, an attempt to
strengthen the Soviet Union for the next round of its historic competition
with liberal democracy, a mere breathing space in a strategy of world
domination. In London and Washington – right up to the moment of
Gorbachev's fall – voices warned that we should not be taken in, that we
should not lower our guard against the Evil Empire.

Almost from the beginning Gorbachev's many critics accused him of
lacking a strategic vision. This accusation was unfair. Gorbachev was determined to defuse the East–West confrontation, sharply reduce the military
burden on the Soviet economy, introduce rationality into the economic
system, and release the creativity and initiative of ordinary people by
breaking the grip of the Party on everyday life. He was determined to do all
this within a framework of law, to create the *Rechtsstaat* which had been the
ideal of Russia's nineteenth-century liberals. Aware that most previous
attempts at reform in Russia had ended in violence, he was determined
neither to use force nor to shed blood. But he was only too aware of the
powerful forces of conservatism and radical extremism which could blow
him off course or remove him from office, as Khrushchev had been removed
before him. What others regarded as lack of resolution he himself saw as the
manoeuvring necessary to promote a noble end. He did not foresee that this
process would in the end fatally weaken the Party to which he had devoted
his life. Neither did most dispassionate observers at the time.

Gorbachev made these points explicitly, and on more than one occasion.
In April 1990 he told an audience in Sverdlovsk:

> When we began Perestroika, we saw our society in simple terms. The
> more deeply we got into it, the more we began to understand that we
> would achieve nothing by a minor repair, a paint job, changing the
> wallpaper. Changes were needed everywhere – in the economy, the
> federation, the Soviets, culture, the whole spiritual sphere, in order to
> renew society, to create normal conditions for everyday life … the old
> structures were holding up the reform, and we set in train the political
> reform to break up and dismantle the command system.

His determination to go down in history as the first Russian reformer to
avoid bloodshed was genuine. 'We must do everything', he told his
Sverdlovsk audience, 'to avoid confrontation and even more – civil war,

force, lawlessness, arbitrariness. The law should be supreme... Some people say: Mikhail Sergeevich, bang your fist. But banging one's fist doesn't help to get out of the vicious circle.' Gorbachev did not have a finished or detailed blueprint of how he would set about these tasks. He himself scorned the idea that such a blueprint could be drawn up, or that it could work in practice. In the complex world of Soviet (as indeed any other) politics, even the greatest statesman could only operate effectively if he laced principle with a liberal dash of opportunism.

I first saw Gorbachev's new Soviet Union when I visited Moscow at the beginning of 1987 for official talks with the economic department of the Soviet Foreign Ministry. It was one of the coldest Januaries for decades, and the view of the Kremlin across the ice-bound river was at its most spectacular. Gorbachev had been First Party Secretary for less than two years. For all the excitement in the West, I did not expect my official talks would go much beyond the usual exchange of cautious and tetchy platitudes. The event far exceeded my expectations. Even the Foreign Ministry officials were bubbling over with anxiety to tell me about their internal debates. I also met Abalkin and Bogomolov, two economists who had contributed to the tentative efforts at economic reform in the 1960s. They wanted to discuss not only the technicalities of economic reform in a state-run economy, but also the role of the Communist Party and the traditional Soviet attitude to work (or rather what they saw as the Soviet preference for avoiding it). They openly said that the Soviet Union was falling behind the West, perhaps fatally. Radical measures would have to be adopted, and they would have to work, because everything else had been tried and failed. The restructuring of the economy could not succeed without a parallel reconstruction of the political system – greater openness, industrial democracy, and the withdrawal of the Party from economic management.

These were revolutionary propositions. There was an obvious corollary. To survive the Soviet Union would have to abandon 'Socialism' and break the political as well as the economic monopoly of the Party. But few people, inside or outside the country, were yet ready to say openly that the experiment of 1917 had failed. Soviet conservatives – but not only they – argued that change could unleash the age-old demon of popular rebellion. Surely, many of them thought, it was preferable to continue as before, tinkering with the system, maintaining internal discipline, building up the armed forces, and giving whatever crumbs remained to the patient Soviet consumer. The people I saw in the streets were visibly better off than they had been twenty years earlier: had they not been, it really would have been an indictment of the system. I concluded that there was no reason to expect the Soviet Union to collapse soon. Gorbachev might be the catalyst for an inevitable change. But he might as easily be overthrown by the conservatives and the hard men from the Party, the army, and the police.

Not all the opponents of change were bad people. They included both decent conservatives and peculiarly unattractive reactionaries. Many leading Soviet conservatives were not, at least to start with, opposed to reform as such. They recognised its necessity, but they passionately wished to preserve what they thought was best in the Soviet system. In this sense Gorbachev himself was a conservative. The reactionaries represented an older and darker tradition, the tradition of extreme nationalism of the right and the left which goes back to well before the October Revolution, and is a most unattractive compound of xenophobia, religious obscurantism, and shameless anti-Semitism. Pamyat, an apparently innocuous organisation set up in 1980 to campaign for the resurrection and preservation of the Russian past, soon degenerated into an extreme nationalist and anti-Semitic organisation complete with its own uniformed bully boys. In the late 1980s Vladimir Zhirinovsky, a provincial eccentric from a very humble background in Kazakhstan, was already beginning to set himself up – some said, with KGB backing – as a 'patriotic' alternative to the democrats. Subsequently demonised in the Western press, Zhirinovsky studied Turkish and English at Moscow University, worked in Turkey in 1969 as a translator, and was expelled from Turkey that same year on suspicion of being a KGB agent. He has naturally denied these and later accusations.

These reactionaries made a lot of noise but had little effect on the course of events. Ordinary Russians were less attracted to them than domestic and foreign observers feared.

Gorbachev hoped that the Soviet Union could be preserved and that the Soviet system could be rationalised and humanised. But fate had finally caught up with the Soviet Union, which was no longer capable of facing up to the challenges of the modern world. Collapse had become inevitable.

Since then, Western and Russian observers have often sneered at Gorbachev's obtuseness. How could he have been so unaware that the Soviet Union was beyond reform?

That is of course unfair. When Gorbachev attained power in 1985, the orthodoxy among Western governments was that the Soviet Union and the Soviet threat would be with us for a long time to come. Western governments were at least as surprised as Gorbachev when the Soviet Union fell apart so quickly. Though the decline of the Soviet Union was irreversible, its detailed course could not be predicted in advance. The hard men might have resisted the inevitable at the price of blood. The Gorbachev revolution – a remarkably bloodless revolution – cannot be appreciated unless you bear in mind how fragile it was from its beginning in 1985 to its end in 1991.

Popular wisdom was close to the mark. By the time Jill and I arrived in Moscow in September 1988 the taxi-drivers were saying that we should not worry about Gorbachev. We should look instead to see what kind of man succeeded him.

3

The Flight of the Bumble Bee

He'd fly through the air with the greatest of ease,
A daring young man on the flying trapeze.

Music hall song

Gorbachev had been in office for three and a half years by the time Jill and I arrived in Moscow for our second stay. As the British ambassador, I had one advantage above all. Everyone in Russia, from Gorbachev down to the man in the street, was fascinated by the British Prime Minister. I got to see people and places in the Soviet Union simply because I was 'Mrs Thatcher's ambassador'. Nevertheless the substance of relations between the Soviet Union and Britain did not match the warmth of the personal relationship. Mrs Thatcher and Gorbachev continued their vigorous and enjoyable political exchanges. She continued to act as a valuable channel of communication with Washington when the direct line became clogged, as it did in the first months of 1989 after the election of George Bush as President. But in the later years neither Gorbachev and Thatcher, nor their officials, engaged in much substantial bilateral negotiation on the major issues of the day. The end of the Cold War was negotiated not by Mrs Thatcher but by the Americans and the Germans. The Americans led the negotiations on arms control, though the British gave them important support. And when Mrs Thatcher opposed the Germans' understandable and unstoppable desire for reunification with a combination of prejudice and false historical analogy, British influence was reduced in Moscow, as well as in Washington and in Bonn. Only in the last year of my stay, from the eve of the coup in August 1991 to the Spring of 1992, did the British government under John Major briefly play a significant role in East–West relations once again.

The central question was whether or not Gorbachev and his reforms would prevail. My first despatch to London marked the beginning of a running discussion with London about whether or not Gorbachev could survive, and whether or not his reforms could succeed. I called it 'Impressions of a Debate' because I had been struck above all in my first two months in Moscow by the remarkable openness of public discussion – in the press, on the radio, on television, and in private conversation.

This debate was already homing in on a central flaw in Gorbachev's political and constitutional approach: the Party's monopoly of power, which was enshrined in Brezhnev's 1977 constitution and buttressed by seventy years of ruthless practice. The press was beginning to argue that as long as the Party retained its exclusive grip, people would fear a reversion to the horrors of the past. Gorbachev was not yet prepared to draw the obvious conclusion: to abolish the monopoly. He did speak of the need for 'pluralism' as early as 1987. But until February 1990 he continued to qualify it with the adjective 'Socialist', by which he meant that different opinions should be allowed to compete: but only within the confines of the Party. Meanwhile he was getting rid of the die-hards – by the humane method of early retirement, rather than by shooting them as Stalin had done, or by turning the mob on them as Mao had done. But the Party was still his instrument of power, and he could not afford to alienate it too far. He argued that the Party should confine itself to 'broad guidance' while everyone else got on with ordinary business. But the idea carried no conviction either among the reactionaries or among the liberals. Many Russians had long ignored, despised, or hated the Party. It was now possible for them to say so openly.

Gorbachev continued to have spectacular success on the international front as he moved to reduce the superpower confrontation, promote conventional disarmament, pull out of Afghanistan, and dismantle the Soviet empire in Eastern Europe. Most of his own people welcomed the relaxation in domestic and international tension, though for the most part they were too preoccupied by their own affairs to pay it much attention. But the Soviet military were – not surprisingly – increasingly disgruntled at the abandonment of everything that they had built up since the victory over Germany in 1945. Gorbachev had little understanding for the rumbling in Eastern Europe, or for the increasingly explosive mood in the Caucasus and the Baltic States. None of us, even then, envisaged that the Soviet Union would soon break up into its constituent parts. But Gorbachev's Micawber-like hope that the Balts and the Caucasians would somehow reconcile themselves to their continued membership of a reformed Union became his most vulnerable point. Summing up at the end of 1988, I told the Foreign Office that even if Gorbachev succeeded in creating a liberal democratic state in Russia – a distant prospect – Russia would remain by far the largest military power in Europe, a problem for Russia's neighbours and partners. The interests of even a liberal Russia would inevitably differ from those of the rest of us.

When people asked us about life in Moscow, then and later, they always began with the same question: What was it like to be continuously observed and overheard by the KGB? It was indeed a constant part of our everyday life. In the 1960s the newspaper *Izvestia* would run – usually about once a month – an unpleasantly snide story about the misdemeanours of some foreign diplomat or journalist. Sometimes these were pure fiction, designed to remind the Soviet people of the need for eternal vigilance in their dealing with the foreign enemy. Sometimes they were nastier than that. The KGB used drugs, sex, and blackmail to entangle otherwise innocent foreigners, and to deter both foreigners and Russians from getting too friendly with one another. Just occasionally they did catch a genuine spy, or at least some brave but foolhardy idealist who was smuggling bibles into the country or underground literature out of it.

At the embassy we were all given fearful warnings by our own security people of what would happen if we were caught in any of these ways. No room – either in the office or at home – could be guaranteed free of the KGB's sophisticated listening devices. The junior staff were instructed to keep well clear of Soviet citizens. The rest of us had to report even the most innocent and accidental contact, so that measures could be taken if a sinister pattern seemed to be developing. The precautions were justified. The KGB often attempted and occasionally succeeded in exploiting the personal weaknesses of embassy officials. They saw no reason to relax their efforts after 1985 just because of the advent of Perestroika. This complicated life inside the embassy itself. We had about a hundred Soviet employees, all supplied through the Foreign Ministry's UPDK. The KGB had many ways of putting pressure on the Soviet staff to report on the embassy's work and on the characters, relationships, and weaknesses – financial, alcoholic and sexual – of the British staff. Jobs for Soviet employees in the embassy were well paid and secure. A simple threat to withdraw permission to work in the embassy was usually enough to bring a recalcitrant member of the local staff into line, without using more extreme measures such as blackmail or threats to relatives. Not surprisingly most of the British staff suffered from paranoia. The occasional foolhardy spirits rebelled against what they thought were unnecessary restrictions, and burned their fingers.

The constant harassment of our staff in Moscow led to continual rows with the Soviet government. So did the British government's determination to clip the wings of the KGB in London. In 1971 the British expelled 105 Soviet officials from London in a massive clean-out of real and suspected agents, and imposed a ceiling on those who remained. More expulsions took place in 1985 when the KGB double agent Gordievsky escaped from Moscow with British assistance. The following year it was the turn of the Americans. Reagan ordered out twenty-five Soviet officials working at the UN. When the Russians retaliated, he expelled a further fifty-five from the embassy in Washington and the consulate general in San Francisco, and followed the British example by placing a ceiling on the overall number of Soviet officials working in the United States. The Russians then withdrew all the Soviet citizens working in the US mission in Moscow. Many of these unfortunates were given no warning by either side, and were simply turned away by the KGB guards outside the American embassy when they came in for work the next day. Some of them were unemployed for months afterwards. American diplomats found themselves having to clean their flats and wash up after dinner parties. The British and American press laughed. But it was an additional and distracting burden on wretched officials who were already desperately overworked as the pace of Perestroika accelerated.

Eight months after our arrival in Moscow, on Friday, 19 May 1989, I called on Anatoli Chernyaev, Gorbachev's diplomatic adviser, with a message for his master. Chernyaev's office was next to Gorbachev's in the Central Committee building on the Staraya Ploshchad, just down the road from the Lubianka. Chernyaev was born in 1921 in Moscow into a liberal-minded family, whose views coloured his future attitudes to power and politics. He was a cheerful man, with bristly grey hair and moustache, like the colonel of an English county regiment of the line. Despite his appearance, he was a bit of a romantic, with an infectious laugh, which easily fell into an asthmatic wheeze. He went straight from college to fight in the war as an infantryman. His asthma nearly cost him his life when it overcame him during a patrol in no man's land. After the war he became a historian at Moscow University, where he specialised in the history of the British trade union movement, and then joined the Central Committee apparatus after Stalin died. His liberal ideas were reinforced by three years working on the staff of *Problems of Peace and Socialism* in Prague, which was a liberal and intellectual haven for many of those who were to become the leading proponents of change in the Soviet Union. During the Brezhnev years he was a deputy head of the International Department of the Central Committee Secretariat. But at the same time he maintained his connections with the political scientists, economists and experts on international affairs who inhabited the prestigious think-tanks, and with the artists, theatre directors, and musicians on the liberal fringe. Like them he was not a dissident. But he and they were part of the intellectual world which forged the 'New Thinking' which came to practical fruition when Gorbachev took over the leadership of the Communist Party.

In 1986 Gorbachev plucked Chernyaev out to become his foreign policy adviser. He accompanied Gorbachev on all the great foreign policy occasions until the very end, and went with Gorbachev into the civilised exile of the 'Gorbachev Foundation' after 1991. There he produced several circumstantial and illuminating memoirs. They make it engagingly clear that literature and women were on the whole far more important to him than official business. They do not suffer from self-justifying hindsight. In the privacy of his diary Chernyaev was often highly critical of Gorbachev, especially in the final year. But he remained wholly devoted to Gorbachev's strategic objectives. He became one of my most useful contacts and eventually a good friend: a straightforward man who would either tell me the truth or discreetly keep his mouth shut.

The message I had to deliver was a letter from Mrs Thatcher to Gorbachev, informing him that she had reluctantly authorised the expulsion from Britain of ten Soviet officials and three Soviet journalists. To soften the blow, she said, she had decided not to follow our earlier practice of making an even larger cut in the size of the Soviet community in London. We would not seek publicity. But the Soviets had been rebuilding their intelligence services in London, and action had to be taken. Chernyaev's response was characteristically sophisticated. He did not bother with recriminations. He asked me calmly whether we really had evidence. Were we sure we had picked on the right people? Why did we think it would be possible to avoid publicity? Why, given the close relationship between them, had Mrs Thatcher given Gorbachev no warning during his visit to London only three weeks earlier (an entirely reasonable though unanswerable question)?

I was unable to deliver a similar message to Uspensky, the head of the Second European Department, who was responsible for our affairs in the Foreign Ministry: he and his people were entertaining mine at the Foreign Ministry's dacha in a gesture of good will. But late the following evening I was summoned to the Foreign Ministry's Stalinist skyscraper on Smolensk Square by First Deputy Foreign Minister Kovalev, a man who always looked at death's door, a poet like so many Soviet officials. He rejected our accusations. Eight British officials and three British journalists were to leave

Moscow within two weeks 'for activities incompatible with their status' – a straight retaliation. In future the Soviets would impose the same numerical ceiling on our staff in Moscow – both British and Soviet – as we imposed on Soviet officials in London. I told him that the Russians had no grounds for surprise or complaint. British ministers and officials, and I myself, had regularly complained about the growing numbers of Soviet spies in London. We would not weaken. It would have to be the Russian policy which changed. Soviet spying in London did nothing to dispel the 'enemy image' which Gorbachev had done so much to combat. At this last remark Kovalev went very cold, and we parted stiffly.

By expelling three journalists the Russians ensured that publicity was inevitable. Nevertheless the briefing I gave to the British press the following morning came as a bolt from the blue. The British journalists had assumed that all was sweetness and light after Gorbachev's successful visit to London. They had picked up nothing, despite the normal leakiness of the responsible agencies in London and the fact that thirty-six hours had already elapsed since I had taken action in Moscow. Rupert Cornwell of *The Independent* – not one of those expelled – left the briefing with his knees shaking.

Despite their tough talk, the Russians were in disarray. Gerasimov, the Foreign Ministry's normally agile press spokesman, was unable to explain how the proposed ceiling would work ('Don't ask me, I didn't write this bit of paper'). The 'press spokesman of the KGB' (a figure apparently invented for the occasion) produced some bedraggled 'evidence' against one of the journalists. But Alexander Yakovlev, one of Gorbachev's chief allies in the Politburo, hinted that all three would soon be able to return to Moscow. Within a couple of days a Foreign Ministry official told us that the Russians wanted 'business as usual', despite 'the baboons on both sides'. Senior officials went out of their way to be friendly. Preparations for official visits went ahead in an even more cooperative atmosphere than before. *Moscow News* published the full text of an article lambasting the KGB which one of the three journalists wrote on his return to Britain.

Meanwhile we tried to maintain the morale of our people. The victims were suffering from shock, apart from the few lucky ones who disliked Russia or who were reaching the end of their official postings. There were farewell parties and farewell trips out to the airport. Even these sad scenes had their comic side. The frontier guards at the airport saw a flaw in the visa of the four-year-old daughter of the Assistant Military Attaché, Nigel Shakespear. They refused to allow her out. I pointed out that as the family had been expelled it was illogical to prevent their departure. The officers, each more senior than the last, were adamant. The matter was only resolved by reference to the Interior Ministry in Moscow.

The Russian staff had the most to lose. I assembled them in my office. I told them that Jill and I greatly liked and would continue to like their country. We appreciated all they did for the embassy. We thought of them as colleagues and friends. We intended to fight the Soviet demands on their behalf as well as our own. I saw no harm in the KGB learning all this, as they undoubtedly did as soon as I had spoken the words. It was a small wedge to drive between them and their catspaws in the embassy. 'The girls' were in silent tears as they served us lunch that day.

We then settled down to negotiate. Rod Lyne, the head of the embassy's Political Section, devised and implemented our tactics with tremendous ingenuity, negotiating skill, energy, and an equable temper. Our long-term aim was to secure a reasonably bankable assurance from the Soviets that they would moderate their intelligence activities in Britain. Both sides could then relax the Cold War restrictions which were getting in the way of mutually valuable business. British ministers did not want the row to get out of hand. Gorbachev was in an awkward position. The expulsions, so soon after his triumph in London, made him look a fool in front of his own hardliners. His friend Mrs Thatcher appeared to have taken him for a ride. But within weeks, in a display of massive common sense, he told a British journalist that the Anglo-Soviet relationship was unaffected. Everyone had trouble about spies from time to time. It was normal for journalists to try to discover more than the authorities wanted them to know. We should not, he said, get the imbroglio out of proportion.

The negotiations lasted for many months and eventually tailed off in a series of explicit and implicit understandings. Some Soviet officials showed a marked preference for negotiating in London parks, rather than in their own offices where they presumably feared eavesdropping. Chernyaev was consistently helpful. For Mrs Thatcher the whole thing was an unfortunate burden on her relationship with Gorbachev. Her people delicately indicated to the British press that the responsibility for the expulsions, and for whatever damage they might have caused to Anglo-Soviet relations, rested with the Foreign Secretary, Geoffrey Howe, and Douglas Hurd, then Home Secretary. But by then the back of the negotiation was broken. The KGB failed to get their revenge, we gave up nothing of substance, and common sense prevailed. It was a small victory both for us and for Gorbachev.

On the eve of our arrival in Moscow Gorbachev demonstrated that he was prepared to go much further along the road to reform than the doubters at home and abroad had thought. At the 19th Conference of the Communist Party of the Soviet Union in June 1988, he put forward a plan for the radical transformation of Soviet politics which – though he surely did not intend that – marked the beginning of the end for the Communist Party and the Soviet system itself. The slogan of the Bolsheviks in 1917 was 'All power to the Soviets', the elected bodies of workers, soldiers, and peasants who backed them in their struggle with the Provisional Government. But popular democracy was not to the taste of Lenin and Stalin. They rapidly reduced the powers of the Supreme Soviet until by the 1930s it was even more impotent than the Central Committee of the Communist Party. It met for a few days a year to hear speeches on the State of the Union from the leadership, to approve unanimously whatever was put before it, and thus to provide a simulacrum of democracy. No delegate risked a dissenting voice. Its members were the Party bosses from the centre and the regions, leading figures in Soviet society – editors, factory managers, leading intellectuals – and a quota of women, veterans, youth leaders, peasants, and workers. They were selected by the Party, stood unopposed at election time, and regularly received well over 90 per cent of the votes cast by an electorate who risked punishment if they failed to appear at the polling stations.

Now Gorbachev proposed a new working Supreme Soviet which would meet and legislate for up to eight months a year. Its Chairman, whose functions had been largely ceremonial, would be given real powers: a deliberate step towards presidential government. The governmental functions which the Communist Party had usurped over the decades would be severely pruned. The old Supreme Soviet would meet in the autumn for the last time to ratify the necessary changes to the Constitution. A general election would be held in the spring, in which the voter would be given a genuine choice between candidates if not between parties. The new body would begin work by April 1989.

The delegates listened in stunned confusion. This was a deliberate plan to reanimate the electoral process and transfer power from the Party to those 'to whom', Gorbachev said, 'it should belong according to the Constitution – to the Soviets'. The aim was to introduce a genuine electoral choice, first within the Communist Party itself and then more widely in the country as a whole. Thus, Gorbachev hoped, he would dislodge the old guard – in the Party, in the government, and in local administration – who were opposed to his reforms either on ideological grounds or on the grounds of self-interest. He knew that the placemen would resist. So he got rid of the conservative Party bureaucrats as quickly as he could, and used the electoral process to build up popular pressure on those who remained.

His liberal critics never understood, appreciated, or forgave the complex and often devious manoeuvring into which he was inevitably drawn.

The second, even more colourful political show which Gorbachev mounted in 1988 was the celebration of the Millennium of the Russian Orthodox Church, the thousandth anniversary of the 'baptism of Russia'. All over the country ruined churches were restored: more than five hundred were opened during the year, compared with sixteen in 1987. In the 1930s the Danilov monastery in Moscow was in succession a concentration camp, a transit camp, and an orphanage for the children of enemies of the people. Now it became the seat of the patriarchate in Moscow, with a refurbished church and a spanking new palace for the decrepit Patriarch Pimen himself. Foreign prelates and the secular leaders of the Soviet state flocked to the celebrations. The Church began to lift up its head, no longer a cowed supporter of an atheist regime. Its buildings blazed with fresh paint, its cupolas with gold. Churches and monasteries were filled with new worshippers. Confirmed cynics such as our driver Konstantin Demakhin began to go to church, and even to contemplate baptism and a church wedding to supplement their long secular relationship with their wives. It may have had little to do with religion as such. But it had a great deal to do with a growing feeling among ordinary Russians that the Soviet system had robbed them of their national heritage.

Pimen died in May 1990. We did not meet his successor Aleksi until a few weeks before we left Moscow in 1992, when he was still glowing from celebrating his first Easter in a non-Communist Russia. He was a handsome man, physically alert, stately but unpompous, with a rosary twined round his pudgy left hand. He shared the deep conservatism of most of his fellow Orthodox churchmen. He resented the way in which other Christian Churches were taking advantage of Russia's weakness to proselytise their views. The years of persecution and anti-religious propaganda, he lamented, had left ordinary people without a great attachment to their own Church. They were vulnerable to foreign ideas. The 'Vatican foreign service', he believed, treated Russia as if it were a heathen country with no Christian tradition, ripe for conversion to Catholicism – nightmares fed by some of the wilder pronouncements of the Polish Pope about the restoration of Christian unity under the Church of Rome. Evangelical sects from America, he complained, were trying to bribe the Orthodox with offers of humanitarian aid in exchange for their allegiance. Hari Krishna groups, astrologers and clairvoyants, and witches' covens were flourishing.

Aleksi was eloquent about the crimes of the past regime: the shootings, the collectivisation, the artificial famines in which millions had died. He worried about the Church's reputation for collaboration with the KGB and had set up a commission of young bishops to investigate. It was difficult to be entirely convinced. The reactionary wing of the Orthodox Church was associated with the crudest kind of anti-Semitism since well before the October Revolution. Some of Aleksi's bishops were still not beyond issuing public statements of a most offensive kind. There were lower depths as well. Those who murdered the liberal priest, Father Men, were never caught. But they were suspected by liberals of having acted either on behalf of the KGB, of extreme anti-Semitic nationalists within the Church itself, or of both combined. But Aleksi assured me unprompted that the Church was not anti-Semitic. He actively opposed all discrimination or pogroms against the Jews, with whom the Church shared its prophets and the Old Testament. Rather unconvincingly he claimed that the Church had no ambition to regain the role and prestige within the state that it had enjoyed before the revolution.

The radical priests resented Aleksi's attempts to break clear of his past. They believed that he was a lifelong agent of the KGB. In the Soviet time, of course, no one could make a career in the Church or out of it without at least the passive acquiescence of the 'organs'. Aleksi would answer that only by taking on his own head the sin of collaboration could he work to preserve the Church. And it was Aleksi who in January 1991 denounced the shootings in Vilnius. It was Aleksi who warned against bloodshed at the time of the attempted coup in August 1991. It was Aleksi who later mediated between Yeltsin and the Russian parliament on the eve of the bloody exchange in October 1993. In a totalitarian state nothing is simple and almost no one is entirely free of guilt.

Even before the 19th Party Conference some of Gorbachev's senior colleagues were beginning to worry that he was going too far too fast, and began their first moves against him. The ejection of Boris Yeltsin from the Politburo in November 1987, and the Nina Andreyeva affair of March 1988, struck fear into the hearts of many liberals. Ironically it was Yegor Ligachev, later one of his bitterest enemies, who first recommended to Gorbachev that he bring Yeltsin to Moscow from Sverdlovsk, where he was Party Secretary. In April 1985 Gorbachev made Yeltsin First Secretary of the Moscow Party, and a candidate member of the Politburo. But Yeltsin's populist methods made no real dent on Moscow's problems, and they alienated his colleagues, for whom his contempt was barely concealed. In Autumn of 1987 he told Gorbachev that he wished to resign from the Politburo and from the Moscow Party. No one had ever done such a thing before. It was, among other things, a serious breach of Party discipline.

Gorbachev was at first reluctant to let him go. Yeltsin was a useful balance to Ligachev and the other conservatives in the Politburo. And the Party was about to celebrate the seventieth anniversary of the October Revolution: just the wrong moment to have a public row. But Gorbachev's colleagues insisted that the challenge had to be faced. The result was one of the most disgraceful scenes during the years of Perestroika. Instead of being allowed to resign with dignity, Yeltsin was subjected by his Politburo colleagues – even the liberals Shevardnadze and Yakovlev – to a torrent of abuse unpleasantly reminiscent of the witch-hunts of the past. He was ejected from his posts in the Politburo and the Moscow Party. A campaign of black propaganda accused him of incompetence and abuse of power. He went into one of the extended periods of depression and inactivity which punctuated so much of his later career. It was a chilling business.

Yegor Ligachev now emerged as the leader of the opposition, a dour, old-fashioned man who believed in Socialism, discipline, collectivisation, and the worker-peasant state. He thought that these, plus a little more investment, were all that was needed to make the Soviet Union prosperous. In the Spring of 1988 the orthodox Party newspaper *Sovietskaya Rossia* published an article 'I cannot compromise my principles' by Nina Andreyeva, a hitherto unknown lecturer in a Leningrad polytechnic. It was an old-fashioned appeal for a return to 'Communist values' and a clear attack on Gorbachev's reforms. Ligachev may have helped to draft it, and certainly encouraged its reproduction in other Party papers throughout the country. Gorbachev was on a foreign trip. On his return he read the riot act, and put the reform process back on track. But for a brief moment silence descended on the chattering classes as they wondered whether they had been lured by the promise of Glasnost into sticking their heads too far above the parapet.

Yeltsin began his political comeback at the 19th Party Conference a few months later. With some difficulty he persuaded Gorbachev to let him take the floor. His speech was apologetic rather than defiant. Ligachev rounded on him, and the mood of the hall was for Ligachev. But the proceedings were shown on television. For the first time in the history of the Soviet Union ordinary people were able to observe a political clash between their leaders, whose intrigues had hitherto always been shrouded in the mystery of the Kremlin. For the first time they were able to draw their own conclusions. Yeltsin ceased to be a non-person. His criticism of the Party and its policies found an instant chord among millions of ordinary people. Ligachev's furious remark: 'Boris, you're wrong' became the ironic rallying cry of the democratic opposition, reproduced on millions of stickers and lapel badges. Politics moved from the smoke-filled rooms into the public arena, and there they remained. It was this, even more than the reforms which Gorbachev had proposed, which gave the Conference its epoch-making significance.

Ligachev and his friends were not content to let this pass. While Gorbachev was on holiday in August 1988, Ligachev stepped up the pressure. He publicly attacked the 'New Thinking' of Gorbachev, Shevard-nadze, and Yakovlev, the idea – at the basis of the attempt to improve East–West relations – that international relations should be conducted on the grounds of interests, not ideology. He insisted on the need for Leninist discipline in the Party. And he said that a market economy based on private property was 'fundamentally unacceptable for the socialist system'. The police began once again to suppress peaceful demonstrations in Moscow. The conservative press stepped up its attacks on liberal causes. Attempts were made to impose administrative and financial restraints on the liberal press.

By now even those who were prepared to trust Gorbachev's motives wondered whether he and his reforms might not at any moment be swept away by a conspiracy. Sakharov warned that Moscow felt as it had done in the days before the fall of Khrushchev. Under a banner headline 'Soviet Reform Programme Facing Defeat', *The Times* of London wrote that 'serious Soviet commentators and Westerners alike are convinced that without a rapid improvement in the supply situation the 57-year old leader could face a dangerous combination of a disgruntled public and unhappy bureaucrats joining forces to overthrow him.' But Gorbachev was still at the height of his political form. He launched an unexpected counterattack to throw his opponents off balance. On 29 September the still largely conservative Central Committee was invited to ratify a *fait accompli*: the removal of several of the old guard from the Politburo, and a redistribution of responsibilities among those who remained. The number of the Central Committee's departments was reduced from twenty to nine, significantly reducing its ability to keep a stranglehold on the life of the country. The next day the Supreme Soviet gathered to elect Gorbachev as its Chairman in place of Gromyko, the dour ex-Foreign Minister whom Gorbachev had kicked upstairs to make room for Shevardnadze. The bewildered deputies dutifully adopted his constitutional proposals and ratified the timetable for their own political demise. Gromyko went into involuntary but honourable retirement, with Gorbachev's praise ringing in his ears. Liberals heaved a sigh of relief. Only the carping remarked that the coup had been pushed through in a hugger-mugger fashion which did not square with the principles of openness and democratisation to which

Gorbachev had committed himself so enthusiastically at the Party Conference only three months earlier.

Despite the new openness, it was hard to get to know the people at the top,
busy men wrestling with a revolution. Sometimes I had official business to
conduct or a ministerial visitor to introduce. Otherwise I had to exploit the
official ceremonies of the Soviet state to engage the leaders and their wives
in informal conversation. Gorbachev held an annual reception for ambassadors in the St George's Hall of the Kremlin: the huge white and gold
room, emblazoned in gold letters with the names of the Imperial officers
and military units who won the Tsar's highest award for gallantry. It was a
bizarre and tedious ceremony, though it brought one a little closer to
Gorbachev, his Foreign Minister Shevardnadze and his Prime Minister
Ryzhkov. Far more profitable were the annual Revolution Day receptions in
the Kremlin's Palace of Congresses, a marble monstrosity built by
Khrushchev on the site of an ancient monastery in an unimaginative style
of genteel Soviet Art Deco. It was designed to accommodate the thousands
of delegates from all over the Soviet Union who attended Party Congresses,
and for lesser rituals such as the annual celebration of Lenin's birthday.
When there was no Congress – that was for most of the time, since
Congress convened roughly every five years – the Bolshoi Theatre used it as
an additional stage on which to mount its most spectacular shows. Formal
receptions were held in a huge room at the top of the building, the tables
laden with caviar, sausage, tomatoes, wine, brandy, and a great deal of
vodka. On Revolution Day in 1988 the whole of the Politburo still stood
with their wives at one end of the room behind a barricade of other tables.
Government ministers, the official intelligentsia, provincial party bosses,
and ambassadors milled around in the body of the hall, wolfing the refresh-
ments and trying to push through to the bigwigs. In later years, apparently
on Gorbachev's orders, the barricade was removed, and the leaders
mingled freely with the crowds.

These ceremonies were matched by the great parades on Red Square.
They took place on Revolution Day and May Day: massed ranks of soldiers,
sailors and airmen goose-stepping past with impeccable precision, the
thunder and smoke of tanks and rocket carriers, the metallic blare of the
military bands. In earlier years the soldiers were followed by more
bedraggled groups of workers, peasants, and youngsters, each with floats or
banners bearing the names of the organisations from which they came. As
the Soviet Union ground to a halt the slogans carried by the parading
workers were increasingly bold. They criticised Gorbachev for prevari-

cating, for reforming too fast or too slow. Some went further, threatening the Soviet leadership with exile or worse, attacking the Jews, proclaiming the virtues of Stalin. On May Day 1990 they booed Gorbachev off Lenin's Mausoleum, from which successive generations of the Soviet leadership had reviewed the parade. In 1990 several cities refused to hold the Revolutionary celebrations at all. And by the following year they had been abolished for good. Thereafter the October Revolution was celebrated only by small groups of mostly elderly Communists, the dissidents of the new era.

It was easy enough, when one met him, to see why Mrs Thatcher thought that Gorbachev was a man with whom she could do business. A man of vivid and quicksilver intelligence, he always seemed smaller than one expected: a big personality should have a big frame to go with it. He was vivacious and ebullient, direct, unpompous, with an infectious smile, hazel eyes with an inner sparkle, an almost Mediterranean charm, and an open and confiding manner as if – for a moment at least – you were his best friend. This openness was perhaps a mask. Anatoli Sobchak, the democratic politician who later became mayor of St Petersburg, once said that anyone who believed they knew what Gorbachev was thinking was mistaken. In his private dealings with his colleagues, he could show the autocratic temper, the salty language, the 'iron teeth' of which Gromyko spoke at the time of his election to the General Secretaryship in 1985.

Critics complained that Gorbachev resented the presence of equals, a weakness not unusual in political leaders. But his Perestroika team contained men of stature in their own right – his Foreign Minister Shevard-nadze, his Prime Minister Ryzhkov, and his theoretical adviser Alexander Yakovlev. Unlike many Russian leaders, with their addiction to noisy male company, heavy drinking, and the Russian steam bath, Gorbachev was a very private person for all his outward ebullience. He did not invite his colleagues back to his official dacha on the outskirts of Moscow, and he used to go on holiday alone with his close family and a couple of aides. He was openly devoted to his wife, Raisa Maksimovna. He obviously depended heavily on her for moral and emotional support, and believed that she should share his official life. Every day she would ring him – and his staff – at the office to press this point or that. When he returned to his dacha in the evening after a long day's work he would walk with her for an hour while they discussed the day's business. When he travelled on official business he took her with him. Russian men thought that all this was one more sign of weakness. But Raisa Maksimovna was unpopular among Russian women as well. They envied her smart clothes and disliked what they saw as her imperious manner. Only a few of them gave Gorbachev credit for making it possible for the wives of senior figures to emerge from the Soviet equivalent of the medieval Russian *terem*, the women's quarters.

Gorbachev had all the ambition, all the energy, all the cunning, and – of course – all the vanity that a politician needs to rise to the top of the greasy pole. His enemies accused him of vacillation and cowardice. But he had the courage to think unorthodox thoughts, to push them through against determined opposition from the old guard, and to change his mind if the circumstances demanded. He loved debate, talk, even chatter. In his first years of power he dominated discussion within the Party. In his dealings with Western leaders he handled the complex issues of disarmament and international politics with a freedom and verve which no previous Soviet leader had been able to match. Even Khrushchev, the most human of them, could not match the flexible sophistication with which Gorbachev tackled the most complex issues. Gorbachev's enemies recognised his immense capacity for work, his powerful memory, his mastery of facts. His first discussions with Mrs Thatcher and Geoffrey Howe in December 1984 demonstrated the breathtaking difference between him and his predecessors. Here was a man who – unlike Brezhnev – had mastered his briefs and could speak without advisers, confident, lively, and intelligent, who obviously enjoyed giving Mrs Thatcher as good as he got in argument. Even those of us who saw only the dry official records could sense the excitement.

The man in the Russian street was at first equally delighted with Gorbachev's direct manner. His walkabouts in Moscow and Leningrad in the early years of Perestroika were triumphant occasions. But he became increasingly long-winded. His reiteration of broad strategic principle was no substitute for decisive action as the country fell apart. He irritated his audiences by his endlessly didactic harangues on the television. Moscow intellectuals sneered unpleasantly at his Southern accent and his abrupt way with some of the finer points of Russian grammar. Everyone resented the time he spent with foreigners, whose company he seemed to prefer as the going got rough at home. The Kyrgyz author, Chingiz Aitmatov, tells how he fixed an appointment with Gorbachev at the height of a particularly noisy session of the new Soviet parliament in order to discuss urgent business. Gorbachev bounced in nearly an hour late: 'Jane Fonda's in the next room. Let's go and talk to her.' The foreigners, of course, were charmed as he built new visions for the future, reran past triumphs, and castigated his critics, sometimes for an hour on end. But on emerging you sometimes realised that despite the charm you had settled very little real business.

It later became fashionable to criticise Gorbachev for being a mere Party apparatchik: a man who – unlike Yeltsin – knew little of the real world because he had made his career in the smoke-filled committee rooms in Moscow. That is a gross over-simplification. Gorbachev and his relatives shared to the full the fate of the Soviet people under Communism. Nearly half his village starved to death during the collectivisation of agriculture in the early 1930s. He and his family went almost as hungry in the near famine which followed the war, a time when, as he later recalled, Soviet peasants were treated no better than serfs under the Tsars. His two grandfathers were arrested in the purges. His father fought in the war, when the Germans briefly occupied his home village. In his boyhood and teens he worked the same long hours on the collective farm as everyone else. He got to Moscow University – an unusual achievement for a young peasant – on merit, not through personal connections. He spent the first twenty-three years of his Party career in his home province of Stavropol. In 1966, at the unusually young age of thirty-four, he became the First Party Secretary of Stavropol City. Four years later he became Secretary of the Province, thus joining the next most powerful group of people in the Soviet Union after the Politburo itself. He rushed around his province like a District Commissioner in British India, jollying people along, bullying where necessary, solving local problems, representing the interests of his constituents in Moscow, an exhilarating frenzy of activity. By the time he joined the Politburo he had as much experience of the grandeurs and miseries of life in the Soviet Union as any of his peers.

In retirement Gorbachev read and reread the Marxist classics. It was only with the very greatest difficulty that he accepted that Lenin, too, was responsible for the horrors. He continued to maintain faith with what he thought were the basic principles of 'socialism'. But long before his fall these had already evolved in his mind to something much closer to the Social Democracy of the West – even though he may never have grasped what that might mean in practice – than to the brutal and incompetent rigours of Soviet Communism. In this he differed from those members of the Party who spent their lives mouthing its sacred platitudes, and then abandoned it without a qualm. Gorbachev's struggle to be true to his past and to maintain some degree of intellectual consistency was not at all to his discredit.

I had my first opportunity to see Gorbachev close to during his visit to London in April 1989. The visit was important for him. He had taken a firm decision to disentangle his country from its overextended positions abroad. But at home his position was already weakening. The Russians saw

Western Europe forging ahead politically and economically, and attracting
the neutrals and even their own allies. For forty years of the Cold War we
had worried that the Soviets would supplant the Americans on the
continent of Europe. Now, like the Red Queen, the Russians were having to
run as hard as they could simply to retain their influence in an area of
central importance to their interests. Gorbachev was worried above all by
the silence which descended on Washington for several months after the
election of President Bush. The new President was conducting a rigorous
review of policy towards the Soviet Union. The Republican Right had
accused him in the past of being too complacent about the Soviet threat.
His new National Security Advisor, Brent Scowcroft, believed that
Gorbachev was potentially more dangerous than his predecessors, and said
on television in January 1989 that Gorbachev's new foreign policy might be
simply intended to throw the West off its guard while the Soviet economy
was rebuilt; the challenge would then be renewed. Robert Gates,
Scowcroft's deputy and later Director of the CIA, said at about the same
time that 'A long, competitive struggle with the Soviet Union still lies before
us ... The dictatorship of the Communist Party remains untouched and
untouchable.'[1] Bush called Gorbachev on the telephone and sent him a
soothing letter. But as the weeks went by, and the Americans continued to
refrain from substance, Gorbachev was beginning to fear the worst. He
hoped, I told London on the eve of his arrival, that Mrs Thatcher might
pass the right message through to Washington, and so restart the process of
dismantling the Cold War.

Gorbachev arrived at Heathrow in the late afternoon of 5 April. The arrival
ceremony was a disaster. Sleet drove across the tarmac where we stood in a
bedraggled and disorderly receiving line. The RAF band played the Soviet
national anthem at half speed. Officials scuttered about like frightened
rabbits. Mrs Thatcher looked grim, and there were consequences.

Mrs Thatcher always kept her ambassador away from her meetings with
Gorbachev. But I was allowed to see the witty and reasonably straightforward records prepared by her private secretary, Charles Powell, supplemented in later years by the full and documented memoirs of Chernyaev.
At their private meeting on the morning after his arrival, I gathered, the
two of them had their usual intellectual workout on regional disputes,
disarmament, and nuclear deterrence. I attended the subsequent 'working
lunch' in the small dining room at Number 10. Mrs Thatcher asked
Gorbachev about the Kharitonenko house. There was some general talk
about international affairs. But little real work was done. In the afternoon
Gorbachev spoke about the Soviet economy to a gathering of business

people at Lancaster House. His airy optimism was larded with fashionable macroeconomic jargon ('budget deficits', 'money supply'), which his predecessors would never even have heard of. But when asked who was in charge of the economy now that enterprises were allegedly responsible for their own affairs, his reply was breathtakingly old-fashioned: 'Ask Gosplan, the State Planning Committee. They can sort everything out.' In his speeches at dinner that evening at Number 10, and at the Guildhall the following day, Gorbachev expressed an obsessive concern that the new American President was being hijacked by 'certain circles', coded language for the reactionaries in Washington. In her replies Mrs Thatcher was generous to her guest and repeated her favourite, and disconcerting, theme that there was nothing like nuclear weapons for keeping the peace.

The final event was lunch at Windsor Castle. It was raining. The Queen and Gorbachev damply inspected a detachment of the Coldstream Guard, and she then showed him her Russian treasures: a portrait by Lawrence of Alexander I, the huge malachite urn given to Victoria by Nicholas I, George VI's collection of Tsarist medals, two-headed Imperial eagles everywhere. During the drinks before lunch, both were stiff and ill-at-ease: constrained perhaps by the ghost of the murdered Tsar. At table the Queen was between Gorbachev and his Foreign Minister, Eduard Shevardnadze, two charming men. Mrs Thatcher was seated opposite, next to a morose Alexander Yakovlev, who was so uncommunicative that she turned to me in despair. But the Queen and her neighbours became progressively more animated until, when a ray of sunshine burst through the clouds after a dramatic clap of thunder and illuminated them all, they positively laughed. It must have been at about that time that he popped the question and she accepted: she would come to Russia 'in due course' ('due course' turned out to be Autumn 1994, when Yeltsin, not Gorbachev, was the beneficiary). By the end of the meal the ghost seemed to have been laid. That evening my mother asked whether the cooking at Windsor had been better than at Downing Street. I couldn't remember what I had eaten at either place. Luckily the details of the menus were preserved for posterity by one of Gorbachev's interpreters in his memoirs.[2]

Gorbachev was genuinely pleased at the warmth shown by the ordinary Britons who had mobbed his car as he left the Guildhall. Chernyaev told me that the most important outcome of the visit was not the standard exchange with Mrs Thatcher about international issues, but her comparative success in convincing him that President Bush was not about to depart from the policy of US–Soviet cooperation. I explained to Chernyaev that the long silence coming out of Washington was not unusual: a new US

Administration often took months to sort itself out. He was not entirely persuaded.

But for all the warmth, I noted in my diary, the visit had produced nothing of substance. The glory days of the relationship between Thatcher and Gorbachev were over. Quite soon, I thought, the main role would pass to the Americans and the Germans, and there would be little but sentiment left. Chernyaev later wrote that Gorbachev was beginning to be irritated by Mrs Thatcher's rumbustious attacks on his political beliefs. But Mrs Thatcher's warm support was a consolation to him, especially in the last bad year of his rule, when she was already out of office. And for Chernyaev himself the magic never wore off. 'Margaret Thatcher was as splendid as ever,' he wrote of the April visit. 'I sat opposite her for three hours in her Downing Street office, and admired her as always. She tried to enchant Gorbachev. He responded to her openness, played up to her, pretended to be taken in by her, but maintained a reserve as well.' On the return flight to Moscow, Chernyaev rebuked Gorbachev.

> She's doing us the best of turns. She's raised your authority and upped the ante, so that Kohl, Mitterrand and even Bush are having to learn to jump higher as a matter of urgency. She's publicly stood out against the wave of pessimism which was beginning to wash off against the image of Perestroika ... No one else is giving us such determined help in changing the international situation. Why do you give the impression that you don't appreciate that immensely? What's more, she's a woman. It's not true that she's a man in skirts. Her whole character, even her political modus operandi, is entirely feminine. And above all she is an *English* woman.[3]

My relationship with Eduard Shevardnadze developed more slowly. I had little of substance to negotiate with him about – except for the disputes about spies, from which he sensibly kept his distance. Shevardnadze was wholly un-Russian: with a mane of white hair, piercing eyes, a thick Georgian accent, and a manner which alternated between genuine charm, vivid Southern emotion, and dour sullenness. He was a man of considerable moral courage, who jeopardised his Party career in order to marry a woman whose father had been shot in the purges. He had great physical courage too. He single-handedly confronted an angry crowd at a football match in Tbilisi, which had disputed a decision by the referee, invaded the pitch, and overwhelmed the militia. Shevardnadze went alone into the mob and calmed them down. Most of his fellow Georgians were proud of his international eminence. But he was not universally popular. His career as head of the Georgian Interior Ministry and Party Secretary left him with many enemies. Our Georgian friends never forgave him for insisting on the execution of a group of young men – from the gilded youth of Tbilisi – who hijacked a plane in 1983 and killed several members of the crew. Shevardnadze and Gorbachev became close while Gorbachev was still First Secretary in Stavropol, which bordered on Georgia. It was then that they agreed that the Soviet Union had to change at home, and that it was overextended abroad. Shevardnadze had no experience of international affairs. Foreigners were surprised, and the Soviet Foreign Ministry was disconcerted, when Gorbachev summoned him to Moscow as his Foreign Minister. But he rapidly mastered the most complex briefs on disarmament and on Central Europe. He forced one compromise after another through a reluctant Foreign Ministry, a defence establishment on the verge of mutiny, and an increasingly hostile legislature. His reward was that the conservative opposition, and many ordinary Russians, grew to regard him as a traitor.

They disliked Gorbachev's other chief lieutenant at least as much. Aleksandr Yakovlev, already an elderly man, was wounded in the war, and that was a useful defence when the military and the reactionaries later accused him of betraying his country. An academic and theoretician rather than a political activist, he too rose through the ranks of the Party. In 1972 his career received a jolt when he published an attack on Russian nationalism and was exiled to Canada as ambassador. Gorbachev met him there on a visit and liked him. He returned to Moscow in 1983 to become Director of the prestigious Institute for the World Economy and International Relations (IMEMO). Gorbachev made him a full member of the Politburo in 1987. Despite his reputation for unorthodoxy he was, even in 1988, still arguing in public that the goal of Perestroika was to lead the country back to Lenin's ideals of socialism. He did not leave the Party until the very eve of the coup, little more than a week before Gorbachev himself. Foreign journalists called him the 'Father of Perestroika'. He did indeed provide much of the intellectual drive for reform. But his reformist and his reactionary colleagues were irritated in equal measure. He was soon at loggerheads with Ligachev and the other conservatives. Kryuchkov, the head of the KGB, is vitriolic about him in his memoirs. In his unflattering photographs he looked like a dyspeptic frog. But in the flesh he was more affable than his reputation or his appearance. Like Shevardnadze, he played an increasingly prominent liberal role in the last years of the Soviet Union, and his relationship with Gorbachev became more erratic as a result.

The Prime Minister, Nikolai Ryzhkov, was close to Gorbachev in the early days. In 1983 the ailing General Secretary Andropov ordered the two men to work on a plan of economic reform. Over the next few years they devised many practical measures. Ryzhkov was a handsome man, vain and thin-skinned. His emotional performances on television earned him the nickname of 'the weeping Bolshevik'. He worked his way up from the shop floor to become General Director of UralMash in Sverdlovsk (now once again Yekaterinburg, as it was before the October Revolution), a heavy engineering plant and one of the flagships of Soviet industry, of whose board I was briefly to be a member many years later. In 1975 Ryzhkov came to Moscow as a minister. Ten years later Gorbachev brought him into the Politburo as Prime Minister. His experience was therefore quite different from the experience of the other Perestroika men: he was a practical manager, not a Party official. He deeply resented the way the Party had interfered with his freedom to manage UralMash, and one of his main objectives was to get the Party out of the economy altogether. He was painfully insistent on his prerogatives as Prime Minister and leader of the government. He believed that the government could and should manage the move to the market in a deliberate and orderly fashion so as to reduce the cost to ordinary people. As the pace of change accelerated and became more erratic, he became steadily less happy with the direction of events. From the middle of 1989 he moved away from Gorbachev, whom he accused of failing to give him adequate support. In Yeltsin's Russia he ended up on the neo-Communist right, despite the comparatively liberal views he appeared to espouse at the height of Perestroika.

Vadim Bakatin was another of those close to Gorbachev. Like most of Gorbachev's team, Bakatin was a career Communist, a 'typical apparatchik', but an unusual one. He was full of liveliness and charm, an amateur painter whose work hangs on our walls, with a broad handsome face, and an open trusting smile, like Ivanushka in the Russian fairy tales, the youngest brother of three, the simpleton who nevertheless wins the Princess. He grew up in Kemerovo in Siberia, where he spent his early career as a Party official. He was brought to Moscow in 1983 to be a Central Committee inspector, travelling the country, cleaning up local Party organisations that had gone off the rails, a task which in Stalin's day had had serious, sometimes fatal consequences for the local officials concerned. Later Bakatin returned to Kemerovo as First Party Secretary: a major step up the Communist career ladder. Gorbachev fished him out in 1989 to be Interior Minister. A liberal despite his background, he championed an enlightened policy of criminal justice. He did not believe that the problem of crime could be solved simply by throwing resources at it. He raised the standards of pay and equipment of the police. He earned the devotion of many of the police themselves, the respect of many liberals, and the sustained hatred of the hard men. They secured his dismissal in the Autumn of 1990 as Gorbachev lurched to the right, and their hatred was redoubled when he was put in to reform the KGB in the dying months of the Soviet Union.

Anatoli Lukyanov was the first of the new leaders whom I met, when I presented my credentials to him in his capacity as Chairman (Speaker) of the old Supreme Soviet. I had always refused to buy myself a diplomatic uniform – an unnecessary, old-fashioned, and ostentatious expense. So I paid my respects in a uniform hired from Nathan and Berman, the theatrical costumiers, a splendid outfit topped with a mangy ostrich plume hat. The ceremony took place in a small room in the Kremlin. Lukyanov was then in his late fifties, a stocky man with an oriental cast to his face and sleek grey hair plastered to his skull. He lacked the ponderous stuffiness of the old Soviet leaders, with their bleak 'jokes' and wintry smiles. He remarked engagingly that it was the first time that he, too, had participated in a credential ceremony. We were equally unsure of the balletic moves required ('Two steps forward, one step back, bow, take your partners …'). He claimed to be closely interested in English poetry – he too was a poet – and to prove it quoted substantial chunks in translation. We chatted on intellectual matters for longer than the allocated time and parted.

Lukyanov studied law at Moscow University at the same time as Gorbachev. He was the archetypal central bureaucrat. He spent most of his career in the Secretariat of the old Supreme Soviet. But in 1983 he moved to the Central Committee Secretariat, where he prospered, especially under Gorbachev. In September 1988 he was promoted to the Politburo as a candidate member, and moved back to the Supreme Soviet to manage it in Gorbachev's interest. Because of his closeness to Gorbachev foreigners were inclined to regard him as one of the main pillars of Perestroika. Shrewd observers like Sasha Motov and Konstantin Demakhin were not taken in, and rightly looked on him with suspicion. He helped organise the plot against Gorbachev in the Summer of 1991. In his prison memoirs he comes across as highly intelligent and perceptive. He too genuinely favoured a kind of limited reform. But he saw that the root-and-branch changes which Gorbachev had initiated would lead to the disintegration of the Soviet Union and the end of 'socialism'. This he was unwilling to contemplate. I met him once or twice in the next two and a half years before he went to prison. But I never again had the opportunity for such a pleasant chat.

Dmitri Yazov, the Defence Minister, was a typical Soviet general. He had a crumpled potato of a face, like so many Russian faces; and like so many Soviet generals, he was red and corpulent, with a rough charm and a bullying manner. He was born in 1923 in Yazovo, a peasant village in Western Siberia – hence his family name. His father died when he was still a small boy. The village elders married his mother off to her late sister's husband, and he grew up in a family of ten children. His simple origins thus matched those of Gorbachev and those of many of his senior colleagues. It was perhaps not surprising that when it came to the crunch he chose to remain loyal to the system which had given him his chance in life. Yazov was one of the last serving officers who had actually fought in the war when Gorbachev appointed him as Minister in May 1987. Neither outside observers nor the deputies in the new Supreme Soviet could understand why Gorbachev relied on him as an instrument of reform. Though at first he seems to have done his best to serve Gorbachev loyally, nothing he ever said to me showed that his heart was in the business. He was thought of as a clod by the outside world, but this was to underestimate his shrewdness and intelligence. He was a fluent master of his brief, and though he would bluster in negotiation, his manner was urbane compared with that of some of his colleagues. Another poet, he impressed Jill by his familiarity with English as well as Russian literature. Emma, a pleasantly Soviet woman, was his second wife, whom he had met in romantic circumstances. More sensible than her husband, she did her best to dissuade him from getting mixed up in the coup in August 1991, but without success.

Gorbachev promoted Vladimir Kryuchkov to head the KGB in September 1988. It soon became fashionable for ambassadors to call on him. But I met him, a small, crinkly-faced man with a dumpy wife, on a couple of public occasions only. I saw no point in a more substantial meeting, since we would merely have quarrelled unproductively over the mutual expulsions or the refusal of the KGB to allow Leila Gordievsky to join her husband, the British double agent Oleg Gordievsky. So I knew him only from his public pronouncements, and from his memoirs. These show him as almost an archetype of a successful, intelligent, but old-fashioned Party official. He began life as a factory worker in Stalingrad, served in the Soviet embassy in Hungary during the Rising in 1956, was brought into the KGB by Andropov, and ran its foreign intelligence operations for fourteen years before becoming its head. Even after the August 1991 coup, in the bitterness of hindsight, he admitted that change had been dangerously delayed because of the fossilised and short-sighted thinking of the Soviet leadership, and because the Party had stifled normal political life and lost touch with the people. He and his fellows believed that change could be achieved by tinkering with the details of the system. But his psychology was deeply rooted in the past. Like his Tsarist predecessor, Count Benkendorf, he seems genuinely to have believed that the true and irreplaceable role of the secret police was to act as the ultimate guardian of the state and its interests. In his memoirs he says of the KGB's eavesdropping: 'I did not and do not see any violation of human rights here, since it was dictated by the interests of the state.'[4]

Kryuchkov was an apologist for Stalin and an admirer of Zhirinovsky. When change really began to get under way he could not cope with it. He came to despise Gorbachev. But he successfully disguised his hostility. As late as March 1991 – five months before the coup – he told Richard Nixon that he was committed to reform. Nixon apparently believed him. But Kryuchkov passed a message to one of Nixon's companions on the trip in which he warned that Gorbachev might soon be overthrown in a parliamentary coup led by Lukyanov and backed by the army and the KGB. I did not hear of this warning at the time: but it accurately prefigured the 'constitutional coup' which Kryuchkov and Lukyanov attempted the following June.[5] Post-Soviet Russia was a forgiving place. After a brief spell in prison, Kryuchkov eventually wound up as senior security adviser to Sistema, a lucrative holding enterprise under the control of Luzhkov, the financially ingenious mayor of Moscow under the new regime.

There was one man with whom it was always possible, and sometimes necessary, to do business: Yevgeny Primakov. Highly competent, slow in speech and manner, with hooded eyes and a veiled sense of humour, Primakov was the Jack-of-all-trades of the last years of the Soviet system. A Russian, though born in Tbilisi, he was everything by starts, and nothing long: an Arabist, a journalist, an academic, head of the International Institute for the World Economy and International Relations (IMEMO). Outsiders assumed that he had close links with the external arm of the KGB. He was close to the centre of most of the confidential discussions and most of the major events of Gorbachev's last years in power. He profited from the clean-out of the Central Committee in April 1989, chaired the Council of the Union later in that year, and was a member of Gorbachev's Presidential Council. He was Gorbachev's envoy during the Gulf War, and earned himself the largely unjustified distrust of the Americans in consequence. He remained at the centre during the Yeltsin years: he took over the external

intelligence service from Bakatin at the beginning of 1992, succeeded
Kozyrev as Russian Foreign Minister in 1996, and became Prime Minister in
1998. In a crisis he displayed an uncanny ability to be on the winning side, at
a time when the winning side was also the right side. Merab Mamardashvili,
the Georgian philosopher who knew him well, once said that Primakov was
known as 'the haryair'. When I asked what he meant, he said: 'You know –
that aeroplane [the Harrier] that can take off vertically.' But for all the
accusations of opportunism that were levelled against him, Primakov was a
solid, reliable, effective, and durable interlocutor.

Since I could not expect more than occasional encounters with the top
leaders, I relied on others to keep me informed and to interpret what was
going on. My best guides were editors and journalists from the leading
liberal newspapers. Ivan Laptiev of *Izvestia* and Yegor Yakovlev of *Moscow
News* warmly supported Perestroika and Gorbachev. They acted as channels
for his views, and often gave me valuable insights into what was going on in
the Party. But they were also willing to criticise him in private and
occasionally in public.

Laptiev was in his mid-fifties, a man of comfortable shape and
comfortable manners, distinguished, grey, with a quizzical smile, always
talkative, and always apparently frank. He was a good journalist and a
professional editor. He was firmly on the liberal wing of the Party and a
plausible spokesman for Gorbachev. He was never disloyal, and never told
me things that he should not have told me. But by reading between the lines
of what he said, I was usually able to get a fair view of what was going on
which was rarely disproved by events.

Yegor Yakovlev's father was an officer of the NKVD who – rather surprisingly – died in his bed at the height of the purges in 1937. Yegor himself was
a professional journalist and writer, whose value to me as a source was
diminished by the extreme speed and obscurity of his diction, which
sometimes made him hard to follow. Until he became the editor of *Moscow
News* he was always in and out of trouble because of his nonconformism.
Even in his new role, his outspoken editorial policy led him into more than
one conflict with Gorbachev. In November 1989 he held a great party in the
Rossia Hotel to celebrate the fifty-ninth anniversary of his newspaper. The
whole of Moscow's liberal intelligentsia seemed to be present. Yegor
explained that he was, unusually, celebrating the fifty-ninth anniversary
because in the uncertain political circumstances of the day it was unclear
that the paper would survive until its sixtieth birthday. There were
elaborate multimedia presentations, folk groups, an Orthodox priest who

lectured us at length on the meaning of the Holy Trinity, and a rabbi. I spoke briefly on the merits of a free press. The show ended with a satirical film about Gorbachev and his family, which included material which had recently been banned from television. This did not endear Yakovlev to Gorbachev, who sometimes found democracy easier to bear in theory than in practice, and who later began to suffer from some of the paranoia of a British politician under attack by the Murdoch press.

Rather to my surprise, and contrary to Jill's fears, the mutual expulsions of May 1989 did not affect our relations with our Russian friends. Sensibly enough they did not much mind what the KGB got up to abroad. Like the rest of us, they thought that there was nothing particularly wrong with spying on foreigners. What they cared about was how the KGB used its power at home. And this power was at last on the wane. Gorbachev relied naively on the information – often deliberately misleading – with which Kryuchkov supplied him almost to the last. But he did one essential thing. He successfully persuaded ordinary people that they need fear the power of the secret police no longer, that they could express their opinions, publish and read writings which had been banned under the Soviet and even the Tsarist regimes, travel abroad, and meet foreigners freely. He thus broke with the age-old political principle that Russia could only be securely ruled if it was isolated from foreign contacts and foreign ideas. He opened up a whole new world for his people. For a time even his sharpest critics among the Russian liberals were grateful.

The new openness transformed our life in Moscow. It is impossible at this distance to convey the sense of excitement as one taboo after another collapsed. To the casual visitor from abroad tiny incidents – a word from a Russian friend, a scrap of news in the paper, a scene on television – could seem trivial beyond belief. They would be a minor drama for anyone who had lived in the country before. We set out to meet as many Russians as we could from all walks of life in Moscow and out of it. In earlier years we had worried about anyone who tried to befriend us. Either they were already working for the KGB; or the KGB would soon call them to account. Now new faces were continually coming to the fore. By the Autumn of 1988 the fear was fading on both sides. Suddenly foreigners became fashionable. Russians invited us to their homes and they were willing to come to ours. I bullied my staff to suggest the names of new contacts – politicians, officials, soldiers, intellectuals, musicians, dissidents, refuseniks, journalists, actors, filmmakers, writers, priests. I hared from meeting to meeting. We went to the theatre, the cinema, the concert hall, and travelled outside Moscow whenever we could. Our diplomatic colleagues were as busy as we were, so that we did not have to bother with the more boring forms of diplomatic entertainment. We could make the friends we wanted to make, and take them as we found them.

Despite this new and heady atmosphere of freedom, our new friends still felt anxious. From time to time they might be asked questions by representatives of the 'organs'. Even before I arrived in Moscow, Garetovsky, the Chairman of the Soviet State Bank, remarked to me over dinner in London that 'We still feel insecure. I'm a Party member of forty years standing. But I don't see how we can have proper guarantees as long as the Party has a monopoly of power': an extraordinarily frank statement for someone in his position.

The centre of our intellectual life in Moscow was Lena Senokosov's kitchen. Yura Senokosov was a philosopher, a compact, mild, and quiet man in his late forties, a man of wise judgements on politics and people, a passionate Russian patriot. The child of peasants, he grew up in a wooden hut in Siberia which he and his father built for themselves. To get himself through university he worked as a construction worker in Moscow and as a dancer in a folklore group touring the most obscure parts of the country during the vacations. Later he worked in Prague on the editorial board of *Problems of Peace and Socialism,* and then at the Soviet journal *Problems of Philosophy.* He specialised in the non-Communist Russian philosophers of the turn of the century who had tried to devise a respectable philosophical and theological basis for Russian Orthodoxy. This brought him into conflict with the KGB. They raided his apartment and confiscated his collection of pre-revolutionary philosophical books. He told the thugs that within ten years the books would be published in Russia itself. They laughed at him. But he was right and they were wrong. By the mid-1990s he was on the editorial board of a massive project to publish the lot.

Lena Senokosova came from a very different background: she was a Muscovite, a born member of the intelligentsia, by training an art historian, who had been brought up on one of the smarter boulevards in north Moscow. Her father, a senior official, was arrested after the war because he knew of Stalin's plan to abandon Moscow to the Germans, but survived. Lena read everything and knew everyone on the liberal side of the literary world. The constraints of the Brezhnev years left no public outlet for her boundless energy. So she organised a literary and political salon in the kitchen of her small flat on Kutuzovsky Prospect, almost opposite the building where we had lived during our first stay in Moscow. Around her table we met many of those who were becoming the leading lights in the new Russia. And when Gorbachev at last relaxed the restraints she was finally able to realise her talents, and set up the remarkable Moscow School of Political Studies to introduce the concepts of civil society to the rising generation of young politicians, journalists, scholars, offocials, and business people.

Ambassadors do not often have the chance to get to know ordinary people in the countries where they work: they are too busy cultivating their official contacts. However, in the Autumn of 1988 I received a letter from someone who had seen the official announcement of my arrival in *Izvestia*. The letter was signed 'Konstantin Viktorovich Braithwaite'. Konstantin lived near Novgorod, several hundred kilometres to the north west of Moscow, and he wondered if we might be related. Even a year earlier, Konstantin Braithwaite ('Breitveit' was the Russian transliteration) would not have dared to write to me at all. He came to visit us in Moscow, bringing with him a small bronze rococo statuette of a dancer which he had found in a German dugout on the Bryansk front during the war. He had had it engraved with our two names.

It turned out that there was a whole nest of Braithwaites around Novgorod, in Leningrad, and in Moscow. They were descended from William Braithwaite, an engineer whose steam engine had come second in the competition won by Stephenson's *Rocket*, and who was subsequently invited to St Petersburg by Tsar Nicholas I. By now, however, they were completely Russified in appearance and speech. Nostalgia remained for the country their family had come from. But it was an inconvenient, even a dangerous, memory during the Soviet period, and had been rigorously suppressed.

Konstantin's cousin Feliks, the elder of the Novgorod Braithwaites, was born in 1915. Until his retirement, he directed a small building materials factory in Novgorod. He and his wife Anna lived in a tiny but respectable flat near the Novgorod Kremlin. His brother Yevgeny had retired from working as the transport manager in another Novgorod factory, and was now reduced to living in a communal flat and working as a night watchman at the local theatre. Feliks's great-nephew Valery had been a professional footballer in Central Asia. By a strange coincidence he knew one of the Residence maids, who had been a nurse and had looked after his team. Now he lived in a scruffy apartment and was trying – very ineffectively – to become a 'businessman'.

Alas, I turned out to have no connection with the Braithwaites of Novgorod, though I did manage to track down their English cousin, Bill Braithwaite of Hertfordshire. He was as English as his cousins were Russian, but his father had fought on both sides in the Civil War and retained a Russian accent to the end of his days. I half hoped that the Foreign Office Security Department would ask me why I had failed to confess that I had relatives in Russia. But they never did.

In January 1989 the Foreign Office asked whether Gorbachev was about to be displaced by a coup. My analysis was as follows. It was already clear that Gorbachev's economic measures were muddled, half-baked, and ineffective. The old system of central planning was primitive: but at least it had worked after a fashion. Now it was being undermined, and nothing was being put in its place. The public debate on economics was now being carried on in categories which before were ideologically unacceptable, even when they were understood: balancing the budget, cutting inflation, controlling the money supply, keeping wage and productivity increases in line. But all the talk was delivering nothing. The economy was not going right – or at all. Goods were disappearing from the shops, factories were going onto short time. Political nervousness was increasing as the election campaign for the new Congress got under way. And Gorbachev lacked the rhetorical skills to inspire ordinary people to sacrifice, as Roosevelt and Churchill had done. His audience was increasingly irritated by his endless exhortations. Some were beginning to say they had eaten better under Stalin. Both Russians and outsiders began to fear that the mob might yet take to the streets. It would not be the first time that a Russian revolution started with a riot over bread.

In these circumstances, I thought, a number of things could happen. Gorbachev might continue his reform policies. He might abandon them to remain in power. He might be replaced by an orthodox Party leader who would try to modernise the country through hard work and Party discipline, as Andropov had done. He might be replaced by King Log, as Khrushchev had been replaced by Brezhnev. There might be a military nationalist takeover, Russian chauvinist, anti-Semitic, the 'aggressive and vengeful conservatism' of which Aleksandr Yakovlev had recently warned in a public speech. Gorbachev and his supporters were a minority in the Party. We might have little or no advance warning of Gorbachev's fall. Even under Glasnost we knew little of the inner workings of the Politburo: Gorbachev might disappear overnight, as Khrushchev had done.

I did not believe that the situation had yet reached crisis point. I thought that Gorbachev's policies would continue to make slow progress against an inevitable opposition. There were as yet no real signs of trouble; or of a change of course, either imposed upon Gorbachev by the reactionaries or self-imposed by the need to manoeuvre. His political skills were intact. He was not wavering in the pursuit of his policies on human rights, military cuts, arms control. His known opponents were not strengthening their positions. There were no signs of economic disorder or bloody repression. He might eventually be forced off course or replaced. But the reactionaries would not be able to solve Russia's deep-rooted problems by reverting to the methods of the past. Even if Gorbachev went, the reforms he had initiated would eventually have to be picked up again. I fixed his chances of success at the conveniently judicious figure of fifty-fifty.

But I was sufficiently worried to go to the embassy's pile of back copies of *Pravda* to check my memory of the way in which Khrushchev's dismissal had been announced. My memory did not betray me. On 15 October 1964 *Pravda* said in its editorial: 'The Leninist Party is an enemy of subjectivism and drifting in Communist construction. Hare-brained schemes, immature conclusions, and decisions and actions divorced from reality, bragging and phrasemongering, commandism, unwillingness to take into account the achievements of science and practical experience, are alien to it.' Useful language, I thought, if I ever had to write a telegram reporting the disappearance of Gorbachev.

One thing I did believe. I described Gorbachev to the Foreign Office as a reformer with the creative energy of Peter the Great, but without his brutality. My colleagues in London challenged me on this central point. I pointed out that Peter was a despot, a bloodthirsty sadist in his dealings not only with the Kremlin guard, the Streltsy, who rebelled against him, but also in his treatment of his own son. Gorbachev was neither a despot nor a sadist. I still thought that he would if necessary use force to quell rebellion within the Soviet Union and perhaps even to preserve Soviet strategic interests in Central Europe. Over the next two years blood was indeed shed in Tbilisi, Riga, Vilnius, and above all in Baku. Gorbachev could not escape all the blame. But in the end he fell out with the men of the reactionary right at least in part because he was not willing to use traditional Russian methods to keep the traditional Russian order either in the Empire or at home. His right-wing critics accused him of weakness, then and since. It was in fact one of his most important virtues.

At the beginning of 1989 a colleague in London remarked that the political system in Moscow, as described in my reports, resembled the aerodynamics of a bee. Nothing in it made sense, but somehow the bee kept on flying. In August 1991 the laws of aerodynamics reasserted themselves, the reactionaries mounted a coup, and the bee crashed to the ground. This was what we had all feared. The paradox, which not even the gloomiest foresaw, was that the coup would accelerate, not delay, the process of change; and that it would lead quickly and comparatively bloodlessly to the break-up of the Soviet Union itself.

4

Democracy Comes to the Soviet Union

The people are silent.

Pushkin, *Boris Godunov*

Russia would have been a very different place if the merchant republic of Novgorod, with its primitive system of democracy, had prevailed in the complex civil wars of medieval Russia, rather than the gloomy, introverted, and despotic system created by the Grand Dukes of Muscovy. Novgorod the Great was as old as Kiev and its empire was more extensive. It was a trading city, a member of the Hanseatic League, Russia's window on the West. By comparison, Moscow was a mere upstart, a forest refuge from the Tatar hordes. Novgorod ran its affairs through an elected official, and the rights of its princes were strictly circumscribed by domestic treaty. Power resided in the town assembly, the Veche, which was summoned by the tolling of a bell. The theoretical powers of the Veche were of course brutally limited in practice by local oligarchies. But by the standards of the age the constitutional arrangements of Novgorod the Great were reasonably enlightened.

They were, however, unacceptable to the Grand Dukes of Muscovy. Ivan the Third and Ivan the Terrible (the first formally to call himself Tsar) massacred the city's inhabitants, suppressed its independence and its liberties, destroyed the Veche bell, and nipped democracy in the bud. From time to time thereafter the more enlightened Tsars and their liberal advisers set up lawgiving institutions. But until the last decade of the old regime, these bodies were appointed, not elected. The laws they passed were regularly overruled by imperial decree or ministerial regulation, a recipe for confusion which persisted long into post-Soviet Russia. One after another the half-hearted attempts to create legislative assemblies collapsed or petered out into irrelevance.

As he set out to change all that, Gorbachev drew on his lawyer's background, even if it was only the background of a man trained in the system of Soviet law. He insisted that the country must at last become a *pravovoe gosudarstvo*, a *Rechtsstaat*, a country where even the highest political authority was subject to the law. Gorbachev may not have understood all the practical and institutional consequences of his ideas: with his background that would have been surprising. Sceptics in the Soviet Union and in the West said that *Demokratizatsia* was not the same thing as 'democracy': the whole thing was just another Communist plot. But when Gorbachev told the United Nations General Assembly in December 1988 that he was determined to bring about 'the democratic reform of the whole power system', he meant exactly what he said. Nicholas II had democracy wished upon him after the 1905 revolution, and he and his reactionary advisers did what they could to subvert it. Gorbachev introduced it voluntarily and successfully. After the Soviet Union ceased to exist it became an accepted myth in Russia itself and in the West that democracy was not introduced into Russia until Yeltsin became President. This did a considerable injustice both to Gorbachev and to the millions of people who took advantage of the opportunities he gave them to express their views.

At the end of October 1988 Gorbachev published for public discussion the constitutional proposals he had foreshadowed at the 19th Party Conference. The political background was becoming increasingly turbulent. There were nationalist demonstrations in the Baltic States and in Tbilisi. The Lithuanians abolished the Soviet flag. The Estonian parliament passed a declaration of sovereignty and gave itself the right of veto over all Soviet laws. At the end of November the old-style Supreme Soviet assembled for the last time in the Great Palace of the Kremlin, the massive building just across the river from the Kharitonenko house, which was built in 1832 as a Moscow residence for the Tsars. In the mid-1930s Stalin hacked out of two elegant halls a long, narrow and ugly chamber, furnished in the pale plywood and plush favoured by the Soviet regime, a decor calculated to depress the most unruly parliamentarian, like the bromide in army tea. The political leadership sat on a high tribunal facing delegates packed like the jurors in *Alice in Wonderland* into row after row of narrow seats. Diplomats, journalists, and anyone else who could get tickets were carefully separated from any contact with the deputies, and penned into tiny boxes like open drawers in a chest. They could observe the proceedings only by leaning out at a dangerous angle and cricking their necks. The chamber was as ill-adapted as it could be to free debate before a national public. That was, as the Soviets used to say, no accident.

The deputies to that last meeting were required to approve the arrangements for voting their successors into the new-style Congress of People's Deputies. They passed the proposals in their traditionally disciplined manner, raising their dutiful hands whenever the vote was called. It was the last such orderly scene in the history of the Soviet Union. Even so the voting was not always unanimous. To comply with its own new constitutional amendments, the government was obliged to submit for ratification by the Supreme Soviet two regulations on the management of public disorder. Members of the Baltic delegations voted against both. It was almost certainly the first negative vote registered in a Soviet public assembly since Stalin had made such protests unfashionable. The incident was a brief sensation abroad as well as at home. It was a foretaste of the unruly democracy which came to the Soviet Union in the Spring of 1989.

On 1 December 1988 the old Supreme Soviet passed into law the electoral measures which brought its inglorious existence to an end.

Yeltsin was the natural focus for all those who hoped for radical change. We first saw him at the Revolution Day party in the Kremlin in 1988. He was standing well apart from the top men of the Politburo and the government. Some people were gingerly going up to him; others were rather carefully avoiding him. Jill wanted to beard him straight away. I felt we should not be seen hobnobbing on our first public appearance in Moscow with a man still in bad political odour: a piece of pusillanimity or diplomatic prudence that I subsequently regretted. Later Jill would simply have ignored me, and gone up to talk to him anyway: and I would have been grateful afterwards. But in those early days she was still inclined to think I knew what I was doing. At least we got an impression of the man: powerful, solid, a man of great physical presence in complete contrast to the volatile Gorbachev. His apparent strength was belied by a history of illness. He had heart trouble, back trouble, and recurrent fits of depression. Even in the early days of his political career he would disappear from public view for days, and sometimes for weeks, at a time. But he looked massively like the ordinary Russian *muzhik* or even the Russian *bogatyr*, the hero of folk tale and popular myth. Ordinary Russians liked him from the start. They liked him because, unlike Gorbachev, he drank and fell into rivers, just like they did. They liked him because he opposed a system which they hated, feared, and despised. And they liked him because he was an underdog, and the Russians have a soft spot for underdogs. He had a touch of personal vanity as well, with his quiff of white hair impeccably brushed and fixed into a wave which seemed to survive even the most strenuous activity on the tennis court or in the swimming pool.

The elections gave Yeltsin the chance to re-establish himself. He was of course still very far from being a market-oriented liberal democrat: he was still advocating 'Socialism with a human face', and had not yet abandoned the one-party system.[1] Indeed it was to be nearly a year before he finally left the Communist Party. But the democrats and the anti-Communists rallied to him in increasing numbers. Yegor Yakovlev, who found Yeltsin unattractive, nevertheless considered that his success in the forthcoming election would be an event of the greatest symbolic importance for the new Soviet democracy. And so it proved to be. Yeltsin fought a brilliantly organised election campaign. People across the country competed to have him as their candidate: in his native Sverdlovsk, and in places like Archangel where he had no previous connection. But his final choice lighted on the Moscow Region constituency, with its electorate of nearly seven million. On election day itself, Andrei Sakharov later told me, Yeltsin had two or three people at each polling booth to observe fair play: nearly ten thousand people in all, a huge achievement considering the disadvantages under which he had been placed.

By going for the Moscow constituency Yeltsin raised the stakes to the limit. Gorbachev, or at least some of those around him, took countermeasures. Black propaganda about Yeltsin's character and conduct began to circulate once again, as it had done at the time of his disgrace in 1987. The reactionaries in the Central Committee tried to nullify his candidature on the grounds that he had broken Party discipline by advocating a multiparty system: a curious anachronism at a time when the political monopoly of the Party was already becoming distinctly frayed. The rivalry between Yeltsin and Gorbachev now became the driving factor of Russian politics. But there was a central paradox. Both men made their way from poverty in the provinces to power at the centre. They did so in the most traditional of Soviet ways, through their talents and through patrons within the Party. Both men loved power, as any successful politician must. But Gorbachev had in addition a sense of strategy – naive and half-baked though it occasionally seemed to be. He had conscious objectives and a set of tactical shifts through which to achieve them. Yeltsin was much more instinctive in his pursuit of power. He claimed to favour the continuation of federal or at least confederal links between the component parts of the old Russian empire right up until the last moment. Yet in practice he used the idea of an independent Russia to emasculate and discredit the Soviet government, and so isolate Gorbachev as a step towards eliminating him. Beyond a few slogans he had no political philosophy. Not for him the sophistications of the law-based state, new thinking in foreign policy, a nuclear-free world. His grasp of economics was fragile. His attention even to the everyday political battle was often intermittent. The *nomenklatura* and their wives despised Yeltsin as a clown or feared him as a demagogue. I myself remained suspicious of him almost until the end, influenced in part no doubt by the gossip and rumours – not all of them untrue – which were assiduously spread against him.

Very unlike Yeltsin himself, many of the new democrats who rose to challenge the system were intellectuals. They mostly came from Moscow and Leningrad, and they were Communist Party members almost without exception. Some were the stalwarts of 'New Thinking', people who had first begun to have unorthodox thoughts in the 1960s. Some were university professors with no previous experience of politics despite their Party membership. Many were remarkably effective on the hustings, on the streets, and in the parliament. They enjoyed the trappings of office. They did what they could to push through reform. But most of them lacked Yeltsin's single-minded instinct for the effective use of power. They started as Gorbachev's allies, became disillusioned with him, and in the end turned against him. Gorbachev himself soon began to call them 'democrats' in quotes, and came to regard them as unreliable and even treacherous. By the end of 1990 they were flagging. After the Soviet Union collapsed some of them remained in the new republican politics, some allied themselves with strange bedfellows on the neo-Communist left or the rabid nationalist right, some went back to the academic world or into business, and some returned to the obscurity of private life.

Yuri Afanasiev was a striking example, a chunky, handsome man who was born in Ulyanovsk where Lenin himself was born. In 1986 he became Rector of the Moscow State Historical Archival Institute which was situated in a battered old neo-Gothic building in Kitaigorod, on the site of the first printing works in Russia and just round the corner from the Central Committee building. From this vantage point he led a ruthless attack on the Soviet version of Russia's history. He believed that no reforms could stick unless the country faced up to the truth about the past. He was one of the first to argue that Lenin was as criminally responsible as Stalin for the disasters that followed the October Revolution. Later he became a highly effective street politician, organising one mass demonstration after another against the old regime and against Gorbachev. But he was not a politician for the working day, and when it was all over he returned to academic life as the Rector of a new and independent Humanitarian University in Moscow.

I first called on Yuri Afanasiev in December 1988. We immediately plunged into a long debate about the meaning of history, and about guilt and repentance. In Russia history has never been politically neutral. Both Stalin and the Tsars persecuted unorthodox historians. Both rewrote history whenever it was politically convenient. The re-examination of Soviet history under Glasnost began as an act of protest. Some were ashamed of what had been done in their name and wished simply to establish the truth. Others wanted to restore some sense of unity to their country's past, to repair the fracture caused by seventy years of Communism. Some understood that the historical debate could be used as one more lever to overthrow those in power. For a while there was a far-reaching rejection of everything that had happened in Russia in the previous seventy years.

Ordinary people, who knew only the version of history that had been taught to them in their Soviet schools, were bewildered by the flood of new facts, new revelations, and new interpretations. They joked that the Soviet Union was a country with an unpredictable past. In the summer of 1988 the history examinations were abolished in the schools because they no longer made sense. By the Autumn the liberal newspapers were vying with one another in their accounts of Stalin's atrocities. One after another mass graves – 200,000 people outside Minsk, a similar number outside Kiev – that had been hidden, or attributed to the German occupation, were recognised as the work of the NKVD from before, during, or even after the war. The figures for those who had suffered in the purges and the collectivisation were debated in public. The works of scientists, authors, economists murdered by Stalin began to be published. For a while Bukharin, the old Bolshevik who had been executed on Stalin's orders in 1938, was held up as the model of a liberal Communist, whose ideas might still save the system; and his widow began to give interviews to the press. The role of Trotsky was explored with increasing objectivity. Soviet foreign policy was put under the microscope as well, as the Balts insisted that the Molotov–Ribbentrop Pact was illegal as well as unjust. The more daring iconoclasts went on to draw in public the ultimate deduction: that the excesses of Stalin were foreshadowed by Lenin, that they were perhaps inherent in the ideology of Marx himself. Solzhenitsyn's *Gulag Archipelago* became a bestseller when it was eventually published in the Soviet Union in 1990. Even more shocking for the ordinary Soviet citizen was Vasily Grossman's scathing indictment of Lenin in *Forever Flowing*, and the comparison he drew between Stalin's regime and Hitler's in *Life and Fate*.

This debate had immediate and powerful political implications. By what right did the Party which had presided over these crimes exercise a 'leading role' in the country's affairs? The democrats exploited the argument to the limit. The reactionaries among the Communists attempted to suppress the discussion. But this issue, like so many others, rapidly escaped from the Party's control.

At our first meeting I attempted to persuade Afanasiev that the revision of history had already made remarkable progress. But all political systems needed myths to give them legitimacy. The British had their monarchy. What would the Soviet Union have if Lenin and the October Revolution were demythologised? Stalin and his crimes had to be exposed and denounced. The Soviet Union must become a law-based state. But was it practical politics for Gorbachev to dethrone the founding myths? Would that not give his reactionary enemies a great lever against him?

Afanasiev wholly disagreed. Gorbachev might have a tactical problem. But horrifying facts had come out and there had been almost no discussion of their significance. Gorbachev was still trying to argue that collectivisation had been a genuine step towards Socialism, even if the price had been far too high. But collectivisation had nothing to do with Socialism at all. And as long as Lenin and the October Revolution were wrapped in myth, as long as it was impossible to treat them as 'cold objects' of scientific historical study, the comparative freedom currently enjoyed by historical researchers could come to an end overnight. Afanasiev did concede that any attempt to impose a crackdown would now be resisted. Blood could then be shed. Many of the Moscow intellectuals I met in those first months shared his pessimism. An article that Winter in *Novy Mir* ended with a call for an unfettered reappraisal of the teachings of the founding fathers of the Soviet state: 'But without bullets and bloodshed. We've had more than enough of that already. Let us do battle instead with arguments and facts.'

Afanasiev had raised a fundamental problem. How does a nation come to terms with its guilt? The psychological dislocation which the Russians suffered with the collapse of the Soviet Union was as great as the dislocation suffered by the Germans and the Japanese after 1945. Many argued, both inside the country and abroad, that Russians could not come to terms with their present until they came to terms with their past.

But the task was even harder for them than it was for the Germans. The Germans struggled with a past that went back only twelve years, which no one except a handful of fanatics was prepared to justify; and they had been unequivocally defeated in war. The Russians had won the war, and the victory seemed to many to be a kind of vindication of the regime.

And however evil the regime was in fact, it drew on a generous tradition. The Europeans who made the continental revolutions in the name of 'The Rights of Man', 'Liberty, Fraternity, Equality', were driven by honourable motives. Contemporaries in Western Europe saw the overthrow of the Tsar as a liberation from tyranny, as part of the wider revolutionary tradition born in Europe out of the Romantic Movement and the French Revolution. These images of revolution still resonate even among the stolid audiences who applaud the musical version of *Les Misérables*.

The ideals of revolutionary socialism were discredited by the crimes committed under its banner. But a kind of romantic tradition lived on in the Soviet Union, right through the purges, the war against Germany, and the postwar years of reconstruction. It gripped the minds and the emotions not only of the Party elite, but of almost all the citizens of the Soviet Union, even of those intellectuals who believed that they had shaken themselves free of their ideological chains. Cut off as they were from the outside world, the Soviet people really did believe that in the most important ways their system was superior to that of the West: Socialism and the ideas of Lenin held the key to a more just and prosperous future for mankind. They had themselves experienced the triumphs, the hopes, and the disasters of the Soviet period. After the collapse they found it almost impossible to accept that their own lives and their many sacrifices had been wasted in the pursuit of a false and destructive ideal. They could not simply dismiss their country's history as an uninterrupted series of disasters.

And so some of them emphasised the Soviet Union's technological achievements, its victories in war, and its successes – transient though these were – in the competition with the Americans. A small minority succeeded in convincing themselves that the crimes of the Bolsheviks and of the Soviet regime were grossly exaggerated by domestic and foreign enemies, or that they did not happen, or that they were not crimes. Inside Russia there were of course very many people who found it offensive that concentration camp commanders, torturers, and secret policemen were living out their lives on government pensions in state-owned apartments while many of their victims were still in misery. From time to time there were calls that the guilty men should be put on trial. The Memorial society, founded by Sakharov and led by Academician Likhachev and other eminent liberal intellectuals, did what it could to expose the record and to put up monuments to the millions of dead. But in the end nothing was done. After the spectacular revelations of the late 1980s and a few vivid speeches by Yeltsin and others in the immediate aftermath of the 1991 coup, Russia's leaders made no formal recognition of the guilt of the Soviet period.

Many people, especially foreigners who had never lived in Russia nor under a totalitarian regime, argued that this was a fatal omission. If the Russians did not put the guilty on trial, if they did not confess their collective sins, there could be no assurance that the sins would not be repeated. This was to apply too harsh a standard. Unlike the Germans, the Czechs, or even the South Africans, the Russians lived for three generations under a regime where mutual denunciation and judicial murder were an inescapable part of everyday life. Few people of the pre-Perestroika generation had a completely clear conscience. A lustration, of the kind which the Czechs set in train, would have exposed the major criminals. But it would also have exposed the innumerable otherwise decent people who under the pressures of the police state had compromised, lied, and informed on their colleagues, or even on their friends and relations. The burden on a society which was already finding it hard enough to cope with the trauma of change could have become more than people could bear. And it was an illusion to think that any sort of acceptable judicial process could have been put in place. For all Russians it would have been no more than the latest in the grim series of political show trials which have disfigured Russian history for centuries. Eventually the painful issue would be dissolved with the passage of time, the departure of the generations which lived under Communism, and the fundamental changes which were transforming the nature of Russian society. It was not a solution to satisfy the tidy-minded, the vengeful, or those who yearned after perfect justice. But it was probably the only one available, and it was the solution preferred by both Gorbachev and Yeltsin.

Unlike Afanasiev, Anatoli Sobchak preferred to operate in the political institutions rather than on the streets. Another professor, he was born in Siberia and later became head of the Law Faculty at the University of Leningrad. He joined the Party – for reasons which remain unconvincing – as late as 1988. We first met him at Vladimir Ashkenazy's triumphant return concert at the end of 1989, a historic event which ended in farce when the recording equipment broke down. (The Soviet audience naturally assumed that it was the Soviet equipment that had gone wrong. They were intensely relieved to discover that the blame lay with the BBC.) Sobchak was there with his wife, a handsome and attractive couple. By then he was already an established politician, an enthusiastic supporter of Gorbachev and Perestroika and an untiring critic of the Party. He fought a brilliant campaign in a Leningrad constituency in the elections of March 1989 as an outsider against the Party's preferred candidate and won by a smashing victory on the second round. He was an effective parliamentary performer, and in many ways a highly skilled political operator. In May 1990 he was elected Chairman of the Leningrad City Council, and Mayor of the shortly to be renamed St Petersburg in June 1991. For a time he was spoken of as a future president of Russia.

But Sobchak had several weaknesses. He proved a poor administrator, and his practical performance in office fell far short of his high promise. Like Gorbachev, he talked too much both in public and in private, and his high-pitched voice eventually got on people's nerves. The people of St Petersburg accused his wife of getting above herself and compared her with Raisa Gorbachev. The radicals in the city council – incapable, like so many Russian radicals, of compromise in a common cause – attacked him ever more viciously. He hung on until his defeat in the mayoral elections in the Summer of 1996. By then his aura had quite faded. He was accused of corruption by political rivals, and sought refuge in France. Shortly after his return to Russia he died in the Spring of 1999. In a gesture of loyalty which was one of his more attractive characteristics, Vladimir Putin, who had worked as Sobchak's Deputy in St Petersburg, was among the tearful mourners.

Gavriil Popov and Galina Starovoitova were closely associated with Sobchak and Afanasiev. Popov was a Communist and a Professor of Economics at Moscow University. He was a shambling figure, with bristling grey hair and a bristling grey moustache. I never knew him to wear a tie, except once, for Mrs Thatcher. An unlikely firebrand, he joined with Afanasiev in leading most of the massive street demonstrations in Moscow in 1990 and 1991. But he too made a stab at government. He was elected Mayor of Moscow in April 1990. His views in office were sensible and moderate. He would tell visitors that the economy would only work properly if the government and above all the Party stopped interfering with it. Democratic freedoms could only be assured on the basis of private property. But he soon attracted envy and criticism. The critics said that his methods were authoritarian and his privatisation schemes ineffective. They accused him of handing out municipal property arbitrarily to his cronies. Falin, the Head of the International Department in the Central Committee Secretariat, called him rather unfairly 'neither a statesman, nor even a professor, merely a minor bureaucrat and a loose cannon'. By the end of 1991 Popov was talking of resignation, and he soon went back into the academic world.

Galina Starovoitova was born in the Urals in 1945, a large, jolly, energetic and uncompromising woman. She studied military engineering in Leningrad, but switched to psychology and ethnography. She specialised in the problems of ethnic minorities, and although she was Russian, she was elected from a constituency in Armenia in March 1989 to voice the woes of the Armenian people, which she did with great force.

Starovoitova was one of the handful of self-made women politicians who rose to distinction in the last years of the Soviet regime. Despite the rhetoric of Socialist equality and the sticky sentiment which surrounded (and still surrounds) events such as International Women's Day, only three women ever sat as full members of the Politburo of the Communist Party, two of them in the Gorbachev years. Women's participation in the Party's Central Committee was never more than 4 per cent. The proportion in the toothless and unelected Supreme Soviet was higher, partly because a quota system operated. The situation was the same in the upper reaches of the Academy of Science, in the universities, and in the organisations which ran Soviet journalism, literature, and culture. Women were trained in substantial numbers for the professions, but the glass ceiling pressed down upon them ruthlessly. One woman who qualified for the Foreign Ministry in the late 1980s left in disgust because the only job she was offered was that of a secretary. Women suffered more than men from the inadequacies of the health service. The absence of contraceptives led to very high abortion rates.

In the new Russia things improved somewhat. Enterprising women were able to launch into business and social projects of their own, and there was a steady trickle of effective women politicians. But the numbers remained exiguous. The leaders of the new politics and the new business were still men. With the abolition of quotas, the Russian parliament elected in 1993 contained an even smaller proportion of women than its Soviet predecessor. The independent women's organisations which had begun to fight for women's rights under Gorbachev lost their prominence under Yeltsin. Some things which had worked well enough under the old system declined in the free-for-all economics of the new. Kindergartens and holiday camps for children closed down for lack of money. Women had to shoulder an even heavier responsibility for their families as their men fell into unemployment and depression. Russia remained a society overwhelmingly dominated by men, and it would be a long time before that changed.

Starovoitova fell out of sympathy first with Gorbachev and then with Yeltsin, who both failed to live up to her fierce ideals. She was spoken of as a possible Defence Minister (improbable as that might have sounded in a country which had never had a civilian, let alone a woman, in charge of its armed forces) and ran for the presidency in 1996. In 1995 she was elected to a constituency in St Petersburg. She was assassinated in St Petersburg in November 1998 for reasons which have never been explained, by contract killers who have never been caught.

Andrei Sakharov was one of Starovoitova's chief mentors. I only met him once, since I was diffident about adding to the number of foreigners who came simply to gawp. But in March 1989 I had to deliver a letter about arrangements for his Honorary Doctorate in Oxford in the Summer. He received me with great courtesy on the sofa of a tiny room in his apartment. His fine face and fine manner radiated an air of purity. He was in the middle of a vicious and distasteful fight to secure election to the Congress of People's Deputies. But he felt – and I believed him – that it was his duty to persevere. His particular concern at that moment was Abkhazia in the Caucasus. The Abkhazian minority wanted to secede from Georgia, and there would be serious trouble. I did not confess that I had only the vaguest idea where Abkhazia was, though I remembered some time later that Jill and I had been there inadvertently in 1964 when the local bus we were travelling on went straight through it and out the other side. It was then an area closed to foreigners, and we were lucky not to be apprehended and sent back to Moscow in disgrace.

Sakharov poured out his energy both in the Congress of People's Deputies and in desperate attempts to mediate in the bloody ethnic conflicts which began to spread like wildfire from one region to another. He was forever warning, haranguing, attacking Gorbachev for not moving fast enough towards a constitutional state. His political naivety occasionally got him into sad scrapes. He suggested in the Congress that Soviet aircraft had bombed their own troops in Afghanistan to prevent them from being taken prisoner, and was viciously abused by two senior officers for his pains. Whether or not the accusation was true, it was bound to provoke the fury of patriots, and was unlikely to achieve any positive result since the Afghan war was already over. One has to be very sure of one's ground before denigrating men in uniform, as the British Labour MP Barbara Castle found out to her cost when she accused British troops of using torture in Cyprus.

I occasionally thought that Sakharov was too critical, that he was making life unnecessarily difficult for Gorbachev, that he would have achieved his ends more easily if he had been less absolute in his judgements. I was wrong. His resistance to the Soviet system, his idea that Russia could only survive if it became an open society, were the indispensable intellectual and political preliminary to Perestroika. His courage, his stamina, his singleness of purpose made one feel small. Unlike Solzhenitsyn, he never joined in the bitter internecine warfare which often disfigured relations between the dissidents. The new Russia which was struggling to be born needed one person like him, the courageous conscience of the nation. After his premature death his voice was desperately missed as Perestroika went increasingly off the rails.

Gorbachev's new electoral system was baroque in its complexity. It was intended to achieve two aims: to give the voter a genuine choice between candidates; and to ensure a preponderant place in the new parliament for the Communist Party. Individual candidates could no longer be sure of election, as they had been in the past. But there was no provision for organised political parties. Gorbachev was still uncomfortable with the idea of a multiparty system, and it was anathema to the Party die-hards around him.

The arrangements were as follows. One thousand five hundred deputies were to be elected in territorial constituencies on the first-past-the-post system. Half of these would come from 750 single-member constituencies, each containing about 300,000 voters, into which the country as a whole would be divided. The other half would come from 750 'national-territorial' constituencies based on the political subdivisions of the Soviet Union: the separate Baltic Republics, Georgia, Armenia, and so on. Moscow, which was divided into a number of normal constituencies, also formed a 'national-territorial' constituency of 6.7 million voters in its own right. The remaining 750 deputies were to be elected from so-called 'social organisations', which were to act as electoral colleges. The largest of these was the Communist Party of the Soviet Union, which had a block of one hundred seats reserved for it in order, as Gorbachev admitted, to ensure that key members of the Party leadership could not be voted down.[2] The smallest was the Union of Soviet Philatelists which had one place only. Others included the Academy of Sciences, the 'creative' unions (writers, musicians, cinematographers, and so on). This self-evidently undemocratic arrangement caused much criticism abroad. My intellectual friends defended it. Without some such system, they said, insufficient intellectuals would be elected to the new body. I countered that in Britain the last thing that most of us wanted to see in Parliament was a lot of intellectuals, too clever by half. My friends were not amused.

The election campaign got under way at the beginning of January 1989. It was the real thing: electoral chicanery and worse, polemics in the press, public rows over the nomination of candidates, attempts by the ruling Communist Party to bend its own rules when they seemed to be working in the wrong direction. Where they could, local Party bosses manipulated the selection procedure to ensure that there was only one candidate for each vacancy, believing that the people – cowed and apathetic as always – would simply fall in with the intentions of their betters. They were wrong. The electoral law laid down two key conditions for a valid result. A successful candidate had to get 50 per cent plus one of the votes cast. And the turnout had to be more than 50 per cent of those qualified to vote. If either of these conditions was not met, there had to be a run-off two weeks later, in which the two most successful candidates in the first round ran against one another. But if there was only one candidate in the first round, and he failed to meet the two conditions, he was disqualified from running again. In a number of key constituencies the voters grasped that if less than half of them turned out, or if a majority of them spoilt their ballot papers, they could block the election even where there was only one candidate.

And so, as in Western democratic elections, the first battle was to get nominated. For the first time, liberals, democrats, political outsiders, and the merely ambitious, had the opportunity to break into politics without trudging through the Party committees. For their part the incumbents of the *nomenklatura* were determined to hang on to their monopoly of power. The battles took place at public meetings, in the workplace, and in the smoke-filled rooms. There were passionate speeches, endless meetings, repeated votes, results falsified and challenged: the messy process of democracy, all closely followed by an increasingly curious and outspoken press. In the big cities of Leningrad and Kiev, and to a lesser extent in Moscow, the local Party machine was strong enough to frustrate or even to block entirely the candidature of people of whom it disapproved. In some cities, and in many rural constituencies, the number of places was the same as the number of candidates, each of whom was a tried and tested member of the *nomenklatura*. Candidates from the 'social organisations' were selected by the Party's placemen, most of whom had been in charge for decades. They too tried by secret manipulation to reduce the lists to the familiar, comfortable arrangement – one place, one candidate.

The hacks had their successes. Many liberals failed to be adopted as candidates. Here and there strong-arm methods were used. An election meeting for Korotich, the editor of the liberal weekly *Ogonek*, was sabotaged by Pamyat hooligans shouting anti-Semitic slogans. But the hacks were far from having it all their own way. In the Communist Party the selection process produced the expected result. There were one hundred candidates for the hundred places set aside for Party leaders. Six hundred and forty one people attended the meeting of the Central Committee which acted as the electoral college for these places. Seventy-eight of them voted against nominating Ligachev and fifty-nine voted against Yakovlev. Indeed they voted against anyone prominent: representatives of both the left and the right within the Politburo; representatives of the liberal intelligentsia; anyone in the public view. Only the unknowns received unanimous support – the statutory factory workers and milkmaids who had always found a place in the Supreme Soviets of the past. There were twelve votes against Gorbachev himself. In the Academy of Sciences, the battles were far more vicious. The selection procedure was run by Academician Kudryavtsev, the Director of the Institute of State and Law. He manipulated the procedures to keep Sakharov and other liberal scientists off the list. But the liberals refused to be railroaded. They voted down the packed list and the selection procedure had to be rerun. This time Sakharov secured his place. All these excitements were fully reported by the Moscow rumour factory and increasingly by the press as well.

In March Jill and I went to the Northern cities of Murmansk and Archangel to see how the campaign was going in the provinces. Murmansk was founded as a base for Allied arms supplies in the First World War. It served the same purpose for the Arctic convoys in the Second World War, when it was bombed to bits. It was not at its best in the warm slushy weather: a line of undistinguished Soviet blocks of flats and offices strung out for twenty-one kilometres along a barren fjord. At its northern end stood a huge war memorial, a massive statue of a Soviet warrior known to the locals as 'Alyosha', where young couples came to pose for their wedding photographs. Only a small section in the middle of the city had any distinction: a street of baroque Stalinist palaces from the 1950s, decorated in St Petersburg colours of ochre, yellow, green, blue. Archangel was a much older city. Ivan the Terrible founded it in 1584, the first English visitors passed through it on their way to Moscow, and Peter the Great made his first experiments in shipbuilding there. Once it had been an attractive place; but Stalin blew up the cathedral and Khrushchev began replacing the wooden streets with high-rise concrete monstrosities. To my surprise, I see that my diary describes the food and service in the Dvina Hotel in Archangel as 'excellent by any standards': an effect spoiled when the hot water and the electric lights failed on the first morning.

The most interesting tourist attractions in both cities were the local museums. For the first time we came across those dedicated women, dressed in pitiful poverty because the pay was so bad, who all over Russia were devoting their lives to the task of keeping the flame alight. Without their quiet heroism the renaissance of Russian culture in the 1980s would have had little to build on. Maya Mitkevich ran the Museum of Plastic Arts in Archangel. Her women colleagues were making expeditions into the deep countryside to find the relics of a dying folk culture and whatever remained of the icons in the ruined churches. Marfa Menshikova – over seventy, a Party worker for fifty years, bright as a button, a tremendous enthusiast for the preservation of local folk art, churches, villages – ran the unpromisingly named 'House for Propagandising Monuments of History and Culture'. It was she who had bullied the town council into preserving the whole street as a museum to old Archangel, with wooden pavements and wooden lampposts, and buildings moved in from other parts of the town: a monument to the past, and to the vandalism of the Soviet period.

Women were also in charge of the monastery on the island of Solovki in the middle of the White Sea, a monument to another kind of heroism. The monastery, founded in 1429, is a fairy-tale place of churches with onion domes, surrounded by a string of defensive towers on a wall of massive rough-hewn rock. Almost as impressive as the Moscow Kremlin, it draws on the older architectural tradition of Northwest Russia. It looked particularly lovely in the pale wintry sun. But it had a sinister reputation. The Tsars used it as a place of exile: Pushkin narrowly missed being sent there. The Bolsheviks turned it into a concentration camp. In *The Gulag Archipelago* Solzhenitsyn describes how the place worked. Middle-class women from St Petersburg were rounded up in the first wave: they arrived in evening dress or whatever else they had been wearing at the time. Later inmates were worked to death on the White Sea Canal, the 'Achievement of Socialism' which Western fellow-travellers used to be taken to see in the 1930s. Every now and again the inmates were shot in batches. Dmitri Likhachev, one of Russia's most respected literary and academic figures, was a prisoner there. He escaped by pure chance on the night that three hundred people were shot – the same as the total number of people who were sent to Solovki during the half millennium before the October Revolution. Ludmila Lopashkina, the museum director, did not speak about the horrors. She preferred to concentrate on the bombardment of the monastery by two British frigates during the Crimean War – HMS *Miranda* and HMS 'Brisk' (*sic*) under the command of Captain Ommakhonei (O'Mahony?) – nine hours, eighteen hundred shells, no damage.

The local officials and journalists were worthy but dull. Klimentiuk, the shifty Secretary of the Murmansk Town Council informed us proudly that Murmansk cows had the highest yields in the Soviet Union, a fact (if such it was) that turned out to have a bizarre significance almost three years later. He and his colleagues were trying, without obvious success, to convince themselves that change, as ordered by the General Secretary, was the right thing. They could not believe that ordinary people were now to be allowed to express their views freely. So they were doing what they could to ensure that the popular choice was exercised 'responsibly' – in favour of the

Party and of candidates with the 'right' experience. One Party boss in Murmansk supported Perestroika – of course. But he saw no virtue in rapid change. Market economics were all well and good. But the Soviet Union was still a long way from the market, and commands would still have to be issued during the transition.

The Party Secretary in Archangel was unavailable: he had broken his leg electioneering, an excuse so original that I was inclined to believe it. His predecessor had been killed by a stray bullet during a demonstration in the mid-1950s. Archangel was obviously a dangerous place for politicians. Under Party pressure the Archangel Electoral Commission had reduced the number of potential candidates from forty-six to twelve: two for each of four constituencies, and three for the town of Archangel. One constituency had been reserved for a single candidate, Gorshkov of the Central Committee. Everyone knew Gorshkov would not be elected if anyone ran against him, and the Electoral Commission had therefore managed to eliminate the other nominees. All the candidates were Party members: several workers, a few Party officials, one youth, one woman, one factory director – an entirely traditional mix.

Back in Moscow on the eve of the poll, Jill and I went to observe the final pro-Yeltsin rally at Luzhniki, an open space in a bend of the Moscow river close to the Novodevichy Monastery where the rigged election takes place at the beginning of Mussorgsky's *Boris Godunov*. The weather was sunny, but bitterly cold. I pulled my fur hat down over my head to make it harder for Soviet secret policemen and British journalists to recognise the British ambassador participating in a political demonstration organised by the opposition. The authorities closed the nearest metro stations, a regular tactic which failed to prevent people from pouring in on foot. One speaker estimated the crowd at forty thousand. All were neatly dressed, good-tempered, and well-behaved. There was even a handful of army officers in uniform among them. A group of soldiers giggled nervously as a middle-class woman exhorted them to vote for Yeltsin. It was as if they were all desperately trying to prove themselves mature enough to be entrusted with a bit of real democracy. The authorities were less sure. Plain-clothes men armed with cameras recorded the faces of the crowd. The place was ringed with soldiers and police. Twenty-eight army lorries loaded with soldiers were parked on the other side of the railway embankment which enclosed the site.

The demonstrators carried few slogans and flags. The red flag was far outnumbered by flags bearing the St Andrew Cross (blue diagonal on a white ground), symbol of Russia's patron saint, of the Imperial Russian

Navy, and of the extreme nationalist right. Disappointingly, Yeltsin himself did not turn up. Speakers called for 'Bread and Freedom', the slogans which triggered the revolutions of 1905 and 1917. They reminded their audience that the Party had fought hard and dirty to limit the choice of candidates and to stop Yeltsin. One man, in a typical Russian simile, compared Russia's sufferings since 1917 with Christ's sufferings on Golgotha. Everywhere people handed out home-made election pamphlets and stickers: the crowd were practically fighting to lay hands on them. How, I wondered, had the activists managed to get hold of the computer, the copiers, the fax machines, equipment which until recently had been kept under KGB lock and key? One carbon-copied poem read:

The Central Committee has shown what it means
By Glasnost and freedom of speech.
Yeltsin stepped half an inch out of line,
And then – Wallop! – got one in the eye.
He'd asked them: 'Come tell us just what you've achieved.
Perestroika is stuck in the mud.
Four years have gone by … Now it's surely high time
For the train to pull out of the station?'
My goodness, how that question enraged those great men,
Every one of those over-fed mugs!
They'd sell their own mothers just so they could keep
All their government cars and their houses.
No, Perestroika won't get us too far
While we still have this Central Committee.

Atrocious verse: but highly significant politics.

Throughout the country, ordinary people were politically active for the first time in their lives. Sasha Motov was in a frenzy of political enthusiasm. He was out on the streets, canvassing votes in apartments and super-markets, campaigning against unpopular candidates. His excitement grew as election day approached. He repeated the rumour circulated that Yeltsin had been knocked down by a car. He was dying – or dead – in the Kremlin hospital. The implication was obvious. Someone was trying to get rid of Yeltsin by the same method that they had got rid of the popular First Secretary of the Belorussian Party a few years earlier. The rumour was unfounded: Yeltsin was alive and well. Had it been true, there might well have been a popular explosion.

Election day in Moscow on Sunday 26 March was a quiet and orderly affair. We looked in on the polling station near the embassy. People were performing their civic duty, in a poll which appeared to be genuinely secret. At least in Moscow, the election officials behaved scrupulously. Each polling station had a lawyer to advise the voters on their rights. Sasha Motov asked whether his vote would be valid if he crossed out all the candidates. The lawyer ruled that it would. Like the other 'little people', Sasha had realised that he could frustrate the Party bosses who had tried to rig the lists by simply crossing every name off the list.

The election results were much more spectacular than anyone had expected. The intrigues of the *nomenklatura* were frustrated by tactical voting in one constituency after another. Thirty-one Obkom First Secretaries – the regional Party dictators who always had their way under the old system – were defeated: nearly one in four of the total. The leadership in Leningrad (including Soloviev, a candidate member of the Politburo) was wiped out. The Mayor of Kiev remarked ruefully: 'I lost because I was unopposed.' The Mayor of Moscow, Saikin, was out. So were the reactionary writer Bondarev, the Commander of the Soviet Forces in Germany, and thirteen other Military District Commanders, including those in Moscow and the Far East. All Pamyat's extreme nationalist and anti-Semitic candidates failed. Here and there the older patterns of subservient voting still prevailed: but it was mostly in the remoter cities and in Central Asia.

Most spectacular of all, Yeltsin had secured over 90 per cent of the vote in the Moscow 'national-territorial' constituency where the voters decided that a vote for him was a handy vote against the leadership and the system. The Party's underground campaign against him had wholly backfired. He was elected by more than five million ordinary people. Gorbachev, on the Central Committee's list of one hundred, was elected only by his colleagues in the Central Committee. Yeltsin now had an undeniable political base and a legitimacy which no one else could match. By contrast Gorbachev had been unwilling, perhaps afraid, to subject himself to the democratic disciplines he was introducing for the rest of his compatriots. The inexorable decline in his political status began from this moment. Less than three years later he surrendered the keys of office to the man whose political career he had once pronounced at an end.

There were of course many ragged edges. Reruns had to be organised in the numerous constituencies where there had been no clear result. The Party hacks, chastened but enriched by the experience of defeat, fought back in the second round. In the ancient West Russian town of Pskov, they got their man elected against no opposition. The Party man in Dushanbe, the capital of the Central Asian republic of Tajikistan, claimed a very old-fashioned score – 70 per cent of the votes in a turnout of over 90 per cent. But the liberals also scored successes. A shamefaced Academy of Sciences finally elected Sakharov. Korotich won respectably in a field of half-a-dozen candidates. Ivanov, the State Prosecutor who had pinned corruption charges on Churbanov, Brezhnev's son-in-law, fought the Leningrad Region on an anti-corruption ticket. On the eve of the poll he went on television to claim that his latest investigations were leading him towards the very top. He had evidence, he said, which implicated Politburo members Romanov and Solomentsev, and Ligachev himself. He secured more than 60 per cent of the votes against a field of twenty-five. His smashing victory, comparable to Yeltsin's, was further evidence of the deep unpopularity of the Party leadership. The authorities tried to discredit him. But he instantly became a popular hero. Sasha and Konstantin furiously believed even his most extreme accusations against the Party bosses, though he never produced the convincing evidence he had promised.

The new Congress of People's Deputies met on 25 May 1989 in the main auditorium of the Congress Hall in the Kremlin. It lasted until early June, and was immediately followed by a session of the new Supreme Soviet, the executive arm of the Congress, which consisted of 542 Congress deputies split between two chambers. The 'Presidium' of the Congress sat on the stage: mostly nonentities, except for the Kyrgyz author, Chingiz Aitmatov; Politburo member Vorotnikov; and Gorbachev himself. The rest of the Politburo and the government ministers sat in pens to one side. The delegates sat in the main body of the hall. Journalists, diplomats, and other hangers-on sat in the gallery. Unlike the hall in the Great Palace where the old Supreme Soviet used to meet, the Congress Hall was well adapted for debate. It was broad rather than long, everyone had a good view, and it was hard not to catch the eye of a scrupulous Speaker if you stood up to demand attention. Diplomats and journalists could even bluff their way into the deputies' canteen if they were sufficiently thick-skinned, to mingle, to gossip, and to question the hitherto inaccessible pillars of the Soviet establishment.

The proceedings of the Congress and the new Supreme Soviet which followed went far beyond even the remarkable limits of Glasnost set by the 19th Party Conference. The delegates decided right at the start that their proceedings should be televised. The result was a political soap opera broadcast across the country at all hours of the day and night. Work ground to a halt as people watched hitherto unknown delegates cross-examine their leaders and attack the sacred cows of the Soviet state without inhibition. Even the procedural debates were excited and at times heated. The proceedings were dominated by Balts, Georgians, and Armenians, and by the disdainful intellectuals from Moscow and Leningrad, to the fury of the right-wingers and the far more numerous delegates from the provinces. People spoke of the country being on the edge of an abyss. It was like the noisy, disorderly debates in Petrograd in 1917 which John Reed describes in *Ten Days that Shook the World*.

On the first day Gorbachev was put forward for election as 'Chairman of the Supreme Soviet' (effectively Head of State). The deputies seized the opportunity to subject him to an unprecedented cross-examination. Why did he want to combine the Presidency and the General Secretaryship? Did he know in advance about the recent massacre in Tbilisi, in which paratroopers had killed nearly twenty people? What about his luxurious dacha on the Black Sea? Napoleon's wife persuaded him to become Emperor: did Gorbachev see a parallel? The last two questions were obviously directed against Raisa Gorbachev, and one woman delegate jumped up to say that in *civilised* countries the wives of heads of state themselves had state functions. An obscure delegate put himself up as an alternative to Gorbachev, because he believed that no candidate should be returned unopposed. Gorbachev naturally survived the challenge. In his acceptance speech he committed himself to respect for the law and for human rights. People should not, he said, have to go onto the streets to pursue their political aims. There should be discipline, but not the heavy hand of the past. All this was dutifully applauded.

Lukyanov, Gorbachev's candidate for the Deputy Chairmanship of the Congress, was treated more roughly. The delegates accused him of mismanaging the preliminary business of the Congress. They tried to implicate him in the Tbilisi killings and the black campaign to discredit the State Prosecutor Ivanov. But in the end they let Gorbachev have his man. It was the first but not the last occasion on which he pushed through the candidature of someone who later betrayed him.

The new arrangements provided that the President (Gorbachev) had the right to appoint his own Prime Minister (Ryzhkov), but that the remaining ministers had to be presented to the deputies for approval. This step towards democracy was unprecedented either before or since the October Revolution. Ryzhkov immediately ran into trouble. He had put his government together with great care, and believed that it was 'the best qualified, the most independent government in Soviet history'.[3] But the deputies showed no mercy. He had to withdraw the nominations of hopelessly unpopular ministers, such as Zakharov, the Minister of Culture. Sobchak accused Kamentsev, the First Deputy Prime Minister for Foreign Economic Relations, of corruption and nepotism. The deputies turned him down, and his political career was finished. Biryukova, a Candidate Politburo member and Deputy Prime Minister responsible for social and consumer affairs, had to spend seventeen hours defending herself before eight different committees. Six out of Ryzhkov's sixty-nine candidates failed to make the grade. He claimed that this was a reasonable proportion. So it was: but Soviet parliamentarians had never been able to exercise that kind of power before.

The Ministries of Foreign Affairs, Interior, and Defence, and the KGB reported direct to Gorbachev, not to the Prime Minister. He was therefore responsible for proposing the candidates. He nominated the incumbents, Shevardnadze, Bakatin, Yazov and Kryuchkov. He too immediately ran into trouble. Vlasov, a former Olympic weight-lifting champion, launched an all-out attack on the KGB and its record of mass murder, torture, and intimidation. He demanded that it should be put under parliamentary control, open its archives, publish its staff numbers and official budget, give up its privileged hospital in the suburbs, and vacate the Lubianka. His speech was published in *Pravda*, and read with amazement throughout the country. Kryuchkov, the KGB's Chairman, was asked endless questions, of the kind 'When did you last beat your wife?' He claimed that torture and telephone tapping were no longer used. He said that it was more important to reform the KGB than to move it out of the Lubianka. He was heard without any sympathy. But when the vote was called, only two brave hands were raised against him, and the onlookers tittered nervously. Defence Minister Yazov was asked if he intended to mount a coup. He denied it stoutly. He tried to cash in on his record as the last general to have served in the Great Patriotic War. They told him roughly that there were younger generals from more recent wars. With Gorbachev's strong support he just squeaked through.

The Soviet ruling class had always been co-opted in secret. Now the intrusive personal questioning inflicted on every candidate for high office destroyed the aura of mystery and menace. The elections brought entirely new faces into the political process. The voters were able to form their own judgement on the people who presumed to govern them. This was what Gorbachev had planned. The practice was more painful than he had bargained for.

The conservatives and the provincial delegates were still in a majority. They were horrified by what was happening, and they were determined to strike back. Gorbachev's new constitutional arrangements provided for the Congress of People's Deputies to elect the new Supreme Soviet from its midst. This gave the conservatives their opportunity. They used their voting muscle to put together what Yuri Afanasiev, with his usual colourful exaggeration, called 'a Stalinist-Brezhnevite aggressive majority Soviet'. Yeltsin and most of the liberal reformers in the Congress were excluded. People took to the streets in protest. Kazannik, an unknown deputy from Siberia who had been successful in the voting, offered to step down if, but only if, Yeltsin could have his place. After some wrangling this ingenious wheeze was agreed: a solution both politic and procedurally improper. Yeltsin entered the Supreme Soviet and moved one step further towards a position from which he could effectively challenge his arch-rival.

The distinction between the 'Congress' and the 'Supreme Soviet' of the USSR was replicated when the Congress of the Russian Soviet Federated Socialist Republic was elected in 1990. It is a confusing distinction which had little significance in practice. It is simpler to use the phrase 'Soviet parliament' to cover both Soviet bodies elected in 1989, and 'Russian parliament' for their Russian equivalents elected a year later. After the 1993 election the Russian parliament was called the 'Duma' to underline continuity with its pre-Revolutionary predecessor.

Right from the opening debates, the delegates started to circle around some fundamental issues. Could the Soviet Union survive without a strong, and if necessary a harsh, central authority? What guarantees could be erected against a new Stalin? How could the rule of law be imposed on a bureaucracy which for centuries had been used to issuing decrees, regulations, and simple orders regardless of the statute book? Nothing and nobody, not even Lenin, was sacrosanct: Yuri Karyakin, a Dostoevsky scholar, proposed that his body be removed from the mausoleum on Red Square. An obscure delegate grumbled that he had not heard the word 'Communist' uttered once. In the Foreign Ministry they shook their heads and muttered that the country was going to the dogs. Nationalist emotion began to rise. The parliament set up a commission to discover who had been responsible for the army's massacre of peaceful demonstrators in Tbilisi. They went into closed session to consider the appalling situation in Uzbekistan, where Uzbeks were murdering Meskhetian Turks deported from the Caucasus by Stalin in 1944. The Balts and the Georgians demanded economic autonomy. The Estonians insisted that their laws had precedence over Soviet law. Russian and Estonian wrangled about who got the most economic advantage from Union membership as each attempted to blackmail the other.

Down in the Caucasus it was bullets that were being exchanged, not words, as Sakharov had feared. The Georgian government decided to open a branch of Tbilisi University in Sukhumi, the capital of the Georgian province of Abkhazia. The Abkhazians saw this as a piece of deliberate cultural imperialism by the Georgians. As tension grew, our friend the Georgian violinist Liana Isakadze had to call off her annual music festival in the Abkhazian resort of Pitsunda, the ancient Colchis. By mid-July sixteen people had been killed. Police posts were raided and there were firearms everywhere. All this was shown on national television. Merab Mamardashvili, sublimely liberal, intelligent, and rational, was passionate to the point of incoherence when someone mentioned Abkhazia at a party at the Senokosovs. The Abkhazians, he said, were a conspiracy, not a nation. They had no culture. The Georgians had had to invent their alphabet for them. This, he declared, was how the Abkhazians repaid Georgian generosity. As in most ethnic disputes, the rights and wrongs of the Abkhazian dispute were highly complex, though those involved reduced them to black, white – and blood red. Outsiders who expressed a view on one side or the other got into serious trouble. Those who implied that blame lay with both sides got into still more serious trouble. It was not safe even to express total neutrality. In real life, philosophy has its limitations.

Even Ukraine began to stir. Shcherbitsky, the Ukrainian Party Secretary, still kept a firm grip on behalf of the 'Muscovites' (a term of abuse in Ukrainian). But an incident in early July was symptomatic. A group of Ukrainians decided to turn the two hundred and eightieth anniversary of Peter the Great's victory at Poltava over the Swedish King Charles XII and his Ukrainian ally Mazeppa into a celebration of Ukrainian nationhood. Ukrainians regard Mazeppa as a hero. Russians see him as a traitor. Pamyat mobilised its bully-boys to disrupt the celebrations. Korotich, himself a Ukrainian, persuaded the Moscow authorities to take countermeasures. Trouble was forestalled – for the time being.

As the Summer wore on, the workers too got restive. Worker unrest was one of the symptoms which, we had told the Foreign Office in January, could mean Gorbachev was in serious trouble. The miners had the best organisation and the most stamina. They went on strike in the Kuzbass in Siberia and in the Donbass in Eastern Ukraine. The Kuzbass mines were richly productive, they made a profit, and the miners wanted to keep the money for themselves. But the coal they produced was piling up at the pithead, because the collapsing transport system could not get it to the customer. Stocks were catching fire by spontaneous combustion. The miners resented their efforts being wasted in this way. By contrast the mines in the Donbass were worked out and making a loss. The last thing the Ukrainian miners wanted was economic independence: what they were striking for was increased subsidies from the centre. But all were living in intolerable conditions. Pilar Bonet, the highly experienced correspondent of the Spanish paper *El Pais*, found that the miners in the Kuzbass were demanding one piece of soap and one towel a month, and carpets in the barracks they lived in. One miner sidled up to ask her if there was a Communist Party in Spain. 'Yes', she said. 'Small and getting smaller.' 'Good,' he said. 'Keep it that way.'

In the Soviet parliament, too, working-class deputies were increasingly insisting that the garrulous intellectuals and the bureaucrats should surrender the floor to them. They demanded genuine workers' representations to replace the existing unions, which had failed to fight for their members' interests. They wanted new laws on property and on workers' rights. They wanted the government to adopt a proper economic programme. Time and again they said they did not trust their factory management, the local authorities, the Party, the Ministries, anyone in authority. Only Gorbachev and Ryzhkov were still sacrosanct.

Ryzhkov, a miner's son, visited the pits, showed the emotion for which he was becoming notorious and of which he was secretly proud, and bought the strikers off by promising massive handouts. These would further have undermined the economy and given another twist to the inflationary spiral. But by now Ryzhkov did not have the resources to do even that much. The miners' independent leaders maintained an impressive discipline. There was no unrest. The pits were properly maintained. For a while at least the miners even refrained from vodka. They became increasingly familiar visitors to Moscow. In the Spring of 1991 their demands became increasingly political. They talked of flooding their mines if the reactionaries mounted a coup. Volynko, one of their leaders, told me that the miners were now insisting – a significant change – on the resignation of Gorbachev and his government. Despite the hardships, Volynko said, the miners were fully supported by their wives, who had given them their sandwiches on the first day and told them not to come home without victory. 'With their shields or on them,' I remarked.

Like everyone else, I was carried away by enthusiasm at the sight of Russian democracy in action. I too followed the proceedings on television, hung around the Congress Hall, gossiped in the corridors. But my reporting to the Foreign Office was more sober. The new parliament had earned high marks for effort, little for achievement. It had posed the questions, but had not provided the answers. It had done nothing for the economic crisis to which speaker after speaker had referred. It had got no grip on the underlying constitutional and practical issues. It risked becoming a mere talking shop, ignored by government and Party alike. Gorbachev's own performance in the early weeks was masterly. He dominated the proceedings throughout. Without his persuasive skill, his willingness to allow debate on the most sensitive issues, his political guile, and his tireless energy, the show would have fallen apart. Gorbachev still stood in public for Lenin, Socialism, and the leading role of the Party. But his political methods, and his strategy for the democratisation and modernisation of the state, were leading inexorably away from all three. I believed that he was sincere in wanting a real parliament, where debate was free but disciplined, where laws were drafted which bound government as well as people, and where the authorities could be brought to effective account for the abuse of power.

But Gorbachev was operating on equivocal ground. He continued to mouth ideological pieties to keep the Party together. His thought processes were moving away from the old orthodoxies, though he still thought of himself as a Communist. But I doubted if he was much concerned with ideological niceties. Chingiz Aitmatov told the parliament that Sweden, Switzerland, even Britain, were closer than the Soviet Union to true Socialism. If Lenin and the Party eventually had to make way for a modern, effective Soviet superpower, Gorbachev, too, would find it easy enough to call the result 'Socialism'.

And so the hectic mood of euphoria which dominated the opening of the new parliament was not long sustained. Gorbachev himself began to flag. His speeches on the economy and on the growing ethnic conflicts were feeble – long on rhetoric, and short on concrete ideas. He resorted to vague threats, telling the parliament that 'the country could find itself in a situation when it would be necessary to consider what forms (*sic*) should be used to prevent the situation getting out of hand.' In the midst of his preoccupations he found time to visit Paris, to go to a Warsaw Pact meeting in Bucharest, and to purge the Party leadership in Leningrad. Even if these trips were a relaxation from Moscow life, they meant that the pace was unremitting. He was stretching the elastic thinner and thinner. The parliament was barely over before gloom began to spread. Moscow intellectuals worried that the Russians would fall into the ancient trap: they would fail to muster the discipline necessary for democratic debate; the hardliners would regain control; and the parliament would be dispersed as Lenin had dispersed the Constituent Assembly in 1918. Sasha Motov and Konstantin Demakhin were cynical and impatient with the posturing of the deputies, the manipulations of Gorbachev and Lukyanov, and the failure of the government to do anything practical about the economy. At the end of July 1989 Sakharov told *Ogonek* that there was a risk of a coup, or an excessive concentration of power in the hands of Gorbachev or his successor. Korotich thought that Gorbachev was panicking, and that a fascist coup was on the cards. The Polish liberal Adam Michnik said that Russia was now back where it was in 1917. Though there was as yet no Lenin and no Finland Station, my mood began to deteriorate in sympathy with that of the Moscow intellectuals. Had the Soviet Union reached the stage which France had come to in 1789: halfway through a process of reform introduced too late to avert catastrophe?

I reported on the change of mood in a telegram to the Foreign Office entitled 'Post Congress Triste'. I fiddled with the draft of a pessimistic letter. But before I sent it, I consulted Jack Matlock, my American colleague. Jack was a Russian scholar, and immensely experienced. He was a regular and effective performer on Soviet television. After I began to appear on Soviet television myself, I would be regularly hailed by strangers in the most remote corners of the country. 'We love to see you on television, Mr Matlock,' they would say, impervious to the improbable thought that there might be two Anglo-Saxon ambassadors who spoke Russian on television. Effendiev, the chief engineer of the Azerbaijan oil company, a man with a black moustache and a sad pockmarked face, like the corrupt Bey in *Seven Pillars of Wisdom*, even asked me a couple of years later to convey his greetings to 'Your Prime Minister, Mr Matlock'. Such is fame.

Jack was much closer to the Soviet leaders than I could hope to be, because of the amount of bilateral business he had to conduct with them. He did not believe that Gorbachev was at risk. There were none of the signs that the KGB was becoming disloyal which preceded the fall of Khrushchev. I still thought that we would get little advance warning of a move against Gorbachev. But for the time being I concluded that I was becoming too prone to the Moscow intellectual vice of rocketing between euphoria and despair. I suppressed the letter. But I kept the draft in case I should need it on a future occasion.

Konstantin Demakhin helped to restore my equilibrium. He thought that some of the rage and resentment was dying down as ordinary people began to think they could influence events after all. He gave a small example. Every evening there were demonstrators outside the parliament and outside the Moskva Hotel where the deputies were staying. They were the mothers of students and young soldiers protesting against the brutality with which the army treated its young conscripts. Konstantin, who was carrying on his own private war against the army, began to demonstrate with them. Soon the women adopted him as an honorary mother. The pressure worked. To the fury of the generals, who muttered that the country was going to the dogs, the parliament resolved that students should be released from military service. The 'Mothers' put up a poster on the hotel: 'Thank you, deputies!' Konstantin was jubilant. For once the 'little people' had got their way.

I called on Laptiev. He dismissed talk of an army coup. Some of the 'law-and-order' people wanted one. But the army was and always had been under political control, and Gorbachev was moving younger officers to the top. There was no candidate for the Man on the White Horse, the general who takes over from the corrupt politicians in the traditional Latin American coup. After the shootings in Tbilisi the army would never again be used for maintaining internal order. That was the job of troops from the KGB and the Interior Ministry. As for the strikes, the degree of discipline shown so far by the strikers was evidence of advance planning. The official unions would have to look to their laurels. But there was little danger of a 'Solidarity' movement developing. Unlike in Poland, the strikers supported the reform programme of the government. Glasnost was in good shape. Now that both Solzhenitsyn and Grossman had been published, it had little further to go. I left Laptiev's office more cheerful than I had been when I went into it.

At the end of Pushkin's *Boris Godunov*, the crowd outside the Kremlin is invited to cheer the new Tsar, the Pretender Dmitri. But 'The people are silent.' Russian scholars still argue about whether it was Pushkin, or Tsar Nicholas I acting as Pushkin's personal censor, who actually wrote the most famous stage direction in Russian literature, the equivalent of Shakespeare's 'Exit pursued by a bear.'

Gorbachev gave the Russian people a voice. The Summer of 1989 marked a giant, though not yet an irreversible, step towards the democratisation of the Soviet Union. What had been said in public – about the mismanagement of the economy, about the secret police, about the future of the empire – could not be unsaid. In March 1989 and thereafter the 'little people' refused to remain silent any longer. In the last days of the Soviet Union and in the new Russia they turned out massively to make their voice heard in national and local elections. They expressed their views on the future of the Union, on the Presidency of Russia, on the shape of national parliaments and local councils. Their elders and betters were not always happy with the views they expressed. Sometimes the voters supported reactionary Communists. At other times they backed extreme nationalists.

The government still tried to manipulate the vote where it could. But one thing seemed to have changed for good. Russian leaders could no longer rely on a subservient electorate to retain them indefinitely in power. That was something qualitatively new in Russian history.

The final collapse of the Soviet Union took place after the fall of the Berlin Wall and the velvet revolutions of 1989 in Eastern Europe. And so the Poles, the Hungarians, the Czechs, the East Germans, and even the Rumanians, have got the credit for being the first to overthrow Communism in their countries. But our Polish friends had been right to predict, even at the height of their euphoria in the late 1950s, that change in Eastern Europe could only be secure if it were preceded or at least accompanied by genuine change in Russia. The lesson was rammed home by the suppression of the Prague Spring in 1968, justified by Brezhnev's doctrine that it was permissible for the Soviet Union to use force in an country where 'Socialism' was threatened, and by the imposition of martial law in 1980 in Poland in the shadow of the Soviet army.

But the Soviet elections of March 1989 were the first elections in a Communist country where the voters were offered a genuine choice, and where ordinary people took the opportunity to deliver a mortal blow to the ruling Party. Another two months passed before the elections in Poland took place on 4 June 1989. They too were rigged in favour of the Communists, and were described by the Western press at the time as no more than 'partially open' or 'semi-free'.[4] In Poland too ordinary voters had the wit to exploit a complex electoral system to get Communists out. And by the time the new Polish parliament met, the remarkable proceedings in the Soviet parliament were already providing the final evidence that a kind of democracy had at last reached the Soviet Union itself. After visiting the two countries in July 1989, President Bush remarked to his aides: 'If there were no Gorbachev, there would be nothing of what we've just seen in Poland and Hungary.'[5] On 25 October 1989, Gorbachev said in Helsinki that the Soviet Union had no right, moral or political, to interfere in Eastern Europe. The Brezhnev doctrine was no more.

The parliament of 1989 was the high point of Gorbachev's domestic political career. From then on he earned plaudits only from foreigners. Criticism spread almost immediately from the Congress Hall, not only into the intimate gatherings of the intelligentsia and into the workplace, but into the press as well. The General Secretary of the Communist Party himself was no longer immune. Gorbachev was forced into ever more convoluted and opaque manoeuvres and compromises. By opening the leadership to popular criticism, he lit a fuse under himself.

5

The Ashes of Victory

In truth, what is it that has essentially upheld Russian statehood? Not only primarily, but exclusively, the army. Who created the Russian Empire, transforming the semi-Asiatic Muscovite tsardom into the most influential, most dominant, grandest European power? Only the power of the bayonet. The world bowed not to our culture, nor to our bureaucratised church, nor to our wealth and prosperity. It bowed to our might.

Sergei Witte, Prime Minister of Russia 1903–6

Seventy miles westward of Moscow, just past the little town of Mozhaisk, the highway to Warsaw passes through wooded countryside, mild and welcoming by the austere standards of Russia. Just to the north of the road lies the tiny village of Borodino with its seventeenth-century church, folded into the steep banks of a network of streams too small to be called rivers. Hard by the church is a wooden hospital – capable of little more than binding up cut fingers – gardens with sunflowers, clean white geese everywhere.

This peaceful countryside is the place where Kutuzov's peasant army fought Napoleon to a standstill. In the centre you can still see the remains of the Great Redoubt, where Tolstoy's hero Pierre Bezukhov watched the battle unfold. Over on the left still stands the great eagle erected by the French on the centenary of the first Battle of Borodino to mark the spot where the Grande Armée met its match. Spurning the less imposing memorials to the Russian imperial regiments, it is to the eagle that young couples now go to have their wedding photographs taken. A nineteenth-century monastery stands a little further on, built by the Countess Tuchkova, sister of one of the heroes of the battle in his memory. Tolstoy stayed there when he was doing his research for *War and Peace*. As a sergeant doing his military service, Sasha Motov took part in the re-enactment of the battle for Bondarchuk's massive film of the novel.

It was among these rolling woods, at the foot of the Great Redoubt and right across the ancient battlefield, that the soldiers of General Lelyushenko's 5th Army dug themselves in as the Germans lunged towards Moscow in October 1941. While they waited for the German onslaught, their officers paraded before them the Tsarist regimental banners preserved in Borodino's little museum.[1] When the Panzers arrived the Russian soldiers fought and died and sullenly withdrew, as their ancestors had done before them. The slit trenches and the observation posts and the Great Redoubt are still there in the unspoilt countryside, convincing testimony to the doggedness of the Russians in two Great Patriotic Wars.

So is the little church in Borodino, the only building left in the village after Napoleon had passed on his way. It was closed down during the Communist period and reopened for worship in 1990. We visited it eighteen months later. The upper storey – the 'summer church' – was still full of rubbish, but the winter church below was being pulled together, with icons brought from the cathedral in nearby Mozhaisk. Father Igor, the young priest, spoke surprisingly good English. He had learned it as a small boy while his father was working in the Soviet Trade Delegation in Highgate. Before entering the Church he had studied at the prestigious Moscow Institute of International Relations, the forcing ground of Soviet diplomats and spies.

The Soviet people paid a huge price for their victory over the Germans. The exact casualty figures are still disputed. But about the order of magnitude there is little doubt. At least thirteen million Soviet soldiers and seven million Soviet civilians died in the war. Many authorities put the figure higher, to a total of twenty-seven million. The big mass graves in the war cemetery in St Petersburg each contain 50,000 civilian bodies: the British lost 60,000 civilians altogether in the whole course of the war. On the war memorial at Orlov, a little village of some three hundred souls just outside Moscow, there are seventy names. Liberal Russians argue that the losses were needlessly multiplied by Stalin's lack of foresight in 1941, and by the indifference to casualties of even the most competent Soviet generals. Conservatives reject criticism as a slur on the glory of the Soviet triumph and on Marshal Zhukov, the architect of the Victory. Either way the figures are beyond the imagination of most Anglo-Saxons: there are too many zeros. Western losses pale by comparison: three hundred thousand British servicemen and about the same number of Americans. Even the German losses do not come close. And so when Stalin exploited the smashing victory of 1945 to carve out a new empire stretching from the River Elbe to the River Bug, and thus give substance to Peter the Great's vision of Russia as a dominant Central European power, the Soviet people accepted their new empire as a just return for the sacrifice they had sustained in tearing the guts out of Hitler's war machine.[2]

You can tell much about a nation's character from the way in which it honours its glorious dead. The British prefer to rob war of its terror and grandeur. Everything is understated – tattered banners in an ancient cathedral, modest memorials on the village green, cemeteries in France nurtured to look as like as possible to an English rose garden. For the Germans war is a dark and passionate thing: their First World War cemetery outside Ypres is a shrine to the ancient gods, to Siegfried, Hagen, and the Nibelungs. The Russian idea of military glory is grandly rhetorical, like the German. Russian war monuments are huge in scale. When they succeed they are uninhibitedly emotional and surprisingly moving, like the huge monuments to the victors of Stalingrad on the Mamaev hill in Volgograd and to the defenders of Moscow in Alma Ata. When they fail, as so many of the monuments belatedly erected in the last years of the Brezhnev regime failed, they are embarrassingly vulgar. But though there are many Soviet war monuments, there are surprisingly few Soviet war cemeteries: the cemetery in St Petersburg is an exception. The rhetoric of Russian glory contrasts bitterly with what actually happened to the Soviet dead. Tens of thousands of them were simply left to rot where they fell, their remains anonymous until pious people began to exhume and identify them four decades and more after the battle.

The Victory brought Zhukov and his soldiers tremendous prestige amongst the ordinary people of the country. The Communist leaders were more suspicious. They feared what they called 'Bonapartism' – the conquest of supreme political power by an ambitious general. Stalin and then Khrushchev drove Zhukov out of the limelight. But the General Secretaries, like Ivan the Terrible and Peter the Great before them, were convinced that the power of the state resided and was reflected above all in the power of the armed forces. Stalin and his successors struck a bargain with the military. If they kept out of politics, they would have absolute first call on the country's resources.

But as the economy began to fail in the late 1970s the Soviet armed forces started to lose ground. Stories of inadequate equipment and declining morale emerged with increasing frequency. In 1975 a Soviet frigate of the Baltic Fleet attempted to defect, got halfway to Sweden, and was bombed into submission by the Soviet airforce.[3] The war in Afghanistan accelerated the decline. Soldiers sold their equipment for drugs, committed vicious atrocities against the locals, and fought, if at all, not for glory, not for the Soviet motherland, not for their officers, but to revenge their fallen comrades. It was a mirror of the travail the American army had gone through ten years earlier in Vietnam.

The Soviet officers were a separate and privileged caste, cut off from the civilian society of their own country, stuck in the attitudes of the Second World War or even of the nineteenth century. They were discouraged, as all Soviet citizens were discouraged, from speculating about the politics of the modern world or about the nature of international relations in the nuclear age. Their ignorance of the world outside their narrow professional sphere was crippling. Zhukov himself wrote in his memoirs: 'I have always had the feeling that my field of knowledge was much narrower than I would have liked and than I felt was needed for my work'.[4] They found it difficult, and in many cases impossible, to adjust to the changes which were about to descend upon their country. As the achievements of the military crumbled at home, in Central Europe and in their global competition with the Americans, the initiative passed to civilians with a better grasp of reality. Civilian analysts published their views on military matters in the public prints. All this aroused at first the contempt and then the anxiety of the professional soldiers.

To hide their weaknesses as well as their strengths, the military made lavish use – even after the reconnaissance satellite had transformed the equation – of what in 1839 the Marquis de Custine called 'secrecy useful and secrecy useless'.[5] The Soviet defence establishment considered it their patriotic duty to mislead not only foreigners, but even their own political bosses. Maps published in the Soviet Union were deliberately distorted so that American bombers – and Russian tourists – would be unable to find their way. When he joined the Politburo in 1980 Gorbachev was shocked to discover that expenditure on defence took priority over expenditure on food. The actual figures were secret: some were kept from him even when he became General Secretary. Ordinary Soviet people were much more ignorant. For them Mrs Thatcher's television interview in Moscow in March 1987 was the beginning of enlightenment.

On the one hand secrecy and lies – *vranyo*. On the other, Potemkin and *pokazukha*. To impress the Empress, so the legend goes (it is rejected by serious historians; but legend is more durable than scholarship), Potemkin ran up fake villages, which bore no relationship to the dour reality of life in the Russian countryside. In the middle of the nineteenth century the *Edinburgh Review* had doubted the reality of Russian military might, hidden as it was behind a veil of secrecy. Soviet military strength was much more genuine. But the Soviet military saw no harm in reinforcing the impression.

And so they dazzled foreign visitors with ostentatious pageant. When Tom King, the British Defence Minister, visited the Soviet Union in May 1990, they took him to Kubinka airbase outside Moscow, where MiGs and Sukhois pirouetted over the airbase in brilliant aerobatic displays. In Sevastopol the impeccably turned-out officers and men of the missile cruiser *Slava* looked as if they had just come off the set of *On the Town*, as rocket launchers shot out of hidden hatches and disappeared again by magic. On the parade ground of the crack Taman Guards Division outside Moscow, the armoured vehicles drawn up on the parade ground for inspection were painted into position. At the Higher Airborne Academy in Ryazan General Slusar, the jackbooted, and scarred commandant, a hero of the war in Afghanistan, stood grimly on the tarmac as ten girls and ten very tough soldiers parachuted in to greet the Minister with flowers. His young men practised unarmed combat *en masse* – the karate chop, the knife thrust, the boot in the balls – all set to music like an open-air version of the ballet *Spartacus* in the rain. At the missile training base at Balabanovo keen young officers chanted in antiphon as they went through the coded procedures to 'launch' their strategic rockets against the 'potential enemy' – namely ourselves. All this parade had more in common with the performances of the Bolshoi Theatre than with the increasingly distressing realities of life in the Soviet armed forces in the last years of their existence.

Because the British were involved in the reunification of Germany, the withdrawal from Eastern Europe, and various measures of arms control, I had regular dealings with the senior military: Defence Minister Yazov, Chief of Staff Moiseyev, Gorbachev's Military Adviser Marshal Akhromeyev, and the Commander in Chief of the Soviet Fleet Admiral Chernavin. The generals were sufficiently influenced by Perestroika and Glasnost to drop some of their traditional wariness. Occasionally we had independent information – not always accurate – which enabled me to press them harder than they found comfortable. Some of our encounters were noisy; but they usually ended with good humour. Visitors helped to tempt the Soviet generals out of their bunkers. They included the Defence Secretary, the Permanent Secretary of the Defence Ministry; the Chiefs of the Defence Staff, the Air Staff, the Defence Intelligence Staff, the First Sea Lord, and our ambassador to NATO. The RAF's Red Arrows went through their aerobatic paces at the British Exhibition in Kiev in the Summer of 1990. *HMS London* helped to celebrate the fiftieth anniversary of the first Arctic convoy in August 1991 and *HMS Fearless* visited Sevastopol in November of the same year. By some quirk of NATO protocol it also fell to me to act as host to General Galvin, the Supreme Allied Commander in Europe, in the Autumn of 1990.

These visits were punctuated by rounds of heavy entertainment in the Ministry of Defence's wooden dacha in the woods outside Moscow. At Yazov's dinner for Tom King, the Russians provided an excellent jazz band which the Chief of the Air Staff, Peter Harding, joined with a bravura demonstration of saloon bar virtuosity on the piano. General Moiseyev, the Chief of the General Staff, drank to Galvin in a string of traditional Cossack toasts: vodka, bottoms up. Galvin replied with an elegant quotation from T. S. Eliot. On the same occasion a gloomy general's wife called Mrs Shein took great care to explain that her surname was not Jewish, whatever it sounded like. She asked if I believed in flying saucers. She was shocked when I said that I did not.

The generals came in droves to the Kharitonenko house. Yazov and Moiseyev, Achalov the parachute general who was involved with Yazov in the putsch in August 1991, the commander of the Rocket Forces, the chief of the Ground Forces, a brace of admirals, all passed through the house at one time or another. As they entered they piled up their caps, with their huge peaks which looked like the halos in paintings of medieval saints, in an indistinguishable pile on the table in the hall. They never picked up the wrong hat as they left. On Trafalgar Night, 1991, the British Naval Attaché gave the traditional dinner in the embassy for his NATO colleagues. There were Russian guests too – Admiral Chernavin and Admiral Alekseyev, a friend of Jill's from the Northern Fleet. All the guests were in full uniform, none more so than Admiral Sir James Eberle, a naturally imposing figure even without the star and sash of a Grand Commander of the Bath. The dinner table was scattered with pastry models of the ships of the opposing fleets, made by Stephen Baldwin, the cook. I toasted the immortal memory of Admiral Lord Nelson. The French naval attaché Commander Maillard replied with a nervous mixture of wit, passion, and stumbling English, and made the entirely legitimate point that the British could not have won so glorious a victory if their opponents had not been so formidable. The Russians were mystified throughout.

I paid my first official call on Yazov in December 1988 in the Defence Ministry, a pompous new construction close to the Kremlin, clad throughout in that peculiarly dead-looking marble which characterised the monumental building of the Brezhnev period. The cavernous corridors which led to the minister's office were decorated with tapestries, mosaics, and medals glorifying the military exploits of the Tsars. Yazov's office was on a scale to match the rest of the building. In one corner was an immense desk, covered with telephones, including the Gorbyphone – the direct line to the General Secretary. Yazov sat me down at a sofa on the other side of the office, and offered me the inevitable glass of tea. The absence of Armenian brandy on morning calls – a dreadful burden in the 1960s – was one of the positive consequences of Gorbachev's anti-alcohol campaign. The campaign was very unpopular at the time and has been much derided since. The accompanying decline in the vodka tax blew a huge hole in the Soviet budget. But alcoholism in Russia is an age-old scourge. Sales of alcohol more than doubled in the last decades of the Soviet Union. Gorbachev's successors have not solved the problem either.

After hinting that he knew from his card index that I had served in military intelligence in Vienna in the early 1950s, Yazov started to bully me about NATO's position on arms control. We got nowhere. I changed the subject. What about the rumour that the armed forces would be put on a professional basis? Yazov said that he was entirely opposed to the use of 'mercenaries': it was a privilege for young Soviet men to serve their country. I asked if he was having any success in cutting back on *dedovshchina*, the vicious bullying of new recruits which – according to the radical press – regularly resulted in more deaths than the Afghanistan war. All that, he blandly replied, was invented by the journalists. He had given instructions that any cases of *dedovshchina* were to be referred directly to him. He doubted if there were more than two or three in a year. It was an insignificant but genuine example of *vranyo*. Both then and thereafter conscripts continued to die or to commit suicide at the rate of hundreds a year.

My main dealings were not, however, with Yazov, but with the Soviet Chief of Staff, General Moiseyev. Handsome (as a colleague remarked) in the style of Burt Lancaster, with piercing blue eyes and bushy eyebrows, he came from a poor Cossack family in Siberia – another simple man for whom the Soviet system had provided a career and prestige to which he could not have aspired in an earlier age. He was emotional, noisy, and a hard drinker in the old style. It was a real pleasure, though of a perverse kind, to do business with him. He could be charming when he wanted, with a rough and ready sense of humour. But he was equally capable of showing his teeth, and switching in a flash to bootfaced aggression. From time to time he would bawl at me like a Regimental Sergeant Major: about the need for peace and friendship, or about the iniquities of NATO, or about the extreme undesirability of fighting a war against Saddam Hussein in the Gulf. He was a Russian patriot of an old-fashioned kind. He wanted to revive the pre-Revolutionary guards regiments, and in his more expansive moments he would relate stories about Russia's military heroes which sounded like something out of the *Boy's Own Paper*. He believed that the Stalin period was good, because in those days people were disciplined and enthusiastic. He deeply resented the criticism to which the armed forces were being subjected. He thought that democracy was all very well provided it was properly managed by those who knew best: he admired Mrs Thatcher, not least for her apparent ability to sack ministers at will.

Moiseyev's fiercely handsome wife, Galina, seemed to find him a bit of a show-off. Yet he was presumably able enough: he was one of five gold medallists in his year at staff college. Mrs Thatcher thought that his 'demeanour marked him out as someone of unusual intelligence and strength of character'. He came readily enough to formal occasions at the embassy, but when I invited him to bring his wife and a number of other military couples to an informal dinner he showed great reluctance to name the day. He finally surrendered when I accused him of chickening out. The dinner was preceded by a tense negotiation first between myself and my defence attachés, and then between my attachés and the Defence Ministry, over the question of whether or not uniforms should be worn. In the end the soldiers decided on civilian clothes. It was a mistake. I hardly recognised Moiseyev in his Soviet-style light grey suit and light grey shoes. They did not become him. He gave Jill roses grown in his own garden, and spoke with his usual enthusiasm about his granddaughter and the Siberian Cossacks. A few weeks later he was in disgrace because of his alleged involvement in the putsch in August 1991. Years later I took him to dinner in London, a bitter man, but with the old charm and a much smarter suit.

Some of the Soviet generals were more reflective. Marshal Akhromeyev, Moiseyev's predecessor as Chief of Staff, was thoughtful, cool, judicious, courteous, militarily correct, and deeply conservative, with a twinkle in his blue eyes, a long face, square skull, and cropped hair. He had served in the defence of Leningrad, and on the Manchurian frontier immediately after the war in conditions so primitive that his next posting to Belorussia seemed, to his wife, almost as glamorous as going to Paris.

General Rodionov had the close-cropped iron-grey hair *en brosse* and the intelligent air of a French parachute colonel. He was the Commander of the Transcaucasian Military District at the time of the shootings in Tbilisi in April 1989. He was made the scapegoat for that tangled business, and sent off to run the General Staff Academy to keep him out of the way. Yeltsin made him Minister of Defence in 1996. He had learned the lessons of the collapse, and put together a sensible plan to redefine the role of the

Russian armed forces, cut their numbers drastically, and give them modern equipment. But he was not a sufficiently skilful politician or administrator to carry through his expensive ideas while Russia was still in a state of economic collapse. Within a few months he was brutally sacked. After the sinking of the submarine *Kursk* in September 2000, he wrote an emotional article in a Moscow paper, attacking the indifference of the military to casualties, and their relentless mendacity. Only a free press, he said, could reveal the truth. That was something I never expected to hear from a Russian general.

General Volkogonov had broken through the intellectual carapace in which so many of his colleagues were trapped. He too had risen from a humble family in Siberia. His father was shot in 1937, and his brother was still an ordinary worker. He first received me in the Spring of 1989 in the full uniform of a Colonel General at the Institute of Military History on the Lenin Hills. Before becoming a full-time historian he had been Deputy Head of the Political Directorate of the Ministry of Defence, responsible among other things for psychological warfare in Afghanistan. Open, frank, humorous, vain, with a twinkling intelligence, it was hard to imagine him as a Commissar, the orthodox Politruk of so many Soviet war films. By the time I met him he was already beginning to argue for the removal of Communist Party cells from the army. He was receiving streams of hate mail for his recently published reappraisal of Stalin, which was based on archives in the Defence Ministry to which he had unique access. Some of the most sensitive papers had of course disappeared as Stalin manoeuvred to preserve his place in history. In the late 1920s, Volkogonov told me, Stalin insisted on seeing the papers about the Soviet-Polish War of 1920, in which he had played an inglorious role. When the archivist asked for them back, Stalin said that they had been destroyed, as of no historical interest: a coded death sentence for the unfortunate archivist.

As Gorbachev's revolution unfolded, Volkogonov moved ever further from his old colleagues. The final break came in March 1991 when he was attacked for his mammoth history of the war by what amounted to a kangaroo court of senior generals. They resented his failure to recognise that the Soviet Union had created a strategic glacis on the eve of the war by 'liberating' the Western Ukraine, fighting Finland, and incorporating the Baltics and Moldavia. They could not forgive him for blaming the Soviet Union's catastrophic defeats in the first months of the war on the unpreparedness of the armed forces and Stalin's massacre of the officer corps after 1937. They called his book unpatriotic, anti-Communist. It was a scene reminiscent of the collective attacks on writers and scientists in the

Brezhnev period and earlier. The history was never published. Volkogonov was sacked from the Institute of Military History. But by then he was already a deputy in the Russian parliament, close to Yeltsin, and able to cock a snook at the dinosaurs.

Gorbachev and Shevardnadze were profoundly convinced that the nuclear confrontation was mortally dangerous and that the Soviet political and economic system was no longer in any shape to sustain it. Shevardnadze in particular realised that 'Fear, mistrust, hatred, constant expectation of a violent eruption, and enormous military expenses [were] leading at last to material privation and a consistently low standard of living. The victors had thus become losers.'[6] He warned his colleagues in the Foreign Ministry that the Soviet Union would fall fatally behind the Americans in military technology if it did not accept the arms control agreements being negotiated with the West and so give itself the breathing space for economic reform to begin to work. These insights were sober, responsible, and greatly to the advantage of the Soviet people as well as of the rest of us. But they led Gorbachev and Shevardnadze into increasing conflict with the military and with the imperialist diehards of the Communist Party.

With hindsight the collapse of Russia's East European empire seems to have been inevitable. It certainly did not seem so at the time. By the 1970s the experts in the Foreign Office in London and the Foreign Ministry in Bonn were convinced that a genuine patriotism was developing in the German Democratic Republic (GDR), and that the rising generation of West Germans had forgotten about the East. *The Economist* announced that the East German economy was more successful than the British. Trust Germans, they thought, to be the only ones to make Socialism work. To one less expert, these arguments were not plausible. It seemed obvious that the GDR was an artificial and ephemeral construction, and that German reunification was inevitable.

But the orthodoxy was deeply rooted. In Autumn 1987 the Foreign Office Planning Staff tried to shift the debate. The division of Germany, they argued, was unsustainable and destabilising. Gorbachev might revive the bargain which the Russians had so often dangled before the Germans in the 1970s: neutrality in exchange for early reunification. This would lead to a new Europe dominated in new ways by a reunited and probably neutral Germany, uninhibited, prosperous, and the natural partner for a reduced Soviet Union. Change meant risks for the Russians too. It could unravel the Russians' military and political position throughout the whole of Central and Eastern Europe, and perhaps in the Baltic States and Ukraine as well. The Russians would oppose this, with force if necessary. So change was not an early prospect. Germany was likely to remain divided, and Eastern Europe to remain under Soviet domination, well into the twenty-first century. Nevertheless, it was not too early to start thinking about how to deal with the situation when it arose.

Some of the senior officials who read the paper in the Foreign Office rejected the premise. They believed that there was no early prospect of the reunification of Germany and thought that its continued division was not necessarily inconvenient. Others, including myself, thought that reunification was not only inevitable, but desirable, since it would eventually help to stabilise Europe despite the obvious difficulties of transition. None of us thought it would occur in any timescale relevant to current policymaking. We were not alone in this view. The leaders in London and Washington, and most of their officials, were of the same mind. In the Moscow think tanks, and in Shevardnadze's close entourage, people were more far-sighted, though of course we did not know that at the time. But events soon began to accelerate faster than even they could have imagined.

In September 1989 – two years almost to the day after the Foreign Office debate, and two months before the Berlin Wall fell – I wrote down some thoughts in my diary which give the flavour of our fears.

> We are witnessing the break-up of the last great European empire ... the post-war period is now finally over. This raises the most profound questions. It is difficult to imagine even Gorbachev (assuming he stays in power) making the leap of imaginative statesmanship involved in withdrawing the Soviet forces in Germany and permitting reunification to go ahead on terms which would inevitably be far more strongly influenced by the successful GFR [German Federal Republic] than by the feeble GDR.
>
> But if the Russians remain immobile, then they cannot rule out the possibility of a major breakdown in Poland and/or East Germany which – apart from the unattractive political implications – could be a real threat to their garrison in East Germany and its lines of communication in Poland. That is a threat to which they would have to respond by force if necessary. By contrast they can afford to be more relaxed about Hungary, Czechoslovakia, and the Balkans. Their defection would not threaten the Russians' basic strategic requirements, however much of a blow it was to their imperial pride.

The prospects are thus very obscure, but not on the whole encouraging. The same is true of the implications for Western policy. Soviet military intervention in Germany or Poland would destroy the improvement in East–West relations; so would massive bloodshed within the Soviet Union itself. But the opposite scenario would be just as unsettling: NATO and 'European Union' would lose much of their rationale if we were to start moving towards a reunified and substantially demilitarised Germany.

On 6 October 1989 Gorbachev left for Berlin to attend the fortieth anniversary celebrations of the German Democratic Republic. It was perhaps the trickiest foreign trip he had yet undertaken. I told the Foreign Office that he had no coherent policy, just a Micawber-like hope that he would be able to improvise something when it came to the crunch. But the GDR was an artificial creation. Improvisation would therefore lead inexorably to a united and non-Communist Germany. And that was something, I still believed, that the Russians could not stomach. *In extremis* they might still use force. But I was wrong. By then Shevardnadze had moved close to his final view that the Soviet Union

> really had only two alternatives. The first was to achieve ... an agreement on a final legal settlement of the German question, which would serve our security interests and the cause of stability in Europe ... The second alternative was to use our half-million troops in East Germany to block unification ... But that would put us on the brink of World War III.[7]

That was something that neither he nor Gorbachev were remotely willing to risk.

On Mrs Thatcher's instructions I called on Chernyaev on Saturday 4 November. The new Party Secretary in Berlin had sacked five septuagenarians from the Politburo the previous day, and was promising liberal new laws. But thousands of East Germans were still streaming out of the country. I told Chernyaev that we believed that NATO and the Warsaw Pact should remain in being, at least for now, in order to help with the orderly management of change. Chernyaev said that change was natural. The Germans must be left to sort themselves out. But excessive haste would destabilise. There was thus, I thought, a sort of agreement between the British and the Soviet governments. But both of us were still without a policy.

The Berlin Wall came down on the night of 9 November. What had been a serious dilemma for the Russians in October now became a crisis. They faced the imminent collapse of their East European empire. Triumphalist voices in the Federal Republic and the United States called for immediate reunification. Gorbachev and his people had said in public and in private that they would in no circumstances use force. But I feared that a spontaneous or provoked incident – for example, an attack by East Germans on a Soviet barracks – could lead to irresistible pressure for forceful action from the Soviet military. Gorbachev sent Mrs Thatcher an incoherent plea for help. I suggested that she should send a supportive reply. She should offer to share her worries with Bush, whom she was seeing shortly. And she might propose as a crisis management procedure the revival of the mechanism used to negotiate the Berlin settlement in the 1970s: the combination of the 'Four' wartime allies, France, Britain, America and the Soviet Union, and the 'Two Germanies', East and West. I like to think that this proposal may have been the origin of the 'Two plus Four' procedure which was later devised for negotiations for the reunification of Germany. The laurels are of course claimed by many others, no doubt with better justification.

Rod Lyne and I delivered the Prime Minister's reply to Gorbachev on 17 November. We met in his office in the Kremlin, furnished in a comparatively tasteful blue and silver rather than the traditional Soviet red and gold. Chernyaev was the only third party. Gorbachev looked pink, plump, and healthy – none of the haggard appearance I had seen on TV in the preceding months when he was addressing (or hectoring) the Supreme Soviet. He was in a cheerful mood – relaxed, unpompous, lively and enthusiastic. After some initial bantering I gave him the Prime Minister's message. The British government appreciated the responsible way the Soviet government were reacting to the events in Germany. The initial problems seemed to be subsiding. But Mrs Thatcher was worried and wanted to keep in close contact. Gorbachev said that our views were at one. What had happened in Germany was a historical turning point. It was impossible to tell where it would lead. His visit to East Germany had convinced him that change there was essential. He had felt foolish standing beside the German Communist leader, Honecker, during the anniversary celebrations in Berlin, while the columns of torch-bearing students marched past, shouting 'Gorby! Gorby! Help us!' The changes that were occurring went very deep. He would encourage them despite the difficulties it would cause him at home. But he would oppose outside interference. The existence of two Germanies was still a reality.

Like everyone else, Gorbachev was lagging behind events. At the end of November someone wrote on a wall in Prague: 'It's over. The Czechs are free.' At the beginning of December the East German Politburo and Central Committee resigned. At the end of the month the people of Romania rebelled. Ceauşescu tried repression. It failed. On Christmas Day he and his wife were summarily shot. All this was shown on Soviet television. Soviet viewers saw the Communist parties of Eastern Europe collapsing one after another, their prestige and pretensions utterly gone. Soviet Communists began to fear for their own Party, for their jobs, and even for their lives. Cold shivers went down the spines even of ordinary people. After Tien An Men Square, after Romania, was the Soviet Union too on the brink of bloodshed? That Winter a British television company kept a team permanently in Moscow to cover the fall of Gorbachev. The following Summer the English National Opera brought its version of Verdi's *Macbeth* to Kiev and Leningrad in June 1990. The production was set in a crumbling Central European dictatorship. In comfortable London it had irritated the audience. In the edgy Soviet Union, on the verge of explosion, it spoke with painful force.

Now there were only two questions of importance left. How and when should Germany be reunited? And what should be the relationship between the new Germany and NATO? Kohl and Bush had already decided the answer. East Germany should be absorbed into the Federal Republic as quickly as possible. A reunited Germany should be a full member of the Western Alliance. Gorbachev and Shevardnadze soon realised that they could now do little more than try to salvage their self-respect. Less than a month after the Berlin Wall came down, they began to meet the Germans with increasing frequency. Genscher and Kohl came to Moscow to develop negotiating positions that they had not always cleared in advance with their allies: to Mrs Thatcher's irritation 'our' Germans were beginning to exercise their independent judgement. There was a breakthrough in February 1990 in the margins of a disarmament meeting in Ottawa. Shevardnadze agreed to the beginning of negotiations on the reunification of Germany, using the 'Two plus Four' mechanism whereby East and West Germany would negotiate a settlement between themselves, while the four wartime allies, Britain, France, the United States, and the Soviet Union sorted out the wider implications. Shevardnadze had probably gone beyond his instructions. He nervously told a gathering of Canadian MPs that reunification should go slowly. The Soviet Union was 'sick' and needed to be handled with care: a remarkable, indeed an imprudent, admission of weakness.

Soviet officials were not so perceptive as Shevardnadze, nor so fleet of foot. Their unhappiness was unmistakable. They warned us that the generals would not abandon the Soviet Union's strategic position in Central Europe. There would be a huge outcry from the man in the street if Germany were reunited. Valentin Falin, Gorbachev's German expert in the Central Committee, had spent much of the 1970s as ambassador in Bonn. He was a craggily handsome man with blue eyes, a lugubrious manner, and many secrets to hide. Now he claimed to have warned Honecker many months before the Wall came down what would happen if he did not adapt. But Honecker had not responded. So the Russians had expected a shock, but not on the scale that was now unfolding. Falin was darkly apprehensive about Germany's long-term ambition to dominate Europe ('Deutschland über alles').

Anatoli Adamishin had succeeded Kovalev as Deputy Minister responsible for Europe. He was scathing to me about both Britain and France. We opposed reunification, he said, but were too frightened to act and expected the Russians to pull our chestnuts out of the fire. In January 1990 he told William Waldegrave, a visiting Foreign Office Minister of State, in an outburst that was almost hysterical, that the West was pushing for the overthrow of Communism all over Eastern Europe, even where the Communists were pursuing sensible policies. The Soviet Union had abandoned the ideological struggle. Now the West had taken it up. Soviet tolerance had its limits. It was unimaginable that East Germany should become part of NATO or that American troops should advance to the Polish border. Ordinary people would not accept a reunited Germany. The issue could split the civilian and military parts of the Soviet government. Gorbachev might be overthrown. We might all be overwhelmed by events.

Chernyaev was more philosophical. On 15 February I told him that Mrs Thatcher believed that the best guarantee for stability in Europe was to anchor Germany in NATO and the EC. She was prepared to contemplate an additional guarantee: NATO's border might remain at the Elbe, while Soviet troops stayed in the former East Germany. Chernyaev said that the Russians did not at all agree that a united Germany should stay in NATO. They were not afraid that one day the Germans would march again. But they remembered the war and could not simply abandon the fruits of victory. It was a real domestic problem for the Soviet leadership. Why, in any case, did we need NATO, now that the relationships in Europe were being transformed? I replied that we all wanted Perestroika to succeed. But there was at least a 30 per cent chance that it would not (Chernyaev indicated that he wished the odds were so good). And geography was immutable. One superpower was in Europe, the other was across the Atlantic, and we needed a balance. Chernyaev accepted these arguments cheerfully enough, even though he was obviously unhappy that we wanted to retain NATO lest Gorbachev fail.

On 23 February I called on him again, this time with Percy Cradock, the Prime Minister's Foreign Policy Adviser, who had arrived for a familiarisation visit. (My German colleague seemed convinced that Cradock had come as a special emissary of the Prime Minister to negotiate about Germany behind the backs of her allies. This was not so.) Chernyaev was particularly (perhaps, he subsequently told me, unduly) open with us. We argued that the Russians should feel more secure if a united Germany were firmly anchored inside NATO, and thus inoculated against the temptation to strike out on its own which had caused Europe so much suffering for more than a century. Why, Chernyaev countered, should the Russians be happy if an alliance set up to oppose them were now expanded? He consoled himself with the thought that reunification would take place more slowly than we thought. After the East German elections in mid-March the political pressure would be reduced, and the West Germans would begin to realise the practical difficulties. That was why the Russians had got over their initial panic. They now thought there would be time for all concerned to organise the architecture of the future Europe satisfactorily and in cooperation.

Kohl's refusal to affirm in public that he had no designs on the ex-German lands east of the Oder–Neisse line sent cold shivers down the spines of even moderate Russians and Poles, and fed the wilder accusations of people like Falin and Adamishin. Even Chernyaev was worried by Kohl's refusal to come clean, though he recognised the pressure Kohl was under from the millions of German voters whose roots lay in the lost lands in the East. With vivid personal memories of how the Poles felt about this issue, I suggested to the Foreign Office that London should reason with Kohl. But this was the opposite of Western policy, which was to leave the running to Kohl, who had domestic reasons for prevarication. Despite my worries, the Polish-German frontier agreement was eventually signed, but a month after reunification had already taken place.

By the Summer the weakness of the Soviet negotiating position could no longer be disguised. On 6 July 1990 NATO declared in London that the Soviet Union was no longer an enemy. The Russians seized on this as an excuse for bowing to the inevitable. Kohl and Gorbachev met in Moscow a week later, and agreed that Germany could join NATO if it wished; Soviet troops would leave Germany in three to four years; the Bundeswehr would move into East Germany immediately on unification, but would be reduced in overall size. Falin's suspicions were undiminished. Some of the people around Kohl, he muttered to me darkly, were already talking of the time when Germany could hope to renegotiate its Eastern borders and seek compensation for Poland in Belorussia and the Ukraine, which would by then no longer be under Soviet management. In making this remark, he became one of the first people to predict the break-up of the Soviet Union in the form in which it actually occurred.

At the end of August 1990 Jill and I drove through East Germany on the way back to Moscow from our summer holiday. It was our first visit to the German Democratic Republic, now on its last legs. As soon as we crossed the old barrier – the watch-towers and barbed wire dismantled, the frontier posts unmanned – the road surfaces deteriorated sharply. We were back in Eastern Europe. We drove into Eisenach, where Bach was born, past run-down factories as depressing as the approach to any Soviet city. In the seedy Park Hotel – a relic of the nineteenth century – the lavatories smelled and the staff seemed defeated by life. In Dresden the centre of the city was still a desert, not only because of the destruction wrought by the RAF and the US Air Force, but also because of the Communists' failure to rebuild more than a few of the major buildings. The Soviet system was as bankrupt in East Germany as it was everywhere else. Even the Germans had been unable to make it work.

But the new life was on its way. In Eisenach the shops were already full of Western goods. The Dresdener Bank had set up a branch in a Portakabin just outside our hotel: it was crowded with people eagerly opening accounts and changing money, fascinated by their new-found Deutschmarks. The supermarket in a small village off the road to Weimar was packed with cheerful and prosperous locals buying Western toothpaste and canned fruit, while perfectly respectable Bulgarian bottled fruit lay discounted and unpurchased on a bottom shelf. The Old Market Place in Dresden was jam-packed with West German cars for sale, shops full of the latest electronic gadgets, and advertisements for courses on how to survive in a market economy. Russians slunk sadly through the streets, no longer the victors. The Russian language bookshop in Weimar and the busts of Pushkin in the streets were now no more than monuments to the failure of Russian cultural imperialism.

On 12 September, three short weeks before the date fixed for reunification, the agreement on Germany and NATO was finalised in Moscow by the

Foreign Ministers of the Four Powers and the two Germanies. The negotiations took place in the Oktyabrskaya Hotel, around the corner from the embassy, another pompous building from the Brezhnev period, which in the past had served as a base for Party delegations visiting Moscow. There were some moments of farce. The British infuriated Genscher and Shevardnadze by insisting on last-minute amendments. The French word processor broke down. The Germans lost their copy of the text. But in the end Gorbachev was able to preside over the signature of the Treaty which ended the Second World War.

By now the Soviet military were increasingly suspicious about what they might have to swallow next. Was the inclusion of united Germany into NATO to be the end of the story? Western politicians tried to calm the Russians' fears. James Baker assured Gorbachev in February 1990 and again in May that NATO jurisdiction and troops would remain to the West of the Elbe. In March 1991 Yazov asked John Major about President Havel's call for NATO to bring the Czechs, Poles and Hungarians into membership. The Prime Minister assured him that nothing of the sort would happen.[8] In April Chernyaev told Michael Alexander, the British Permanent Representative to NATO, that Gorbachev himself wanted NATO to remain as a force for stability now that the Warsaw Pact had collapsed. But NATO should not move closer to the Soviet border or stoke up old fears of the Soviet threat: that threat was over, whoever came to power in Moscow. The real threat would come from the proliferation of nuclear weapons if the Union disintegrated. Marshal Akhromeyev deployed similar arguments. The East–West relationship had to build on trust. The Russians did not want a confrontation with the Americans: indeed (a striking admission) they could no longer sustain one. The Soviet Union would remain a major power. But with no allies of its own, it still confronted a large and integrated alliance. As a soldier, Akhromeyev could not ignore these military realities.

The assurances which Western politicians gave about the future of NATO were not binding, they were not written down, and they were given by people in a hurry, intent on achieving more immediate objectives. They were not intended to mislead. But the Russians inevitably interpreted them to mean that there would be no further expansion of NATO beyond Germany's new Eastern boundary. For them the later policy of NATO enlargement was a clear breach of faith.

The British role in these great events was minimal. The lead on the Western side naturally fell to the Germans and the Americans. As one of the Four victorious Powers, we were involved in the negotiations on Germany as of right. But Mrs Thatcher resolutely refused to face up to reality. I called on her in Downing Street at the beginning of September 1989. When I tried to develop some thoughts about what was happening in Germany she stared disconcertingly at the floor. The Germans, she said, would go for neutralism or reunification or both. She had written them off.

A couple of weeks later she arrived in Moscow on her way back from Tokyo. It was the first time she had visited us: she came back once again as Prime Minister and once more after she had lost office. Any Prime Ministerial visit is a worry. Ambassadors have been sacked because they failed to please. But there are compensations. Prime Ministers are supported on their travels by a highly professional and experienced team: the Private Secretary, the Press Adviser, secretaries, paper handlers, and a small squad of Royal Military Policemen to ensure security. Mrs Thatcher would pass through our house like a cleansing whirlwind. Her staff would take over my office and were fed non-stop by the residence kitchen. The embassy secretaries took the Prime Minister's secretaries to tour the sights. Then they would all leave. The embassy would heave a collective sigh of relief as the Prime Ministerial aircraft lifted its wheels off the tarmac, and we could revert to normal.

Because Mrs Thatcher's visits were properly organised, they were less of a headache than the visits of more junior ministers with inexperienced staff and ideas above their station. And as a guest she was a pleasure, interesting, frank, and relaxed in conversation. Above all she was invariably kind and thoughtful to the junior staff, which is by no means true of everyone who reaches high office. As Prime Minister she was accompanied by Charles Powell, her outstandingly able Private Secretary and confidant; Bernard Ingham, her pugnacious Press Secretary; and Crawfie, her dresser. She would be up at crack of dawn to have her hair done by Nina, one of the Russian women on the residence staff. After breakfast we would brief her – in a very small group, because she was then less likely to show off, and more likely to listen. Then she would rush off on her punishing schedule, accompanied usually only by Charles and her interpreter.

On this first visit she landed shortly after midnight on 23 September, having made a refuelling stop at Bratsk in Siberia where she had charmed the hard-bitten local Communists off their perches. Tireless as ever, she settled down happily with a whisky and soda for an hour's gossip before going to bed. The next morning she met Gorbachev in the elegant St Catherine Hall in the Grand Palace of the Kremlin, and conveyed a reassuring message from Bush. Gorbachev was, she told me later, relaxed and confident despite his difficulties. The army was tense, he said. But he had strong support. It was standard, bullish stuff: though he was franker with her than with others, particularly because (as Chernyaev noted) 'he knew that she followed the situation closely, and that it was dangerous to try to pull the wool over her eyes.'[9] The most significant part of the discussion was on Germany. Mrs Thatcher believed, as she said in her memoirs, that Germany was 'by its very nature a destabilising force in Europe'. She explained to Gorbachev that Germany's allies were apprehensive about German reunification despite their traditional statements in support. Gorbachev said that the Russians did not want German reunification either. 'This reinforced me', she later wrote, 'in my resolve to slow up the already heady pace of developments.' But she had misunderstood Gorbachev: he did not intend to stand uselessly against the tide of history. His problem was a different one: to extract the best bargain he could in exchange for Russia's inevitable retreat.

Exactly a month before the Wall came down I attended a conference in the Foreign Office. By then there were massive demonstrations in East Germany and the Hungarian Communist Party had just voted itself out of existence. We all knew that, whether we liked it or not, the two Germanies would converge on the West German model. Suddenly the political justification for our defence arrangements began to look shaky. If the overwhelming Soviet conventional forces in Europe were slashed through negotiation or withdrawal, how would we justify deploying nuclear weapons to deter them? How would our own conventional cuts be divided among the allies to give each a fair share of the 'peace dividend'? Christopher Mallaby, by now our ambassador in Bonn, reported that Genscher wanted to bring Austria and eventually Poland and Hungary into the European Community. The comfortable simplicities of the Cold War were over.

Mrs Thatcher had, however, decreed that officials were not even to think about German reunification. She believed that Gorbachev and Mitterrand would help her to stem the tide. At a summit in Paris at the end of November 1989 she told her European colleagues that 'any attempt to talk about either border changes or German reunification would undermine Mr Gorbachev and also open up a Pandora's box of border claims right through Central Europe ... we must keep both NATO and the Warsaw Pact to create a background of stability.'[10] For good measure she added that she was very gloomy about Gorbachev's prospects. Rumours of her attitude began to circulate in Moscow. Her relations with President Bush deteriorated. People began to sense that her days were numbered. The envious and the offended saw the chance to get their own back.

At the turn of the year the Prime Minister finally took her head out of the sand, and accepted that Germany would reunite. Her ideas were still grandiosely unrealistic: NATO and the Warsaw Pact, she thought, should remain in being to balance one another. But their roles would change fundamentally. The Americans might pull out of Europe. She now demanded that her officials think about alternatives to NATO. In February 1990 she admitted to Vadim Medvedev, a visiting Politburo member, that the aspirations of the Germans would have to be respected.

But if her head accepted that German reunification was inevitable, her heart was still unable to do so. Right after our meeting with Medvedev, she confessed to me that she was appalled by the speed of events. James Baker was wet. Gorbachev was wavering, despite what he had told her in Moscow. Soviet troops should be allowed to stay in the former GDR. The final settlement should make it clear that the Germans were still not fully trusted. A month later she called a group of academics to Chequers for her notorious seminar on the German question. Several of the participants expressed old-fashioned anti-German sentiments. The proceedings leaked. The Germans were offended. But by then nothing Mrs Thatcher could do could affect events. The seminar fed her prejudices, but did nothing to forward the process of sensible policy making. In June 1990 Mrs Thatcher came to Moscow for her last visit as Prime Minister. By then her position had changed, and she tried to convince Gorbachev that the presence of a united Germany in NATO would be of positive advantage to the Soviet Union. She was slightly surprised when he did not react negatively.

It was too late to repair the damage. Mrs Thatcher's futile attempt to stand against the course of history undermined Britain's international position and its relationship with the Germans. Along with her mishandling of European affairs and her miscalculation over the poll tax, her prejudice against German reunification showed that her political instincts were no longer in working order. Less than two months after Germany was reunited she lost her job.

The Soviet generals were not brought into the negotiations about Germany, although they had to cope with the consequences: the withdrawal of half a million troops, their dependants and their equipment, to a country which lacked the means to accommodate them. But by the time the German treaty was signed in September 1990, they were already in trouble. Nearly two years earlier, on 7 December 1988, Gorbachev had announced in a stunning speech to the United Nations General Assembly that the Soviet Union would reduce its armed forces by 500,000 men, and cut its forces in Eastern Europe in proportion. In future the Soviet Union's foreign relations would be based on interdependence rather than the class struggle. He promised to strengthen the rule of law and the provision for basic freedoms at home – what he called a 'law-based socialist state'. The style, the language and the content of his speech were wholly different from those of his predecessors. The CIA's chief Soviet analyst told the US Congress a few days later: 'Had we said a week ago that Gorbachev might come to the UN and offer a unilateral cut of 500,000 in the military, we would have been told we were crazy.'[11] My embassy colleagues nevertheless thought that it was no more than the old Soviet claptrap: 'peace propaganda' designed to undermine the will-power of an incautious West. I pointed out that Gorbachev was proposing to cut just those offensive forces in Central Europe that we had been pressing him to cut: six tank divisions, assault bridging and landing units, the numbers of tanks in motorised rifle divisions. My colleagues were unconvinced, and I began to doubt my own judgement. But Jack Matlock, the US ambassador, agreed with me. He had been in New York, he had heard Gorbachev speaking live, and he was amazed that he should have lived to hear a Soviet General Secretary speak in such terms. I felt better.

The withdrawals which Gorbachev had ordered were already under way by the time we had our first military visitor. Richard Vincent, the Vice-Chief of the Defence Staff, came to Moscow at the end of November 1989. Friendly and sympathetic, he was well suited to the pioneering task. In Krivoi Rog in the Ukraine, he visited a tank division scheduled for destruction under Gorbachev's unilateral cuts. Krivoi Rog is 120 kilometres long – an endless strip of open-cast mining with a town straggling along its edge. Vincent got to the tank park in a blinding snowstorm, after driving for three hours past knots of people huddled in the snow waiting for buses or queuing outside empty shops. It was beyond belief dreary and rugged. After slithering around frozen tanks for an hour, Vincent was taken to a party in a tent. The atmosphere became unconstrained. The Major General commanding the division rose to say: 'Some people are beginning to say that the whole army is being thrown on the scrap heap ... [pause] I agree with them.' His superiors did their best to cover up, but the thing was said.

The general's problems were compounded by the resumption of serious negotiations for the mutual reduction of conventional forces in Europe. The MBFR negotiations, of which I had seen the beginning in Vienna in 1973, had languished thereafter. In April 1986 Gorbachev suggested ways of relaunching them. His proposal was endorsed by the Warsaw Pact in Budapest in June. NATO followed with its own proposal in December 1986.

Negotiations for a Treaty on Conventional Forces in Europe (CFE) began in Vienna on 9 March 1989 and were concluded with great ceremony at the Paris Summit of November 1990 – Mrs Thatcher's last appearance as Prime Minister on the world stage.

This was the issue on which Moiseyev and I locked horns most often. Almost immediately it had been signed, the Treaty became a subject of contention between the Russians and the West. NATO accused the Russians of trying to evade or pre-empt its provisions. Naval forces were outside the Treaty: the Soviet military reassigned a number of army bombers to the navy, and redesignated three divisions of infantry as marines. The Treaty provided for the destruction of surplus weapons in the Treaty area: the Soviets withdrew masses of tanks and guns behind the Urals so that they would not be counted. These moves contravened the letter of the Treaty, or its spirit, or both. But the Treaty had been negotiated at a time when the Warsaw Pact still existed. Now the Warsaw Pact was no more. The Soviet military firmly believed that the Treaty gave the West a grossly unfair advantage, and that they were entitled to use every loophole to salvage what they could of their military position.

The Americans and the British were equally determined that the Treaty should be observed to the last detail. In January 1991 I took Moiseyev a letter setting out our concerns. His favourite defensive tactic was to overwhelm his interlocutor with a cascade of words and facts delivered with his particular brand of hectoring charm. As I got through the door of his office, he opened up with a tremendous tirade about the impending war in the Gulf. I interrupted to point out that his government supported the UN's policy in the Gulf: was he against it? Of course not, he said. But war was dreadful, and people were getting killed. I forbore to remark that he should have thought of that before he became a professional soldier.

Moiseyev and his colleagues were upset about the Gulf War not for humanitarian but for professional reasons. The war demonstrated just how far their military technology had fallen behind; and it showed yet again that the Americans, unlike themselves, were able to use military force with impunity, whether under cover of a UN mandate or – as in Panama a year earlier – with very little legal justification at all. Soviet officials disliked the war because it threatened the political, commercial and industrial links they had built up with Iraq, links they were determined to restore once the war was over. A few days earlier I had called on Belousov, the Deputy Prime Minister responsible for the arms industry. He told me he had never met a Western diplomat before, and I had certainly never come across him. He had recently been in Baghdad to negotiate about the repatriation of Soviet citizens trapped in Iraq on the eve of war. The Iraqis had promised Primakov to send them home. But nothing had happened and the Soviet parliament was getting restive. Belousov had made sure that this time the arrangements were agreed by Saddam Hussein personally. A contingent of Soviet maintenance engineers would stay behind to stop the projects deteriorating. None of them, said Belousov, was a military adviser. In return he had agreed with Saddam Hussein that Soviet construction contracts should be suspended, not abandoned, and that they would be resumed when the crisis was over. But he was quite frank that his aim was to preserve the position which the Soviets had built up in Iraq over several decades. I never saw him again. Gorbachev's last-minute attempt to negotiate Saddam's withdrawal with the minimum of bloodshed might have succeeded had the American military juggernaut not by then been unstoppable. He and Shevardnadze kept faith with the West, which did them no good with the reactionaries in their own country.

After Moiseyev had calmed down, I delivered the letter. I assumed, I said, that the Russians believed that the CFE Treaty was in their interest, as we believed it was in ours. But it would not work unless both sides had confidence in it. This sparked off another tirade. The Treaty was one-sided, roared Moiseyev. NATO was using it to steal a march on the Soviet Union. Lots of people in Moscow thought that 'our chief negotiator' (that is, Shevardnadze) had given away too much. The Supreme Soviet might well refuse to ratify the Treaty if NATO kept up its unreasonable pressure. His colleague General Denisov chipped in to say that the Treaty was in the interest of NATO only, not the Soviet Union. I asked if I was to report to London that the Soviet General Staff considered that a Treaty signed by the Soviet government was contrary to the Soviet interest? Denisov backtracked, thus losing the high moral ground. Moiseyev attempted to recover by lambasting the Poles. They were obstructing the Soviet withdrawal: they should remember the 650,000 Russians who had died to liberate them. I responded that I had spent three years in Poland and knew the Poles well. They remembered many things: for example, three partitions, three Warsaw Risings, and the betrayal in 1939. I was struck, as so often, by the way Russians, like the English, find it hard to understand why their neighbours dislike them so much. Some years later I suggested to Dmitri Ryurikov, Yeltsin's foreign policy adviser, that it might be no bad thing if Poland joined NATO and so ceased to be a temptation to either of its great neighbours. 'But we're not going to invade Poland,' he said. 'I believe you,' I replied, 'but the Poles don't know that.' I rehearsed the history, culminating in the imposition of martial law in Poland in 1980. 'Why do you keep on dragging up all that old stuff?' he spluttered.

But there was no point in having a row with Moiseyev about three hundred years of Russian-Polish relations, so I wrenched the discussion back to the matter in hand. I went through our various complaints and concluded by saying that the spirit of the Treaty was as important as its letter. Either there was a real muddle about the facts; or the Russians faced genuine practical problems over meeting their obligations; or they were deliberately trying to evade those obligations. The first two could no doubt be dealt with by discussion. The third would be very serious. Moiseyev did not explode again, as I thought he might, and agreed that the details should be discussed between experts.

In the months that followed, Yazov and Moiseyev continued to bluster. But Akhromeyev assured us in April that the Russians would keep to the agreed figures. They did not like them, he said, but it was their own fault that they had failed to negotiate more effectively because of their own internal disagreements. Using an ancient political device, Gorbachev sent Moiseyev to Washington to negotiate directly with the Americans: the general would thus be landed with the responsibility whether the negotiations succeeded or failed. On 14 June 1991 the negotiation was finally concluded in Vienna, the city where it had begun almost eighteen years earlier.

The Russians, like ourselves, are obliged under the 1972 Biological Warfare Convention not to produce biological weapons. The Convention suffers from a fundamental snag. You do not need elaborate equipment to do the research, and a covert research programme is hard to detect even with the most sophisticated methods. And once you have done the research it is comparatively easy to produce the weapons. We had always suspected that the Soviets were up to something. In 1979 the Americans announced that a lethal outbreak of anthrax in Sverdlovsk (now Yekaterinburg) was the result of an accident with a biological weapons programme. In Autumn 1989 Vladimir Pasechnik defected from a Leningrad scientific institute to tell us that illegal weapons research was being concealed behind the ostensibly 'commercial' activities of an organisation called Biopreparat. A few years later he repeated the whole story on British television, perhaps as part of a manoeuvre to keep up the pressure on the still shifty Russians.

Obviously we could not let this pass. But London saw a serious tactical problem. How could we put pressure on the Russians without revealing our source? I thought that the difficulty was exaggerated. Our source was now safely in England. The Russians had presumably noticed that he was no longer coming in to work. We could reveal what we knew without harming him. And unless we made it quite clear that we knew what we were talking about, the Russians would easily evade our questioning. My views did not prevail. But Tom King was due to visit the Soviet Union in May 1990: the first visit by a British Defence Secretary in living memory. We had to act, but we feared that a row would spoil the visit. Jack Matlock and I warned Chernyaev and Bessmertnykh, the Deputy Foreign Minister, what was in the wind. King questioned Yazov at a private meeting. His manner was hopelessly oblique. Yazov muttered to his aide that the British had presumably learned something from 'that defector', went red in the face, but blandly denied all knowledge.

Mrs Thatcher tackled Gorbachev much more directly during her last visit to Moscow as Prime Minister a month later. He claimed to know nothing but promised to investigate. Intelligence analysts in London and Washington, many of whom still thought that there was little to choose between Gorbachev and his predecessors, believed that he knew perfectly well what was going on, and was party to his generals' deliberate deception. Chernyaev, with whom I pursued the issue in April and December 1991, argued that it made no sense for Gorbachev to deceive the West. Gorbachev himself passionately believed that transparency in the military field benefited the Soviet Union as much as it benefited the rest of the world. I suggested that the military had deceived Gorbachev over their biological weapons programme, as they had deceived their civilian masters over their anti-ballistic missile programme[12] and over their withdrawal of conventional forces from Europe. Chernyaev considered the possibility, but was willing to give the generals the benefit of the doubt. I was more sceptical. Gorbachev may well have been unaware of what the generals were up to. But the generals were perfectly capable of misleading him out of a sense of misplaced patriotism, firmly believing as they did in the old principle: 'Secrecy useful and secrecy useless.' Gorbachev could not, and did not, know everything that was going on in the country. But by that time he was in any case no longer in a position to assert himself.

When Douglas Hurd called on the Russian President in January 1992, Yeltsin said without prompting:

> I know all about the Soviet biological weapon programme. It's still going ahead, even though the organisers claim it's merely defensive research. They are fanatics, and they will not stop voluntarily. I know those people personally, I know their names, and I know the addresses of the institutes where they're doing the work. I'm going to close down the institutes, retire the director of the programme, and set the others

to doing something useful. When I've checked for myself that the institutes have stopped work, I'm going to ask for international inspection.

We were stunned, and could do no more than thank him. Yeltsin repeated his promises when he visited the United States in May 1992. But even that was not the end of the story. The Russian military ducked and weaved, as they had done when they still wore Soviet uniform. Delegations of experts were exchanged, but their missions produced no decisive evidence. The Americans as well as the Russians pleaded considerations of commercial secrecy as a reason for not opening their books. Civilian watchdogs warned of the dangers. But the essential problem remained: research into biological warfare can be concealed beyond the capacity of the outside world to detect.[13]

Because nuclear issues were a matter for the Americans and the Russians at the strategic level, and for the NATO alliance as a whole at the tactical level, the British had no independent role in the nuclear arms control negotiations which took place throughout the Gorbachev period. Their role was confined in practice to attempting to influence American or Alliance policy. Under Mrs Thatcher, they exercised this role with force and effect. The Soviet leaders were baffled by Mrs Thatcher's enthusiasm for nuclear weapons, which she expounded with verve whenever she met them. In June 1990 she asked to meet the generals in order 'to see how they were thinking and also to let them know precisely what my own views were'. The meeting took place in the great conference room of the Defence Ministry, encrusted with scenes of Russian victories. Yazov appeared with Moiseyev and several of their colleagues: safety in numbers. They were tickled pink at the prospect of meeting her. But they were apprehensive and carefully briefed. They knew her formidable reputation in debate, and doubtless remembered how she had wiped the floor with the Soviet defence correspondents on television three years earlier. Yazov kept a very tight grip on his team, slapping Moiseyev down when he tried to intervene. Mrs Thatcher announced that it was nuclear weapons that had kept the peace: their great advantage was that once you had them no one wanted to attack you. The generals nodded sagely. Fighting to get a word in edgeways, Yazov broke in to say that nuclear weapons might have helped to keep the peace in Europe. But they hadn't been very successful in keeping the peace elsewhere. And since the explosion in the nuclear reactor in Chernobyl in 1986 the Russians were much less keen on nuclear weapons in general.

Yazov expanded the argument when he met the Supreme Allied Commander in Europe, General Galvin, in November 1990. Life on earth could be made unsustainable with far fewer weapons than the existing nuclear powers already possessed. He no longer understood why the military on both sides had built themselves so many. Nuclear weapons should be eliminated, or they would be used. Galvin countered with arguments about the value of minimal deterrence and the impossibility of uninventing the bomb. Yazov was not convinced. General Karpov, the Head of the Main Operations Department of the General Staff, remarked that the underlying Soviet strategy had always been defensive. But the Soviets had been attached to an operational doctrine of attack. They had therefore multiplied their armour and their nuclear weapons. But they had failed to appreciate the consequences of nuclear warfare, and the impossibility of victory in a Third World War. All this had exacerbated the Cold War and led to the nuclear stalemate. In the end the economic burden had become unbearable. The changes since 1985 had been designed to bring Soviet foreign, defence, and economic policy into line. It was a neat exposition of the underlying rationale of Perestroika and the only time that a Soviet general admitted in my hearing that the Soviet Union shared responsibility for the Cold War.

As their conventional superiority crumbled away the Russian generals began to wonder whether nuclear weapons were such a bad thing after all. In earlier years NATO had seen its nuclear weapons as a means to compensate for its inferiority to the Soviet Union in conventional force. It was hard to see why Western commentators should be so outraged when the Russians adopted a similar doctrine in April 2000. After all, as Chernyaev told Percy Cradock in February 1990, as long as the Russians kept their nuclear weapons they could look after themselves. What was more, Chernyaev had added with his characteristic grin, no one would bother to talk to the Russians in their current political and economic difficulties if they gave up their nuclear weapons as well.

The Treaty on Germany was the death knell for Stalin's empire in Europe and for the old Soviet army as well. At the beginning of 1988 there were twenty-six Soviet divisions in Eastern and Central Europe. Six years later all were back in what had been the Soviet Union. The withdrawal of the Soviet legions and their equipment in such a short period of time was a logistical *tour de force* for which the Soviet General Staff was never given credit. But the facilities for the soldiers' reception back home were wholly inadequate. Only a tiny minority were lucky enough to move into the new blocks of flats built with German money. Tens of thousand of officers and their families were accommodated in squalid tents and shipping containers. The ragged Soviet armies which returned from Europe in 1945 and 1946 had been in even worse case. But they were buoyed up by the knowledge of victory. Their successors were comprehensively defeated without firing a shot. Baffled and deeply humiliated, the generals blamed the civilians for what they saw as an outrageous and unnecessary failure of will.

For the time being they ground their teeth and continued to accept civilian control. None of us could be sure that their patience would not eventually snap. As early as March 1989 the *Washington Times* reported gossip from the American intelligence community that Yazov had tried to kill Gorbachev, and had then disappeared from public view. The story was spoiled when Yazov turned up at the polling station to cast his vote. But the Moscow intellectuals grew steadily more nervous. They feared bloodshed: a military coup, or a replica of the Chinese massacre on Tien An Men Square. Gorbachev and his advisers, and the experts in London, pooh-poohed the idea of a military coup. That had never happened, they said (inaccurately), in the long course of Russian history. I did not entirely share the optimistic view. By the Spring of 1990 Gorbachev's stock had sunk very low. He had given the people political freedom and they had lost the awe in which they had previously held the pillars of the totalitarian state – the army, the Party and the KGB. He did not understand or sympathise with the generals, nor did he even seem to think it politically expedient to give them moral support or comfort. On 8 May, on the forty-fifth anniversary of the Victory, he spoke in the Bolshoi Theatre to an audience of senior officers and Party leaders. He was lucid, balanced and historically accurate. He spelled out the need for military reform with impeccable logic. But he showed no concern for the soldiers' real problems, and made no appeal to their patriotism. He got no more than routine applause, and more than one elderly general sat on his hands. Mrs Thatcher, living in a Western democracy, always took far more care of her military constituency.

Yazov and his colleagues were dimly aware that economic failure meant substantial reductions in budgets, troop levels, and equipment. But the old faith that God, the Tsar, or the Party would provide died very slowly. I asked General Lobov, who was briefly Chief of Staff in the autumn of 1991, where the funds for his proposed military reform would come from. He replied: 'How should I know? I'm not a businessman.' Now the East European empire – the fruit of the Victory – was slipping from the soldiers' grasp. As unrest increased within the Soviet Union itself, the politicians called on them to aid the civil power in Tbilisi, in Baku, in Riga and Vilnius. But it was the soldiers, not the politicians, who were blamed when things went wrong. Their sons and grandsons no longer regarded it as a privilege – or even as a profitable option – to serve with the colours. Their own unity was declining as disagreement grew between elderly generals and up-and-coming field officers, and between soldiers of different ethnic groups. Desertion and draft dodging were on the increase. The professional honour and competence of the military were routinely pilloried in the liberal press. So were their clumsy attempts to defend themselves in public. In September 1989 one admiral told me that he could not encourage his sons to follow him into the armed forces, a sad admission in a country where you could still find officers whose families had served the Russian military for eight generations.

All this made me think that the old constraints against 'Bonapartism' were weakening as the Party's prestige declined. A purely military coup still seemed unlikely. But a *frisson* went through the intelligentsia in the Summer of 1989 when they read *Nevozvrashchenets*, 'The Non-Returner', a scenario by the film writer Aleksandr Kabakov, about a military takeover in Moscow after the collapse of Perestroika, the breakdown of law and order, and the disintegration of the Soviet Union into its constituent parts. Even short of a military coup, I told the Foreign Office in May 1990, I could imagine a creeping increase in military influence over arms control, over military budgeting, and over the steps needed to preserve the integrity of the Soviet Union. A coherent and disciplined armed force capable of maintaining order might eventually seem attractive to all those Russians who feared chaos more than they feared authoritarian government.

There was evidence to feed these apprehensions. At the time of the street demonstrations in Moscow in February 1990 there were rumours that the army was poised to intervene. In September 1990 paratroops wearing combat gear and carrying ammunition were brought to the outskirts of Moscow. Deputies demanded to know why. Yazov told them that the soldiers had come on manoeuvres, or to help with the potato harvest, or to practise for the November parade. He promised that there would be no coup, and sacked the Deputy Commandant of the Ryazan Airborne Academy for saying that his troops were 'ready for battle'. I paid too little attention to the affair at the time: with hindsight it looked like a logistical rehearsal for the coup in August 1991. A couple of weeks later Yazov said on television that the army would defend itself against harassment, if necessary with arms. In December fifty-three prominent personalities – they included Generals Varennikov and Moiseyev and Admiral Chernavin – called publicly for a state of emergency and presidential rule in conflict zones if constitutional methods proved ineffective.[14] At the turn of the year – I was later told by a Russian friend – twenty marshals and generals, including Akhromeyev, presented a handwritten ultimatum to Gorbachev setting out their dissatisfactions and demands. At the end of March 1991 tanks were deployed with massive efficiency in the streets of Moscow. Violence hung in the air.

In public the generals protested to the last that they would not get mixed up in politics. In June 1991 Moiseyev told me that the Russians had made their final concessions on conventional disarmament to refute growing speculation that the Soviet military were 'imposing their will' on Gorbachev. Talk about a possible military coup was absurd. The Soviet military already had their work cut out reshaping the Soviet armed forces and upgrading their quality. They had no time to engage in politics, said Moiseyev, still less to 'lie around as if they are on a desert island waiting for the bananas to drop into their mouths'. The coup – which found the military divided – took place five weeks later.

Against this background the relationship between Gorbachev and the military grew increasingly tense. By the Autumn of 1990 he was being frequently and viciously attacked in public and in private by the two 'Black Colonels' Alksnis and Petrushenko, who regularly accused him and Shevardnadze of outright treachery. When Gorbachev got the Nobel Peace Prize, furious Party members wrote in to accuse him of betraying Eastern Europe, destroying the Soviet Union and the Soviet Armed Forces, and handing over the country's natural resources to the Americans and the press to the Zionists. The letters were carefully collected by the KGB. Kryuchkov made a point of letting Gorbachev see them.

Shevardnadze fought back fiercely. At the height of the negotiations on German reunification and arms control in the Spring of 1990 he appealed to the Communists in the Foreign Ministry to support his candidature to the forthcoming XXVIIIth Party Congress. He was accused, he said, of lacking patriotism. Like everyone else, he believed that the Soviet Union was a great country.

> But great in what way? The extent of our territory? The size of our population? The number of our weapons? Or the national disasters? The absence of human rights? The disorganisation in our everyday life? Why should we be proud that we have almost the highest infant mortality rate on our planet? ... Do we want to be a nation which is feared, or a nation which is respected?[15]

People whispered that he had undermined the country's military security. Shevardnadze warned his audience that if the arms control negotiations failed, and Perestroika got nowhere, the Soviet Union would soon be unable to compete technically. The argument was impeccable. It was not very different from what General Karpov had said to Galvin. But its underlying thrust – that national greatness does not depend only on armed might – contradicted the whole course of Russian state thinking since Ivan the Terrible. Shevardnadze won the vote. But 20 per cent of his listeners voted in preference for the official driver of one of his deputy ministers. And by the end of the year he had resigned.

The Soviet Foreign Ministry conducted their own polls in Moscow and elsewhere, and were surprised – and doubtless mortified – to discover that even among the military ordinary people did not feel strongly about German reunification.[16] Sasha Motov's view was that whatever the Germans had done during the war, it made no sense to keep them divided fifty years later. A cheerful pair of Soviet army drivers we met in Weimar in the Summer of 1991, tickled to be addressed in Russian, were perfectly content that the Germans could now get themselves properly organised without the Russian on their backs. Ordinary Russians did resent the unseemly speed with which their soldiers were bundled out of Eastern Europe, and the squalid conditions to which they were forced to return. But the risk of an unmanageable popular backlash remained a figment of the politicians' imagination. The Russian people fought Hitler, as they had fought Napoleon, to cleanse their homeland of the invader. But it was the ambition of their leaders in 1813 as in 1944, rather than an understandable desire for revenge, that mainly drove the Russian armies beyond the Russian border and deep into Central Europe. When the time came the Russian people relinquished the conquests without pain. They had far more pressing things to worry about at home.

Every year on 9 May the Russians still celebrate the Victory. In 1991 Michael Alexander, Jill and I went in the spring sunshine to see the veterans in Gorky Park. Everywhere stands sold doughnuts and sausages: no hint of the food shortages which were spreading through the country. Old men and women in medals and faded uniforms gathered in knots round the flags and banners of their wartime units. An old man wandered with a placard on a pole which read 'Is there anyone here from the 213th Guards Rifle Division?' In one corner a plump old woman in a private soldier's uniform played the accordion while two others sang raucous *chastushki*, rude and improvised couplets satirising the onlookers. The new veterans were there too: young Afghantsy in their tropical uniform, berets, and striped vests. Two weedy young men in jackboots were selling extracts from the *Protocols of the Elders of Zion*. Two others were peddling a nationalist newspaper from a wartime lorry marked 'Berlin or bust', with a picture of Stalin on the windscreen. An earnest man of middle age buttonholed me: 'Do you believe it is possible to create a society that is wholly just?' A lean, elderly, and slightly drunk man staggered up to tell me that the first man to die in his arms was an Englishman. He had been fifteen years old and a mechanic on a torpedo boat moored in Murmansk when they landed the wounded from a convoy that had been attacked in the Arctic Sea. One sailor's innards were coming out as he was lowered over the side of his ship: the boy had to stuff them back. The British crew had wrapped the man in two blankets. When he died, the boy's bosun told him to sell the blankets and drink the proceeds. His hangover lasted two days. When he recovered his boat was due to go out on patrol. The bosun told him to stay ashore. The boat never came back.

Anatoli Pristavkin, the author, told us a few days later that the memory of the Victory was the only thing of which Russians could still be proud. But the instruments of the Victory were disintegrating. As the century drew to a close, divisions which at the height of the confrontation with America had numbered ten thousand men could muster no more than five hundred, and four hundred of them were officers.[17] Conscription had all but collapsed, there was insufficient fuel to train the navy or the airforce, and the supply of new equipment had diminished to a trickle.

For some of the professionals, it was more than they could bear. Marshal Akhromeyev, a decent, honourable man, foresaw it all. After the coup of August 1991 he committed suicide in despair at the ruin of the institution to which he had given his life.

6

Fraying at the Edges

I don't see why we should be independent. We've done nothing wrong.

Today we will vote for Ukrainian independence, because if we don't we're in the shit.

Deputies speaking in the Ukrainian Rada, 24 August 1991

Few aspects of the Soviet collapse have benefited more from the resolute application of hindsight than the process by which the Soviet Union disintegrated into fifteen separate nation-states. Gorbachev was pilloried for failing to tackle the crisis earlier or more effectively. Foreigners criticised him for not managing the transition more smoothly. Russians criticised him for not holding the Union together. Gorbachev himself believed that his policy towards the nationalities was amongst his greatest failures. All of them were probably wrong.

All the European empires fell apart in the twentieth century. In each case the process was similar and the collapse followed much the same path. The imperial power believed that its rule was legitimised – by racial superiority, by superior civilisation, by the mandate of heaven. For years, perhaps for centuries, the subject peoples accepted the myth. Then quite suddenly they ceased to do so. Once the idea of national identity and the ambition for national independence took root, it could no longer be eradicated, even by the most draconian measures. That is what happened with the overseas empires of Britain, France, Holland, Portugal and Belgium. It is what happened with the Turkish and the Austro-Hungarian empires in Europe itself. It is what happened to the Russian Empire, which in the last seventy years of its existence was thinly disguised as the Soviet Union.

From time to time Russians would ask me in private and in public for a bit of British advice on how to dismantle an empire. But most of them found it hard to accept that the Soviet Union was an empire at all. They believed, with Dostoevsky, that Russia's 'destiny is a universality to be won not with the sword, but with the strength of brotherhood and our brotherly aspirations for the unification of mankind'.[1] For years after the Soviet Union had become little more than a memory, ordinary Russians were still echoing the kind of sentiments which Gorbachev expressed on television in the Spring of 1991: 'History decreed that a number of bigger and smaller nations became united around Russia ... The process was assisted by the openness of the Russian nature, its readiness to work with peoples of other nationalities.'[2]

The reality was, of course, that Russian and later Soviet imperial rule was at least as brutal as that of other imperial powers. In their campaigns of Russification the Tsars imprisoned and exiled Finns, Ukrainians, and others who dared to practise their national language and sustain a national culture. The Communists continued the practice even more brutally under the guise of eradicating 'bourgeois nationalism'. Large numbers of intellectuals, especially in Ukraine and the Baltic States, were killed or exiled by Stalin. Under his successors the executions were fewer but the pressures continued. Communist Parties, with their own local First Secretaries, existed in all the fifteen constituent republics of the Union save for Russia itself. Russians saw this as discrimination. In fact it was a sign that the Russians did not need their own party, since they dominated the Communist Party of the Soviet Union and exercised effective central control over the republican parties. Throughout the Soviet period discontent flared up from time to time in one or other of the constituent republics, and was brutally suppressed.

But it was not entirely a myth that the peoples of the Union shared common interests and a common citizenship. No more than half the inhabitants of the Soviet Union were ethnic Russians, and over twenty million of these lived outside the RSFSR, the Russian Soviet Federated Socialist Republic. Many of the other ethnic groups, of whom the Ukrainians were by far the largest, had their own Soviet Republics separate from the RSFSR. The Tatars, the Chechens and other small mountain peoples of the North Caucasus, the Yakutis, the Buryats and others, had their own Autonomous Republics within it. The Soviet regime brought law and order of a kind, universal education and a primitive welfare system. Bright youngsters from the republics could make their careers at the centre of imperial power in Moscow. Their sense of 'Soviet citizenship' helped to banish any guilty feeling that they were serving the imperial oppressor.

After the Soviet Union broke up Russians constituted four-fifths of the population of the Russian Federation. The word *rossiyane* – 'Russian citizens' – was used to cover all the country's ethnic groups. Ethnic Russians were called *russkie*. The distinction is similar to that made in the United Kingdom between 'British' and 'English'. It too can lead to misunderstandings if improperly used.

From time to time the non-Russian peoples of the Soviet Union dreamed of independence; the prospect was daunting for almost all but the Balts, and especially for the republics in Central Asia which had no real history as nation-states. It is just conceivable that Moscow could have preserved a form of Union if it had followed more imaginative and timely policies. Gorbachev's concessions, like Lord North's in the American colonies, were too little and too late. The sense of a common citizenship was not strong enough to resist the pressures of reviving nationalism. Even those who thought that Soviet domination in Eastern Europe could not last did not foresee how quickly and completely the Union itself would collapse. In the Spring of 1989 moderates like Beekman, the Chairman of the Estonian Writers' Union, who accompanied Gorbachev to London, still thought that the relationship of Estonia with the Union could be acceptably renegotiated. By the Autumn his ideas would no longer seem outspoken. In Estonia itself they would have been seen as conservative, even treacherous. Russians – even radical Russians like Yuri Afanasiev – still believed that the Union would hold. It might be necessary to use military force in the Caucasus. If so, it would work. Force would not work in the Baltics, and so they would have to be persuaded to stay in the Union voluntarily. Afanasiev was both wrong and right. Eighteen months after he made these remarks to me, force was indeed used in the Baltics. But – as he had predicted – it failed of its purpose.

Even with the benefit of hindsight it is not easy to see what alternative policies Gorbachev could realistically have pursued. He was genuinely reluctant to shed blood to repress nationalist aspirations in the Republics. Most of his colleagues were not prepared to let him bring the Union to a peaceful end. Nor did he want to. Like Churchill, he did not believe that he had been elected to preside over the dismantling of the empire. And it was not only the Soviet government who hoped that the Union would hold together. Shevardnadze regularly warned his Western colleagues that the Soviet Union could disintegrate in blood – Yugoslavia on a continental scale, but this time with nuclear weapons. Western governments were terrified at the prospect. Until the very last minute they did what they could (in practice very little) to help Gorbachev hold things together. But the Russians discovered, as others discovered before them, that the genie of nationalism cannot be put back into the bottle. The subject peoples were no longer content to accept Russian rule. And the Russians had lost their imperial will. All that was open to Gorbachev was to prevaricate, to minimise the bloodshed, to attempt to put together a new relationship between the parts of the old Union, and in the end to accept the inevitable as gracefully as he could.

By September 1989 the signs of disintegration were becoming hard to ignore. I noted in my diary:

[It] is very hard to envisage any policy which can effectively stem the national unrest. The nationalities sense that their Russian imperial masters have lost the will to govern. But decolonisation for a land-based empire is infinitely more complicated and difficult than it is for a maritime empire. The British people could forget pretty quickly that they once ruled India – it was a long way away, and most of them had never been there. By contrast most of the republics contain substantial Russian minorities, and the Russians regard it as their natural right to holiday, mine, or build dirty factories in their colonies regardless of local views. If civil war is to begin, it could well be started by an incident in one of the republics involving the killing of numbers of Russians. The pressure in Moscow on Gorbachev to put down the unrest could then become irresistible. But that would lead the Russians (and I mean Russians, not Soviets) into a quagmire of Algerias, Rhodesias, Ulsters, far worse than anything we or the French had to face. The key could be the Ukraine. It has remained comparatively – and ominously – quiet so far. If it is now on the move, the con- sequences could be grim indeed.

A year later, on the day that he signed the agreement on German reunifi- cation that marked the end of the Soviet Union's East European empire, I told Douglas Hurd that the Union could hardly survive in its existing form. There might be a core Union consisting of the three Slav republics, Russia, Ukraine, and Belorussia, in a reasonable negotiated arrangement with the three independent Baltic States. The Caucasus and Central Asia might decline into endemic clan warfare. I did not see the Russians fighting to recover their old empire. But I could imagine much blood being spilt if the Russians had to fight to cover the retreat of their women and children – the large Russian communities in Kazakhstan and elsewhere. My views were not changed by the bloodshed in Vilnius in January 1991. The following May I told a conference of NATO's senior military commanders that the Soviet Union could hardly survive in its present brutally centralised form; but it was unlikely to fly apart into its fifteen constituent parts. It was not one of the most accurate of my predictions. Only seven more months were to pass before the Soviet Union dissolved, and the problem for Western policy was merely how soon, and in what order, to recognise the new states that came into being as a result. Even at that late stage people were still trying to construct an association of the three Slav states linked with the other Republics of the former Soviet Union. Most Russians still believed that was the natural order of things. It was what Yeltsin thought he wanted, and what his Ukrainian colleague Kravchuk pretended to offer, when they signed the death warrant of the Union in the Belovezha forest on 8 December 1991.

One Western scholar did predict that the Soviet Union would be brought down by a rebellion of its Muslim peoples, whose superior birth-rate would ensure that they soon outnumbered the Russians.[3] It did not turn out like that. The Muslims remained passive, and the Union was destroyed by the determination of the Balts to regain their independence, the resentment of the Ukrainians at the centuries-old domination from Moscow, and by the feeling of the Russians themselves that their empire had brought them far more burdens than benefits. But the violence started in the Caucasus.

The wild people and the wild scenery of the Caucasus inspired Pushkin to some of his best work. Lermontov was exiled and fought his fatal duel there. The poet-diplomat Griboyedov married a Georgian and is buried in Tbilisi. For a thousand years the Caucasus was the strategic buffer between Russia and the hostile empires of Turkey and Persia. Russian soldiers captured Baku in the tenth century. The great Queen Tamara of Georgia married a prince of Muscovy in the thirteenth century. Boris Godunov and Peter the Great sent expeditions to the Caucasus. By the early years of the nineteenth century, Armenia, Georgia, and much of Azerbaijan were under Russian control. To the modern eye, the final conquest of the Caucasus a hundred and fifty years ago was a classic imperial campaign: brutal, and concerned only with the aggrandisement and interests of the imperial power. But judgements change with the passage of time. A British historian writing at the beginning of the twentieth century believed that the campaign was necessary in order to rescue the Christian states of the Caucasus 'from the total ruin threatened by the unspeakable Turk, and still more unspeakable Persian ... as righteous a cause as ever inspired a military or political undertaking; and, by the force of circumstances, it was imposed upon Russia, the only Christian Power that either would, or could, move in the matter.'[4]

The First World War brought about the collapse of Austro-Hungary and Turkey, two of the three great multinational empires of Europe and the

Near East. The third empire, Russia, tottered and nearly fell. But the Bolsheviks soon rallied and reincorporated into the Russian Empire (now renamed the Soviet Union) the independent states which the Armenians and the Georgians had briefly created. Perestroika revived the aspiration towards independence and soon led to bloodshed. There were clashes with the imperial power in Tbilisi in April 1989 and in Baku in January 1990. Ethnic conflict broke out in Georgia. And the dispute between Armenia and Azerbaijan over the mountain enclave of Nagorny Karabakh led to ethnic cleansing on both sides, and a state of undeclared war between the two Union Republics. This was no longer a rebellion against the imperial power, but an international event, a real war between two Soviet republics. The Soviet Union was beginning to break up.

Gorbachev's attempts to cajole and bully the Armenians and Azerbaijanis back to reason were ineffective. His lack of touch was cruelly demonstrated in the aftermath of the tragic earthquake in Armenia which occurred on the very morning of his triumphant speech to the United Nations in December 1988. In the first hours after the disaster the Soviet authorities were almost overpowered. The response from abroad was immediate and overwhelming. The Italians sent a trained emergency unit of carabinieri. The French sent a company of soldiers in a specially equipped aircraft. The Germans set up an air bridge. The British relied as usual on volunteers – enthusiastic, but uncoordinated and meagrely supported by the government. As the first wave arrived – firemen and some burly characters from the International Rescue Corps – I spent the night at Sheremetievo Airport, helping get them and their equipment onto one of the rare planes for the Armenian capital Yerevan. None of the volunteers spoke Russian, so I put David Ludlow, a tough Ulsterman from the Political Section of the embassy, onto the plane with them. I did not bother to ask permission from the Soviet authorities or from our own Security Officer. No one complained about this breach of the rules. Ludlow was followed a few days later by Nigel Shakespear, an Assistant Military Attaché, and Adam Noble, one of our Russian experts from the Research Department of the Foreign Office. Though it was not a consequence of their work in Armenia, both were expelled from the Soviet Union in the exchange of intelligence courtesies which occurred in Spring of the following year.

Within four days the International Rescue Corps team had returned from Armenia. Their elderly doctor said it was worse than what he had seen in Aachen and Dresden at the end of the war. The team calculated – on basis of their experience in Salvador, Mexico, Columbia – that the total number of dead could be as high as 200,000. The first official figure was

40,000. The final death toll was set at about 20,000: a lesson in the unreliability of statistics. The team had great admiration and sympathy for the Armenians. But they were critical of the Russian system of command and control. Even the simplest decision would generate half an hour of argument. Sloppy rescue work meant buried survivors were crushed or suffocated before they could be freed. Many people had been killed very quickly by the dust alone. One woman was still sitting at breakfast with her child, unwounded but dead. Even the birds had no time to fly away, and lay dead in the streets.

The IRC team were certain that there was no hope of finding more survivors, nothing more for rescue teams or doctors to do. What was needed now was earth-moving equipment, tents, food. But British firemen, doctors, nurses continued to flood in. Some soon complained that they had no real role. Within ten days most of them had gone. They did a good job in appalling conditions. But on the British side, too, coordination was not what it might have been. Some of the volunteers ignored the instructions of the local authorities, on the grounds that they knew best. Others accused their fellows of publicity-seeking and drunkenness. There were threats of libel actions. I recommended to London that the British government should set up a permanent rapid reaction organisation for natural disasters, based on the armed forces and with its own transport. I got the expected answer. What Italians and Frenchmen did was no guide. Our system might look odd but (so I was told) it worked. In any case there was neither the money nor the will to make the change.

Ordinary people inside the Soviet Union were surprised and moved by the outpouring of Western sympathy and support. Olga Dmitrieva, the embassy's Russian teacher, and Sasha Motov had always been taught that the outside world and the capitalists hated the USSR. They were convinced that the West could only be hostile, and that our natural reaction would be to welcome and exploit the disaster. When the opposite happened, they and many others began to believe that the Cold War was indeed coming to an end.

But the disaster did not have the effect, for which I and others had naively hoped, of bringing the Armenians and the Soviet government closer together. Ryzhkov, the Prime Minister, performed well. The viewers saw him mingling with the dispossessed victims, warm, human, on the verge of tears. This was the beginning of his reputation as 'the weeping Bolshevik'. But Gorbachev struck exactly the wrong note. He went down to Armenia shortly after his return from New York. In private and in meetings of the Politburo he expressed warm sympathy for the Armenians. But the television showed him accusing Ter-Petrosian and other members of the Armenian Committee for the Defence of Nagorny Karabakh of exploiting the disaster for political purposes. Armenians were said to have spat on him in the streets. Foreign and domestic cynics commented that for Gorbachev the five million Armenians weighed little in comparison with the fifty million Azerbaijanis and other Muslims living in the Soviet Union. In a display of shocking but no doubt widely shared Great Russian chauvinism, one of the embassy's Russian staff told me that Gorbachev had been quite right to put those whining, corrupt, ungrateful Armenians in their place. All this fed the deep, almost paranoid suspicions of the Armenians. Some believed that the earthquake had been triggered off by a secret Russian nuclear test. Others thought that the evacuation of homeless and orphaned children to Russia was a trick: a deliberate policy of deportation, from which the children would never return. Years later even sophisticated Armenians had still not forgiven Gorbachev.

In June 1990 we flew with Mrs Thatcher to Leninakan, one of the cities worst hit by the earthquake, to open the school which had been built there by the British. We were met by what *Private Eye* would call 'amazing scenes'. One hundred and fifty thousand people turned out to meet Mrs Thatcher: more than half the population of the town, crowding the streets and perched on every tree and roof. The security arrangements were in tatters. We had to get out of our vehicles and fight our way through the crowd. I wondered what would happen if someone panicked. It was like the arrival of the Great White Mother in British India – even to the arrogant way Zamyatin, the Soviet ambassador in London, and the other Russians treated the locals ('Such chaos! But what can you expect from a bunch of wogs?').

Jill and I had first seen Armenia in the 1960s. Unlike Baku and Tbilisi, Yerevan is almost wholly Soviet, though some of its buildings are comparatively attractive. Outside the city you find the Hellenistic sites and the ancient churches of the Armenian faith, the oldest of the Christian state religions, with a sense of orderly intellectual enlightenment which compares favourably with Russian Orthodoxy. In April 1991 we returned on an official visit. Levon Ter-Petrosian, former dissident and jailbird, was by then the President, young, handsome, intelligent, with his collar undone under his tie in the Caucasian fashion. He was born in Syria, where his father helped found the Syrian and Lebanese Communist Parties. A scholar by profession, he was imprisoned in 1988 for his membership of the Committee for the Defence of Nagorny Karabakh, and thus arrived in national politics with a very respectable record.

Ter-Petrosian was so reasonable and balanced in his analysis of Armenia's problems – he was almost unnaturally rational about Nagorny Karabakh – that I wondered how he could possibly have risen to the top in the cauldron of Caucasian emotions. Armenia would certainly become independent, he said. But unlike the Balts, the Armenians would proceed according to the protracted process laid down in Gorbachev's secession law of 1990. There would be plenty to negotiate about meanwhile. The Armenian economy was almost completely integrated with the rest of the Soviet Union. This limited Armenia's freedom to go its own way, or to pursue economic reform as fast as he would like. But even though the Armenians were prepared to be reasonable, and to play the game according to Soviet law, Gorbachev had run out of steam, and was unlikely to make any voluntary concessions to the republics. The conservatives in Moscow were on the counterattack. But the Communist Party no longer had any influence in Armenia, and Ter-Petrosian claimed to have come to his own understanding with the Soviet military and the KGB.

The leaders of the parliamentary opposition met us in the building of the Armenian Supreme Soviet. The Communists were not there: the others said they were afraid to show their faces. The most articulate of those present was Airikyan, a man in his mid-forties, handsome, bearded, and snappily dressed. He had spent many years in prison for 'terrorism'. In July 1988 he was arrested and bundled out of the country by Gorbachev, and had only recently returned. Unlike Ter-Petrosian he believed that Armenia should go for independence straight away, rather than plod its way through the Soviet legal labyrinth. Armenian independence should then be guaranteed by the Five Permanent Members of the UN Security Council. I warned him against reliance on foreign guarantees. The Poles had still not forgiven the British for the meaningless guarantee which they gave Poland in March 1939. I thought the Armenians would need to remain on reasonable terms with the Russians as a counterweight to the sea of Muslims by whom they were almost surrounded. So indeed they did once they became independent.

We also called on Prime Minister Manoukian, a small, bespectacled, neat intellectual. He insisted on speaking Armenian, so that we lost a lot of time with interpretation. I tried to persuade him that the republics would strengthen their eventual negotiating hand with Moscow if they were to set up working parties now to devise practical ways of dividing economic and other responsibilities as they drew away from the centre. But Manoukian, like most of the others, was obsessed with the politics. The practical problems of breaking up the Union were well illustrated when we went to visit a project –

the largest factory for programmable logic controllers in Europe – which the British firm Simon Carves was helping to build in the suburbs of Yerevan. The factory was of course owned and financed by the Union. Its market and many of its component suppliers were in Russia. The Armenians could never afford to buy Moscow out. So what would happen if they got independence? Apart from Ter-Petrosian, the politicians had evidently not thought about such problems. But the mavericks were right and he was wrong in one important respect. Armenia was independent by the end of the year.

In April 1989 Gorbachev returned from another foreign visit – this time to London – to face another crisis in the Caucasus. But this time the tragedy was man-made. On the morning of Sunday 9 April we heard on the BBC that sixteen people had been killed in riots in Tbilisi the previous night. They were said to be have been demonstrating in favour of Georgian independence. Adam Noble, who was on duty, contacted the British teachers in Tbilisi: they were safe. One of them had been in the centre of the town at 4 a.m. when the fight occurred. Paratroopers, he said, had waded into the crowd with shovels. Nearly twenty people had been killed, mostly women. The story emerged piecemeal.

In Autumn 1988 students had set up a tent city opposite the parliament in the centre of Tbilisi. They wanted more autonomy for Georgia, and less autonomy for the smaller ethnic groupings, such as the Abkhazians, who also lived in the republic. The demonstrations were peaceful. But the Georgian Party leaders were irritated by the protracted challenge to their authority. Patiashvili, the Georgian Party Secretary, asked Moscow to help. Just before Gorbachev got back from London, Ligachev and Yazov ordered additional troops to Tbilisi. They did not inform Prime Minister Ryzhkov, and Gorbachev only learned what they had done when he landed at Vnukovo. The next day the Georgian Party leaders panicked ('shat in their pants', as Gorbachev elegantly put it). Patiashvili called on the local Military Commander, Colonel General Rodionov, to send in the troops: both in due course became the natural scapegoats. Gorbachev accused Yazov, Kryuchkov, and the others of ignoring his authority, sticking to the old forceful methods, believing that persuasion signified weakness. Did they not understand that democracy required new methods? He did not convince them, either then or later. In his diary that night Chernyaev wrote prophetically: 'Gorbachev has a choice: either [military] occupation and the empire again; or a federation, or rather a confederation. ... Is Gorbachev ready for that? Or does he think that the others won't let him?' By the time Gorbachev found the answer, it was too late.

But for the first time a Soviet massacre became the subject of a public enquiry. The Congress of People's Deputies set up a commission of investigation. Sobchak was one of the members. So was Alexander Maksimovich Yakovlev, a constitutional lawyer who served on the Commission (not to be confused with Alexander Nikolaevich Yakovlev of the Politburo or Yegor Yakovlev of *Moscow News*). Yakovlev told me some months later that Moscow did indeed give permission for troops to be used – but only to guard strategic points in the town. The Georgian Party leadership decided to clear the square in the early hours of the morning, when there would only be a few people around. But then everything went wrong. The preparations of the security forces were so ostentatious and so protracted that thousands of people flocked to the square before the troops arrived. They erected barriers on the approach roads to prevent further troops arriving: but these impeded their own escape when the trouble began. The troops, who were without firearms, were deployed in a second line, behind riot police with shields and truncheons. They came into action when demonstrators made a breach in the line of riot police. That was when they used their spades. They were of course totally untrained in crowd control, and had no specialised equipment. Some riot control gas ('Cheremushka') was used, but nothing more lethal. The casualties were mainly due to panic and pressure in the crowd.

I remarked that this account sounded suspiciously like whitewash. But Yakovlev assured me that the commission had cross-examined all the relevant people, including Ligachev and Yazov, who had cooperated fully. The Georgians themselves, he said, were not dissatisfied with the report. Sobchak later wrote perceptively that the decision was an inevitable result of the 'collective irresponsibility which in the language of Party officials is called "collective decisionmaking". That is how the notorious "collective thinking" is born, the hive mentality of the System, which is more like an animal instinct than anything else.'[5]

Whatever the truth of the final report, the mere fact that a parliamentary commission had been able to take evidence and report on the activities of the executive branch was a breakthrough. Alas, the experiment was not repeated after the other bloody incidents which disfigured Gorbachev's last two years in office. By the standards of the twentieth century the Tbilisi massacre was a minor affair, comparable with the 'Boston Massacre' of 1773 when British troops killed eight Americans in a scuffle. But just as the American revolutionaries gained the martyrs they needed to lever the British out of North America, so the deaths in Tbilisi were a watershed in the increasingly volatile ethnic politics of the last years of Perestroika.

Even after the vicious little civil war which destroyed much of the main street around the parliament in the winter of 1991, despite the dreary Soviet-style suburbs built long after our first visit in 1964, Tbilisi remains a very beautiful small town, with its castle, its churches, its synagogue, and its wooden houses with balconies clinging to the crags of a ravine through which flows the River Kura. When we went there in the autumn of 1990 the Georgians were already sweeping away the traces of the old regime. In the centre of the town there was a green lawn opposite the City Council in Freedom (formerly Lenin) Square, where the statue of Lenin had stood until a few weeks earlier. The Institute of Marxism-Leninism was now the headquarters for the numerous parties and groupuscules which had been created in recent months. Our generous hosts were Bachi Begishvili and his wife Nino. Nino's brother, Alexander Toradze, a successful concert pianist, defected in 1983 while on tour in Spain. His father died a few weeks later from the shock. At first none of his friends would risk paying the traditional funeral respects. But then Shevardnadze, who was the Georgian Party Secretary at the time, ostentatiously came to the funeral, and all the friends flocked back.

Bachi and Nino showed us how much better the tight-knit Georgian elite lived than their opposite numbers in Moscow. They themselves lived in a private house built for Bachi's grandfather, an eminent Academician, near the centre of Tbilisi, with its own garden, vines and a fig tree. Nino's mother lived with them: a former actress, with the remains of quite exceptional beauty. A family friend, the elderly composer Aleksei Machavariani, lived in a large apartment on a tiny square between a Russian Orthodox church and a twelfth-century Georgian church. The music room was so large that it dwarfed the two concert grand pianos there. Machavariani came from Gori, Stalin's birthplace. Stalin's mother used to work in his parents' house. He was of the generation which believed that everyone was much more disciplined and honest in Stalin's day. Bachi pointed out that this was barely surprising: they were sent to the camps otherwise. Machavariani was not convinced.

The Georgian upper middle classes and intelligentsia spent their holidays in the sanatorium in Borzhomi, where Bachi's father had been deputy director. On the way there we called at Gori. The tiny house where Stalin was born was preserved under a marble canopy to protect it from the weather. The museum next to it had been 'closed for repair' for the last two years. But the huge statue of Stalin outside the town hall was still there in all its glory: perhaps the last in the whole of the Soviet Union. As we approached Borzhomi, the countryside became more beautiful. The valley narrowed, and at almost every turn a small castle dominated the road. The trees were just turning to Autumn. Great fat pigs wandered across the main road in the mountain villages. The petrol stations had notices saying 'Petrol' in English and Georgian, but not in Russian. Petrol was very short, as it was in Moscow. But Bachi had got the petrol for the trip from a friend – which is the way everything is done in Georgia. In Borzhomi we stayed in the middle of an extensive park in a small mock Renaissance palace which was built by a Romanov Grand Duke in 1893. The Romanov furniture and crockery were looted in the late 1960s by the local Party bosses. One of the remaining desks had a nail driven into it: Stalin used to hang his cap there during his visits. On the terrace outside was a small niche. On it was written: 'This bust of V. I. Lenin was placed here in September 1951 by order and in the presence of J. V. Stalin.' Only there was no bust, only a half-finished graffito in Georgian, the equivalent of 'Lenin woz here.'

Within a few months, by the Spring of 1991, public order, political behaviour, and relations between the Georgian majority and the South Ossetians, Abkhazians and other peoples who formed part of the Georgian 'empire', had all deteriorated. Violence was on the increase. Georgian national emotions were unscrupulously exploited by Gamsakhurdia, the intellectual and former dissident who had spent some time in a KGB prison, where evil tongues said he had learned to collaborate. We returned to Tbilisi on 31 March 1991, the election day for the Presidency of Georgia. I was buttonholed at the airport by a man skulking in a corner, who claimed to be from the Georgian Supreme Soviet. He gave me an invitation from Gamsakhurdia to his birthday party that evening. Carolyn Brown, the embassy's expert on the Caucasus who was with us, strongly advised me to turn it down – Gamsakhurdia was probably trying to exploit my presence. I thought the party would be fun and interesting, and accepted Carolyn's advice with great reluctance. But she was of course quite right. So we spent the rest of the day eating with Bachi and his family. In the late afternoon we called at the polling booth – set up in Bachi's old school – to watch him vote.

Gamsakhurdia won a smashing victory. We called on him the next day – April Fool's Day – at the parliament building. A knot of scruffy members of the new Georgian National Guard, in ill-fitting khaki uniforms with red berets, hung around the entrance fingering submachine-guns. Gamsakhurdia had recently survived an assassination attempt (though his enemies said he had staged it to gain the sympathy vote), and the security was doubtless necessary. But it produced an unpleasant effect. Gamsakhurdia himself was wearing a neat blue suit, and a carefully clipped grey moustache. He was surrounded by sycophants. He asked me if Georgia was losing sympathy abroad.

I told Gamsakhurdia that Western opinion supported the expansion of democracy and human rights in the Soviet Union. It sympathised with the desire of the republics to redefine their relationship with Moscow. But Western governments disapproved of his assault on human rights, and their sympathy for Georgia would certainly wane if he did not mend his ways.

Gamsakhurdia defended himself vigorously. It was all Moscow's fault. The Soviet government would not allow any Republic to secede. The shootings in Tbilisi, Baku, and Vilnius showed how far Moscow was prepared to go. Western support for Gorbachev simply helped to sustain Soviet imperialism. Foreign governments should recognise Georgia's independence immediately.

I answered that we could only recognise a state that had the practical attributes of independence. We were telling both Moscow and the republics that the way to independence was through negotiations which took account of the interests of all concerned.

Much of what Gamsakhurdia said was superficially reasonable. He was on his best behaviour, buttoned up both literally and figuratively: in superficial appearance far from the fanatic I had expected. But his eyes were cold blue and wild. There was an undertone of dangerous, even insane, extremism in everything he said. He was the nearest thing I ever met to a mad dictator. It was his policies that triggered the fighting which destroyed the centre of Tbilisi at the end of 1991. He later found an obscure death in a byway of the civil war which he had done so much to unleash.

The most brutal exercise of Soviet power in the last years of the regime occurred in Baku. It was far more bloody than Tbilisi, and is much less well remembered in the outside world. Following a massacre of Armenians in the Azerbaijani town of Sumgait, Azeri refugees from Nagorny Karabakh carried out a pogrom in Baku on 13 January 1990 in which about fifty Armenians were brutally killed. The next day there was a mass rally of protest in Yerevan, and an upsurge in the fight around Nagorny Karabakh with both sides using heavy weapons they had acquired from corrupt units of the Soviet army. The National Front, the anti-Communist Azeri independence movement, was now in charge in Azerbaijan: the Communist Party had been swept aside. On 18 January Moscow sent the army into Baku. The violence went far beyond anything that had happened since Gorbachev had come to power. Even the official reports admitted that about ninety people had been killed, including a dozen soldiers and two army wives. The real figure was almost certainly in excess of two hundred. Russians, Armenians, and Jews began to leave in droves. BBC television showed Russian mothers protesting against the call-up of reservists to fight in Azerbaijan. Two of the cleaning ladies at *Moscow News* told Yegor Yakovlev that they would make their husbands go into hiding rather than let them rejoin the colours.

Gorbachev and his officials told the outside world that the Soviet army had had to intervene to protect the Armenians from further massacre. Gorbachev was doubtless sincere. Western governments had no desire to make life difficult for him. The Americans had made it clear to him after the shootings in Tbilisi that they would understand if the Soviets used troops to restore law and order; but would condemn them if they used them to prevent free expression.[6] Mrs Thatcher repeated this assurance to Vadim Medvedev, the Politburo member, when he called on her in London a month after the Baku massacre. An effective central authority, she said, had to ensure law and order.

The truth was more complex. Shortly after the shootings, Vorontsov, the First Deputy Foreign Minister, told William Waldegrave that both sides were equally to blame. The Armenian decision in early December to incorporate Nagorny Karabakh formally into Armenia was bound to infuriate the Azeris who still lived there, and their relatives who had been forced into exile in Azerbaijan. For the sake of the one hundred and fifty thousand Armenians in Nagorny Karabakh, the Yerevan government had put at risk two hundred thousand Armenians living peacefully in Azerbaijan, who might all now become refugees. Moscow could not understand why the Armenians had been so rash.

But some people in Moscow had another agenda. Yazov boasted – indiscreetly, in public – that the troops went into Baku to clean up the National Front. Falin confirmed in private that Moscow's real objective was political and imperial, not humanitarian. The National Front, he said, was militarised, disciplined, hierarchical. It was seeking weapons, money and political contacts from Turkey, Iran, and 'further South'. Moscow had used moderate force to avoid thousands of casualties later. Falin did not dwell on the fact that the intervention had had the incidental advantage of restoring the Communists to power in Baku.

Baku is a charming and ancient city. There is a medieval fort in the centre, an old palace, ancient Turkish baths, mosques, and old houses. Along one side of the old city are the mansions built by Nobel, Gulbenkian and the other oil barons at the end of the nineteenth century. When we first went there in April 1991 all was in a sorry state of late-Soviet disrepair. And Baku has one disadvantage. It is built on an escarpment overlooking the flat seashore which is covered with nodding donkeys pumping out oil. The associated gas is not flared off, but simply escapes into the atmosphere, so that the whole place smells as if it will go up in a puff of smoke if somebody lights an incautious match. Nevertheless the first work of restoration had begun. Neat little restaurants were being set up in the old caravansarais. Communist symbols no longer dominated the city. Instead there was the new flag of Azerbaijan: blue, red, and green in horizontal stripes, with a star and crescent in the centre. Most of the shop signs were still in the Cyrillic script. But here and there the Turkish version of the Latin alphabet was coming into use, as a symbol of the country's reorientation.

President Mutalibov was a handsome and powerful man, put in by the Russians after the massacre the previous January. Quiet-spoken to the point of inaudibility, his discourse was larded with half-hearted appeals to Islam. His ambition was to build up Azerbaijan's links through Turkey to Europe. He criticised Gorbachev for not slapping the Armenians down when the troubles started in Nagorny Karabakh. Gorbachev talked plati-tudes about the Leninist policy of friendship between peoples. But Lenin was now outdated and irrelevant. Azerbaijan had enjoyed only 'puppet sovereignty' hitherto. That needed to change.

By contrast Prime Minister Gasan Gasanov was a noisy man, very plain, with spectacles. He talked very fast and in the broadest of generalities: the official bully who prefers to bluster rather than to commit himself to a concrete and possibly risky proposition. He believed that Azerbaijan could be the Abu Dhabi of the Caspian if the Russians would only get out of the way. At dinner he hardly stopped talking for a moment: anyone of any importance in European or Middle Eastern history was in fact a Turk; there was no risk of Islamic fundamentalism; but Islamic countries were more moral than Western ones because polygamy reduced the pressure for extra-marital affairs. His wife, remarkably blonde for an Azerbaijani, remained bored and silent. I found it hard to judge whether he was a serious figure. But his proven capacity to hang on to office of one kind or another despite subsequent changes of regime showed that he had important political skills.

In May 1991 we stayed in Kabardino-Balkaria, one of the five 'Autonomous Republics' of the North Caucasus, with our friends Sasha and Marina Chudakov. Sasha was a member of the Soviet Academy of Sciences. For nearly twenty years he had been conducting a massive experiment deep in a huge artificial cavern hollowed out of the mountain granite in the shadow of Mount Elbruz, the highest peak in Europe. The experiment was intended to catch and to count neutrinos (elusive sub-atomic particles emitted by the sun) as they flashed through dozens of tanks of petrol armed with photoelectric sensors. So far Sasha had had few significant results. Neither had the Americans who were conducting a similarly grandiose experiment on the other side of the world.

In 1943 the Balkash were deported to Central Asia with the Chechens, the Ingush, and the other peoples of the North Caucasus whom Stalin considered less than whole-hearted in their opposition to the German invasion. Many thousands died on the trains and on the march: our friend Anatoli Pristavkin described the scenes in his semi-autobiographical novel *The Little Golden Cloud*. Marina's friend Djemiliat, who lived just up the valley, had had to leave her cattle and all her possessions behind when the soldiers came. She took four small children with her, and acquired seven more in Central Asia. When she and the others returned home in 1958 they had to rebuild everything from scratch. Djemiliat's youngest daughter Asiat, a plump young woman with red boots and a baby, had recently got married in the traditional way. A young man from a neighbouring village kidnapped her and carried her off into the mountains on his motorbike: in earlier years it would have been a horse. Her family thoroughly approved: Asiat was already becoming too familiar with the married men of the village. Djemiliat's youngest son Khazir was getting restive in a different way. Despite Perestroika no real elections had yet been held in the valley. Everything, he said fiercely, was still being run from Moscow in the same old way. He was sick of it.

For centuries the Russians thought it essential to hold the North Caucasus as a jumping off place and barrier against the Turkish and Persian empires to the South: the equivalent of India's North West frontier. They were not too subtle about the means by which they held it. In his short novel about the Russian conquest of the Caucasus, *Hadji Murat*, Tolstoy describes a Chechen village ruined by Russian soldiers.

> The village elders gathered on the square and squatted down to consider their situation. Nobody spoke of hating the Russians. From the youngest to the oldest, every Chechen experienced a feeling that was stronger than hatred. It was not hatred, but a refusal to recognise that the Russians were even human. It was a feeling of such revulsion, of such disgust, of such incomprehension in the face of the absurd brutality of those

creatures, that the desire to destroy them, like the desire to destroy a rat, a poisonous spider, or a wolf, was as natural as the instinct of self preservation.[7]

As the Soviet empire frayed to pieces, it was increasingly clear that the real fighting would take place on the Caucasian watershed.

Ukraine was the core of all that was ambiguous about the old Russian empire. Even sensible Russians found it hard to accept that Ukraine was a separate place. They were brought up to believe that Russian history flowed in a direct line from medieval Kiev through Muscovy to the Empire of Peter and Catherine, to the Soviet Union, and to the Russia of today. The very word 'Ukraine', they would tell you, meant 'Borderland': it was not the name of a real country. The Ukrainian language, they added, was no more than an old-fashioned and inadequate dialect of peasant Russian. That is why Ukraine's best authors, they believed, preferred to write in Russian rather than their native tongue. Russians could not understand why such a non-country should be separated from the Russian heartland. In their heart of hearts hardly any of them believed that the separation could last.

Many Ukrainians also lacked confidence in the durability of their country, and with some reason. After the Kievan empire was shattered into fragments by the Tatars, Ukraine rarely had more than a few brief and unsatisfactory years as an independent state. The Ukrainian lands were exposed to perpetual invasion from Russians, Turks, Tatars, Cossacks, Poles, Swedes and Germans. The Poles and the Jesuits attempted to subvert the Ukrainian Orthodox Church by creating the Greek Catholic (Uniate) Church, which preserved the Orthodox liturgy while recognising the authority of the Pope. What started as the product of a political manoeuvre became a genuine Church, for which its adherents were willing to lay down their lives. The Ukrainian lands were reunited from 1569 to 1648, but only under Polish sovereignty. The Cossack Hetman Khmelnitsky tried to break free from Poland and signed a Union with Muscovy in 1654. He exchanged the frying pan for the fire. After his victory at Poltava in 1709, Peter the Great stripped Ukraine of its remaining pretensions to autonomy. The Tsars did what they could to russify Ukraine. Even the liberal Alexander II banned the printing of books in Ukrainian and its use in higher education. Taras Shevchenko, Ukraine's most famous writer, was sent into exile in Central Asia as a common soldier. Only in Western Ukraine, which the Austrians had carved out of Poland at the end of the eighteenth century, were the Ukrainians able to develop in comparative freedom.

Despite these oppressions, Ukrainians found the strength and organisation to create an independent state after the Tsarist collapse. But after briefly allying themselves with the Poles against the Bolsheviks, they were double-crossed by both in 1921, and their country was divided once again. Western Ukraine became an underprivileged and oppressed part of the Polish Republic. The fate of Soviet Ukraine was very much worse. Some six million Ukrainians died in the artificial famine which Stalin induced to enforce collectivisation in 1932 and 1933. The whole of the Ukrainian Communist leadership and much of the Ukrainian intelligentsia were killed in the purges. Khrushchev – secretary of the Ukrainian Party from 1938 – reimposed a brutal policy of Russification. When the Soviet Union annexed Western Ukraine under its agreement with Nazi Germany in 1939 hundreds of thousands of people were deported, exiled or murdered during the two years before the German invasion. It was not surprising that many Ukrainians welcomed the Germans when they came in 1941. But their hopes were misplaced. The Germans intended to use Ukraine simply as a source of raw materials and slave labour. Between five and seven million Ukrainians died in the fighting and the massacres. And when the war was over, a guerrilla war continued between Ukrainian nationalists and the Soviet army, and the repressions resumed.

After Stalin's death there was a respite. Shelest became the first Ukrainian to head the Ukrainian Communist Party. In 1954 the Soviet authorities celebrated the three hundredth anniversary of Khmelnitsky's Treaty, and made Ukraine a present of the Crimea, which the Russians had taken from the Turks in 1783, and where few Ukrainians had ever lived. But by now a younger and less docile generation of Ukrainian intellectuals was emerging. Under Brezhnev the repressions resumed. Dissidents were exiled, imprisoned, and in a few cases executed. Shelest was sacked to make way for Shcherbitsky, a hardliner loyal to Moscow. Once again Ukrainian-language periodicals were closed, and the Russification of education was resumed. These actions continued into the 1980s. Meanwhile Russians, already preponderant in the East around Kharkov, in the Crimea and on the Black Sea coast, were moving into Ukraine in ever larger numbers. Until Gorbachev removed Shcherbitsky from the Politburo in September 1989, Ukraine remained to all appearances the model of an old-fashioned Soviet republic. The appearance was deceptive. The superficial calm that Shcherbitsky had maintained was rapidly coming to an end.

Kiev stands on a green escarpment on the West bank of the Dnieper River. As you approach it across the flat plain, you see the golden domes of the ancient monastery, the 'Lavra of the Caves', the tower of Santa Sophia, founded in the eleventh century in imitation of its namesake in Constantinople, one church after another shining out dramatically from the dark foliage. It is one of the great cityscapes of the world. The effect is marred by the huge victory monument of 'Mother Ukraine'. It towers over the whole, a memorial to the vulgarity of Brezhnev's last years, vast, tasteless, and ripe to be dismantled after the last veteran is finally laid to rest. Young couples come to be photographed at its base on their wedding days, as they come to 'Alyosha' in Murmansk. Several lucky couples were photographed with Mrs Thatcher when she visited the place in June 1990, a matriarchal blessing they will never forget.

Kiev feels quite different from Moscow. The stately apartment buildings, the boulevards lined with chestnuts, could come from nineteenth-century Vienna. In the summer the youngsters stroll and eye one another along the city's central street, the Kreshchatik, or laze on the golden banks of the Dnieper. It is pure Mitteleuropa, a city on a human scale. Little cafés, theatres, and picture galleries – a small dilapidated Chelsea – run down the steep cobbled street where Bulgakov, the author of *The Master and Margarita*, had his home. His house at no. 13 was the scene of much of *The White Guard*, his novel about Kiev in 1918. It is now a charming museum, run by the usual enthusiastic women. By 1990 the new Museum of Lenin – an anachronism almost from the moment it was built – was showing an exhibition of contemporary Russian paintings saved from the destruction to which they had been condemned by a Soviet judge. The historical museum had an exhibition about Solzhenitsyn, 'From Gulag to Nobel Prize'. A series of small snooks cocked at the Soviet regime. There was also, so we were assured by a local driver, an exhibition about flying saucers. Part of it, he said, was devoted to the metre-long rats which had recently appeared in Moscow. These rats had bullet-proof skins, and could gnaw though the bars if they were imprisoned in cages. We would have liked to visit the exhibition, but had no time.

There are other monuments to the past as well: the mass graves at Borispol, where the NKVD buried over two hundred thousand victims; and the ravine at Babi Yar, now a park in a suburb of the city not all that far from the centre, where one hundred and fifty thousand people, mostly Jews, were killed by the Germans.

The British planned to hold a major commercial exhibition in Kiev in June 1990. We feared that it might get caught in the political crossfire as the Ukrainian nationalists began to make their presence felt. Like the Balts, they were flaunting their traditional colours: the yellow and blue flag of independent Ukraine. Would they cause trouble if we failed to use it in the exhibition logo? Would the Soviet authorities cause trouble if we did? William Waldegrave went down to Kiev to sort things out. Our official calls showed that the wind was already blowing in a new direction. Anatoli Zlenko, the smooth and handsome Deputy Foreign Minister, asserted that everyone in Ukraine now wanted greater political autonomy. Indeed, he admitted, ever more people were pushing for full political independence. This was not yet a majority view, he said. But he did not seem to find it shocking. Yelchenko, the Second Secretary of the Ukrainian Communist Party responsible for ideology, a huge, florid elephant of a man, the very picture of a provincial Party boss, gave us a lumbering rendering of the Perestroika tune. It did not come easily to him. The Ukrainian Party leadership had been accused, he said, of excessive conservatism. But Ukraine too was exposed to the storms of change: the miners' strike, Chernobyl, environmentalist pressure, increasing nationalist emotion. Ukrainians had died fighting in both just and unjust causes. The Ukrainian intelligentsia had been all but wiped out by three waves of terror since the October Revolution. The Ukrainian Party had now come to terms with the existence of the main nationalist movement, Narodny Rukh. But the wounds of the past were being inflamed, especially amongst the young, by separatists and others, who were anti-Party, anti-Soviet, and secessionist. Ukraine's future lay in maximum political and economic autonomy within the Union. The situation in Ukraine was fundamentally stable. The Party was in control. It was trying to find common ground with other political elements. But it knew where the 'negative forces' were. That final remark held an obvious note of menace. But as a whole it was a remarkable statement for an orthodox Party official. Yelchenko seemed genuinely moved. Perhaps, I thought, he was a real Ukrainian after all.

That evening we dined in a hunting lodge on the edge of Kiev with his political opponents, Ivan Drach, the president of Narodny Rukh and his colleagues. The older men were cautious. The younger ones muttered about national independence. The evening ended with folk-dancing and innumerable toasts. Waldegrave incautiously raised his glass to 'Ukrainian independence'. In an echo of *Yes, Minister,* a British official intervened to suggest that what the minister *really* meant to toast was 'Ukrainian cultural independence'. 'Not at all,' said Waldegrave firmly, and raised his glass again. In later years I used to remind the Rukh leaders that it was the British who first gave official support to the independence of Ukraine.

Princess Anne opened the exhibition in Kiev at the beginning of June. We stayed in a government guesthouse in the centre of the city, round the corner from the Ukrainian parliament, a handsome neo-classical building built after the Second World War. The parliament (in Ukrainian, the Supreme Rada) were in the throes of electing a new Chairman. There were nine candidates, including Drach and Ivashko, Shcherbitsky's successor as First Secretary of the Ukrainian Party. The building was picketed by demonstrators carrying the Ukrainian national flag and slogans denouncing Ivashko as a Party hack. Slightly farther off, in October Square by the monument of Lenin, knots of people were growling about independence. In the Supreme Rada itself rows flared between the Ukrainian-speakers and Russian deputies. The nationalists committed a classic error. They had insisted that Ivashko renounce the Party Secretaryship before standing as Chairman. When he refused, they stormed out of the hall. So he got about 270 votes, and the next candidate about 40. If the nationalists had stayed on to vote, they would have formed a solid bloc against Ivashko. He would have had to take account of them even if elected.

When the results came out, the crowds roared in protest. They jeered at the deputies as they crept back to their hotel. One indignant woman was haranguing a militiaman: the Party apparat had fixed the result; her son and daughter-in-law had been held by plain-clothes men after the demonstrations. The militiaman seemed sympathetic. Konstantin Demakhin joined us. I asked if this was a revolution or merely another riot. He said that the people were just getting into practice.

A week later we flew back to Kiev with Mrs Thatcher. Ivashko inveigled her into addressing the Rada. To her surprise she found the hemicycle full (why it should have been a surprise, given her reputation, I do not know). But, she wrote later, 'I managed well enough, as I always do.' She improvised a firm lecture on the rule of law and took successful evasive action when a bearded representative of the parliamentary group of ex-political prisoners asked her to comment on the local politics. She was less successful when she was asked to open an embassy in Kiev. She replied that she could no more open an independent embassy in Kiev than she could in San Francisco. The nationalist deputies never forgave her.

In the evening we attended a gala performance by the English National Opera of Handel's *Xerxes*. We were all staggering with fatigue. Afterwards the over-officious KGB security officers tried to prevent the Prime Minister going backstage to meet the cast, on the grounds that they had not reconnoitred the route. We brushed them aside. A young student invited me home to tea, but was disappointed to discover that I was not, after all, Jack Matlock. After the show we drove twenty miles out of Kiev to the official guesthouse built by Shcherbitsky for himself: huge tasteless luxury in wooded parkland. The furniture and decorations were dreadful, stags at bay in every room. The buildings and woodland were guarded by at least a company of uniformed and plain-clothes KGB, despite the absence of any conceivable threat. The security on the road to the airport next day was equally heavy. Konstantin Demakhin said that the Ukrainians were more disciplined and harder working than the Russians: 'They make the best corporals in the army. They always carry out any order to the letter, however stupid.'

As the exhibition ended the Ukrainians went over to Ukrainian time, one hour ahead of Moscow: another gesture of independence from Russia.

Two months later, on our way back from our holiday in the Summer of 1990, we drove to Lvov: Austrian before 1918, Polish before 1939, now the capital of Soviet Western Ukraine. We were turned away from the old-fashioned hotel in the centre of the city, because it had entirely run out of water. So we stayed in the huge Soviet hotel on the top of the hill, dominated by two immense radio aerials, formerly used for jamming foreign broadcasts. Lvov was pure Central Europe, quite unlike the Soviet Union apart from the empty shops. Before the war a third of the population had been Jewish – now there were only 14,000 Jews left. The Polish population had also largely disappeared, though there remained two Polish churches. There were mass graves outside Lvov, as outside Minsk and Kiev: and here too the NKVD were as guilty of the massacres as the SS. Postwar industrialisation trebled the population to over a million. In the centre of the city were the offices of the Pushkin Society and the Sakharov Society. The latter, our Ukrainian guide told us, was 'progressive'; the former was definitely not. In Lvov, as in Weimar, the Russian nationalists used Pushkin as a symbol of imperial power, and the locals did not like it.

Hard by our hotel on the hill was the baroque St George's Cathedral. The Russian Orthodox Church took it over when Western Ukraine was annexed to the Soviet Union. Now it had been returned to the Greek Catholics. I was shown around by their Metropolitan, Volodymyr, a plump eighty-year-old, with a white beard, in a black cassock. He studied theology in the West, was imprisoned by the Soviet authorities after 1946 for five years and then worked as storekeeper and watchman. He practised under cover and did not openly declare his priesthood until 1988. From St George's, he took me to the Cathedral of the Transfiguration in the centre of the city. The Uniates had taken it back in the Spring without fuss: one fine day the Orthodox congregation and all the Orthodox priests but one simply announced that henceforward they would regard themselves as Greek Catholics. Afterwards Volodymyr took me to his home: one small room in which he had been living for thirty years. Since he had became a bishop the courtyard of his block of flats had been paved in his honour.

The representatives of Rukh had assured us that there would be no ethnic unrest in an independent Ukraine, despite the country's history of anti-Semitism and bloodshed between Poles and Ukrainians. The Chairman of the Lvov Town Council said the same thing. My doubts were not allayed when we called on the offices of the local nationalist newspaper, *Za Vilnu Ukrainu* ('For a Free Ukraine'). It had been set up only three months earlier, and its tone was extreme. The editor was a smooth, foxy-faced man with a beard and an untrustworthy manner. His deputy was a mad archaeologist. He claimed that the Scots and the Ukrainians were both descended from the Scythians. The Russians, he said, were 'genetically' different, which is why they were uncivilised, brutal, and had an inbuilt propensity to run concentration camps.

The bust of Lenin had already been removed from the front hall of the old municipal building. The leaders of the local Communist Party now occupied only one floor. They were a shadow of their former selves, defensive and apologetic. They admitted that the Party had committed crimes in the past. They accepted that it could no longer expect a privileged position in the competition with other parties. They had been big, confident men of power. Now they had no real role in the life of the city. I felt almost sorry for them.

The men who had usurped their position now occupied the rest of the building: Davymukha, the Chairman of the Regional Council, an impressive young man who had been an electronics engineer, and his three deputies, Ivan Hel (who had spent seventeen years in the camps); Mikhail Kosiv, a poet; and Igor Yukhnovsky, a physicist and leader of the opposition in the Rada. Davymukha believed, he said, in a gradual and orderly progress towards a market system and towards full sovereignty for Ukraine. Ukraine should have its own money, bank, and customs as soon as possible, even though this was against the trend in Western Europe towards greater integration. Ukraine could not have cooperative common market arrangements with other republics or with the Soviet Union until it had sufficient real sovereignty to negotiate on an equal basis. In Lvov this was the general view. Even the Communists on the floor above agreed with the declarations on sovereignty and economic autonomy which had been passed by the Supreme Rada on 16 July. These ideas were not yet fully accepted in Kiev, where Party hacks like Ivashko were still desperate to hold the Union together. But within a year they had become commonplace.

In the Spring of 1991 I went back to Ukraine with Douglas Hurd. As a result of the political upheavals of the previous Summer and Autumn

Kravchuk had replaced Ivashko as Chairman of the Ukranian Supreme Soviet, and the smooth Zlenko was now Foreign Minister. They radiated a feeling of confidence in themselves and their country's future. Kravchuk had the thickset Ukrainian look and a benign air. He had the reputation of a Party hack: as regional Party Secretary he had been one of the most active agents of Russification in the Western Ukraine. He now told Hurd that there should be no iron curtain between Ukraine and Moscow. But Ukraine must be an equal partner. It must own and control all the capital assets and natural resources on its territory. It must collect all taxes, passing on an agreed portion to the centre. Direct taxation by the centre must come to an end. For seventy years the Party and the government had been amalgamated in a cruel and totalitarian system. The bureaucrats at the centre were hanging on to their positions 'like fleas in wool'. The Ukrainian deputies were still servile when they had to tackle difficult issues, 'round-eyed with fear' at the thought of what Moscow or the Central Committee of the Ukrainian Party might say. All this was from a man who had spent his whole career loyally executing Moscow's policy in Ukraine. I nevertheless found him a refreshing and formidable politician. Nine months later he would manoeuvre his country into independence.

Even as the rest of the Soviet Union opened up, the politics of the Central Asian republics remained obscure. Ostensibly they had the same state institutions as the other Union Republics: a Communist Party, a Supreme Soviet, an Academy of Sciences, a Ministry of Foreign Affairs, and their local branch of the KGB. But this was in part a facade behind which the politics of powerful and ancient clans continued to operate in the shadows. In the Perestroika years there was violence in Central Asia too. In 1986 there were riots in Alma Ata against the imposition of a Russian as First Secretary of the Kazakh Party. Otherwise the violence was usually sporadic, and communal rather than political. In 1992 a destructive civil war began in Tajikistan, fuelled by intrigues across the border with Afghanistan. But for the most part the Party leaders in the Central Asian republics were confident of their power, conscious of the advantages of the Moscow connection, willing to bide their time and to change their spots when that seemed expedient.

In April 1990 my family and I travelled to Kazakhstan and Kirghizia, half work and half play. My departure was held up at the last minute by official business. Jill and the others went off in advance. Conveniently this meant that I missed a ceremony at which I would have had to carve up a sheep's head and eat the eye. Jill conducted herself gallantly in my place. I arrived in Alma Ata in the late evening and went straight from the airport to visit the parents of Marat Bisengaliev, the young Kazakh violinist with whom I used to play music in Moscow. The Bisengalievs, whose family had been musicians for two hundred years, lived in a small bungalow on the outskirts of the city, with a yurt, sheep and goats in the back garden, and pictures of the British royal family inside. The old man had been a railway engineer, and showed us a photograph of himself and his wife as young students in St Petersburg. Now he wore a *tiubeteika* on his head, and accompanied his wife on the two-stringed *dombra* while she sang Kazakh songs with such enthusiasm that her false teeth shot out, and she had to shove them back in mid-phrase. Their five-year-old granddaughter sang *Alouette* in English. A small grandson played *Twinkle, Twinkle, Little Star* on a miniature violin: ten years later Amir was already becoming a formidable concert soloist. Marat lent me a splendid Tyrolese viola which he had borrowed from the Conservatoire, and we played Schumann with two of his friends. Afterwards we had a huge meal – sheep, pasta, and dozens of toasts. A 'representative of the Foreign Ministry's Protocol Department' hung around throughout, an offensive young man who persisted in lecturing the Bisengalievs on the correct way to address me. Marat told me years later that the local authorities had visited them in advance to offer a complete set of new furniture to make the place suitable for entertaining an ambassador. The Bisengalievs had naturally refused. During the evening itself the surrounding woods had been full of watching police cars. In such ways the secret policemen reminded people that things hadn't yet changed all that much. But even in Kazakhstan there were no longer serious consequences.

In Frunze, the capital of Kirghizia (now Bishkek, the capital of Kyrgyzstan) we spent a night in a luxurious government guesthouse in an orchard outside the town, and were then driven to Lake Issyk Kul in a caravan consisting of two police cars, a Chaika limousine, three Volgas, and a special ambulance containing three nurses, whose particular responsibility was to ensure that I did not drop dead of a heart attack. We stayed at another marble guesthouse in the resort village of Cholpon Ata. We were given a huge double bedroom with a sunken bath, had the run of a winter garden, a cinema, a banqueting hall and an excellent restaurant, and above all a stupendous view over the lake and the Northern slopes of the Himalayas. Other recent guests had included two Presidents of Finland and Rajiv Gandhi. The luxury was positively Romanian.

These pleasures left me little time for official business. In Alma Ata my main official call was on Nursultan Nazarbaev, the First Party Secretary and Chairman of the Supreme Soviet of Kazakhstan. I found him formidable but not charming: he improved on subsequent occasions. He believed that rapid reform was needed to solve the country's many problems. He still thought that the Party knew best. 'We will keep our hands on the reins of power. No one in Kazakhstan seriously wants to set up rival parties.' He favoured economic autonomy for the Republic and much greater freedom for business. He was standing for election as President of Kazakhstan a few days later. No one expected him to lose.

In Bishkek I called on the Prime Minister and the Foreign Minister. Prime Minister Djumagulov was a softer, more talkative man than Nazarbaev. He too spoke of the growing economic autonomy of his Republic. There was an immense ethnic mix, but no ethnic strife, he claimed, and little demand for alternative political organisations (murderous communal violence broke out the week after we left). People wanted to restore the Kyrgyz traditions. An edition of *Manas* was coming out at last, the national epic about the liberation of Kirghizia from the Chinese, which was a thousand years old and longer than the *Odyssey* and *Iliad* combined. I found it difficult to know what to make of him. He must have been tough, despite his mild exterior. And he was less informative than he seemed. At the Kyrgyz Foreign Minister's lunch the most talkative speaker was Nedet Shiremkulov, the Second Secretary of the Kyrgyz Central Committee. He spoke in honour of Lenin, whose birthday was the following Sunday. Some thought that Lenin was a dictator, some that he was responsible for the repressions, but Shiremkulov thought that Lenin was the great leader who had introduced Socialism, the future for all mankind. Even in April 1990 that was an anachronistic view.

At the beginning of 1990 London asked for my assessment of the state of the Union. I repeated my standard line. Reform bred resistance. A coup against Gorbachev was possible. By definition, a successful coup would be one whose manner and timing no one had predicted. I drew particular attention to the worsening situation in the Baltic States, especially Lithuania. Moscow might allow the Balts to leave the Union in peace. But we needed to decide in advance our public line if Gorbachev used force. We might be able to acquiesce in a forceful restoration of law and order. But the use of force to suppress the legitimate political aspirations of the Baltic peoples would be another matter. I commented that it would be a difficult distinction to make. Two weeks later we faced just that difficulty over the shootings in Baku.

Throughout 1990 Gorbachev's room for manoeuvre got steadily narrower. Moscow applied economic pressure against Lithuania. It produced no effect. Lithuania declared its sovereignty on 11 March. Russia followed suit on 12 June; Ukraine on 16 July; Belorussia on 27 July; Tatarstan in August. These acts were symbolic. Even at that stage 'sovereignty', for all except the Balts meant autonomy within a confederation, rather than outright independence. But on 13 January 1991 Soviet special forces stormed the television tower in Vilnius, the capital of Lithuania. Thirteen people were killed, more than a hundred wounded. The casualty list was far smaller than it had been in Baku a year earlier. But the outrage both abroad and at home was far greater. Chernyaev asked me sarcastically whether the West worried less about dead Muslims in Baku than about dead Christians in Vilnius.

The Vilnius shootings marked the turning point. Opinion in the republics became intransigent. Gorbachev had finally lost the initiative. But he fought on. In a desperate attempt to rally public opinion behind him he announced a referendum on the future of the Soviet Union. On 17 March 1991 the Soviet people would be asked: 'Do you consider it necessary to preserve the Union of Soviet Socialist Republics as a renewed federation of equal sovereign republics, in which the rights and freedoms of people of all nationalities will be guaranteed in full measure?' These rights and freedoms, Gorbachev announced, would be preserved and protected by the new 'Union Treaty' which he would negotiate with the fifteen constituent republics of the USSR.

A month before the referendum I called on Yeltsin with Tony Longrigg, the head of the embassy's internal political section. For the first time I noticed the fingers missing from his left hand, blown off when he played as a boy with a hand-grenade he had found. He looked fitter than usual, and his judgements were statesmanlike. But he was less ebullient and less sure of himself: possibly, I thought, a result of the relentless campaign of denigration and dirty tricks to which he was still exposed. He spoke quietly for nearly an hour, referring to Gorbachev only as 'Him'. He repeated his conviction that the Union should be preserved. But it needed to be organised on a new basis: from the bottom up, not from the top down. Russia was developing direct relationships with other republics. He would not try to stop the referendum going ahead. But in addition to Gorbachev's question, the voters in the RSFSR would be asked if they wanted to elect their own President by universal suffrage.

The proposal was a masterstroke. Gorbachev tried to prevent Yeltsin from advocating it to the electorate. He was denied time on the television. Instead he spoke brilliantly on Radio Russia. He repeated his support for the Union. But the real question was: What sort of Union? Were the various Republics to be kept in by force? Or was it to be a voluntary Union, which

Republics could leave if they wanted? Gorbachev was asking people to vote for a Socialist Union. But what if they wanted a non-Socialist Union? Gorbachev was asking people if they wanted the Union to observe human rights. But, Yeltsin justly observed, the government should guarantee human rights whether there was a Union or not. Were we to assume that people who voted against the Union were therefore in favour of violating human rights? Yeltsin concluded with a rousing appeal to the people to vote for himself as President of Russia.

On the eve of the referendum we went with Olga Trifonova, the widow of one of the best Soviet authors of the 1970s, to see Chekhov's estate at Melikhovo, about sixty miles south of Moscow. In the nearby town was a churchyard with the graves of Pushkin's son and daughter. Pushkin's daughter died in 1919, two years after the October Revolution. Despite the Pushkin cult which dominates every physical trace of the poet's life, the graves were in a state of almost total disrepair. The weather was horrid: rain, slush, and mud. Chekhov's dacha was set in lovely and typical Russian countryside. But it was a fake. It had burned down several times, and was reconstructed by Avdeyev, a scholar blinded in the war. His wife guided him through the long battle with the authorities to get a state farm off the land, and restore it to what it had been in Chekhov's day. He had since died, and the new curator was another heroic museum lady.

Olga asked me how she should vote the next day. I said that I did not know, the diplomatically correct answer: it was not for me to interfere in Soviet domestic politics. But it was also true: I had no idea what would be the best vote for Russia. Gorbachev had tried to turn the referendum into a vote of confidence. If he 'won', that is if he got a 'Yes' vote from more than half of those eligible – it would mean very little. He might claim he had a mandate for harsh action on the economy and against the dissident republics. But that would cut little ice with ordinary people who already objected to their economic suffering, or with the dissident republics, most of whom had said they intended to ignore the result anyway. If he got less than half the votes it would be a disaster for him: Yuri Afanasiev suggested that he might then try to fake the result. As for Yeltsin, it would be a triumph if he got substantially more than half the votes for the creation of a Russian presidency; and a disaster if he got less. But he would have little difficulty in demonstrating that the vote on the Union was meaningless, whatever the result. Perhaps, I thought, the best thing would be a majority for both questions.

That is indeed what happened. A substantial number of the Soviet electorate supported the Union. But the Russians were equally in favour of electing their own President. Four days later I called with Douglas Hurd on both Gorbachev and Yeltsin. From time to time Gorbachev radiated his usual shafts of charm. But in the longer stretches between he looked gloomy and unresponsive: a notable change. He thought the opposition would now try to destabilise the situation. There would be fierce political battles. He would permit no further disintegration in the structures of the state. But he was determined to press ahead with change. The process would take more than one government and more than one generation. Nevertheless, 'We're crawling into a profound reform.' The referendum had shown that most people wanted the Soviet Union to survive. With amazing self-deception – based on the distorted information fed to him by Kryuchkov – he claimed that even the Balts and the Caucasians wanted to stay in the Union: it was the local authorities who prevented them from voting freely. Now there would have to be negotiations for a new 'Union Treaty', in the first instance with the nine Republics that had clearly voted 'Yes'. Different Republics could negotiate different arrangements for themselves: in the Tsarist empire, after all, Poland, Finland, and Bukhara had all had a different status. He now reluctantly accepted that Republics which wanted to leave the Union should be able to do so, provided they were prepared to negotiate about such matters as minority rights, strategic affairs, and economic links. The process would be painful. But 'we'll have to travel this road in the near future.' Hurd told Gorbachev firmly that we disapproved of what had recently happened in the Baltic States. But the disintegration of the Soviet Union would be bad for all of us. He told the press that Britain therefore strongly supported 'a renewed and voluntary Union'. When we compared notes afterwards, I said that I still did not believe that Gorbachev was about to institute genuine negotiations with the Balts. Hurd disagreed.

Yeltsin told us ponderously that everything had turned for the worse since Hurd had last called on him in September 1990. Gorbachev had thrown in his lot with the conservatives. He had persuaded the Soviet parliament to reject the 500 Days plan for rapid economic reform. After the Baltic shootings he had acquiesced in a frontal attack on Glasnost, worse than in Brezhnev's time. Yeltsin had been forced to distance himself. Russia, he said, was now working on its own economic reform plan: and he gave us a lecture on supply-side economics that was breathtaking in its simplicity. But Yeltsin too, insisted yet again that the Union should be preserved. He had never doubted that most people would vote for the Union. He was prepared to negotiate. But the draft Treaty proposed by Gorbachev was inadequate. The proposed distribution of functions between the centre and the republics would not do. Six republics would not remain in the Union at all. Several others would refuse to call themselves 'Socialist'. The central leadership would then adopt even more severe policies. He and Gorbachev represented two irreconcilable approaches. He believed that the totalitarian system now had to be destroyed: not by force, but by legal and constitutional means. There was no risk of civil war, he said, though Gorbachev kept trying to make everyone's flesh creep. The important thing now was the election of the Russian president, an idea which 70 per cent of the Russian electorate had supported in the referendum.

As we left Hurd remarked that Yeltsin was a 'dangerous man', barely under control. But Yeltsin's analysis was after all correct. Gorbachev was by now living almost entirely in cloud-cuckoo-land. The referendum did nothing to clarify the relationship between the centre and the republics. At the best it provided a basis for Gorbachev's gallant, tortuous, and ultimately abortive attempt to negotiate a 'Union Treaty', a federal or confederal agreement between the republics which would preserve the shadow of the Union. By far the most significant result of the referendum was that it opened the way to the popular vote on 12 June 1991 which propelled Yeltsin into the Russian presidency, and gave him the moral supremacy over Gorbachev and the legitimacy to defy the putsch in August.

The Russian empire was an organism with very tough roots, put together over nearly a thousand years by a complex process of war, peaceful colonisation, exploration and settlement. Russians lived not only in the metropolis, but in large numbers outside the ancient lands of Russia itself, where they felt as much at home as they would have done in Moscow. The Russian empire was not a maritime empire, where the distinction between colonies and metropolis is absolute and defined by the oceans. Thus the comparison was not with British India, where at the end all the colonists had to do was to get onto their ships and sail home. It was with the continental empires of Austria-Hungary and Turkey, with Canada and North America.

These comparisons are not easily accepted by those who believe that the Russians are a uniquely imperial people. They forget that, as Samuel Huntingdon remarks (in a no doubt unconscious echo of Sergei Witte's musings on the nature of Russian power in the epigraph to chapter 5), 'The West won the world not by the superiority of its ideas or values or religion (to which few members of other civilizations were converted) but rather by its superiority in applying organized violence. Westerners often forget this fact; non-Westerners never do.'[8]

The collapse of the Russian empire was attended by much less bloodshed than the collapse of the European empires overseas. Most of that blood was shed, not by the imperial power, but as a result of strife between ethnic groups which the imperial power was unwilling or unable to prevent. The largest single massacre committed by Soviet forces – the killings in Baku in January 1990 – resulted in substantially fewer deaths than the massacre at Amritsar committed by British troops in 1919. The casualties inflicted by Soviet troops in Vilnius in 1991 were similar to those inflicted by British paratroopers on Bloody Sunday in Londonderry in 1972. The Russians continued to intrigue beyond the frontiers, in the Caucasus, in Moldova, in Central Asia. In Western Europe we learned fifty years ago that it is no longer acceptable to invade Belgium or Luxembourg whenever we feel like it. Russian rhetoric, especially about the Baltic States, gives the impression that the Russians have not yet learned the same lesson in the East. Until they do, they will continue to be feared by their neighbours. But when it comes to deeds, not words, they have not – apart from the bloody and bungled intervention in Chechnya – made a serious attempt to reassert their imperial claims. Like the corpse of a frog connected to an electric battery, the remnants of empire gave the occasional galvanic twitch. But the imperial drive was dead.

7

The Lurch to the Right

Things fall apart; the centre cannot hold;
Mere anarchy is loosed upon the world.

W. B. Yeats, *The Second Coming*

Gorbachev's strategic aim was always reform – how far-reaching he was not at first sure. But his tactic was to occupy the centre ground. He drew support from the radicals or the reactionaries, whichever served his purpose of the moment, and he set the extremists against one another whenever it seemed expedient. But from the Summer of 1989 this tactic began to turn sour. Gorbachev was less and less the master of events. He no longer manoeuvred. He vacillated, inclining now to the one wing, now to the other. By the end of 1990 – what Chernyaev called 'the lost year' – he was roundly distrusted by both.

Funerals punctuated the decline. Gromyko died in July 1989. The political turmoil in Moscow was at its height. Stalin's European empire, to the preservation of which Gromyko had devoted his career, was beginning to break up. Stalin recruited Gromyko into the Soviet foreign service in 1939 as part of an urgent drive to replace the old Bolshevik diplomats whom he had systematically shot. As Foreign Minister, Gromyko was associated with many of the Soviet Union's worst crimes and follies. Now he lay in state in the ponderous neo-classical House of the Soviet Army. A mile-long queue of workers and peasants waited outside to pay their respects. The columns of the great hall were covered in red and black cloth. The mirrors and chandeliers were draped in black. A military band played funereal music. Soldiers stood to attention everywhere. Obsequious young men from the Protocol Department of the Foreign Ministry wore expressions of contrived grief. Gromyko's coffin was placed high on the catafalque, at such an angle that I found myself staring up his nostrils as I stood in front of him. His medals – dozens of them – were laid out on crimson velvet before him. I patted his widow on the hand: she mumbled

English at me and I mumbled Russian at her. Gromyko may not have been a nice man, not a constructive nor an imaginative man. But that was not her fault and she was in tears.

The end of 1989 was marked by a far more important death. Gorbachev admired Sakharov but never found him easy to deal with. He was too independent, too oblivious of the rules of sensible politics, too inclined to reduce complex tactical issues to moral simplicities. The two clashed regularly in the Congress of People's Deputies. On 14 December 1989, in a brutal exercise of the power of the Chair, Gorbachev refused to let Sakharov discuss the Communist Party's monopoly of power under Article Six of the Soviet Constitution. Sakharov was not prepared to give up. The last thing he said that night before going to bed was 'Tomorrow we'll have a fight.' He died of a heart attack in his sleep and was found by his wife in the morning.

Three days later he lay in state at the huge 'Palace of Youth' on the Lenin Prospect. It was a political event as well as the occasion for an outpouring of popular emotion, such as had accompanied the funeral of Tolstoy. The nearest metro stations were closed, as they always were when the authorities hoped to deter people from gathering without official sanction. Large numbers of troops waited in buses in the side streets, ready to go into action if things got out of hand. The mourners – perhaps as many as 250,000 of them – queued for up to a kilometre in temperatures of minus 20 degrees to pay their last respects. Inside the building the Borodin Quartet played chamber music, as they had done at the funeral of every General Secretary of the Communist Party since Stalin. The Moscow intelligentsia took turns to stand in the guard of honour. Gubenko – the actor from the Taganka Theatre who was now Minister of Culture – sat on the dais. As we watched, an elderly woman started to shout: 'They killed him – the dictatorship and the usurpers.' She was gently moved away. A group of young men wore Ukrainian colours and hatbands saying 'Chernobyl!' Others wore armbands with a figure '6' struck through: abolish Article Six of the Constitution and the monopoly of the Communist Party, the cause for which Sakharov was fighting when he died.

As we got up on the morning of the funeral itself we heard the first reports from the BBC about rioting and demonstrations in Romania. The bitter cold of the previous day had changed into slush, greyness, fog. For two hours or more Jill and I waited with our children Kate and Julian in the great square in Luzhniki for the cortège to arrive. There were groups carrying the cancelled '6' symbol, others with the Russian nationalist flag of St Andrew, and others carrying placards saying 'Forgive us – we should have demonstrated for you in 1980', when Sakharov was sent into exile in Gorky. The good-tempered crowd grew all the time until there were perhaps eighty thousand people there. But the young policemen who encircled the crowd were under no obvious command, and had no idea how to manage. As the crowd swayed aimlessly backwards and forwards, we feared that someone might slip and fall on the slushy ground, that there would be panic and deaths. It was only with great difficulty that a passage for the coffin was cleared to the tribunal. Sakharov's widow Yelena Bonner took the microphone and shouted: 'You are carrying banners saying "Wisdom, Honour, Conscience". Why don't you show a bit of wisdom, honour, and conscience yourselves, instead of milling about like animals. Remember all those who were crushed to death at Stalin's funeral in 1953.' It was not a happy note to strike.

Academician Likhachev was the first to speak: the only man in Russia who could command even a part of the respect in which Sakharov was held. He praised him as one of the finest representatives of the Russian intelligentsia (he emphasised 'Russian') and compared him with Tolstoy, another fighter for justice. Yevtushenko read a bombastic and self-indulgent poem. Sobchak reminded us that Sakharov had died on the anniversary of the Decembrist Rising, the first liberal rebellion against the Tsars. Yuri Afanasiev called on everyone to fight, as Sakharov would have wished, against Article Six and for the creation of a proper democratic opposition. Then the body was taken away for burial to the sound of Albinoni's *Adagio*, his favourite piece of music. As we left a tiny woman in a red beret recognised us. Her name was Yelena, and she offered to introduce us to Dmitri Mitlyansky, the sculptor who had done Sakharov's death mask. Later she was as good as her word: and he gave us a copy of the mask.

That evening we were invited to a wake in the great restaurant of the Rossia Hotel. There must have been at least a thousand people there. They queued up for the microphone to share their memories of Sakharov – Afghan veterans, invalids, people for whom he had found apartments, representatives of all the people he had helped unstintingly. The speakers insisted that Sakharov was not as politically naive and impractical as he seemed. He had been right to refuse to compromise. I had thought that his time was past. It was no longer a time for heroes, but a time for practical statesmen like Gorbachev, for whom Sakharov had made life unnecessarily difficult. Now he was dead, I was no longer at all sure. The coming year was to show that Russia still needed its conscience, and that the liberal opposition had no other leader to compare with Sakharov for moral stature and purity of motive. It was far less important that from time to time he may have misjudged the tactical situation. His death was a major blow to the democratic process. Later I read his *Memoirs*. His courage, his singleness of purpose, and his stamina, his conviction – expressed in the writings he addressed to the public and to the Soviet leadership directly – that Russia could survive only if it became an open society, were the indispensable intellectual and political preliminary to Perestroika. The tragedy of 1990 was that the democrats who succeeded Sakharov were unable to sink their differences, or to swallow their suspicions of Gorbachev enough to give him and his reforms the consistent support they needed to stem the wave of reaction from the Communist hard men. Instead they switched their support to Yeltsin. If Sakharov had lived, he just might have proved the catalyst for a broader cooperation among the democrats and the liberal Communists which could have saved the country much later travail.

Meanwhile the old guard in the Communist Party were getting restive. They had originally supported Gorbachev because they thought he could get the old system going again on the old lines. But at the 19th Party Conference in 1988 he had given them fair warning that they would have to rely for their political influence in future on merit and on the support of the public, rather than on secret manoeuvring in smoke-filled rooms. He knew that neither confrontation nor persuasion would unclench their grip on power. He therefore resorted to salami tactics, slicing away at the reactionary majority in the 'mini-coup' of September 1988, and again through the elections of March 1989. As Party bosses were voted out of office in one city after another, they realised that Gorbachev's aims and theirs were not compatible. A spirit of rebellion was born. Over the next two years it brought together leading figures in the Party, the military, and the secret police. They hoped to bring Gorbachev back under their control. In the Winter of 1990–91 they nearly succeeded.

In the immediate aftermath of the elections in March 1989, the Central Committee of the Communist Party met in plenary session. In a tactical manoeuvre of great elegance, Gorbachev took the opportunity to engineer the 'resignation' of one hundred and ten of the Committee's members, one in six of the total. They included such heavyweights as Gromyko; Aliev, the former First Party Secretary of Azerbaijan, an elderly man of sinister charm who reappeared in 1993 as President of an already independent Azerbaijan; and Marshal Ogarkov who as Chief of the General Staff had tried to explain away the shooting down of the Korean airliner in 1983. It was the biggest clean-out since Stalin had purged the delegates to the XVIIth Party

Congress in 1934. For the victims the essential difference was that on this occasion they were not shot, but induced to go quietly with offers of generous pensions and a silent veil over the past. Those promoted to fill the gap included Yevgeny Primakov, Academician Velikhov, the nuclear physicist and arms control expert, Valentin Falin, the Head of the International Department of the Party Secretariat, and Yuli Kvitsinsky, the Soviet ambassador in Bonn. All played distinctive roles in the last stage of Perestroika. Primakov survived beyond that into the new era, and became Yeltsin's antepenultimate Prime Minister.

Gorbachev thus got rid of a dead weight of conservatives. But those who supported him in the Central Committee were still a minority. The discussion at the Plenum was noisy and protracted. The loyalists were confused, angry at the mounting criticism of the Party in the press, and above all incensed and apprehensive at the growing possibility that the Party might lose its political monopoly. Gorbachev was attacked in terms which had never before been used of an incumbent General Secretary, and there were rumours that he would be removed. Lengthy excerpts from the record appeared in *Pravda*, which was still in the hands of his opponents. Saikin and Soloviev, the former bosses of Moscow and Leningrad who had been beaten at the election, spoke with particular bitterness. The economic reforms were incoherent, they said. Private business was enriching itself at the expense of state enterprise. These criticisms were not unjustified. Gorbachev fought back firmly and at characteristic length. The economy was indeed in a mess. 'We have to look the truth in the face: many people have forgotten how to work. They've got used to the idea that they're often paid simply for turning up at their workplace.' Ordinary people needed to take responsibility for the welfare of the country. That was what democratisation was for. The Party had led the way. But reform was being driven from below, not imposed from above. That was not a threat to the Party, nor to Socialism. 'If it is weakness to conduct a dialogue with all levels of society, then I don't know what courage is.'

Gorbachev quelled the mood of rebellion for the time being. But the pattern of the April 1989 Plenum was repeated at Plenums in February 1990, and in April and July 1991; at the first Congress of the Russian Communist Party in June 1990; at the XXVIIIth and last Congress of the CPSU a month later. Each time Gorbachev fought back, cajoling, bullying, and if necessary threatening to resign. Each time he was left with less real power than before.

The Party was faced with two immediate issues. Could it retain its constitutional monopoly of power, against which Sakharov and his friends had been campaigning? And was there room within the same Party for Ligachev and the reactionaries on the one hand, and Gorbachev and his followers on the other? The two questions were closely connected. On the answers depended the very nature of the Soviet Union as a political organism.

Article Six of the USSR Constitution – the 'Brezhnev Constitution' of 1977 – described the Communist Party as the 'leading and guiding force of Soviet society, the nucleus of its political system and of state and public organisations'. In practice the Party had of course dominated the country's political life even without the benefit of this formula. But the formula had more than symbolic importance, since it was the legal obstacle to any form of multiparty democracy. Even within the Party there were those who thought it was time for a change. At the end of 1985 Aleksandr Yakovlev tentatively suggested to Gorbachev that the Party should be split into two parties, one social democratic and the other Communist, which would compete for the favour of the electorate.[1]

At that time Gorbachev thought the idea premature, but he continued to play with it. By January 1990 his associates were telling me openly that the Party might split. Laptiev thought that a multiparty system was now inevitable. The very word 'Communist' could become an electoral liability. At the end of that month CNN reported that Gorbachev was about to resign as General Secretary and to use a strengthened Presidency as his power base instead. I was sceptical. But Yegor Yakovlev of *Moscow News* said that this idea was indeed in the air. The Party was so discredited that it was no longer essential as an instrument for running the country. Gorbachev could push ahead with Perestroika as President of the parliament: he had after all threatened to resign from the Secretary Generalship three times in 1989. Yakovlev did not think that Gorbachev would make the move soon. The hardliners were still too worried about the popular reaction to force his hand. But Gorbachev could no longer continue to manoeuvre between the radical and reactionary wings of the Party. He must now lead from the front if the political process was to remain controllable. Otherwise the Soviet Union faced 'one or other of the East European versions': Romania or Yugoslavia, bloody insurrection or disintegration.

Reassured by these exchanges, I told the Foreign Office that Gorbachev was determined to break the grip of the Party bureaucracy and its political monopoly, and that he had everything under control. My confidence was jolted by the Plenum which the Party held at the beginning of February 1990. I was in London when it began, preparing for a visit by a delegation of parliamentary deputies led by Vadim Medvedev of the Politburo. I heard on the BBC that Gorbachev had failed to get his way on the first day. Ligachev had attacked his policies on the economy, on the nationalities, on Germany, and on the unity of the Party. Brovikov, the Soviet ambassador in Warsaw, had launched a vicious personal attack on Gorbachev himself. The television showed streams of boot-faced generals emerging from the Kremlin with no comment. And yet once again Gorbachev mounted a successful counterattack. He persuaded the whole Central Committee, except for Yeltsin who had ideas of his own, to vote for a constitutional amendment abolishing the leading role of the Party, and to approve a liberal draft of a new Party Programme for the XXVIIIth Congress which was planned for later in the year. The language of this draft departed significantly from the blinkered incantations of earlier Party documents. Gorbachev himself at last used the word 'pluralism' without the adjective 'Socialist'. Phrases like 'Socialist market', 'Socialist legality' and other Orwellian circumlocutions were dropped. To the outside world these changes seemed insignificant, mere Talmudic obscurities. But they marked the abandonment of a whole set of ingrained ideological formulae which had made it impossible for the Party to talk political and economic sense about the real world.

Gorbachev's opponents within the Party now began to contemplate a new strategy, a strategy which was curiously like that of their arch-enemy Yeltsin, since it involved mobilising the institutions of Russia against those of the Soviet centre. Yeltsin was at least able to build on the shadowy governmental institutions of the Russian Soviet Federated Socialist Republic (RSFSR). But the RSFSR, unlike the other Soviet Republics – Ukraine, the Balts, the Caucasians, the Central Asians – had neither its own Communist Party, nor its own security organs, nor even its own Academy of Science. Russians did not mind this apparent discrimination as long as the Soviet Union continued to function as an effective substitute for the old Russian empire. But as the Union decayed they began to agitate for the creation of specifically Russian institutions. Demands for a Russian Communist Party grew from the beginning of 1990. Gorbachev's people were aghast. When I asked why, Laptiev told me that a Russian Communist Party would fall into the hands of the Right, the imperialists, the conservative law-and-order men, the quasi-fascist extremists – a fear justified by the event.

In the last years of the Soviet Union, indeed, political factions could not easily be categorised into 'Left' and 'Right'. Hitler's was a 'National Socialist German Workers Party.' Mussolini was a socialist before he became a

Fascist. Because *les extrémités se touchent*, the extreme Right in the Soviet Union included Communist hardliners as well as virulent nationalists. Both were reactionary, chauvinistic and authoritarian, and their views were sometimes indistinguishable. The views of moderate Communists like Gorbachev – men of the Left – evolved into something very close to the Social Democracy of Western Europe. Many of Yeltsin's earlier supporters were 'liberals' in the English, rather than the American or Continental sense.

Gorbachev tried to stem the move to set up a Russian Communist Party but failed. The new Party held its founding congress in Moscow in June 1990. Gorbachev opened badly, insisting at excessive length that the new Party should be subordinate to the CPSU. He was subjected to a malevolent attack by the Commander of the Urals-Volga Military District, General Makashov, who became an extreme nationalist of the worst kind in the years that followed. To the dismay of the liberals Gorbachev failed to sack the General for this grossly improper intervention in domestic politics. Rejecting more liberal candidates, the delegates elected Polozkov, a reactionary Party Secretary from Krasnodar, as General Secretary of the new Party. Various people told me that this obscure Party bureaucrat was a force to reckon with. But when I called on him in the Spring of 1991 in the office of the Russian Communist Party, an old building on the edge of the Central Committee complex in Kitaigorod off Red Square, he seemed to be a little man in all senses of the word. My impressions were borne out by his subsequent undistinguished career.

The reactionaries made further gains at the XXVIIIth – and as it turned out the last – Congress of the Soviet Communist Party in July 1990. The issues were clear: Would the apparatchiks still accept Gorbachev's leadership? Would they still be willing to go along with his reforms? Was there still any place in the Party for the reformers themselves? By the time the Congress was over it was clear that the Party was lost to reform: but also that it had been damaged beyond repair. The right-wingers were noisy and abusive. But their champion Ligachev was voted out of office, and his effective political career brought to an end. Despite their misgivings, they reluctantly voted for Gorbachev's social democratic Party Programme. Equally reluctantly – a quarter of those present voted against – they re-elected him as General Secretary. They acquiesced in a massive reshaping of the Party organisation, which severed almost all the remaining links between the Party and the state. For the first time since the October Revolution no member of the new Politburo held a post in the state system except Gorbachev himself. The Politburo and the Party were finished as instruments of state power. It was at this belated moment that several of the most radical reformers finally plucked up the courage of their convictions and resigned from the Party. Yeltsin warned the apparatchiks that if they did not modernise the Party, they and it would go the way of the Communist Parties of Eastern Europe. He, Sobchak and Popov then marched out of the hall to cries of 'Shame!' They were not followed by many others. Shevardnadze and Alexander Yakovlev remained in their places. But Yeltsin's dramatic departure from the Party encouraged all those – such as Sasha Motov – who had delayed handing in their Party cards for fear of losing their jobs or worse. From now on the trickle of defections became a torrent.

But though the Party was emasculated, the apparatchiks still controlled the instruments of local power: the offices, the telephones, the local press and, for the time being, the television. I warned the Foreign Office that they should not be underestimated in defeat. In my diary I wrote that 'it is not clear that [the apparatchiks] have much support in the country as a whole: to judge by the attitude of the miners, very little. So they could mount a coup, but not a counter-revolution.'

The struggle within the Party was paralleled by the struggle on the streets. In the first years of Perestroika, public demonstrations were still forbidden and were dispersed by the police and the KGB, often with considerable brutality. But as 1989 wore on Yuri Afanasiev and his democratic colleagues began to shift the political debate onto the streets. Hundreds of thousands of disciplined Muscovites turned out at their call. Now the police stood passively by as ordinary people began to voice their profound hatred for the Party. To everyone's surprise, it turned out that the Russian people were as politically sophisticated and as capable of orderly protest as the East Germans. Even as the official parade took place on Red Square in November 1989, a rival demonstration demanded an end to the leading role of the Party: its banners said 'Workers of the world – forgive us!' Miners struck in the Northern city of Vorkuta to demand the abolition of Article Six. In December the people of Moscow demonstrated in response to Sakharov's last appeal. The Volgograd Party, in a paroxysm of misplaced and atavistic ideological fervour, ordered the destruction of a number of private greenhouses on the outskirts of the city on the grounds that they were 'illegal speculation'. Tomatoes promptly disappeared from the Volgograd markets, the people went onto the streets in fury, and at the beginning of the new year the Party Committee was dismissed *en masse*. The local Party leadership in Tyumen followed suit. In Chernigov an official car was crashed by its drunken driver. The boot burst open: it was full of food from a Party delicatessen. Party bosses began to wonder if the 'elemental forces' of popular anger would sweep them away as they had swept Ceauşescu.

On the evening of 4 February 1990 several hundred thousand people gathered on the Crimea Bridge near Gorky Park. They marched round the Garden Ring, down past the Museum of the Revolution on Gorky Street to Manege Square just under the walls of the Kremlin: the first time that an opposition demonstration had been permitted so close to the seat of power. Some were carrying Tsarist flags and flags of the February 1917 provisional government, in a deliberate attempt to create a bridge with the pre-Communist past. Others were carrying slogans such as 'Down with the KGB', 'Army, don't shoot' and 'Party Bureaucrats: Remember Romania!' Konstantin Demakhin marched with them. So did Jill, who had gone to watch, but ended up by joining the throng. In Manege Square they were harangued by Yeltsin, Gavriil Popov, Korotich, and the poet Yevtushenko. Most of the marchers were decent middle-aged people from the middle classes. There were comparatively few young people among them. Several recognised Jill, who had recently appeared in a television chat programme: 'Ah, you're the wife of "our" English ambassador.'

A second demonstration took place on 25 February – the anniversary of the fall of the Tsar in 1917 – to mark the culmination of the election campaign to the Russian parliament. The authorities began to increase the tension deliberately. The Soviet parliament warned against 'civil confrontation'. *Pravda* published an appeal from the Central Committee to the people to behave themselves. Jill reported rumours from the university, where she gave regular English conversation classes, that the army was concentrating around Moscow and that the demonstration would be forcibly suppressed. On television Ryzhkov spoke gravely but menacingly about the need for law and order. I wondered whether Yuri Afanasiev was about to go too far.

On Saturday 24 February – the eve of the democrats' demonstration – the Moscow Communists and the military organised an anti-Yeltsin meeting in the centre of Moscow. Their slogans read: 'The People and the Army are One!', 'Russia for the Russians', 'Yeltsin and Co. are the Servants of Zionism'. Though I did not know it at the time, Kryuchkov, Yazov and Pugo were present, the men who later organised the 1991 coup.

Early the next day, the radio announced that Moscow was surrounded with troops. Doctors were on alert. An Orthodox bishop called on people to spend the day at home. Jill and I walked over the Great Stone Bridge which leads across the river to the Kremlin, through the park below the Kremlin walls, and into the centre of the city. Everything looked peaceable as people wandered around in the unseasonably hot weather. But in the side streets there were troops and police in waiting, lorries parked ready to block the roads, and large numbers of closed vans marked ДЕТСКОЕ ПИТАНИЕ ('Detskoe Pitanie' = 'Children's Food'), a transparent disguise: in Solzhenitsyn's day the KGB's Black Marias were marked ХЛЕБ ('Khleb' = 'Bread'). Snipers in flak jackets manned the roofs. In a side street at the bottom of Gorky Street we looked in on the well-kept and fashionable Church of the Resurrection, hung with splendid icons rescued from churches and monasteries destroyed during the 1930s. A well-groomed and intelligent-looking priest was delivering a deeply subversive and highly sophisticated sermon on the relationship between God, man, and history. Man went wrong – in the Garden of Eden and in the twentieth century – when he tried to put himself in God's place. Hence all the horrors of the recent Russian past. Now Russia was being given another chance to recognise God and God's role in history.

The demonstrators conducted themselves in the orderly and disciplined fashion that had become their hallmark. They made no attempt to break through the steel ring of troops around the Kremlin. But once again they turned out in force despite the menaces of the authorities. Liberal politicians claimed on television that 'the people have overcome their fear.' In the Kremlin they saw things differently. When the Politburo met to discuss the day's events, Ryzhkov claimed a victory. Kryuchkov said that the people now knew who was master. It was left to Bakatin, then still Minister of the Interior, to protest. Yes, he said, the people had been frightened. Otherwise there would have been one million people on the streets, instead of only three hundred thousand. Next time they would not hold back. They would march straight on the Kremlin, and the Party would have to secure its 'victory' with tanks. Instead of talking about 'victory' the authorities should negotiate with all those who favoured reform. Gorbachev rounded on him. Those who had led the demonstrations – Popov and others, whom he called 'political scoundrels' – represented nothing, and there was nothing to discuss with them: 'The real working class has not yet spoken out.' Bakatin was isolated. The rest of the Politburo lined up behind Gorbachev.[2]

So far the demonstrators had not criticised Gorbachev. But this now began to change. In a further liberal gesture which misfired badly, Gorbachev allowed independent political groupings to march onto Red Square for the May Day parade. They were a motley collection of Democratic Unionists,

Socialists, Constitutional Democrats and others – these names, too, reminiscent of the Tsarist regime's brief flirtation with democracy at the beginning of the century. Some demonstrators carried slogans which deliberately and crudely threatened the Party bureaucrats: 'Get out of your armchairs and into the concentration camps', and – once again – 'Remember Ceauşescu'. They booed Gorbachev. He stormed off the podium in a rage. It happened again at the Revolution Day Parade in November, a grey day of melting snow. Gorbachev started well enough by addressing everyone as 'fellow-countrymen', not 'comrades'. But then – as so often – he burbled on for twenty inconsequential minutes and the people lost interest. The military parade was as impeccable as ever. The civilian parade which followed was another break with precedent. Gorbachev, Lukyanov, Yeltsin and Popov descended from the podium to lead the demonstrators through the square. Despite the careful organisation, there were a number of anti-Gorbachev slogans ('Remember you're still the General Secretary', 'When you go abroad, don't lose sight of your own country'), demands for unity against chaos and civil war, attacks on economic reform and on falling living standards. Groups of elderly people carried portraits of Stalin, and viciously anti-Semitic banners. Once again there were rival demonstrations in the surrounding streets. Halfway through there were a couple of bangs from the other side of Red Square. We thought that some balloons had burst. But we later learned that a madman from Leningrad had pulled out a sawn-off gun, and fired two shots into the air. No one was hurt.

At the usual reception in the Kremlin that evening Gorbachev and Raisa came over for a chat. He said very earnestly that the process of Perestroika was now deeply rooted in the minds of the people: I should not attach too much importance to the froth of today's demonstrations. I assumed that he wanted me to convey an upbeat message to Mrs Thatcher and others in London who were wondering how far he was still the right man to support. It was the last such reception, and the last November Parade, in the history of the Soviet Union.

Although he could not nerve himself to abandon the Party, Gorbachev too understood by the Spring of 1990 that he could not rely on it to carry through his reforms. He therefore moved to create a new post of Executive President, to which he would be elected by the Soviet parliament acting as an electoral college. This would still not give him the legitimacy of a direct popular election which Yeltsin had enjoyed since his victory in March 1989. Vadim Medvedev hinted to me that an additional reason why Gorbachev was putting himself forward was that he feared that Yeltsin might stand in his absence and win. Chernyaev subsequently told me that Gorbachev had reluctantly come round to the idea of an executive presidency for two reasons. The new democratic institutions, the Soviet parliament and the multiparty system, had taken root surprisingly quickly and at the expense of the executive. A strong Presidency would rectify the imbalance, and manage the upheaval which change was bound to bring. The parliament itself was not enthusiastic. Stankevich, a leading young liberal much loved by Western television because he spoke excellent English, insisted on proper guarantees to prevent any abuse of power by the new Executive President. Gorbachev tried to cut him off, but he was supported by Sobchak. Bakatin and Ryzhkov were put forward as alternative candidates but withdrew. Academician Likhachev reminded the deputies that he was probably the only one present to remember the fall of the Tsar and the horrors which followed. Any further delay would mean civil war. He appealed to Stankevich and the others to withdraw their opposition. When the vote was taken, barely 60 per cent of the deputies voted for Gorbachev. Sergei Karaganov, one of Moscow's best-known analysts and men-about-politics, remarked to me that evening that Gorbachev probably would not have been elected at all if there had been any further delay.

Just as Gorbachev was trying to strengthen his own position by building up the institutions of the Soviet state, Boris Yeltsin was exploiting the hitherto feeble institutions of the RSFSR for a similar purpose. A new Russian parliament was elected at the beginning of March 1990, and lasted until it was suppressed by Yeltsin's tanks in October 1993. As in the elections to the Soviet parliament the previous year, the electorate was once again allowed a choice of candidate. This time the Communists knew what to expect. They organised themselves effectively and did well in the provincial towns and the countryside. But in the big cities well-known liberals were elected: the human rights campaigner Sergei Kovalev, the dissident priest Gleb Yakunin, Stalin's controversial biographer Dmitri Volkogonov, and Vladislav Starkov, the editor of the successful weekly *Argumenty i Fakty*, a journal which Gorbachev found particularly distasteful because it had run an opinion poll allegedly documenting the decline in his popularity.[3]

When the new Russian parliament met, Yeltsin ran for election as its Chairman. Gorbachev tried to persuade Party members that they should vote against Yeltsin as a matter of discipline. His efforts backfired. After several ballots Yeltsin was finally elected Chairman on 29 May. His acceptance speech that evening was (I noted in my diary) 'in his usual content-free, bull-headed, uncharming manner'. But he now had a firm base from which to grasp at real power and to build up 'Russia', its state institutions, and its laws as a sovereign counterweight to Gorbachev's Soviet Union.

In another sensational upheaval Gavriil Popov was elected in April as Chairman of the Moscow City Council, another key position in the old Communist power structure. Stankevich was his deputy. In June Mrs Thatcher called on him in his new office in the Moscow Town Hall on Gorky Street. This ponderous edifice was designed for the first Governor General of Moscow under Catherine the Great. In 1939 it was – as every Intourist guide would tell you – moved fourteen metres back when Stalin widened the street, and two extra storeys were added, turning what might perhaps have been an elegant town palace into yet another monument to bureaucracy. Inside it smelled of new paint – symbolic of the new management. Popov shambled into his office wearing a tie in Mrs Thatcher's honour. Behind him was the new chairman of the Municipal Executive Committee, the chunky populist Yuri Luzhkov, later his successor. The Soviet Union, said Popov, was like a small boy who had climbed a tall tree, and did not know how to climb down again. Democracy had been broadened, but it lacked an economic base. The present wave of radical populism could flip and become a populism of the right, which would lead the country back to bureaucratic socialism. Gorbachev was very good at international diplomacy. But he was less good at diplomacy within the country. He could not lead on his own, his room for manoeuvring was diminishing, and the leadership was now unpopular at all levels. Mrs Thatcher was delighted: she recognised in Popov a pure Thatcherite, a true devotee of Milton Friedman and the Chicago School.

The popular press was becoming increasingly impatient. *Komsomolskaya Pravda*, the organ of the Communist youth movement which had become a major vehicle for liberal opinion, published Solzhenitsyn's manifesto 'How we should transform Russia'. By now Solzhenitsyn's ideas were no longer particularly original. Many had become part of the common discourse in Moscow. And he offered no practical thoughts on how his ideas should be implemented. But the manifesto contained some splendid invective. His opening phrase was reminiscent of the first sentence of Marx's *Communist Manifesto*: 'The clock of Communism', said Solzhenitsyn, 'has struck for the last time.' The reference to 'five years of noisy Perestroika' was an unkind dart aimed at Gorbachev. The September issue of *Ogonek* published the 'Manifesto of the Peasant Party of Russia'. There was no evidence that such a party existed in the real world. But the language of the 'Manifesto' was inflammatory.

The country is on the verge of famine. In a year when the harvest has been unprecedentedly rich, the shops in the towns are empty. Millions of tons of our own grain are rotting, and we are buying foreign grain for gold. This is not the result of the stupidity of some minister: it is the death throes of the system, the retribution for decades of abuse and coercion against the workers on the land and against the land itself. As the consequence of a monstrous social experiment, the Russian countryside is approaching the twenty-first century ruined, depopulated, beggared. The importation of food is a lifeline for the AgroGulag. No one except the Russian peasant can feed Russia. It is time to stop trying to save the collective farms – we must save the people!

The process of building an alternative Russian state culminated nine months later on 12 June 1991, when Yeltsin was elected President of the RSFSR in a fiercely contested election. A legitimate authority had been created as an alternative to the old Soviet system. Without it, the attempted coup two months later might have succeeded. I did not fully appreciate the significance of the event – I was more moved by the vote in Leningrad to restore the historic name of 'Saint Petersburg' – but my diary entry was judicious enough:

People have been saying that these were the first democratic elections in the Soviet Union. Of course they weren't: the elections to the Supreme and local Soviets were also genuinely democratic. But in this election the choice was much clearer. The policy issues were personified in the candidates and so people knew what they were voting for. Yeltsin stood for change and democracy, Ryzhkov for caution and the old ways, Bakatin for Gorbachev and liberalism, Makashov for the iron hand. The fifth candidate, Zhirinovsky, head of the Liberal Democratic Party, was widely thought to be a clown or – alternatively – the candidate of the KGB (!). So it is highly significant that Yeltsin got about 56%, Ryzhkov about 20%, and Bakatin and Makashov about 3%. Zhirinovsky took a strongly Russian chauvinist line. He did quite well in some places and got about 7% overall; but no conclusion can be drawn from his performance.

A few days after the election we gave a small dinner for Stankevich and his wife and two other Russian couples. The Tatarstan government, he said, had boycotted the election. Russian deputies who went to Kazan as observers were confined to their hotel while a hostile mob demonstrated on the street outside. After two days they were advised to leave the city for their own safety. Stankevich was in the grip of a mystical Great Russian chauvinism. Russia could afford to lose the Baltic States and Ukraine. But for Tatarstan and the other Autonomous Republics to escape from subordination to Russia, he said, would mean the end of Russia as a historic state. He made everyone's blood run cold when he added that this would have to be prevented by all means, including military force. For a moment I thought that this humourless man might become the St Just of the Second Russian Revolution. His fate was less dramatic. In Yeltsin's Russia he was involved, or possibly framed, in a scandal about the misuse of money for a concert on Red Square, and sought political asylum in Poland.

And so by the Autumn of 1990 Gorbachev had lost the initiative. He had failed to exploit his new powers as Executive President either to push through an economic reform or to assert himself over the extremists to his left and his right. His tactic of operating from the centre no longer worked. The most prominent reformers had lost faith in him, and had thrown their weight behind 'Russia' and Yeltsin. The reactionaries deeply resented the damage he had done to the Soviet Union's international position and to the integrity of the Union itself. Ordinary people were thoroughly bored and irritated by his endless harangues on television, and no longer placed their hopes in him. But he did not give up. In November he asked the Soviet parliament for additional powers, a 'cabinet' of ministers directly responsible to him, and a Vice President. The parliament voted him the powers he wanted with a strange docility. It looked like another triumph. I believed it to be a sham. I saw no reason to think that Gorbachev would exercise his 'new' powers any more effectively than those he had been granted in the Spring. He was ducking the issues, reacting to events instead of anticipating them. His authority was waning visibly. Alksnis, one of the 'Black Colonels' who had put themselves at the vocal head of reaction within the armed forces, rammed the point home when he got up to tell Gorbachev that if he had not restored order in the country within thirty days, the parliament would call for his removal.

I got a glimpse of Gorbachev's mood at this time when I took General Galvin, NATO's Supreme Commander, to meet him on 13 November 1990. He was raw and defensive. He told us that he had just spent five hours with military deputies from all over the country. 'One Colonel' (it was Petrushenko) had attacked him for accepting the Nobel Prize. In the olden days, remarked Gorbachev, that Colonel would by now be neither a

Colonel nor a deputy. He then launched into a passionate defence of Perestroika. It was not a superficial paint job, but a fundamental process of change, affecting the interests of everyone in the country. When he had embarked on the process, there had been plenty of enthusiasm. Now that real change had begun, things were getting difficult – including of course for the army. Some people were even asking if they should ever have set off on this path. But a transformation on this scale could not be smooth. With much justification Gorbachev pointed out that Mrs Thatcher had found it painful enough to restructure the British steel industry, a tiny task by comparison. No one before had ever tried reform in Russia without the shedding of blood or civil war. Foreigners criticised him for not going faster. But surely he knew his own country better than his foreign critics? Did they really not see how much had been achieved since 1985? Was it their business to criticise his tactics as opposed to his strategy? He would press ahead with his priorities: the market economy; the law-governed state; and a new relationship between the States of the Union. He would be patient and tolerant. But he would act decisively if the constitution were in danger. This menacing theme was by now increasingly frequent in his statements.

A lurch to the right now seemed inevitable. Gorbachev had gone very far towards breaking the power of the old baronies, especially the Party. He had provided the space for liberal forces to organise themselves in effective bodies, with genuine political programmes of reform and the discipline and determination to put them into practice. But instead of supporting him the liberal intelligentsia spent much of their time in futile internecine warfare, the weakness of the Russian intelligentsia for a hundred years and more. Because the liberals failed to put together a convincing show of organised unity, it was hardly surprising that the baronies began to raise their heads again. They were the only people who still occupied positions of real power, and they had the experience to exploit it. Yegor Yakovlev commented at the end of November that Gorbachev was behaving like a man who had been driven into a corner. He was having to ally himself with the forces of the right: the army and the KGB. The liberals were unable to provide him with adequate support. Ominously, Yakovlev said that Lukyanov – the man whom we had all thought was one of Gorbachev's closest allies – had now gone over to the right.

The figures from the first bright days of Perestroika began to fall away. The first to go was Bakatin, the liberal Communist whom Gorbachev himself had put in charge of the Interior Ministry and whom he now sacked as a gesture to the reactionaries. The 'Black Colonels' were openly exultant. They boasted in public that Shevardnadze was next on their list.

And indeed on 20 December Shevardnadze announced to the parliament that he was resigning as Foreign Minister. He spoke with great emotion, accusing the democrats of running for cover and warning of the threat of a new dictatorship. He concluded: 'I believe that to resign is my duty as a man, as a citizen, as a Communist. I cannot reconcile myself to what is happening in our country and the trials awaiting our people. Yet I believe that a dictatorship will not succeed, that the future belongs to democracy and freedom.'

By the time I got to the Congress Hall that day, the deputies were emerging from their stunned silence. Academician Likhachev said that Soviet foreign policy had been the one wholly successful area of Perestroika, and asked the deputies to vote to persuade Shevardnadze to stay. Other liberals called for a common stand against the threat of dictatorship and civil war. They accused Gorbachev of being taken hostage by the men in uniform, and attacked Shevardnadze for abandoning his post under fire. The 'Black Colonels' spluttered with emotion. Then Gorbachev spoke, calmly and without drama, rising to the occasion as he had not done for some time. He knew of no evidence that a 'junta' was preparing to take over. Order did have to be preserved in a time of difficult transition. But strong leadership was quite different from dictatorship. Shevardnadze was wrong to abandon the struggle: he still had a valuable contribution to make. Gorbachev concluded by inviting the parliament to vote for the continuity of Soviet foreign policy and the continuation of Shevardnadze in office. The bemused deputies dutifully did so, but Shevardnadze was not to be mollified.

I was not clear what kind of 'dictatorship' Shevardnadze feared: an overpowerful Gorbachev, or a Gorbachev who had been taken hostage by the generals. He did nothing to enlighten me when I called on him a couple of months later in his new Foreign Policy Institute. Perhaps the simplest explanation was that he was aware of the plans for a forthcoming crackdown on the Republics, could not reveal them in terms, and chose this dramatic gesture instead.

Gorbachev had now lost his most prominent liberal advisers. Bakatin had been sacked, Shevardnadze had gone, Yakovlev had faded away. In mid-December Ryzhkov told the parliament that 'Perestroika as we conceived it has failed', had a heart attack, and resigned. By the turn of the year the original Perestroika team had gone. To replace them Gorbachev looked to the men of the right – conservative hacks in the old Soviet mould. The first was Boris Pugo, who took over as Interior Minister from Bakatin. Pugo had been Chairman of the KGB in Latvia, and later First Secretary of the Latvian Party: a mild, plausible and soft-spoken figure, with a benign expression, a bald head, and a tuft of hair above each ear, a decent enough man in Chernyaev's eyes. The new Foreign Minister was the likeable Bessmertnykh, a career diplomat hauled back from his new post as ambassador in Washington, together with his tearful wife and a new baby. The candidate for the new post of Vice President was Gennadi Yanaev, a former trade union leader of breathtaking obscurity. He too was quiet-spoken, a chain smoker, with a grey haircut so carefully arranged that I suspected a wig. The parliament approved his appointment only after intense pressure by Gorbachev.

But the prize figure in the new government was Valentin Pavlov, Ryzhkov's successor as Prime Minister. Formerly the Finance Minister, he looked like a plump and cheerful gnome (Jill thought him much more sinister – perhaps a troll), with hair *en brosse*, a foolish giggle and a twinkle in his eye. Disrespectful Russians called him 'Svinoezh', which means 'Porcupig'. Of all the Soviet politicians I met, he was the least attractive. He was cynical, miserly with the truth and – as he showed in his meetings with John Major and Mrs Thatcher – incompetent as an economist as well. Soon after taking office, in a remarkable display of ignorance, fatuity, irresponsibility and xenophobia, the Prime Minister of the second most powerful country in the world publicly accused Western banks of plotting to flood the Soviet Union with roubles in order to engineer the collapse of the government and the fall of Gorbachev, thus enabling Western businessmen to buy up Soviet industry at rock-bottom prices. Kryuchkov supported this bizarre proposition on television and radio, claiming that the KGB had the evidence. Pavlov boasted that he had foiled the plot in the nick of time – 'a matter of hours, not days'. I lost no opportunity to point out to my contacts in government how badly such statements could damage the Soviet Union. But despite Pavlov's unattractive qualities, my friends warned me not to underestimate him. They described him as a 'a very clever fellow with figures', a powerful, ruthless, and effective politician, of whom even Gorbachev had reason to be wary. On 14 January – at the height of the Baltic crisis – the parliament voted him into office with never a murmur.

Thus by the middle of January 1991 Gorbachev had put into place all the people who were to betray him seven months later.

At the end of 1990 some small bombs exploded in public places in Latvia. The authorities blamed them on Baltic nationalists: I thought they were at least as likely to be a deliberate provocation by the Soviet special services or local Russians. On New Year's Day my Italian colleague told me that, after talking to Chernyaev and others, a visiting Italian Communist had concluded that the Russians would use the impending war in the Gulf as a cover for action in the Baltic Republics, just as they had used the Suez crisis to mask their assault on Budapest in November 1956. I was sceptical. Gorbachev publicly supported the Americans over Iraq. Repression in the Baltics would severely damage his reputation abroad and at home. I thought that he would resist the pressure to keep order by force. I was wrong.

On 2 January 1991 Interior Ministry troops occupied the state publishing houses in Riga and Vilnius. The next day I called on Chernyaev. He affected to believe the official line. But he said, as he had often done before, that the Balts were bound to leave the Union eventually. He was adamant that Gorbachev would not use force. I warned him about the serious effect that the use of force would have on the Soviet Union's relations with the West. In London a few days later Douglas Hurd asked me what we should do if there were a crackdown in the Baltics. I reminded him that the previous year we had accepted the Soviet claim that the army's bloody intervention in Baku had prevented even greater violence. But we had made it equally clear we would not acquiesce in the suppression of democratic and human rights. The bombs in Latvia looked like deliberate provocation. If force were used we would have to speak out. Even so, the failure of Perestroika was not inevitable. We should not be overinfluenced by individual incidents, whether encouraging or discouraging. As I left the Foreign Office, news was already coming in of a much more serious development. Soviet paratroopers were entering Latvia and Lithuania 'to round up draft-dodgers' – a feeble excuse. Perhaps, I thought, Gorbachev was at last becoming a prisoner of the army as I had feared.

This was not the first time something like this had happened. The previous Spring of 1990 Moscow had launched a sustained campaign of economic pressure and political intimidation against Lithuania, while going through the motions of negotiation with the Lithuanian President Landsbergis. At the height of that crisis the Foreign Ministry had closed Lithuania to foreign diplomats. This time they did not object when I arranged for David Manning, the Head of the Political Section, to go to Tallinn and for David Logan, Noel Marshall's successor as Deputy Head of Mission, to go to Riga and Vilnius to contact the local politicians and to report on events as they unfolded. Throughout the crisis my colleagues telephoned from the Baltic capitals – sometimes from within the besieged parliament buildings – supplementing the information which flooded in on the embassy's rickety fax machine. The Baltic leaders were grateful for their presence. Our contacts with them had been carefully nurtured by Sian McLeod, our Baltic expert, and we were among the best informed of the Moscow embassies in consequence.

On Thursday 10 January Gorbachev sent a menacing message to the Lithuanian parliament. He referred to 'demands' from Lithuanian workers and others for the imposition of Presidential rule. He 'proposed' to the Lithuanians that they revoke all their 'anti-constitutional' acts. His message set no deadline, but it was ominously reminiscent of the language the Russians had used before invading Czechoslovakia. The next day the Lithuanian Foreign Ministry rang the embassy to say that paratroops had taken the press building and the 'Ministry of Defence' in Vilnius, on the grounds that these buildings technically belonged to Moscow or to the Soviet Communist Party. The soldiers had not tried to occupy the parliament or to arrest the government. So ostensibly they were acting within the bounds of the law. But they had fired live ammunition. Although no casualties were reported, one of our journalist friends phoned his wife to say that he had seen the soldiers shoot at a man who was pouring water on them from an upper storey. I warned London that Moscow was increasingly likely to use force. At midnight, BBC television – which we could now receive in the embassy – showed the streets in Vilnius: tanks, resentful crowds, just like Prague in 1968.

Early the following morning, on Sunday 13 January, tanks and troops stormed the TV centre in Vilnius. About thirteen people were killed. The Soviet military claimed that they had been called in by a 'Committee of National Salvation'. The Lithuanian parliament remained defiantly in session. The Soviet government was in disarray. Civilian and military spokesmen issued increasingly contradictory statements, some of which were clearly lies. Late in the afternoon I was called to the Foreign Ministry to see Kovalev, the elderly and ailing Deputy Foreign Minister, with the air of a bedraggled vulture, who had been so angry with me over the expulsions in May 1989. I got to the deserted Ministry building as night fell to find that the American, German, French, Italian and Finnish ambassadors were there as well. Kovalev came panting in. I had expected him to bluster. Instead he was uncharacteristically nervous. Gorbachev had personally ordered him to explain that he was determined to defuse the tension in Lithuania by political not military means. No one in Moscow knew who was in the 'Council of National Salvation'. The local garrison in Vilnius had acted on its own initiative. There were only three dead, two of them military. Kovalev asked us to assure our governments that Soviet policy was unchanged. It was a distinctly odd and unconvincing performance. Many of the facts were wrong. And that evening on the television news Pugo contradicted almost everything that Kovalev had said.

Next there was trouble in neighbouring Latvia. Another anonymous 'Committee of National Salvation', backed by the military, threatened to take over the government centre in Riga. Attempts to organise protest rallies by the Russian minorities in the Baltics were a flop. The Latvian citizens responded by erecting defensive barricades. The Latvian Prime Minister told David Logan, 'They remember 1940 [when they failed to resist the Soviet invasion] and intend to be more responsible this time.' On 15 January the Soviet military stormed the police academy and a police station, and demolished some of the barricades. Here too people were killed.

The Soviet press and broadcasting exploited the freedom which Gorbachev had given them to lambaste him and his government. At first the official news programmes reverted almost to pre-Glasnost standards of tedious bias. But the critical viewer could read between the lines. One newscaster ostentatiously announced that she was reading out the official bulletins because no other information was available. On Leningrad TV Sobchak ridiculed Gorbachev's claim that he did not know who had been responsible for the massacres. And the written press was uninhibited. *Moscow News* published a front page, entitled 'Bloody Sunday', which attacked Gorbachev in the most wounding terms. Blood dripped down from the masthead of the organ of the Moscow Communist youth organisation, *Moskovsky Komsomolets*. *Komsomolskaya Pravda* printed an interview with Bakatin, now out of office. He asked why Gorbachev had not dissociated himself from the killings, and wondered why it was that the KGB and the Interior Ministry had been unable to discover who was behind the shadowy 'Committee of National Salvation'. Only *Pravda* gave prominence to the appeals for Presidential rule from 'peasants and workers' in the Baltic States.

Pugo, Yazov, and Gorbachev himself became increasingly entangled in a web of contradictions. Did the 'Committees of National Salvation' exist or did they not? Had the Balts shot first? Had the local troops been acting on their own initiative or on orders from Moscow? In the parliament Gorbachev was almost incoherent with rage at the press criticism and proposed the suspension of the law on press freedom. He admitted – as he had done before – that the Balts had the right to secede. But it must be done according to the law, and after a referendum. The deputies listened in stunned and gloomy silence. Gorbachev himself was living in cloud-cuckoo-land. Fed by biased information from Kryuchkov, he still believed that the majority of Balts wanted to stay in the Union, a belief that was shortly to be shattered when the referenda held in Latvia and Estonia produced a massive turnout and a 73 per cent vote for independence. To my American colleague Gorbachev admitted that he was under 'hellish' pressure.

His closest colleagues put on the best face they could. Laptiev, Petrovsky, Primakov pleaded with me that the West should not desert Gorbachev, that we should trust him, and not play into the hands of the hardliners. Chernyaev was more depressed than I had ever seen him, uncharacteristically touchy and defensive, though as courteous as ever. Tamara Aleksandrova, his delightful middle-aged secretary, was equally gloomy. Chernyaev was bitter about the 'desertion' of Shatalin and Petrakov, Gorbachev's economic advisers, who had resigned in a blaze of publicity. With great emotion Chernyaev said that he himself would stick by Gorbachev. If Gorbachev's basic policies had really changed, he too would have left. Gorbachev could not control everything; but he was being universally blamed. Without properly checking their facts, people were questioning his policies and even his good faith. The Western leaders were fair weather friends only. Now Gorbachev was in real difficulty, they no longer supported him. Chernyaev wondered wistfully if things would have been different if Mrs Thatcher had still been there. I did not then know that he had written a passionate letter of resignation to Gorbachev immediately after the shootings, in which he told Gorbachev, in the harshest language, that he had lost the trust of the people, that he risked destroying everything that Perestroika had achieved, that he had handed a huge political advantage to his rival Yeltsin, and that it was the beginning of the end of the Soviet Union itself. The letter was never sent. At first Tamara Aleksandrova refused to type it; then she locked it in her safe and prevaricated until she had convinced Chernyaev that now was not the moment to desert his embattled leader. It was her arguments that he had used with me.

To cheer him up I sent Chernyaev an extract from the speech made by Turgenev when the first public statue to Pushkin was unveiled in 1880:

[O]nly the short-sighted, those who are fixed in the past, will be disconcerted, mourn the purely relative calm of earlier days, and attempt – if necessary by force – to make others return to the past. In those periods of the nation's life, which we call transitional, the task of a thinking man, of a true citizen of his country, is to go forward, despite the difficulty and often the dirt along the way, but to go forward without losing sight for one moment of those fundamental ideals, on which is built the whole essence of that society of which he is a living member.

Gorbachev later passed my note to Bessmertnykh, Yazov, and Moiseyev. They did not recognise the quotation and assumed that it was written by a Perestroika author.

It was Yeltsin and – surprisingly – the Orthodox Church who mounted the most effective opposition to what had happened. Yeltsin flew to Tallinn straight after the shootings, signed a joint statement with the three Baltic leaders, and spoke on television of a massive threat to democracy going well beyond the Baltic States. In what was in effect a call to mutiny, he appealed to the Russians in the Soviet army not to take part in the suppression of democratic institutions. Patriarch Aleksi's statement was just as strong, and was carried all over the country by *Izvestia*. He said that both sides had made mistakes: but the government carried the greatest responsibility. He reminded the soldiers that they were not in a conquered foreign country, and that the inhabitants of Lithuania were their fellow citizens whatever their nationality. 'With all deliberation,' he thundered, 'I have to say that the use of military force in Lithuania is a major political mistake. In the language of the Church, it is a sin.' Chrysostom, the Orthodox Bishop of Lithuania, was even more forceful. At the funeral of the victims of the Vilnius shootings he said: 'The Russian authorities are guilty for what is happening here. The Russian people should be ashamed.' And on TV he accused Gorbachev of deceiving the people. Such language from the traditionally sycophantic Orthodox Church was an unprecedented appeal to very profound Russian instincts.

And so for the first time since the October Revolution, a major Soviet crisis was conducted in the full glare of public opinion. No one could claim that he did not know what the issues were. A demonstration called by *Moscow News* on 20 January was attended by up to half a million people (later estimates put the figure at 100,000, still a very large number). One of them was Sasha Motov. It was the first time he had ever voluntarily taken part in a political demonstration. He demonstrated because he disapproved of the shooting of civilians by the army.

A week after the shootings I put my thoughts into a letter to the Foreign Office, as much for my own benefit as for theirs. Gorbachev's policy towards the Baltics had wavered for eighteen months. Under any of his predecessors the tanks would of course have gone in at the first sign of

indiscipline. As Soviet politics lurched to the right, the chances of negotiation in good faith had faded. The military and the reactionaries in the
Party increased their pressure on the government to restore order in the
Republics. Gorbachev must have concluded that he had to go along with
them to preserve his authority. The hard men adapted the plan that worked
so well in Czechoslovakia in 1968: set up a 'Committee of National
Salvation', call in the army, and restore orthodoxy. But the execution of this
simple plan was bungled. The army moved in before the local Quislings
could be organised to welcome them. The government's public line was
contradictory and implausible. Gorbachev could not escape the responsibility. Either he had initiated the plan, as a necessary action to preserve
the Union; or he had supported and acquiesced in an initiative of the
reactionaries; or he was their prisoner and had lost control of events.
Perhaps he believed that only he could ride the whirlwind. Perhaps he
thought that his alliance with the reactionaries was a necessary and
temporary manoeuvre, after which he could continue with his long-term
strategy to modernise and democratise the Soviet Union. But such extreme
tactical opportunism was highly dangerous.

My judgement would have been even harsher if I had then known that
almost a year earlier, on 22 March 1990, the Politburo had listened approv-
ingly to a plan by General Varennikov to declare an emergency in the Baltic
States, introduce Presidential rule, deploy three regiments of troops at the
request of local 'patriots', and arrest the leadership. It was the Prague 1968
scenario almost to the letter. The plan was not adopted, but Chernyaev
heard the exchanges with deep dismay. Next day he protested to
Gorbachev, who told him to calm down and mind his own business.[4]
General Varennikov experimented with elements of his plan straight away.
It came to nothing then, but in January 1991 he set it in motion almost to
the letter. Years later Chernyaev told me that he had come to believe that it
was Varennikov who gave the order to shoot in Vilnius, without reference
to Gorbachev or anyone else. That was in Varennikov's character. But it
does not absolve Gorbachev from the moral responsibility.

But that was not the whole story. After five years of Perestroika it was far
harder to assert the old authority in the old way: Shevardnadze had
resigned demonstratively and survived. Yeltsin had appealed to Russian
soldiers to disobey their orders. The liberal press had attacked the Soviet
President by name in the strongest language, and called not only for the
government, but for the whole regime, to leave the scene. This was a qualitative change. In the good old days the inadequacy of the plan would not
have altered the end result. The Republics would have been brought into

line after as many deaths as were necessary for the purpose. But Soviet politics were now too complicated for a would-be authoritarian government to manage in the old way.

There was, I thought, a further, even more profound factor at work. Old-fashioned chauvinism was still strong. But the attitudes of the Russian people seemed to be changing. They might, I suggested to London, be losing their imperial will. Further repression of the Balts might encourage the other Republics and especially Ukraine to defy Moscow, undermine whatever prospect remained of a successful economic reform, and alienate the West, with all the political, economic, and security consequences that would follow. If the Baltic crisis spun out of control, it could combine with the breakdown of the economy to mark the beginning of civil strife on an increasing and possibly massive scale, in which even a determined authoritarian attempt to impose order might fail. Faced with these alternatives I thought both sides might now be prepared to negotiate not about the principle of Baltic independence, but about its timing and circumstances.

The West's first reactions to the events in Vilnius were not impressive. On the night after the shootings President Bush appeared on television, looking feeble and exhausted – not at all like a man about to lead his country into war in the Gulf – and admitted that he had not discussed Lithuania during his long talk with Gorbachev earlier in the day. John Major, visiting his soldiers in the Gulf, was almost as shifty. I assumed the two men did not want to damage their relationship with Moscow on the eve of the war: if so, the Soviet hardliners had made the right calculation. Douglas Hurd was rather more robust: if Moscow continued its repression in Lithuania, he said, our bilateral relationship would inevitably be affected.

I myself believed that we needed to keep open our line to Gorbachev, tattered though he now was. So did the British government. Two months after the shooting, in the first week of March, John Major made his first visit to Moscow, met the Baltic representatives over breakfast and spoke to Gorbachev. Douglas Hurd visited soon afterwards. As a result of these visits, our relationship with Gorbachev was resumed. But Gorbachev never again enjoyed the same trust and goodwill in the West. Among the Russian liberals he was finally discredited. The balance of influence, if not yet of power, was slipping towards Yeltsin. In the second half of February there were two more massive demonstrations in Moscow in his support, and his status as a popular hero was reinforced by his regular appearances on television.

Gorbachev himself was learning from his mistakes, but very slowly. On 26 February he spoke in Minsk, his first visit outside the capital for a long time. It was a strong attack on the 'democrats' (his quotes) – depressingly old-fashioned and ill-judged. He flayed Yeltsin and Popov for mocking the country's 'socialist choice', for embarking on an openly anti-Communist path, for trying to boost their popularity by appealing to the people over the heads of the government and the parliament. These 'neo-Bolshevist' tactics could bring the country to civil war. The odd thing about this tirade, I thought, was that it played into the hands of the 'democrats' themselves. People in the Soviet Union were by now thoroughly sick of the 'socialist choice' and were looking for alternatives. I was struck, too, by Gorbachev's use of the word 'Bolshevik'. In the past he would have employed it as a term of the highest praise. But the pejorative tinge he now gave it became common usage.

A month later Gorbachev very nearly went too far. The loyal Communists in the Russian parliament called for a vote of no confidence against Yeltsin. The debate was to take place at an Extraordinary Session in the Kremlin on 28 March. Yuri Afanasiev and the other leaders of 'Democratic Russia' (a political movement which was not yet a party) planned a demonstration in support of Yeltsin for the same day. Kryuchkov told Gorbachev that the demonstrators intended to storm the Kremlin. Gorbachev banned the demonstration. The democrats insisted that it would go ahead. It was the first time they had defied a presidential decree. What everyone had feared, and what had so far been avoided, looked as though it might now happen: the shedding of blood in Moscow itself. On the morning of the proposed demonstration, I warned the Foreign Office that no one knew how the people would respond, or how the army and police would react if the government nerved itself to order the use of force. Gorbachev and his opponents had hitherto always drawn back from the brink. I suspected they would do so again. But there was a real danger of violence

Throughout the morning troop carriers and armoured vehicles assembled at the key points of the city. Battle tanks in groups of three – the tanks which Bakatin had predicted a year earlier – guarded the bridges across the river by the embassy. Some 50,000 police and interior troops were deployed throughout the city. Sobchak came to lunch. He had spent the morning at the Russian parliament. He believed that Afanasiev and his fellows were wrong to push for a confrontation. He had failed to persuade them to hold the demonstration at Luzhniki, instead of attempting to break into the centre of the city. If the government did not draw back, there could be shooting by the evening and blood would be shed. That would be the end for Gorbachev. But Gorbachev was a busted flush anyway. It was now clear that Yeltsin could get himself elected as Russian President, even if he lost today's vote of confidence. Meanwhile the real decisions were being taken by those in the shadows behind Gorbachev, above all by Lukyanov. Lukyanov looked like a grey official. People called him a creep. In fact he was highly intelligent, a reactionary with a very powerful will. 'Like Stalin,' I commented.

By six o'clock CNN television was showing tens of thousands of disciplined citizens (Konstantin Demakhin was of course amongst them) pouring onto the streets and assembling by the Mayakovsky statue in Gorky Street despite the government's clear warning. The Russian deputies, by an overwhelming vote, decided to send their Speaker, Ruslan Khasbulatov, to tell Gorbachev that they would not continue their session under the barrel of a gun. After a highly emotional exchange Gorbachev promised to remove the troops. When they heard the news, the deputies abandoned their session to join the demonstrators. Snow was falling on the city as, by late evening, the troops were on their way out of town.

It was a huge defeat for Gorbachev. The reactionaries no doubt accused him of having collapsed under the pressure of the crowd. The crowd itself now hated and despised him. It seemed only a question of time before he was replaced, perhaps by a genuinely new government under Yeltsin. But I did not believe that Lukyanov, Kryuchkov, Pugo, and the others would give up so easily. I woke up in the middle of the night to find myself composing in my head a telegram for Gorbachev's political epitaph.

All was not politics at that difficult time, though everything had a political overtone. During the years of Communism, Easter was celebrated with the minimum of pomp, hugger-mugger even in the major churches, the priests and congregation harassed, especially in Khrushchev's day, by hooligans set on by the KGB. But in April 1991 the streets of Moscow were hung with posters wishing the people a Happy Easter for the first time for seventy years. We ourselves celebrated the festival that year with Father Oleg in his parish of Tatishchev-Pogost. As we drove the hundred miles north from Moscow the countryside looked at its very worst: stuck between Winter and Summer, dirty snow in the shadows, the trees bare, the grass grey or overwhelmed by mud and melting water, the villages wholly unkempt, wooden *izbas* at crazy angles, interspersed with the worst kind of agro-industrial slum.

Tatishchev was no exception. The newly painted neo-classical church and Oleg's new brick house were stranded in a sea of mud. Oleg was in his early thirties, very fat as a result of some hormone imbalance. He had been exiled to Tatishchev by the Bishop of Yaroslavl for insubordination. He had been threatened, and his car had recently been crushed between two lorries in what looked like a staged accident of the traditional kind. His guests for Easter included Galina Kharitonovna, a small neat woman, the director of the profitable local concrete factory, who looked more like the headmistress of a minor English public school for girls; the chairman of the local state farm; and the Deputy Chairman of the Yaroslavl Regional Council. A Colonel of Militia hovered in the background for reasons which were never clear.

Before the service we had a massive meal, even though it was still formally the Grand Fast (Lent). We needed it for the ordeal to come. By ten o'clock the church was packed with people who had come from miles around, young and old, men and women. In a short sermon Father Oleg bitterly attacked the regime for its crimes against Russia. No one, he said, could escape guilt, neither those who committed the crimes, nor those who had failed to oppose them. He then announced to a baffled congregation that they would now be addressed by the British ambassador. Equally baffled and wholly unprepared, I mumbled something about hoping that the Resurrection of Christ would be matched by the Resurrection of Russia. I was followed by an equally confused Deputy Chairman.

We then got into the serious business of the service. A clutch of tough and raucous old ladies did the singing. Father Oleg did everything else. At midnight we cried 'Christ is risen', kissed one another, and carried the cross around the church. The whole thing lasted more than five hours. We began to wilt, and made increasing use of the chairs which Oleg had thoughtfully provided. The tough old women stood throughout, immovable, like rocks: the ocular demonstration of why Napoleon, Hitler, and even Stalin had failed to break the Russian nation. The service ended with the rustling of paper as the old women opened bags full of hard-boiled eggs to be blessed. The holy water sprinkled us too. We kissed the cross and embraced the priest. Everyone perked up, the choir sang with renewed enthusiasm, and the day dawned.

We went back to Father Oleg's house to break our fast. Again there was a feast, this time with lavish vodka. After the toasts, Oleg started chanting the gospel. The rest of the table joined in: they knew the gospel by heart, and they picked up the music as they went along. The melody and the harmony seemed straight out of *Boris Godunov* or *Khovanshchina*. (Musicologists like to argue that the tradition of Russian church music is a myth, largely invented by Romantics in the nineteenth century. The argument is probably exaggerated, and leaves the evocative power of the music undiminished.) After three hours' sleep we got up to find that Father Oleg was still on the stump, his enthusiasm and dedication and humour undiminished as he held short services in all the local cemeteries. People were putting paper flowers, birdseed and sweets on the little tables by the graves of their relatives. The raucous old women, still in full voice, supported Father Oleg in the chanting. None of them seemed to have had any sleep for thirty-six hours and more.

The events surrounding the great demonstration of 28 March 1991 were a turning point. For the reactionaries they were another trial run for a decisive blow in Moscow itself. For Gorbachev they were a serious warning that he risked being swept away by a reactionary flood, losing all claim to the respect of his compatriots, of his foreign partners, and of history. He deliberately drew back and tried to repair his links with the democrats. Over the next months he met time and again with Yeltsin and the other republican leaders at Novo-Ogarevo, a villa outside Moscow, in order to hammer out an agreement on the distribution of powers between the Union and its constituent parts. It was a task difficult enough in itself. How were the political, fiscal, and economic powers of a formerly centralised state to be divided up? What was to happen to the Soviet armed forces, the Soviet central bank, the unified Soviet transport and energy systems, and the other instruments of central power? The task was made much more difficult because Yeltsin and the Ukrainians were determined to use the process to promote their own independent power. The Balts and the Georgians, each determined on a complete break, refused to participate in the talks at all.

In the middle of these negotiations Yeltsin achieved his stunning victory in the elections to the new post of President of the RSFSR. Time was running out for the reactionaries They believed that the talks at Novo-Ogarevo and the existence of two presidents in what they still thought of as one country threatened the Union, and was more than they were prepared to tolerate. On 17 June Pavlov took advantage of Gorbachev's absence in Novo-Ogarevo to ask the parliament for emergency powers to implement his anti-crisis plan for the economy. He admitted that he had not consulted the President in advance. Reactionary deputies launched a stormy attack against Gorbachev. The meeting went into closed session: but its proceedings leaked within hours. Pugo, Kryuchkov and Yazov all said that the country was going to the dogs. Kryuchkov repeated his dire warnings about sinister foreign forces, and said that he was prepared to act to save the system 'rather than any particular leader'. The nationalist deputy Kogan proposed an extraordinary Congress of People's Deputies to strip the President of his executive powers. The newspapers called it a 'constitutional coup'.

The Queen's Birthday Party in the Kharitonenko house two days later was a day of sweltering humidity, preceded by a cracking thunder-and-rainstorm. It seemed as if Russia now had a monsoon climate, unlike the old days when Queen's Birthday Parties took place on the lawn, and Khrushchev and his friends struggled with strawberries and cream. Laptiev, Afanasiev and Starovoitova were there, deeply depressed and full of the 'constitutional coup'. I reminded them that when the reactionaries went on the rampage at the two Party Congresses in 1990 we had asked ourselves whether they were making a last stand or trying to mount a counterrevolution. Was history repeating itself as farce? But all three were convinced that a genuine conspiracy lay behind the interventions of Pavlov, Yazov, and Kryuchkov. Gorbachev had been totally taken aback. A coup could happen at any moment. The troops in the Moscow military district were put on alert following Yeltsin's victory. General Rodionov came up to me and said cheerfully that the Moscow military commanders had agreed over the weekend that one president in the country was enough, and that he shared their views.

But at the end of the week Gorbachev stormed back into the parliament, flayed the conservatives, and nailed his flag firmly to the mast of reform. Yazov shuffled and weaved. Pavlov looked like a whipped boy and complained he had been misrepresented in the press. Lukyanov produced the ingenious explanation that Pavlov had merely been trying to get a better grip on the fiscal and banking system. This was apparently sufficient to calm everyone down. On the whole, observers were inclined to think that the week's events had indeed been a farce, not a tragedy. At supper a few days later, Mary Dejevsky, the correspondent of *The Times*, thought the reactionaries might still try to embarrass Gorbachev before he attended the London Economic Summit in July. Shootings in the Baltic States or more random bombings would serve the purpose. Fyodorov, the Deputy Foreign Minister of the RSFSR, said that the reactionaries were under pressure to act before it was too late. Colonel Shlykov, the Chairman of the RSFSR Committee on Defence, said that many middle-ranking officers were Russian chauvinists who supported Zhirinovsky. Others supported Yeltsin, who was now calling for the creation of a Russian army. The generals were terrified that Yeltsin would appeal effectively to the troops over their heads. But everyone agreed that the 'constitutional coup' was over.

One more storm signal appeared that Summer. On 26 July *Sovietskaya Rossia* – the paper which had published Nina Andreyeva's notorious article in 1988 – carried a 'Message to the Nation' signed by Varennikov and other generals, Bishop Pitirim, and a number of conservative writers. It attacked 'scheming, eloquent leaders, cunning dissidents and greedy rich exploiters … who hate this country and are now slavishly seeking advice and blessing from overseas … Let us all rise up in unity and challenge the destroyers of the Fatherland … Russia, unique among nations, is calling for our help.' In my diary I noted that this was 'Strong language, from people who could do something about it if they wished.' The coup occurred three weeks later.

My own views had been crystallising throughout the year. The Western press and media had personalised the confrontation between Gorbachev and Yeltsin. But the issue went much deeper than the merely personal. Of course the two men hated one another. Of course both of them wanted to be leader in a situation where in the end there was room for only one. But it was a gross oversimplification to characterise Yeltsin as a democrat and Gorbachev as a reactionary. Both favoured reform and democracy. But their strategic approaches were profoundly different. Yeltsin believed that only radical and urgent reform could save the country from chaos. Gorbachev was a gradualist, who believed that generations would have to pass before the process of change was complete.

Even though things were now going badly wrong, Gorbachev had already wrought a remarkable transformation. In 1988 the Soviet Union was still a unitary state, ruled by the authoritarian leaders of an authoritarian Party through a disciplined government machine, massively and unequivocally backed by the army and the KGB. By 1990 some of the institutions of a genuine democracy were taking root, the Party was discredited, the machinery of repression was in decay, the Union was being willy-nilly transformed. The Soviet Humpty Dumpty could not be put together again.

But since the middle of 1990, Gorbachev had signally failed to drive the process forward. Worse, he was toying with the idea that he could stem the symptoms of economic decline by temporarily reverting to the mechanisms of administrative control. If the old-fashioned paranoia and voodoo economics of Pavlov and Kryuchkov came to dominate policy, the country would be in for a period of introverted and authoritarian rule. It would not work, and sooner or later the path of reform would have to be resumed. A further crackdown in the Republics or a more general suspension of democratic rights would freeze East–West relations. But it would not alter the realities of the international balance of power. I did not believe that the

Russians would try to return to Eastern Europe, or that they could succeed if they did try. The East–West settlements of 1989 and 1990 would stand. And even if Gorbachev had lost his former glamour, his ultimate failure was by no means a certain thing.

Yeltsin, the obvious alternative, was by the end of 1990 by far the only politician of comparable stature to Gorbachev. But despite his rapidly increasing political profile, he still had no effective basis of power. He claimed to speak for a 'Russia' which had not yet acquired the attributes of a real state. His lack of serious interest in the details of economic reform was the despair of his advisers. His personal weaknesses – his drinking habits, his attacks of depression, his disappearances from public view – were not simply black propaganda invented by Gorbachev's friends. People could legitimately wonder if he was a genuine democrat, or whether he was driven above all by a lust for power and by his obvious (if entirely under-standable) desire to get his revenge on Gorbachev for the disgraceful way he had been treated in 1987. Some of these questions were still to hang over him after the Soviet Union had collapsed and he had finally become the undisputed President of Russia.

By the middle of 1990 Western critics were already asking themselves whether it still made sense to back Gorbachev. Was it not high time that Western governments should abandon 'Gorbymania' and switch their support to Yeltsin, a much more authentic democrat? Mrs Thatcher's private concerns about Gorbachev's staying power filtered back to his entourage. Douglas Hurd wondered if it was time to distance ourselves from him.

From time to time governments do find themselves wondering whether they have backed the right horse. Should we abandon the Shah of Iran as the opposition to him mounts? Should we continue to dally with the dreadful Ceauşescu because he is a usefully disruptive element within the Soviet bloc? For the outside critic the issue is usually clear: on grounds of morality or expediency we should ring out the old and ring in the new. But governments have to deal with those currently in power, however unattractive they may be and however shaky their hold on office. To switch favours, to ditch one's friends, to change horses in mid-stream even with the best or most cynical of motives, is an operation usually beyond the bounds of practical politics. We had invested a lot in Gorbachev's success. He stood for a European settlement and East–West cooperation abroad, and for political and economic liberalism at home. Despite his wavering, he continued to stand for all of these things until he finally left office. In no sense was he a Shah or a Ceauşescu. I did not think in 1990, and I do not think now, that the West should or could have turned away from him at that time.

In the last months of the old year a Bulgarian clairvoyant predicted that Gorbachev would lose his nerve in 1991 and put a bullet in his brain, after which the Soviet Union would begin to prosper. Many Muscovites were said to believe her.

8

Diary of a Coup

The nimble political high-wire artist simply failed to notice how long the other end of the wire on which he was balancing had already been in the hands of people who did not want to see him as head of state.

Anatoli Lukyanov's memoirs

In July 1991 Gorbachev came to London to meet the 'Heads of State and Government' of Britain, France, Germany, Italy, Japan, Canada, and the United States at the Economic Summit of the Group of Seven (the G7). John Major took him afterwards to see Rossini's *Cenerentola* at Covent Garden. He was cheered inside the theatre as he entered, and again in the street outside as he left, popular enthusiasm that he could no longer command in his own country.

The candlelight dinner afterwards was held at Admiralty House in Whitehall in the small dining room with the dreadful wallpaper and the ostentatious pictures of naval victories over the French. Gorbachev and Raisa entered hand-in-hand. Gorbachev was on his very best form: charming, lively, frank, optimistic, but serious as well. He insisted that he would not be deflected from his strategic aim of transforming the country and building a market economy. But each country had to find the forms best suited to it, and in Russia there was great resistance to change. Much had been made by foreigners of the need to privatise land. But Russian peasants believed that the land came from God. They preferred the commune and the medieval strip system which had had been swept away by collectivisation. It would be much harder than Westerners thought to change these attitudes. He was right. Despite the expectations of foreigners, Yeltsin never managed to get a law on the privatisation of agricultural land through parliament. And even in Putin's Russia the Communists were still opposing it.

Gorbachev firmly believed, he said, that Russia would end up with a mixed economy. The transformation would not be completed in his lifetime. He knew that he was widely criticised for being indecisive. But he could not go faster than the people could bear. He was not prepared to use the forcible methods of the past. If he succeeded, people would forget the criticism. If he failed, the criticism would be the least of his worries. 'Then ten angels will not be able to save us.'

Major asked about rumours of a possible coup. Gorbachev laughed. People were always worrying that he was about to be overthrown. Bush had telephoned him only the other day about some coup or other. But he was confident that everything was going to be all right.

Nothing sensational ever happens in August, apart from the odd World War. Gorbachev had faced down the 'constitutional coup' in June and gone on holiday to the Crimea. My diplomatic colleagues in Moscow agreed that all was quiet: I told the visiting Mayor of Cardiff as much when he came to lunch on 18 August. That evening Jill and I left for a brief trip to Vologda, an ancient city North of Moscow on the seventeenth-century trade route through the Northern river system and Archangel to England and Holland.

There was one odd note. A couple of days before we went off on holiday I received a visit from Misharin, a plump, middle-aged and bearded intellectual who edited *Voskresenie*, a new magazine backed by Gorbachev. He wanted me to write an article on the need to combine democracy with discipline, and on the importance of countries being true to their national traditions. As he warmed up, he asked if I realised how unpopular Gorbachev had become. Did I not understand how dangerous was the division of power symbolised by Yeltsin's Russian flag flying over the Kremlin right opposite the embassy? Did I not understand that everything was now on a knife-edge? It was an odd performance for one who claimed to be a Gorbachev supporter. I drew no particular conclusions and I never saw him again.

The planes to Vologda leave from a small airport at Bykovo to the east of Moscow. As we drove out to the elegant Yak in which we were to travel, it taxied away and took off without us. Konstantin bullied the air traffic controller into putting us onto another plane for Cherepovets, about a hundred kilometres from Vologda. Konstantin was convinced that it was not an accident: someone was determined to prevent us leaving Moscow. But he was unable to think of a rational explanation. At Cherepovets airport – a wooden hut – we settled down to wait for Sasha, who had driven ahead to Vologda, and was now on his way to meet us. Tikhomirov, the pilot who had brought us there, felt personally guilty that we had been let down by Aeroflot, and kept us company while we were waiting. He told us that he had been flying on the route Moscow–Cherepovets–Vologda for ten years. But he didn't have a car, and had never learned to drive.

Monday: the First Day

And so that is how, when the coup began on Monday 19 August, Jill and I came to be spending the first hours not in Moscow, but in the Party hostel in Vologda: the 'best' hotel in town, all cheap plush, plywood furniture, concrete corridors and potted plants, reeking of provincial Communism and generations of Party bureaucrats travelling the country on their petty affairs, next to the huge provincial Party headquarters and the brand-new headquarters of the KGB. Our small radio was set to deliver the BBC news at eight o'clock every morning. Surprisingly, Vologda was within range. 'The Soviet leadership', we heard, had declared a state of emergency 'in connection with the impossibility, owing to his state of health, of Mikhail Sergeevich Gorbachev fulfilling his duties as President'. It was practically the same as the language that *Pravda* had used at the time of Khrushchev's fall in 1964, which I had looked up in the embassy's library nearly three years earlier. An 'Emergency Committee' had been set up. It included Kryuchkov, Pavlov, Pugo, Yazov, and Yanaev, all of whom owed their jobs to Gorbachev. At the other end of Russia, in the Southern city of Astrakhan, Mikhail Afanasiev heard the news as he queued to buy milk for his sick mother. All the women in the queue except one thought it served Gorbachev right. Afanasiev, a young student with links to the reformers, thought the coup could easily succeed. The conspirators need only to shoot a dozen people in Astrakhan – fifty in larger places like Saratov – to establish their rule. He wondered when the KGB would come for him. All over the country people were wondering the same.

Oleg Bobrik, a small businessman in Vologda – one of the first of a new breed – had been intending to act as our guide. Now he came to the hotel to tell us the news. The Vologda City Council were all at sixes and sevens: Should they resist the commands from Moscow? Should they go along? Should they keep their heads down in the hope everything would blow over? He himself was hostile to the Emergency Committee, though he thought that Gorbachev had brought many of his troubles upon himself. Meanwhile the indispensable Sasha fixed us up on the midday plane for

Moscow. Bobrik and Tikhomirov came to see us off at the airport: a brave gesture, perhaps an early sign that the coup leaders would not have things all their own way. Sasha at least was sure that those 'samozvantsy' would soon be thrown out. (*Samozvanets* – a pretender – is a winged word to a Russian. From time immemorial rebels have appeared in the distant provinces claiming to be the true heir to the Russian throne. The most famous *samozvanets* is the First Dmitri who challenged Boris Godunov, and figures in Mussorgsky's opera.)

All over Russia other people, too, were scurrying back to their places of work. Vadim Medvedev was in a sanatorium in the Crimea. He woke up to hear the conspirators' announcement. The telephone in his bedroom was cut off. But all the phones in the other bedrooms were working. He flew back to Moscow with no difficulty, though he expected to be arrested at every moment. He went home, and then to his office in the Kremlin. There too the phones had not been cut; and for the rest of the week he, Laptiev, Primakov, and Bakatin worked at one end of the Kremlin corridors, while Yanaev and the conspirators worked at the other.

Sobchak had become Mayor of Leningrad on the same day as Yeltsin became President of Russia. He was in Moscow when the coup began. After discussing the plan of campaign at Yeltsin's dacha, he set off to return to Leningrad. At Moscow airport three obvious KGB operatives bore down upon him. But instead of arresting him they told him they were there to ensure that he got safely on his plane. On arrival he went straight to the Headquarters of the Leningrad Military District by the Winter Palace. The commanding general, Samsonov, had already announced his support for the coup on TV. He was now conferring with his officers and with the local KGB. Sobchak burst in on them to say that the coup was illegal: he knew, because he himself had helped to draft the constitutional laws. If the generals tried to arrest him they would ruin their careers. The generals argued shiftily that they were only obeying orders. That's what they said at Nuremburg, replied Sobchak, and the generals subsided. He then summoned a meeting of the City Council at the Mariinsky Palace and told them that Gorbachev had been arrested by 'criminals'. He was the first of their opponents so to describe them. In the evening he persuaded Leningrad TV to show scenes from the film version of Kabakov's *The Non-Returner*, depicting Muscovites being rounded up by a military regime in the not-too-distant future. In distant Perm they took the fiction for reality, and briefly panicked.

Yavlinsky, the young liberal economist and politician who had seen me several times during the Summer about his scheme for a Grand Bargain for economic cooperation between the Soviet Union and the West, had just gone on holiday. He was arriving in Lvov on the night train when he heard the conspirators' announcement. Its Stalinist language led him to fear the worst. He got straight on the train back to Moscow. He too expected to be arrested at any moment, so at each stop he handed a written account of his views to the bemused people on the platform. When he heard the plotters' fumbling press conference on his radio, he knew the coup would fail. The question was, how much blood would be shed in the process? He went to the White House, the seat of the Russian parliament, where he helped maintain contact between the Russian and the Soviet KGB.

We ourselves arrived back in Bykovo just after lunch, barely twenty hours after we had left it. Konstantin was in a high state of triumphant excitement. Had he not been right about last night's incident at the airport? The air traffic controller had had a portrait of – guess whom? – Stalin over his desk. My new private secretary Julie Bell was also there, and showed me the first clutch of reporting telegrams from the embassy: the text of the Emergency Committee's 'Decree No. 1', banning political parties and ordering the people and the economy to behave themselves; Yeltsin's appeal to the soldiers to disobey them, and his call for a general strike.

We drove into Moscow along the Ryazan highway past a parked column of over a hundred military vehicles: lorries, armoured personnel carriers, a few tanks, canvas-covered objects that might have been guns. The soldiers were lounging in the sun. One carrier was broken down by the road. In Moscow itself, things seemed surprisingly normal: civilian cars in their usual chaotic jam, people going about their normal business, women shopping. Military vehicles nosed through the traffic. Tanks in groups of three commanded the entrances onto Red Square, as they had done at the time of the demonstration in March. Their crews were gloomy and uncommunicative. Stuck to the back of one tank was a copy of Yeltsin's appeal to the soldiers. People were mystified and curious rather than fearful. Neither the soldiers nor the civilians seemed to have any idea what was going on. It did not feel like a besieged city expecting violence

The embassy seemed almost empty when I got back. The young men from the political section were enjoying themselves on the streets as they observed what was going on, struggling to report back from the battered telephone kiosks, because this was before the age of the mobile phone. John Major had already announced that we would have nothing to do with the Emergency Committee. I tried to ring Chernyaev at home and in his office: his phones were not working. Meanwhile Jill set off with her Social Secretary Ann Brown and her video camera to see what was going on. They came back a couple of hours later. There were protest meetings on Manege Square, where Jill had met one of the young Soviet cosmonauts we knew. The troops and the people were now talking to one another, friendly and relaxed. Armoured units were on the move – the KGB's Dzerzhinsky Division, the elite Taman Division, the paratroopers from Ryazan. It was rumoured, and then denied, that paratroopers had taken over the Moscow City Council.

As the day wore on the Emergency Committee issued a stream of announcements and appeals, strengthening the grip of the security organs, banning all political activity, and reasserting central control of the economy. The Committee appealed to the Soviet people for support in restoring the Soviet Union to its rightful place in the world. It assured the international community that the Soviet Union would continue to uphold its international obligations.

But it soon became clear that there was something very odd about the coup: no action on the streets, no one arrested, Yeltsin in the White House stoutly maintaining that only he, and not the putsch leaders, had authority on the territory of Russia. The forces facing Yeltsin were overwhelming in their numbers and their firepower. But the columns of armour were not backed up by the hordes of footsoldiers which had dominated earlier attempts to intimidate the Moscow streets and there was none of the aggressive military hysteria which had accompanied the bloodshed in Baku and Tbilisi.

At teatime the conspirators – people were already calling them 'the junta' – gave a televised press conference: a performance so bizarre that Jill immediately christened it 'The Muppet Show'. A nervous – perhaps a drunken – Yanaev tried to explain their position. He promised that the junta would continue with reform, and expressed the hope that after a good long rest Gorbachev might be able to resume his duties as President. He then foolishly agreed to take questions. A young journalist from *Nezavisimaya Gazeta*, Tanya Malkina, asked if he realised that he was acting against the constitution. Another journalist asked what he thought of Yeltsin's call for a nation-wide strike: thus enlightening millions of Soviet viewers who didn't know Yeltsin had called for any such thing. The junta's credibility was thus destroyed at its first public appearance. On the evening news a grim woman announcer rose from the Soviet past to read the decrees of the Emergency Committee. All the independent newspapers were banned. Yeltsin was chided like a naughty boy for his rebellious remarks earlier in the day. But the same news programme showed Yeltsin making those very remarks, demonstrations in Leningrad and Moscow, a tank flying the Russian flag, a soldier waving an unloaded gun and swearing that he would never fire on the crowd, men building barricades outside the

White House, saying that they were determined to defend the parliament which they themselves had elected.

By that evening the coup was already degenerating into farce in Leningrad. The journalist Ivan Sedykh drove out along the motorway on a rumour that the Pskov Airborne Division was approaching the city. He found a group of policemen constructing a barricade of buses on the carriageway into town. The outward carriageway was free: the policemen assumed that the armoured column would obey the traffic regulations and keep to the right side of the road. Further on he saw one cannon and four mobile army kitchens abandoned in the middle of the road. The soldiers had got lost and were now shacked up in a nearby village. The policemen arrested the soldiers and took them in triumph to Leningrad.

By then it was clear enough what had happened. The reactionary barons had tried for a year to reverse the course of reform. They now feared the tide was turning against them. They moved when the leader was on holiday, to prevent the signature of the Union Treaty and the breakup of the Empire. Their timing was predictable. Unfortunately neither Gorbachev nor we predicted it.

This was not after all simply an action replay of the fall of Khrushchev in 1964. That was a palace coup within the Communist Party. This time the Party played no formal role. There was no meeting of the Central Committee, no *Pravda* leader, no black limousines driving in and out of the Kremlin. The Central Committee headquarters looked deserted throughout the day. The Emergency Committee failed to mention the Party in any of its public pronouncements. No one even bothered to tell us whether Gorbachev was still General Secretary, and if not, who was his successor. Gorbachev had made the Party irrelevant. The main aim of the barons was not to restore Communism. It was to impose law, order, political and economic discipline, and to restore the prestige of the Soviet Union in the only way they knew.

And so the attempted coup of 1991 was a public affair. It sparked public indignation from the very beginning. Despite the mass of armour on the Moscow streets, the first day had an oddly tentative, even gentlemanly air about it. By the evening of the first day, I thought it was still too soon to judge whether popular outrage would swell into full-scale resistance, whether Yeltsin could continue his defiance while lacking any of the normal attributes of power, whether the confused mood of the troops would lead to disobedience, mutiny or to violence, whether the hardliners in the Emergency Committee would overbear their colleagues who had been exercising restraint. I did not think it inevitable that Russia would now relapse into sullen acquiescence or enter a new time of troubles. I doubted if we could do much to influence the outcome. But I recommended to the Foreign Office a number of measures that would hurt the new regime without damaging our Russian friends or denying them hope for the future.

By midnight all was quiet. Even Ekho Moskvy, the independent radio station broadcasting from within the White House itself, had fallen silent. A steady drizzle had set in, dampening the morale of the soldiers without apparently affecting that of the growing number of people gathering round the White House. That evening I wrote in my diary:

> The reactionaries will be unable to make the economy work by decree, any more than Canute could make the tide flow back. So the economy will go from bad to worse, perhaps after a brief lurch for the better as people work harder under the influence of fear. That is on the assumption that the reactionaries can make their will prevail. After this first day, that is still not yet entirely clear.

As I went to sleep I seemed to hear the keening of liberal intellectuals regretting that they had not supported Gorbachev while he was still there.

Tuesday: the Second Day

Guy Spindler and Richard Astle, two of the embassy's young men, had spent the night at the White House. Early on the morning of the second day they reported that about forty armoured personnel carriers and seven heavy tanks were now around the building. They were from the crack Taman Division. Earthmovers from the City Council were helping to construct more solid barricades. There were paratroopers from Tula under General Lebed, who said they had come to support Yeltsin and Russia. The account in Lebed's memoirs is hilarious. At 4 a.m. on 19 August he was ordered up to Moscow with his paratroopers with orders to defend the White House. His superiors were unable to explain whom he was meant to defend it against. Since his command vehicle had no adequate radio receiver, he did not hear the initial statement by the junta and had no idea what was going on even after he got to Moscow. So he led his men to the White House, and persuaded Yeltsin with some difficulty that he was there to help.

The junta had still not established their control over the media. When they tried to prevent *Izvestia* from printing Yeltsin's appeal the printers threatened to strike and the message was carried. Even *Pravda* reported

Yeltsin's statements, the scenes on the streets, and the foreign criticism. The Committee on Constitutional Supervision announced that the State of Emergency would be legal only if it secured a two-thirds majority at the meeting of the Soviet parliament called for 26 August.

British businessmen came in for a briefing. I told them that anything could happen, from the collapse of the coup through inanition to a bloody civil war. But the conspirators had made a serious mistake by not acting more ruthlessly and they now seemed to be losing the initiative to Yeltsin and the democrats. Several of the businessmen asked if they should bring their employees to Moscow from the distant construction sites where they were working, or even send them home. I advised them to do nothing for the time being. They would look pretty silly if the coup fizzled out, and it would be harder to get their people back than to remove them.

Rumours began to spread that democrats had been arrested, that the Emergency Committee was falling apart. In the afternoon the tempo quickened. Friends in the White House phoned to say they expected an attack imminently. At teatime a panicky Stankevich appealed over Ekho Moskvy for all women and children to leave the White House and the area around it. It was frustrating to hang around in the office while history was being made. Everyone else was out on the streets. I had already suggested to Stephen Wall, Major's Private Secretary, that I should show solidarity by going down to the White House. He promised to ring back. Meanwhile I drove off in a Russian jeep with David Manning and Geoff Murrell, the head of the embassy's internal political section. Jill set off separately in another jeep with Stephen, our cook, and Ann Brown.

We parked on the embankment opposite the White House, an absurdly pompous building built at the height of Brezhnev's vulgar reign, faced with lifeless white marble, a rectangle standing upright on another rectangle with the usual multiplicity of inconsequential entrances, most of them – as always in Soviet buildings – locked firmly shut. Up until now the White House had been a symbol of the fraudulent Soviet Union, with its fake national Republics and their nameless Prime Ministers and powerless 'governments'. From now on it was to become a powerful symbol in its own right: a symbol of a new and very turbulent Russia. Facing the White House on the other side of the river where we were parked was the Ukraina Hotel, one of Stalin's neo-Gothic fantasies, imaginative, powerful, menacing, everything that the White House was not. The embankment was crowded with parked cars. I wondered that so many Russians appeared to be willing to risk their valuable cars in the middle of what could become a very nasty affair indeed.

The Kutuzovsky Bridge leading to the White House was blockaded with tanks flying Russian and Ukrainian flags. It was not clear which side they were on. People crowded across the bridge in a subdued mood of festivity and excitement mixed with apprehension. Crowd stewards were ineffectively trying to prevent them from moving towards the White House. At the other end of the bridge there was an inadequate barricade. Cranes were being brought along to help with the construction of more barricades. There were a couple more tanks, their young crews clambering around doing their housekeeping. The parachutists and their armoured personnel carriers, who were supposed to have come in the previous night, were now nowhere to be seen. Ambulances waited in clutches. Mobile toilets were being used both as part of the barricades and for their proper purpose.

In contrast to the middle-aged demonstrators of 1989 and 1990, this time most of the crowd were in their twenties: at last the youth of Moscow was on the move. People stood in knots around anyone with a portable radio. Some had guitars and were singing quietly. A passionate young man jumped on a tank with a loudhailer. He cried: 'Foreigners are taking photographs and asking questions: Where are your weapons? How are you going to fight the soldiers? But we aren't going to fight the soldiers. The soldiers are our friends and countrymen. We are going to greet them and reason with them.' The crowd cheered when he told them that the Ryazan Airborne Academy had declared itself for Russia, and would persuade the incoming troops not to fire.

By now we were increasingly convinced that the coup would fail. Geoff Murrell remarked that it was another October 1917: only this time it was the Soviet power that was crumbling. Neither of us had expected to live to see it. In the square behind the White House we met Guy Spindler, who had been prowling around the building for most of the previous twenty-four hours. He said that there had been perhaps two hundred thousand people there earlier in the afternoon. People were milling about aimlessly, some building flimsy barricades out of park railings, bits of tree, and climbing frames from children's playgrounds. The cobblestones had been dug up in the classic revolutionary fashion. But there was no sign of organisation and no sign of serious preparation for resistance. Rumours swept the crowd. A column of tanks was on the way; there would be an assault from the air; gas would be used. People seemed cheerful despite the rumours and despite the drizzling rain. But it was hard to imagine those unarmed people and those pathetic barricades resisting an even halfway serious assault. At most they could achieve the status of martyrs.

Geoff and I walked back to the embassy through the gathering dusk. There was a cordon of troop transporters at Manege Square. The crews were standing around or sitting on their vehicles. They seemed mostly very small and very young. Many were wearing badges with the Russian flag. They looked confused and unhappy. A woman asked one intelligent-looking boy what he thought he was doing. He said that he and his comrades were told in the middle of Sunday night that they were going on a training exercise. They took a minimum amount of food and ammunition with them. It was only when they arrived in Moscow that they heard that President Gorbachev was ill, and that they were there to preserve order. The boy got more and more unhappy with the relentless questioning, until he put his hands over his ears and said that his nerves were fraying. Someone then put a tape recorder radio on his vehicle. It was replaying Yeltsin's appeal to the soldiers not to sully the glory of Russian arms by shedding Russian blood. I thought: if only Gorbachev had been capable of that kind of patriotic rhetoric. A youngish man in a grey three-piece tweed suit with a brief case was angrily defending the army: 'Aren't you ashamed of attacking Soviet power? Aren't you afraid of being arrested?' 'Look at him,' a woman sneered, 'the last surviving remnant of Soviet power.' A smart and handsome young captain was arguing with a civilian about the shortage of sausage. The civilian grumbled about the privileges of the military. The officer countered that, unlike the civilian, his duties prevented him from taking time off to queue in the shops. The officers made no attempt to shield the young soldiers against the attacks on their morale: one more indication of the half-hearted nature of the coup. As we moved off, a youngish man in a suit ran up, crying: 'Everyone to the White House! Everyone to the barricades!' People started to drift back up Kalinin Prospect towards the White House.

We walked across the Great Stone Bridge to the embassy. Groups of heavy tanks squatted on the approaches. An olive-green assault bulldozer lurked ponderously in a turn of the road. It could have swept away the barricades around the White House in the twinkling of an eye. Back in the embassy they told me that the Russian radio had reported that Chernyaev had been arrested at the same time as Gorbachev. No wonder I had been unable to get through to Chernyaev. I felt sick at the thought of him stuck down there in unknown danger.

By the second evening the junta had begun to get some grip on the television. One clipped announcement succeeded another. Black-market-eteers were being arrested; Pavlov had been taken ill; individuals would still get foreign currency to travel (a sop to the privilegentsia). A young worker-writer made a sentimental appeal to soldiers and civilians to be nice to one another, and deplored Yeltsin's rude language about the junta. A nervous and uneasy General Kalinin, the Military Governor of Moscow, announced that a curfew would be imposed in Moscow, starting immediately.

But the Soviet radio and television no longer had a monopoly of the news. Russian Radio reported that Bakatin and Primakov were now in the White House. Fax reports were flooding into the embassy from the Russian press agencies. Support for the junta was crumbling throughout the country. After wavering for a day, Nazarbaev, Kravchuk, and the Belorussians had now come out against them. The Leningrad naval base was supporting Sobchak. Rostropovich flew to Moscow and was in the White House. Mrs Thatcher, from the safety of London, encouraged the people of Moscow to go onto the streets. Rumour said that Kryuchkov and Yazov had resigned, and that Moiseyev was now Defence Minister. Jill rang from the Senokosovs' apartment. She had met them outside the White House and heard the cheers when it was announced that the Prime Minister had telephoned Yeltsin, and again when Shevardnadze came into the building. We agreed that the junta would soon lose the initiative if they did not assert themselves decisively. I told her about the curfew and warned her to stay indoors.

Some time after midnight the embassy started to get phone calls about sporadic small arms fire around the White House. The Russian radio reported that a dozen tanks and some twenty troop transporters had moved past the US embassy, towards the White House, and over the first barricade. One person had been killed and several wounded. A fax came in from the White House itself. The defenders were expecting an infiltration attack by special duties officers of the KGB. To oppose them there were three hundred armed militia inside the White House, the same number of Afghan veterans, and some unarmed students. It was the moment of highest tension. Yavlinsky told me later that he had rung his wife to say farewell. But by then the Soviet KGB were trying to reassure the defenders of the White House that no attack was intended. They took Yavlinsky to see their assault force, the crack Alfa group. The soldiers were armed to the teeth in a school hall within striking distance of the White House. But they were lying around, many were sleeping, others were reading comic magazines. It was clear that they had no thought of a fight. Yavlinsky then knew that it was all over.

I reported by telephone to the Resident Clerk in the Foreign Office. He told me that the Prime Minister wanted me to inform Yeltsin that we had reason to believe he would be attacked during the night. Although the shooting had already taken place, I got through by phone with no difficulty to Sukhanov, Yeltsin's assistant in the White House, a man I had never met, and never did meet. The quality of the line was far better than normal for Moscow – Sukhanov sounded as if he were in the next room. He said that he knew that armoured vehicles were on the move. But he couldn't see them from the White House, and had no details of the shooting. He assured me that Yeltsin's supporters were getting ready to defend themselves. He agreed I might ring him again if I needed to. He would do the same. Needless to say, he did not. He had more important things on his mind. I went to bed.

John Major's message was too vague and too late to be useful. Even if it had arrived in time, it would have had to compete with the thousands of other items of information which were flooding into the White House. Almost everyone there – politicians, soldiers, secret policemen – was in touch with their professional colleagues on the other side about the rumoured assault. They had too much information, not too little. And of course the British message was incorrect. There never was an attack on the White House. But the message was at least, as I told Sukhanov, a genuine gesture of solidarity.[1]

The next day Jill admitted that instead of observing the curfew she had gone with the Senokosovs to the defenders on the barricades. Now was the time, she had argued, for the liberal intellectuals to stand up and be counted. She was on the bridge when the shooting started. At first the crowd had thought it was some kind of fireworks. But a woman standing next to her said it was gunfire: she had heard the same eighteen months ago during the massacre in Baku. All's well that ends well: Jill wasn't killed, and the wrong side didn't win.

Wednesday: the Third Day

I woke at 6 o'clock on the third day of the coup to find the rain still pouring down in buckets. It was not the weather for mass demonstrations. Perhaps God was on the side of the junta after all.

But Ekho Moskvy was still on the air, after an attempt to suppress it during the night. The White House was still unstormed, and the crowds of defenders were still camped around it. But the armoured column which broke through the first barricade, the announcer said, had crushed three people to death and wounded others with machine-gun fire. Rutskoi, Yeltsin's Vice President, came on the air to attack the junta and call on Russians to stand up and be counted. Yevtushenko unburdened himself of a piece of manufactured emotion and appealed to the shades of Pushkin and Tolstoy (who but the Russians would broadcast poetry on such an occasion?). Bakatin and Primakov, in their capacity as members of (Gorbachev's) National Security Council, called for the reinstatement of the President. Numerous Russian towns and regions expressed their support for Yeltsin. The BBC reported that Kryuchkov had twice telephoned Yeltsin's chief of staff, Burbulis, during the night to assure him that the White House would not be attacked.

As she brought me breakfast, Liuda started talking about politics for the very first time. The junta's arbitrary assumption of power was a disgrace. They had no right to do it, and they would not succeed. I pointed out that it would not be the first time that a dictatorial regime had taken power in Russia. She replied that in those days ordinary people did not understand what was going on. They had really believed their leaders' propaganda. Now they knew better. They themselves had elected the Russian President and the White House, and they would not give them up.

London finally agreed that I should call on Yeltsin. I decided to attend the morning's extraordinary session of the Russian parliament in the White House, which was due to call for the dissolution of the Emergency Committee. It was still not at all clear that the conspirators were beaten. They had the firepower. If they chose to use it, and prevailed, they would no doubt hold my support for Yeltsin against me. My usefulness as an ambassador would be over. But Russia under the junta would no longer be much fun to live in, and I would no longer want to stay there.

Sasha drove me to the White House, which he had spent the previous night helping to defend. He had been made a 'centurion' (*Sotnik*) on account of his unblemished military service as a sergeant, and had been put in charge of a company. He told me that a squad of Afghan veterans went out during the night to suppress a sniper on one of the buildings overlooking the White House, for fear he would try to pick off some of the tank crews loyal to Yeltsin. The barricades were more substantial now, though none would have stopped a determined tank. The people were still packed outside, bedraggled with the night's rain, huddling in makeshift shelters, but cheerful, stoical, Russian. Inside the White House there were numerous smart militiamen and rather less smart civilians, many in bits and pieces of the uniforms they had worn in Afghanistan. They were armed with submachine-guns only: I saw nothing more sophisticated. The atmosphere was hectic, emotional, people milling about everywhere, aimlessly purposeful. The Smolny Institute in Petrograd must have been like that when Lenin and Trotsky launched their coup d'état in October 1917.

More than half of the deputies, including the Communists, had dared to come to the session. The galleries were packed with journalists. The Swedish ambassador, Orjan Berner, was there too: the most ingenious and knowledgeable of my colleagues, with endless contacts among Russian public figures. If I ever went to a public occasion and he was missing, I always assumed that he had gone somewhere more interesting.

The Speaker, Khasbulatov, began with a call for silence for the previous night's dead. He then turned his attention to the junta, colourfully, sarcastically, aggressively. He reported on the demands which he, Rutskoi and Silaev (the Prime Minister of the RSFSR since June 1990) had put the previous day to Lukyanov, who was hovering on the edge of the junta, though he was not formally a member. Gorbachev was to be examined by a team including doctors from the World Health Organisation and other foreign observers; he was to be restored immediately to power; the curbs on press and TV were to be lifted; the Emergency Committee was to be dissolved. The deputies cheered when he called for the junta to be punished.

Yeltsin then came forward: ponderous – an assault bulldozer in himself – confident, and apparently unaffected by the tension and two sleepless nights. His speech was tough and well structured. The junta had failed to recruit even a single democrat to give them respectability. He had set up a shadow government to replace him if he was arrested. But elements of three divisions of the occupying troops now supported him. General Lebed had led his paratroopers from Tula to defend the White House instead of storming it. Yeltsin had appointed new commanders of the Moscow and Leningrad Military Districts, and Major General Kobiets as his Defence Minister. (Kobiets, a handsome fleshy man, was standing in full uniform in a corner of the podium.) The Patriarch Aleksi had put out a strong statement of support during the night. Messages had flooded in from abroad: from the British Prime Minister and Mrs Thatcher among others. He did not mention Mitterrand's ill-judged hedging of bets with the junta on Monday. He then reported that Kryuchkov had offered to come to the White House, and to fly down with him to see Gorbachev in the Crimea. 'Don't go, Boris,' the deputies roared unanimously. But they accepted his alternative suggestion that Silaev and Rutskoi should go instead, with a medical team to check the story that Gorbachev was ill, and with foreign journalists and diplomats to observe fair play. It sounded to me like a classic KGB trap. I wondered if it made sense for the Russians to risk losing two of their top people. But the presence of foreign observers would presumably help.

Silaev broke in with a dramatic announcement. The junta were reported to be on their way to Vnukovo, apparently intending to fly to the Crimea and to leave Moscow at the mercy of the troops. Yeltsin immediately ordered the Russian KGB to arrest them. Yavlinsky and some colleagues were sent off to Pugo's apartment to supervise his arrest. Yavlinsky told me later that armed militiamen who were meant to conduct the actual arrest never turned up. So he and his colleagues broke into the flat. Pugo and his wife had shot themselves and were lying dead on their bed.

In another room of the White House, Kunadze, one of the deputy foreign ministers of Yeltsin's Russia, was giving a press conference about the previous night's violence. A column of six armoured personnel carriers travelling along the inner ring road had been trapped by demonstrators in an underpass at Kalinin Prospect. Three civilians, two soldiers, and a US journalist had been killed: either crushed to death, shot, or burned when the last vehicle was set on fire by a Molotov cocktail. These figures later turned out to be inaccurate, like much of the other 'information' bandied around during the putsch. The final count was three civilians, no journalists, and no soldiers; though there was a persistent rumour that a solider had been killed, but not honoured because he was on the losing side. Kunadze added that the soldiers had been at risk of lynching. Oleg Rumyantsev, the Social Democrat deputy, had negotiated their surrender on discretion. The vehicles, and the prisoners who included a General Smirnov, were then taken in triumph to the White House. 'General Smirnov' was never identified more precisely. I wondered whether he ever existed.

Even after the surrender of the small column, Kunadze said, the defenders around the White House had still expected an assault. There had been about fifty thousand of them deployed in six cordons around the building, ten tanks and ten armoured personal carriers as well. This armour was not a serious military force, but it was enough to provide vital psychological support. A number of other military units had given assurances that they would not shoot. But it was only after Kryuchkov had been contacted in the small hours that the defenders had begun to relax. Now, Kunadze said, the troops appeared to be withdrawing.

On the square outside, a Russian Orthodox hymn swelled up full-throated from many thousands of ordinary people.

Back in the embassy confusion broke out about the plan to send diplomats with Silaev to the Crimea. The Russian Foreign Ministry phoned to say that the plane was due to take off in half an hour. Douglas Hurd insisted I stay by my post in Moscow, so I rushed off to Vnukovo in the Rolls-Royce with Geoff Murrell to put him on the plane instead. For mile after mile we passed armoured vehicles driving at great speed out of the city: some twenty miles of tanks, roaring along and grinding up the muddy roads. One had careered off the road and the soldiers were trying to haul it back. Smoke and dust hung like a fog. More tanks and military vehicles were laagered in the fields to both sides of the road. It was a dramatic and menacing sight of great power, a sight I never expected to see and never expect to see again. It was also a tribute to the ability of the Soviet General Staff to deploy huge masses of armour at great speed. But there was no disguising the fact that I was watching a humiliated army in retreat: Afghanistan, East Germany, now this. Nothing could have been more damaging to the prestige of the generals: so many Dukes of York.

At the airport gate I got into an absurd and entirely Russian argument with a young man in sneakers and golf blouson who was acting as security guard at the VIP terminal. He had, he claimed unconvincingly, never heard of a special government flight to the Crimea. He had no telephone nor any other way of finding out what was going on. As I argued, the other European Excellencies arrived in dribs and drabs. We milled about ineffectively until we learned that the plane had gone without us from the other terminal. The young man in the blouson apologised with a cheerful laugh: 'It isn't every day we have a coup d'état.' We had wasted three hours. It was particularly galling to discover later that the French ambassador had accidentally gone to the right terminal and – by an infuriating combination of good luck and good judgement – got his man onto the rescue aeroplane, along with Jonathan Steele of the *Guardian* and a couple of other enterprising Western journalists. Bakatin later told me that even he had only got onto the plane by the skin of his teeth: the doors were already shut and the engines starting as he drove onto the runway.

The comedy did not end there. I had just got to sleep when someone rang from London to ask if I knew the telephone number of the Kremlin: the Prime Minister wanted to ring Gorbachev when he got back from the Crimea, and the Cabinet Office had lost the number of the hot line. I had just got to sleep again when the Dutch embassy rang to say that Gorbachev was due back at Vnukovo in half an hour, and that the European ambassadors were going out to meet him. I drove myself hell for leather out to the airport. It was another wild goose chase. Gorbachev sensibly decided he could do without having to make conversation with a gaggle of ambassadors. We were not allowed into the airport building, and merely saw his motorcade sweep out of the other gate.

Thursday: the Aftermath

I got up at crack of dawn the next morning to pull some thoughts together for the Foreign Office. Jill and I then drove in the Rolls-Royce, with the flag flying, to observe the session of the Russian parliament in the White House. The building was still surrounded by the detritus of the defence: the remains of barricades, the encampments of the defenders, scraps of meals taken in the rain. We bumped and nosed our way through the obstacles, to park by the square where the victorious people were still gathered in their thousands. Inside the White House the atmosphere was no longer one of apprehension, fatigue, and dour courage. Russia had won its victory, and the Russian people and their leaders were determined to celebrate.

Inside the building Yeltsin and his comrades-in-arms – men who had been consciously risking their lives for the last three days – spoke in legitimate triumph: of what they had achieved, of the end of the seventy-year-old nightmare, and above all of the rebirth of Russia. Yeltsin listed his new decrees, well beyond the limits of his authority as Russian President, trespassing on those of the Union government as he staked out his claim to power.

The other speakers poured out their scorn of the coup leaders, the collaborators, those who had failed to oppose the coup, and those who were now trying to claim that they too had fought valiantly against the defeated Communists. They jeered at Gorbachev for appointing the people who later betrayed him. They attacked Lukyanov, 'the ideologist of the putsch'. Khasbulatov demanded that the Communist Party be stripped of its property. Someone else called for the punishment of the Russian Communist deputies who had opposed the calling of Wednesday's emergency session. I thought I heard the unpleasant undertones of an incipient witch-hunt: France after the Liberation. Silaev suggested that the St George's Cross, the Imperial Russian equivalent of the Victoria Cross, be revived to honour the courage of those who had stood up for Russia in the last three days. Deputies demanded that the flag of Soviet Russia be replaced by the Russian tricolour which had flown over the White House during the siege, and which the defenders had worn in innumerable plastic badges mass-produced in the emergency.

The feeling of Russian fervour grew still greater as we pushed out onto the terrace overlooking the square. Tens of thousands of people were streaming in to join those already there. I congratulated my friends on their victory. The economist Shatalin and I hugged one another. By this time the myth had already been created that I too had been in the White House throughout the siege. An obscure French deputy pushed his way to the microphone to make a Gallic speech comparing the Russian revolutionary tricolour with that of France.

Then Yeltsin appeared on the terrace. His bodyguards held bullet-proof glass shields to protect him against snipers as he made his victory speech. Russia was born again; Russia had saved the world. He promised the crowd the biggest firework display they had ever seen. They shouted in reply 'Ros-si-ya! Ros-si-ya! Ros-si-ya!' They jeered the conspirators. Some shouted 'Shoot them'. They called for Gorbachev to resign. They cheered again when Yeltsin announced that the parliament square was to be renamed 'The Square of Russian Freedom'. Yeltsin smirked when Popov proposed that he be awarded the medal of 'Hero of the Soviet Union' (what an irony!). Shevardnadze suggested that those who were killed on Tuesday night be buried in the Kremlin wall, where the dignitaries of the Soviet regime had been buried. 'We can dig up some of those who are already there to make way for them.' The atmosphere of vengefulness and Russian nationalism continued to grow. But unlike Mark Antony at the Forum, Yeltsin kept the crowd under control. Neither then nor later was he vengeful in victory. The witch-hunt I feared did not take wing.

Back at the embassy Stephen Wall caught me on the telephone from Downing Street: What was going on? Could we help set up the Prime Minister's phone call to Gorbachev? He revealed that Major had spoken the previous day to Shevardnadze, Yeltsin and Yakovlev. I said it would have been nice if we'd been kept informed. He apologised, but said rather sharply that I ought to understand that Downing Street had been very busy over the last few days. Ho, ho, I thought.

I called on Laptiev in the Kremlin. He was his usual friendly self. For an hour and a half he rattled on, giving me my first insider's account of the week's events. He was slightly on the defensive and made a point of telling me that his attack on the junta failed to appear when *Komsomolskaya Pravda* was banned along with the other liberal newspapers. As leader of the Upper House of the Soviet parliament, he had remained in his office in the Kremlin, but had been in regular contact with Aleksandr Yakovlev and Yeltsin's other allies throughout. His daughter was on the barricades for all three days. He did not need to convince me: he was a decent liberal man, if not a natural hero.

Laptiev confirmed that the trigger for the coup had indeed been the imminent signature of the Union Treaty. Representatives of the junta – Varennikov, Boldin, the head of Gorbachev's personal secretariat, and

Plekhanov, the general in charge of Gorbachev's bodyguard – had flown to the Crimea on Sunday to present Gorbachev with an ultimatum. After Gorbachev rejected their overtures, they had come back to Moscow on Monday to confer with Pavlov, whose subsequent illness was genuine. The junta had realised that they faced failure when the crowd around the White House continued to increase, and it became clear that none of the military units in Moscow could be relied on to storm the building. The conspirators' essential misjudgement was that they genuinely believed that ordinary people wanted an 'iron hand'. The coup collapsed when this turned out to be wrong.

Lukyanov, Ivashko, Yazov and Kryuchkov had flown to the Crimea the previous afternoon, just ahead of Rutskoi, hoping to persuade Gorbachev to do a deal. He refused to see them until after Rutskoi and the others had arrived. The coup leaders were now all under arrest, except Yanaev who enjoyed parliamentary immunity but was 'helping the police with their enquiries', and Pugo who was dead. Lukyanov had failed to distance himself satisfactorily from the conspirators and had been suspended from his position as Chairman of the Soviet parliament. Laptiev had assumed his functions for the time being.

Now, Laptiev thought, the pressing issues were the choice of new people to replace those who had disgraced themselves; the relations between the two Presidents; the Union Treaty; and the economy. The junta had taken all Gorbachev's power. And then they had let it drop. Yeltsin was now picking up as much as he could. Gorbachev was greatly weakened. The fact that the conspirators were all his own people was particularly damaging. But he would remain more than a symbolic figure. The other Republics would see him as a counterweight to Russia, and he would regain some of his former powers. Meanwhile the Communist Party was finished. It had played no overt role, but the conspirators were all Central Committee members. Not all the KGB had supported the coup. But it should be split up and put under civilian control.

I asked Laptiev why the junta had failed to cut off the telephones more effectively. Foreigners, he grinned, always laughed about the number of telephones top people in the Soviet Union had on their desks (gesturing towards his own). The reason was that the technology was so primitive that special networks had to be set up for special purposes: for Gorbachev, for the KGB, for the Central Committee, and so on. It wasn't possible to cut them all off at once: one more reason why the coup failed.

That afternoon the European ambassadors were summoned to the Kremlin to see Gorbachev, a symbolic affair intended mainly as compensation, I suspect, for the runaround we had been given at Vnukovo the night before. Gorbachev was beaming, with that tan of his that always looked as if it had come out of a bottle – quite different from the wan and exhausted figure we had seen on television stumbling down the aircraft steps in the middle of the night. We exchanged banalities. Chernyaev was there. I gave him a big hug.

Next, Geoff Murrell and I called on Aleksandr Yakovlev in the Moscow City Council building on Gorky Street. For once Yakovlev was cheerful and relaxed, not the dyspeptic frog. Like Laptiev, he criticised Gorbachev for his choice of advisers. He too thought the KGB should be brought under civilian control and broken up, lest it continue to act as a force on its own. The political police should be disbanded. The foreign intelligence service should be retained. All countries had one, though as an ex-ambassador he could say from experience that most foreign intelligence was useless. I replied that as a still serving ambassador he wouldn't expect me to be able to agree with him. As we left, he said with disapproval that the crowd were already breaking the windows of the Central Committee building on Staraya Ploshchad. Geoff and I wondered how long it would be before the Muscovites tore down the statue of Iron Feliks in front of the Lubianka. They did so later that night, to the cheers of a huge crowd.

Back in the embassy we organised a champagne party for the Russian staff. I congratulated them on their victory, a peaceful popular victory unique in Russian history, the third great battle of Moscow after 1812 and 1941. Even the hard-faced KGB stooges among them seemed genuinely pleased.

Jill and I spent the evening watching Gorbachev's press conference on television. It was an honourable performance, very human, but a political disaster. In his measured opening statement he described the pressures he was under while he was in isolation. If he had left it at that, he would have commanded the human sympathy of his audience. But as usual he talked too much for his own good. He fell into two particular traps. He refused to distance himself from the Communist Party, which he still hoped to reform from within. He refused to explain why he had insisted on appointing to high office the men who had subsequently betrayed him. He gave the impression that he had learned nothing, and forgotten nothing. By this one misjudgement he greatly accelerated the rate of his inevitable decline.

The evening ended with the firework display which Yeltsin had promised the people that morning. It was the noisiest we had ever heard.

Friday: Power Passes to the New Men

On the next day I woke up feeling depressed, cowardly and incompetent. Tens of thousands of ordinary people had risked their life for their principles. Their leaders had shown will, courage, and stamina. If I had been a senior Soviet official, instead of a mere British voyeur, I would probably have gone the way of the Foreign Minister, Bessmertnykh: a decent but cautious official trying to do the right thing without the right person to guide him. Of course my feelings were of no importance against the measure of what had happened. But it was not pleasant. I was glad that Jill had saved the honour of the family, and had had the guts to support our friends on the barricades.

That afternoon I was in the office of the Russian Deputy Foreign Minister, Fyodorov, when his television began to show the proceedings in the Russian parliament. Gorbachev was making his first political speech since his return from the Crimea. He was in better command of himself than during his press conference the previous day, and performed with dignity and aplomb. The deputies treated him with a mixture of respect, sympathy, and hostility. Their questioning was brutal and abrasive. One deputy asked him to agree that Socialism should be proscribed and the Communist Party banned as a criminal organisation. He answered that the banning of parties and political opinions was not compatible with democracy and pluralism: a fair answer, but not one that won him any friends. Yeltsin was determined to make it clear who was now the boss. He gave Gorbachev a summary record of the meeting of the Soviet Council of Ministers on the first day of the coup, and roughly ordered him to read it out. Almost all the Ministers whom Gorbachev had appointed had supported the putsch. It was a crude and vivid demonstration of the shift of power. In earlier times Gorbachev had found it difficult to handle criticism in public. Now he swallowed his pride and kept his temper. He had little choice. He had returned to a world unrecognisably different. Power had passed from him, crudely and demonstratively.

Saturday: the Day of the Funeral

Saturday 24 August was the day of the third political funeral I attended in Moscow, the funeral of the three young men killed on the second night of the coup: Dmitri Komar, twenty-three, a Russian decorated for service as a paratrooper in Afghanistan; Ilya Krichevsky, twenty-eight, a Jewish architect, who had served in a tank regiment; Vladimir Usov, thirty-seven, a Russian accountant, married with one daughter.

By that morning the statue of Kalinin, the first President of the Soviet Union, had already been removed from its place on Kalinin Prospect. The Central Committee building was quiet. There was a notice on the door: 'This building is sealed.' The scrawl on the statue of Marx, 'Proletarians of the world, unite – against the Communists', had been replaced. It now read simply: 'Forgive me.' There were two red flags floating over the Kremlin: but the hammers and sickles had been cut out. The day was warm and dry. Jill, Julian, David and I joined the crowd gathering on Manege Square. There were said to be a million people on the streets. Armenians and Azerbaijanis, Georgians and Lithuanians marched with their national flags to comm-emorate the people that they too had lost. A group of people were carrying an immensely long Russian tricolour which had been donated by the newly created Stock Exchange. Two Orthodox priests carried a portrait of Nicholas II, Tsar and Martyr. Other priests carried icons: they looked like a tableau from Repin's picture *The Religious Procession*. Beside the priests was a small group of uniformed Cossacks, scruffy ruffians who looked ripe to launch a pogrom. Michael Gavin of the Cheshire Homes was carrying a Union Jack. He had been lent it by young Igor Garashchenko, who had got it through the BBC's rock music fan club. It was the solitary foreign flag until a couple of young Russians rushed off to bring a French tricolour as well. The ambas-sadors of the European Community also marched, gallant but uncertain.

The funeral orations took place on an improvised tribune in front of the Manege. The three coffins stood before the tribune. Gorbachev spoke with dignity and merciful brevity. Yelena Bonner (Sakharov's widow) made a moving and emotional appeal for tolerance, the more effective because her voice had so often been raised in passionate denunciation. Bob Strauss, the new American ambassador, gatecrashed the tribunal to quote Patrick Henry ('Give me liberty or give me death'): a brilliant gesture much envied by his professional colleagues from Europe. An Afghan veteran recited some of his own poetry. An Orthodox choir sang magnificently: the bass worthy of *Boris Godunov*. A Rabbi intoned the Kaddish in Hebrew in memory of Jewish Krichevsky. It would be harder now, I hoped, for Russia's anti-Semites – the pseudo-Cossacks and others – to claim that the Jews were always Russia's enemies.

Throughout the speeches an elderly officer in a crumpled uniform stood alone before the coffins, crossing himself and bowing.

As we started marching behind the coffins towards the Vagankovskoe Cemetery, Kozyrev, the Russian Foreign Minister, came up to say with great emotion that Yeltsin had been told how Jill had helped to distribute food to the defenders of the White House. Russia would never forget the support it had received from Britain and its Prime Minister in the moment of crisis. The crowd marched slowly, cheerful and orderly. There was a sense of seriousness, of elation, but not of tragedy. The marshals – many of them Afghan veterans – were courteous and effective. Disciplined files of people of all ages linked hands to split the crowd into manageable groups. The marshals warned us in advance of tramlines and potholes, so that we shouldn't trip up. We felt far safer than we had done during the Sakharov funeral, when the bungling militia proved so incompetent.

The marchers swapped their experiences on the barricades. Those who had not been there explained defensively why they had unfortunately been prevented. Many criticised Gorbachev for his misjudgements and indecisiveness. But they also recognised that it was he who had launched the whole process. They all thought that the Communist Party was finished. By contrast with the scenes outside the White House in the middle of the week, there was a welcome absence of vengefulness or Russian chauvinism. A surprising number of the marchers talked about the prospects that had now opened for them to start up their own businesses. How ironic, I thought, if the last revolution of the twentieth century turned out to be a revolution in favour of free enterprise.

A plump bearded man in his thirties marching beside me had been a career officer in a chemical warfare unit. He was now a specialist in the history of the Imperial officer corps at the turn of the century. He had been on the barricades for three nights, and gave me a miniature Russian flag to pin on my suit (later the Belgian ambassador pointed out that I'd pinned it on upside down). Ludmila Doronina, a diminutive librarian who was walking on my other side, later came to tea at the embassy with a set of the leaflets put out by the defenders of the White House. A little old man who insisted on repeating out-of-date political jokes was told to shut up and show more respect for the dead.

In the river to our left the ships lowered their (Russian) flags and sounded their sirens as the procession with the coffins moved along the embankment. The procession stopped at the White House for an address by Yeltsin. We were too far away to see him or hear him. Jill and I never got to the cemetery itself: the crowd by then was impenetrable. By the time we finished marching we had spent seven hours on the streets.

Back in the embassy the rumours grew and were then confirmed that Gorbachev had banned the Party and resigned from the Secretary General-ship. The *Daily Mail* rang from London: they had a picture of my wife on a tank waving a flag. They wanted an interview. What did my wife look like? I asked. Blonde and wearing sneakers, they said. Not my wife, then, I replied. The same boot-faced television announcers who had read out the junta's decrees on Monday were now reading out Yeltsin's decrees in the same deadpan way. Michael Gavin came to supper with Igor Garashchenko. The last week already seemed like a wholly unreal dream.

But for months afterwards people would ask one another when they met: 'Where were you on the 19th of August?' In the first half of 1991 the BBC had shown a brilliant television series on *The Second Russian Revolution*. After the coup the producers updated it with remarkable speed. The new instalment was ready by the end of September. We invited some of the protagonists for a preview at the embassy: Aleksandr Yakovlev, Laptiev, Chernyaev, and Gorbachev's political adviser Shahnazarov with his wife. They were like schoolboys at a treat, refighting the battles of August with undiminished enthusiasm, an orgy of reminiscence.

The Shahnazarovs and the Pugos had been on holiday in the same Crimean sanatorium, just across the bay from Gorbachev's villa. The day before the coup holidaymakers had seen security troops converging on the villa. 'What are you up to?' they asked. 'We're on our way to arrest Gorbachev,' the soldiers answered, and the people laughed. The Shahnazarovs' phone was cut off from the beginning and they were confined in their sanatorium. Mrs Shahnazarov spent her time photo-graphing the ships blockading the bay, in case a record was ever needed. Before it all began she saw Pugo walking along the beach with his grand-daughter. The little girl was saying: 'You're the best grandpa I've ever had; you're the best grandpa in the world.' Chernyaev believed that even at that late stage Pugo still had no idea what was afoot: his suicide was that of an honest man caught up in events beyond his control.

Yakovlev confirmed the rumour that the air force under Shaposhnikov had prepared to bomb the Kremlin if the White House was assaulted. Given the propensity of modern smart weapons to miss their target and hit something nearby, I wondered whether it had after all been so clever to insist on hanging on to the embassy building. Next time someone wanted to bomb the Kremlin we might not be so lucky.

Laptiev was worried that the conspirators would use their trial as a public platform to justify their actions. The defence lawyers were already trying to portray them as decent men with their country's best interests at heart. I commented that this was what defence lawyers were for. Laptiev said that my comments showed that I didn't understand Russia after all. The conspirators never came to trial. By the time they were released from jail a year later they were almost heroes to those who could still be bothered to remember who they were. Some people regretted that justice had not been done. But many welcomed the break with the bloody political practice of the past.

Time and again the Russian people have rebelled against authority. Time and again Cossacks, peasants and soldiers have risen up to destroy their masters and what they stood for. Time and again the authorities have answered blood with blood and prevailed. But rarely have the people been prepared to stand up peacefully to defend their rights. Perhaps the first time they did so was when Father Gapon, the equivocal priest, led a peaceful demonstration to present a petition to the Tsar at the Winter Palace in St Petersburg in January 1905. That time the authorities kept their nerve. They shot down the demonstrators and triggered off the 1905 revolution.

The August coup failed for three reasons. It was an attempt to destroy political and human rights which the people had come to savour, and were prepared to defend if necessary at the cost of their own lives. Their determination was fed by the freedoms brought by Glasnost and political change, and matured through the long series of demonstrations which began in 1989. As Liuda remarked, they had for the first time been allowed – by Gorbachev whom they now disliked so much – to vote for their own president and their own parliament. They were not now going to let them be taken away. Gorbachev gave the people their chance. His angry refusal to compromise with the conspirators cut the ground from under their feet. Yeltsin's courage, will, uncompromising clarity of purpose, even his ponderous physical presence, inspired the ordinary people and formed a rock of opposition which the junta could not ignore and in the end could not break. The two men share an equal credit for the failure of the coup.

If the conspirators had kept their nerve the coup need not have failed. Both at the time and later they portrayed themselves as moderate conservative patriots, acting more in sorrow than in anger in the best interests of the Soviet Union. They hoped that reason would appeal to those who feared that the relaxation of traditional Russian disciplines would lead to the dissolution of the empire. Hence their failure to arrest potential leaders of opposition, to storm the White House, to disperse the demonstrations. They were beaten before they began, and showed it in their press conference on the first day. And by then they must have realised that the rot of democracy was not confined to the intellectual middle classes. On the contrary, it had spread to the army and the KGB, who were divided among themselves throughout the coup, and on whom the conspirators soon learned they could not rely. Kryuchkov claims in his memoirs that he and his fellows decided in advance that they would halt their action if it looked like leading to bloodshed. It is hard to believe that any serious group of conspirators could have taken such a self-defeating decision. General Jaruzelski could have taught them a thing or two had they not (as Sasha Motov said sourly after a night on the barricades) been far too arrogant to take lessons from a former satellite. Their essential failure was a failure of will. They put more tanks onto the streets than most Russians had seen since the Battle of Kursk. But they never had the guts to strike home.

Cynics, deconstructionists, neo-Communists and right-wing chauvinists later argued that the resistance came only from a small number of middle-class inhabitants of Moscow and Leningrad, and that the mass of the people was apathetic, especially in the provinces. Anecdotal and some substantial evidence points the other way. Many Russian provincial cities came out for Yeltsin and Russia against the Soviet Union and the Communist Party. But it is scarcely surprising that the majority of ordinary people went about their ordinary business and watched to see which way the cat would jump. The mobs who stormed the Bastille were a small proportion of the French people in 1789. And of Americans in 1776 it has been calculated that one third were for the Revolution, one-third were for the King; and the rest only wanted to be left alone.[2] The number of people who were on the streets of Moscow in August 1991 was at least as great as the number who were on the streets in Petrograd in October 1917. Yet neither the French nor the Americans nor the Russian insurgents in 1917 faced a ruthless despotism of the kind imposed by the Communists at the height of their power.

Conspiracy theories multiplied in the days and months after the coup. Gorbachev, went one version, was himself in the conspiracy. He had not really been isolated from the outside world; he gave the conspirators at least a nod and a wink; he encouraged them to go ahead, in the belief that a return to the old ways would enable him to regain control. Alternatively the whole thing was somehow engineered by Yeltsin, as a way of discrediting Gorbachev and accelerating his own progress towards supreme power. Both theories violate Occam's rule that the simplest explanation is the most plausible. Russians are peculiarly prone to conspiracy theories. But it is not only Russians who rebel at the thought that human affairs are the product of chaos and chance, and who prefer to believe that they are directed if not by the Deity, then by some malignant intrigue of Jews, Freemasons, Communists, Roman Catholics, financiers, multinationals, speculators, or secret policemen.

There was another fundamental reason for the failure of the coup and the inability of the reactionaries to reassert their hold over ordinary people. The computerised leaflets handed out during the great demonstrations of 1989, the illegal broadcasts of Radio Moscow, the faxes from the White House, the endless telephone calls – the international messages of support direct to Yeltsin himself, calls between military and KGB colleagues on both sides of the barricades – all this was possible only because of modern technology. A qualitative and perhaps irreversible change had been introduced into Russian politics. In the old days the KGB and their Tsarist predecessors could track and destroy illegal printing presses with little difficulty. They could prevent people from knowing what was happening inside the country, let alone what was happening outside it. This was no longer possible in the days of satellite television, email, and the fax machine.

The outcome of the coup enormously enhanced Yeltsin's prestige and influence. I still had my doubts about his judgement and competence on matters of everyday politics and administration. But from now on he would have a central part to play. Gorbachev's power would decline at an increasing rate. But he and Yeltsin complemented one another. Perhaps, I thought, the working partnership which had so long eluded them might now be in their grasp.

The basic tasks had not changed: to reform the economy and the relationship between the Republics. The political victory would not get bread into the shops. But it had discredited many of those who yearned for a return to the command economy. Ordinary people might now be more willing to accept, at least for a while, the immense pain and difficulty of economic reform. The balance of power had now swung towards the Republics. The use of force against the Baltic governments was now impossible, and their prospects of a negotiated independence much improved. Reaction in Russia was not dead. No political system would be complete without it. But the Party was now irrelevant, the reactionary generals had been humiliated, the KGB's own leader had tried and failed to overthrow the legitimate government, and the bureaucrats and the industrial barons had performed ingloriously, to say the least. None of these, I thought optimistically, would be able to resist reform for a long time to come.

In the West people debated endlessly about whether governments should have foreseen the coup and whether they should have done something to prevent it. Had there been yet another massive intelligence failure? Western governments had of course worried for years that Gorbachev might be toppled by a combination of reactionary Party bosses, disaffected secret policemen, and generals humiliated beyond endurance. From time to time people predicted coups which then failed to materialise. When the real coup finally happened, it took everyone by surprise, from Gorbachev down to the young officers and soldiers who were bundled into their armoured vehicles early in the morning of 19 August to make the long journey to Moscow. Among those who failed to predict it were Yeltsin, Aleksandr Yakovlev, the former KGB General Kalugin, and the Joint Intelligence Committee in London, for whom it came 'out of a clear sky'.[3] And this was scarcely odd, because potential coups about which the authorities have firm circumstantial warning tend not to get to first base. Kryuchkov and his colleagues were professionals, and they ensured that there were no leaks.

President Bush's warning, about which Gorbachev was so dismissive in Admiralty House, was based on a brief and cryptic message which Gavriil Popov gave to the American ambassador on 20 June, three days after Pavlov, Yazov and Kryuchkov mounted their 'constitutional coup' in the Soviet parliament. Popov warned that a coup was to be mounted the following day to remove Gorbachev, and named Yazov, Pavlov, Kryuchkov and Lukyanov as the conspirators. Although he had contacts among the reformers in the army and the KGB, there is no obvious reason why Popov should have had inside knowledge of the conspirators' plans. They regarded him as a dangerous radical, who two months later was to figure on their hit list. At that early stage the operational planning for the coup had not even begun And even before the 'constitutional coup' took place, the four men Popov named were already widely regarded as the obvious people to lead a coup if there was to be one. Bush's warning told Gorbachev nothing that he could not work out for himself.

Aleksandr Yakovlev, the 'Father of Perestroika', did announce on 16 August that a coup was imminent. It was the day he was expelled from the Communist Party, and he was furious. Within a couple of days his prediction apparently came true. But he told me later that he had had no inside knowledge, and no idea that a coup would actually take place so soon. He had simply judged that things could not go on as they were much longer. He had of course been predicting a coup since the winter of 1988.

The CIA perhaps got nearest to the mark. In a series of assessments from Spring 1991 onwards they warned that Gorbachev's dominance of the Soviet political scene was at an end. A coup could happen at any time, though it would be unlikely to prosper in the long or perhaps even in the short term. That was no different from what others were arguing. But in mid-August, they told President Bush that the signature on 20 August of the Union Treaty could well trigger action by the reactionaries. This was a competent piece of work. But the relevant information was equally available to any analyst or journalist who wished to make use of it. The rest of us failed to do so. But despite the CIA's perspicacity, the first reaction of the American government was still to hedge. There was, after all, no guarantee in the first hours that the coup would not succeed or that Bush would not have to deal with the men who had ousted Gorbachev. And in any case, there was not much that foreign governments could do about it one way or the other.

The fuss about 'intelligence failure' was misplaced, as it often is. The future retains one gritty and irreducible characteristic. You cannot predict it. People have tried since the beginning of history – Roman augers and Western intelligence agencies alike. They have never been able to crack the problem. As the House Armed Services Committee of the US once put it, 'Policymakers and private citizens who expect intelligence [agencies] to foresee all sudden shifts are attributing to [them] qualities not yet shared by the deity with mere mortals.'[4]

9

The Rubble of the Dictatorship

My Friend, have faith: that Star will rise,
The Star of captivating joy.
Russia will shake herself from sleep,
Autocracy will crash in ruins,
And on the rubble they'll write our names.

Pushkin, *To Chaadaev*, 1826

The conspirators of August 1991 achieved exactly the opposite of what they had intended: the collapse of the old Soviet Union. Now the task of the survivors was to construct something durable out of the rubble.

No one performed with distinction. Inside Russia the vanquished – above all the old baronies of the army, the KGB, and the Party – were discredited, stunned, and powerless. The victors seemed overwhelmed by the magnitude of their task and by the huge responsibility which had been thrust upon them. Yeltsin's first aim was to consolidate his own power which, on the principle of connecting vessels, meant draining Gorbachev of what little power remained to him. The Russian liberals were split. Many – such as Sobchak and even Popov – still hoped that some form of Union could be retained, for economic and in some cases for old-fashioned imperial reasons. But a younger, more sophisticated, and more professional group around Yegor Gaidar was already working out ways in which the Russian economy and Russia itself could be brought to stand on its own feet without the encumbrance of empire. Foreign governments now accepted that Yeltsin commanded the crucial position. But they still hankered after a continuing role for Gorbachev, partly for reasons of grateful sentiment. And they were deeply fearful of the consequences of a break-up of the Union. They had heard Shevardnadze warn of chaos and bloodshed far exceeding Yugoslavia. What would happen to the nuclear and conventional arms control agreements which they had negotiated with such difficulty? What would happen to the nuclear weapons if there were civil war? The continuation of a more civilised Union seemed by far the lesser evil. Almost on the eve of the coup, Bush praised Gorbachev in a speech in Kiev, warned the Ukrainians against 'suicidal nationalism', and told them that they would be wise to remain within a Soviet federation: 'Freedom is not the same as independence.' The Ukrainians were not pleased with what a right-wing American commentator subsequently called his 'Chicken Kiev speech'.

Quite soon the euphoria of victory began to disperse. The old, debilitating atmosphere of Russian pessimism gathered force amongst our friends, a feeling that things were now bound to go wrong, the hangover after the victory. After his triumph, Yeltsin was in a position to impose his will on events. The problems were daunting. What was to be done with the remnants of the Communist Party, the KGB, and the army, which were demoralised and disordered but still potentially dangerous? How were the institutions to be created – ministries, a central bank, local government bodies – which would be needed to govern the new Russian state? What could be done to tackle the mounting crisis in the economy? How were the increasingly complex relations between Russia and the other republics of the Union to be managed, now that the centralised institutions of the Union no longer commanded respect on the periphery? For several weeks Yeltsin did nothing. Instead he disappeared from public view to restore himself in the holiday resorts of the South. On his return he, like Gorbachev before him, began to issue decrees which had no application in the real world. His supporters began to fall out with one another. Yuri Afanasiev threatened to bring the crowds back onto the street. Gorbachev seized the opportunity to reassert himself in a bravura but doomed attempt to re-establish his position and repeat his previous triumphs.

A week after the coup, on 29 August, Vadim Medvedev phoned me just as I was about to go out for supper with the Senokosovs. Could I come to the Kremlin immediately? I protested. I was busy. I had no driver. How would I get into the Kremlin? 'Give me your registration number so that I can warn the guards to let you in,' he said. I couldn't remember it (it was 'CMD1-002': about as simple as you can get). 'Fly your official flag,' he said. I couldn't find it. Needless to say the guards let me in nevertheless, through the great Borovitsky Gate into the deserted precincts of the Kremlin itself. When I arrived at Medvedev's office in the nineteenth-century office block where Lenin had lived and Stalin had worked, he informed me without ado that Gorbachev wanted to see me. After a lengthy wait, during which he told me about his experiences during the coup, we walked along the dim high-ceilinged corridors towards Gorbachev's office. The shadowy figures of security guards stood in darkened niches at every ten paces. I imagined the ghosts. Stalin working late into the night, his fearful colleagues hovering around him: Kamenev – shot; Zinoviev – shot; Bukharin – shot; Yezhov – shot; Kirov – murdered; Ordjonikidze – murdered; Trotsky – murdered.

We sat, just the three of us, in Gorbachev's sober grey office. Gorbachev was overwrought, almost incoherent, his Southern accent stronger than ever, his sentences even more complex and elliptical. I could barely understand him. Both men seemed close to panic. The strain of the coup was still upon them. Gorbachev started with a confused account of the political situation. Things were calming down after the upheaval of the previous week. The conspirators were being charged with treason, which carried the death penalty: but – he said with obvious approval – his post-box was full of letters demanding the abolition of the death penalty. For the first – perhaps the only – time I heard him praise his rival. Some people criticised Yeltsin for acting unconstitutionally, he said. But that was unfair: it was not possible to observe all the proprieties in the middle of such a crisis. He then got to the point. The country was on the brink of financial collapse. The Soviet Union's debt obligations for the remaining four months of 1991 amounted to $17 billion. Exports over the same period were expected to bring in $7.5 billion. Another $2 billion could be raised on existing credit lines. The gap was $7.5 billion. Gorbachev therefore needed $2 billion new credits from the West in the next couple of weeks, and rescheduling of the Soviet debt thereafter. The Soviet Union would also need urgent help with food and pharmaceutical supplies.

Before the coup, he reminded me, two arguments were advanced in the West against giving credits to the Soviet Union: credits would reinforce the country's totalitarian structures and so delay reform; and the money would simply disappear into a black hole. But with the democratic victory the first argument fell away; while the answer to the second was primarily technical. He repeated his earlier argument. The West had paid out at least $100 billion to finance the Gulf War. Surely it could help finance the greater prize of a stable Soviet democracy? I promised to report, without much hope that his requests would be met.

John Major visited Moscow three days later, on Sunday 1 September, the first foreign statesman to do so after the coup. The previous evening Moscow had been gripped by a pop festival: rock groups on the steps of the White House and the usual young and middle-aged poets. Transport was paralysed. The crowd on Red Square was good-humoured and festive, but quiet. No one was wearing patriotic symbols, though a group of young people was roller-skating very fast through the crowd with Russian flags streaming from their backs. There were no police at all. A balloon hung in the dark over Manege Square. A huge picture of George and the Dragon – Moscow's patron saint – covered half the front of the Moskva Hotel.

The Russians were as eager to meet Major as he was to meet them. He saw almost everyone of importance in Moscow who was not in prison. He called first on the man who was still President of the Soviet Union. Gorbachev was in his Kremlin office, tanned and cheerful as always. Norma Major and Jill gave him a big kiss of relief at seeing him again. He explained that the coup had failed because the plotters had underestimated the President, the Russian government, the ordinary people, and their own hold over the army. The affair had been a lesson to him: he had misjudged the need to support the liberals. He was heartened by the way the young people had stood up for democracy. Now the guilty should be punished according to the law. But he believed in clemency: there should be no punishment for those who were merely confused. Ordinary people were worried that the Union might disintegrate. He and eleven republican leaders were preparing a joint statement covering an economic agreement, joint control of the armed forces, and a new role for the Republics. Repeating many of the arguments he had just put to me, he told Major that the Soviet Union urgently needed Western help: to maintain imports, to help with the debt, to train managers for the private sector, to supply food and medicine for the Winter. The West had spent billions on the Gulf War. It should not stint on this much greater prize. Major gave him the message which had been agreed with the Group of Seven and the International Monetary Fund: pay your debts, tighten your belt, and then we might be able to help. It was orthodox stuff – but not much comfort for Gorbachev.

In the White House Yeltsin was in a cut-and-dried, self-confident mood. He did not rant, but he made it brutally clear that he was the master now. He still insisted that the Union must be preserved. 'As of today we need Gorbachev to hold the Union together.' All fifteen Republics should preserve a 'single economic space'. Otherwise foreign economic assistance would be wasted. Even the Baltic States agreed, he claimed – wrongly. The G7 had promised economic assistance to the Soviet Union if political reform became irreversible. The defeat of the coup was the guarantee for which they had asked. They should now come up with the goods. Somewhat inconsistently Yeltsin warned that the domestic situation was not yet under control. When the Soviet parliament met the following day, the remaining reactionaries might attempt to remove Gorbachev (the interpreter used the word 'impeach') and mount another 'constitutional coup'. Major asked about the military. Who was in control of the nuclear forces? What about the future defence relationship between the centre and the Republics? Yeltsin said that there would have to be Union defence forces with the nuclear weapons under central control. The Soviet air defence system would have to remain in place for many years even in the Baltics. Russia did not want its own armed forces: there was no point in setting up separate armed forces so that the Republics could fight one another. All Russia itself needed was a national guard of five thousand men to defend its democratic institutions against future coups.

Within little more than six months of these confident predictions Yeltsin had ridden to sole power over the dismembered corpse of the Russian Empire, the armed forces of the Union had disintegrated, and nuclear weapons were stationed under dubious control in four of the successor Republics. On Victory Day 1992 Yeltsin proclaimed the new 'Armed Forces of Russia'. And by 1995 the 'Forces for the Protection of the Russian Federation' under his direct command numbered twenty thousand, a bloated Praetorian Guard.

The collapse of the coup had left the Soviet Union without a recognisable government: the Soviet Prime Minister was in prison and almost all the Soviet ministers were compromised. 'Russia' had a Prime Minister – Ivan Silaev – but little in the way of ministerial apparatus, and no authority over the other Republics. Gorbachev therefore put together a task force consisting of Silaev, Yavlinsky, Luzhkov, Moscow's chief executive, and Volsky, formerly a Party official and now a representative of the growing entrepreneurial class. Their task was to run the Union economy until a new government could be set up. Major called on this committee in the absence of a prime ministerial interlocutor. Once again the theme was economics. Silaev said that the defence budget would be cut substantially in 1992. This turned out to be true, though the axe was wielded not by him, but by his successor Gaidar. Yavlinsky launched into a passionate harangue. The first task was to put together an economic agreement between the Republics – whether or not they decided to stay in the Union. Thereafter there had to be a genuine and viable reform programme. Three-quarters of the country's GNP would be generated in the private sector in four to five years (an estimate which turned out to be less wildly optimistic than I thought at the time). Until this programme was in place, there was no point in the West giving massive financial aid. The money would be wasted or counter-productive. This, to Silaev's chagrin, was the exact opposite of the message that Gorbachev and he were trying to get across.

At the end of the day we gave a dinner for the visitors. It was only a modest success. Major was not there: he was off again with Gorbachev. The new political Moscow turned up in force: Silaev, Nazarbaev, Rutskoi, Primakov, Yavlinsky. But they insisted on sitting together, destroying Jill's careful placement. Throughout the evening there was a whispering of political intrigue. To prevent the 'constitutional coup' against which Yeltsin had warned, Gorbachev, Nazarbaev, and Yeltsin were cooking up an emergency resolution with eleven republican leaders. It contained a commitment to a Union of Sovereign States with a coordinated economic management and centralised armed forces, and confirmed all the Union's international political and economic obligations. It was, in fact, a restatement of the policies Gorbachev had striven for since the Spring. The next day Nazarbaev read it out at the beginning of the session of the Soviet parliament, which went into immediate recess. The deputies were given no opportunity to attack Gorbachev, and dutifully voted for the resolution. Whatever plans there had been for a 'constitutional coup' were successfully stifled.

The Prime Minister's visit ended in farce at midnight. Half of his personal staff dawdled about in the embassy and did not reach the airport until after the Prime Minister had already made his farewells, boarded the plane, and was ready to take off. Silaev, the new Foreign Minister Pankin, and the rest of us lined up and waited, as the engines roared and half a dozen secretaries and Military Policemen scuttled past us onto the plane like frightened rabbits.

A general restructuring of institutions now began as 'Russia' started to acquire substance and the Soviet Union went into terminal decline.

Yeltsin's first move was to close down the Communist Party of the Soviet Union. The operation was ruthless and immediate. The local Party office on Tchaikovsky Street in Leningrad was housed in a small but ornate palace built by a German merchant at the end of the nineteenth century. Fifteen minutes after Yeltsin made his announcement, militia armed with machine pistols arrived to seal the building. At a stroke the local Party Secretary, an attractive and able young man in his thirties, became what he ruefully called 'one of the new class of Soviet unemployed'. The scene was repeated all over the country. But there was no systematic repression. After a brief interval the Communist newspapers which Yeltsin had closed down after the coup were allowed to reopen. The Communist Party successfully challenged the legality of the ban against them. And although I never met him again, I have no doubt that the young Party Secretary soon found himself alternative employment, probably in what became wryly known as the 'commercial structures', new businesses, some of dubious propriety and often started up with Party funds diverted from their original and now non-existent purpose.

For a while the Parliament of the Soviet Union, where it had all begun in 1989, remained the theatre for public politics in Moscow. Two days after the funerals, on Monday 26 August, I went to the Kremlin for the extraordinary session of the parliament. The deputies were streaming back from the requiem for the three young men which the Patriarch had just conducted in the Kremlin's Cathedral of the Dormition. People were milling about in the foyer. Ryzhov, a leading democrat, bounded up to thank me for my personal support at the height of the crisis. The Russians, he said, were particularly grateful for my appearance on the barricades at the time they were expecting an assault. My boldness surprised them. On the contrary, I said, I risked nothing – unlike the thousands of ordinary people who were risking their lives. Shcherbakov, the First Deputy Prime Minister responsible for economics in the last government before the coup, was standing by himself. I shook his hand and asked him how he was. He looked sick. In the circumstances it was about the most inappropriate thing I could have said. Gerashchenko, the Chairman of the Soviet State Bank, had been criticised for continuing to finance the Soviet government during the coup. He too was looking lonely, and was pleased when I came up to him. 'All these unjustified accusations,' he mumbled. Because of his professional experience, Gerashchenko was reinstated on the insistence of foreign bankers and governments, who claimed that international confidence in the Soviet Union would otherwise collapse. In 1992 he became Chairman of the Russian Central Bank. It was only then that the foreigners began to call him 'the worst central banker in the world'.

Georgi Arbatov, the head of the Institute for the United States and Canada, was also there. He had been one of the group of intellectuals who had worked on the 'New Thinking' which had been the basis of Gorbachev's foreign policy. Now he was viciously critical. It was under Gorbachev that Muscovites had got used to seeing tanks on the streets. It was under Gorbachev that the special police and military forces were created, the OMON and the *Spetsnaz*. It was under Gorbachev that the Lithuanian killings took place. It was Gorbachev who had appointed the leaders of the coup. He could not escape direct responsibility.

The Chamber was jam-packed and expectant. I barely managed to squeeze to a place. Laptiev conducted the meeting with patience and skill, quite without Lukyanov's trickery and manipulation. The meeting was calm and orderly, as if everyone wanted to pretend that life was after all going on as usual. Gorbachev spoke first, in measured tones. He admitted that he had returned to a wholly different country, which he could now see through wholly different eyes. He accepted blame for what had happened: picking the wrong people, compromising too much, failing to appreciate the liberals, failing to press ahead sufficiently hard with reform. He proposed the early signature of the Union Treaty; general and presidential elections immediately thereafter; talks with Republics that wanted to leave the Union about the continuation of economic ties; and measures to strengthen the authority of the civilian arm over the army and KGB. His ideas were civilised and sensible, but wildly out of date. Even his ally Nazarbaev announced firmly that the idea of a Federation – a group of states clustered round a Union centre – was now dead. Kazakhstan would only join a confederation, whose centre had a minimal function.

The extreme right was in full voice. Outside in the foyer Colonel Alksnis, one of the 'Black Colonels' who had demanded Shevardnadze's departure, was giving interviews to all and sundry. Sooner or later, he said, the tanks would have to be brought onto the streets again. But – a remarkable prophecy – next time it would be Yeltsin who gave the order. Nearby there was a display of telegrams from pensioners and other members of the public. Many attacked Gorbachev viciously for destroying the Party and seventy glorious years of Communism. All seemed to be signed: people were not afraid to declare themselves even on the losing side. Colonel Petrushenko, Alksnis's comrade-in-arms, was in the chamber itself. In full uniform, he was arguing that the country needed a state of emergency. It should have been introduced by constitutional means, but Gorbachev was unwilling to act. So the leaders of the putsch had been quite justified in acting unconstitutionally. This too was a sign that the old fears were dissolving, and that everyone was determined to preserve the legal and democratic proprieties. On no previous occasion would those defeated in a Russian putsch have been allowed to get away with it.

The next day I looked in on the Chamber again. The members of the old government were defending themselves. The most impressive was Shcherbakov, who had been Deputy Prime Minister for the Economy. He described how Pavlov had called the ministers in on the first day of the coup. He had told them that a plot had been uncovered to overthrow the government. Armed bands had been infiltrated into Moscow. They had a list of people to arrest. 'All of you', said Pavlov, 'are on the list.' He had then asked the ministers if they would continue to carry out their duties. Almost all had said yes. Shcherbakov told the Chamber that no one should be surprised. Soviet ministers had never been real ministers, only technical managers who always conformed to whomever was in charge. Even so it was unjust to tar them all with the same brush. Gubenko, the Minister of Culture, had warned Pavlov that the whole thing smelled of the purge year of 1937, and had resigned the next day. Vorontsov, responsible for the environment, had also behaved decently. Gerashchenko had had to act to prevent the collapse of the banking system and was now being unfairly vilified. As for himself, he had every respect for Gorbachev. He had, however, joined the government not to serve an individual, but to serve the country. The story of Gorbachev's illness had been hard to believe. It smelled of the intrigue surrounding the deposition of Khrushchev. But someone had had to stay in office to keep the country going. He concluded: 'This is the last time I shall speak from this tribune. We all failed to appreciate that Gorbachev was trying to preserve a balance between the conflicting forces in the country while edging it towards reform and change. I warn you that the worst is yet to come.' He was heard in silence, and left the tribune with dignity.

That meeting of the Soviet parliament was the last time that it played a significant political role. When it met again on 21 October there were delegations from only seven Republics – not including Ukraine. Laptiev chose that day to announce his resignation as Speaker. When I called on him a couple of days later he said that everyone was now bored with the parliament. Perfectly sensible people, who had performed well in earlier sessions, had got up on the tribune and spouted rubbish. At best the Soviet parliament, like the Union itself, might still have some value as a bridge across which Ukraine and others could find their way back to a structured relationship with Russia once they discovered that independence was less attractive than they had hoped. Gorbachev's real role was rapidly diminishing. His speech to the parliament had been perfunctory. He had announced that he would take 'constitutional measures' if the Republics tried to nationalise or 'privatise' bits of the Soviet armed forces on their territory. But no one knew what this could possibly mean in his present weakened state. He no longer had a full day's work to do. Laptiev had recently called on him on a minor matter, and the meeting had lasted for over three hours. I commented that Gorbachev had always been bad at managing his time and had always talked too much. Laptiev grinned. He thought he knew why. He had recently been rung by Raisa Maksimovna, and it had been three-quarters of an hour before she had put the phone down. Obviously Gorbachev never got a word in edgeways at home, so he turned his eloquence on those he dealt with in the outside world.

The political initiative had now passed wholly to the Russian parliament. It was there, at the end of October, that Yeltsin made his long-awaited speech on economic reform. In a matter of days, the parliament had approved the principle of reform; blessed his request for special powers to override the local bureaucracies; and agreed to look at constitutional change. The main democratic parties signed a declaration of willingness to support the reforms: the 'unified political bloc' for which Yeltsin called in his opening speech. A week later Yeltsin appointed his new government. His Chief of Staff, Burbulis, became the First Deputy Prime Minister, and Gaidar and Shokhin were the two Vice Premiers, the first responsible for economic reform, and the second for social policy including unemployment. This was the public curtain-raiser to the radical economic reforms which Yeltsin and Gaidar initiated in the first days of the new year.

As the parliament of the USSR – Gorbachev's triumphant democratic construction of a mere two years earlier – faded into insignificance, the state institutions of the Soviet Union were following suit. The shadow 'ministries' in the Republics, which had been the symbolic attributes of a phantom 'sovereignty', began to acquire real substance. In April 1991 Andrei Kozyrev, the Foreign Minister of a 'Russia' which had not yet assumed reality, came to lunch with his wife. He was the son of a Soviet diplomat. He had himself served in the Soviet Foreign Ministry. He had enjoyed working with Shevardnadze to turn Soviet foreign policy around, and had helped to draft Gorbachev's historic speech to the United Nations. But the Soviet Foreign Ministry was still dominated by the Party, which interfered with policymaking at all levels, even after it lost its privileged position under Article Six of the Constitution. He found this increasingly intolerable. In October 1990 he decided to abandon a successful career, join Yeltsin, and commit himself to what was still an uncertain and shadowy 'Russia'. I commented that this must have taken courage. He replied that he did not feel like a hero. One member of his tiny staff, who was responsible for human rights, had spent years in the camps. Kozyrev felt guilty each time he looked at him. Kozyrev was not particularly critical of Gorbachev, or particularly enthusiastic about Yeltsin, an unpredictable boss. Both men were still constrained by their Party background, and their capacity to absorb new ideas was limited. Kozyrev and his wife stayed with us for three hours: a measure of the small amount of real business waiting for him in his cramped 'Foreign Ministry' in one of the less fashionable parts of Moscow. He struck me as an intelligent and decent man. I wondered how, with his air of a slightly depressed dormouse, he would fare in the rough and tumble of Moscow politics. But although he became very unpopular in the new Russia, where the nationalists accused him of selling out to the

West, he proved tough enough to survive for five years, until he was replaced by Yevgeny Primakov.

After the coup Kozyrev moved into much grander quarters in the old Central Committee building. In September Geoffrey Howe, the former Foreign Secretary, and I called on him in a large committee room furnished in Karelian birch. Howe asked how the relationship between the Soviet and the Russian foreign ministries was developing. Kozyrev said that all depended on the outcome of the negotiations on the Union Treaty. If there were to be a Union President and a State Council of the Union, then there would have to be a Union Ministry. It would have to hold the Soviet Union's old seat in the UN Security Council, and deal with politico-military matters, some international macroeconomic matters, and the apparently trivial but actually important matter of the appointment of Union ambassadors.

None of this happened. As Autumn advanced the Soviet Foreign Ministry withered on the vine as the Republics developed their own external relations. After the coup, Boris Pankin, who was thought to have performed well as Soviet ambassador in Prague during the coup, replaced the unfortunate Bessmertnykh as Soviet Foreign Minister. Morale hit rock bottom when the rumour spread that Pankin was going to sack all the Deputy Foreign Ministers because of their association with the old regime. By the end of the year, Yuri Fokin, the Head of the Second European Department, who dealt with our affairs and later became a successful ambassador to London, had gone on extended holiday. His deputy went off to work in the expanding bureaucracy of the Russian state. Two others went into private business. But fewer careers were ruined than the diplomats had feared. On 18 December Yeltsin decreed that the Soviet Foreign Ministry had ceased to exist (though the Union which it was supposed to serve had not yet been abolished), the Russian Foreign Ministry moved into their Stalinist skyscraper, and most of the old-fashioned senior diplomats were reinstated.

Yeltsin and Gorbachev both agreed that something had to be done at once about the KGB. Laptiev and Yakovlev had forecast that the KGB would be broken up. The job was given to Bakatin as soon as Gorbachev got back from Foros. Bakatin believed that the KGB and its philosophy of 'Chekism' – the claim that the Party was justified in using unlimited force against anyone who failed to conform with its demands – were the core of the totalitarian regime. Without it, that regime simply could not exist. He accepted that the state needed good intelligence. But much of what the KGB supplied from abroad was rubbish; and the biased domestic intelligence served up by Kryuchkov had helped to push Gorbachev to the right in the Winter of 1990. Douglas Hurd and I called on Bakatin during John Major's visit. He looked tired and red-eyed, and his face was sagging: he was working seventeen or eighteen hours a day in his new job. But he perked up as the meeting went on.

Hurd congratulated him on the outcome of the coup. Bakatin said that it was too early for congratulations. He was still trying to get his bearings and looking for people whom he could trust. He would reduce the KGB's power severely. All its troops would go to the army and the Interior Ministry. Its communications directorate (the codebreakers) would go to a new and separate agency. Foreign intelligence would be the responsibility of a separate agency under Primakov. Senior officers involved in the putsch would be sacked. Morale among the others was very low: they saw their careers in ruins. He was reassuring them that the KGB would still have important tasks: external intelligence, counterintelligence, counter-terrorism, organised crime. But the new KGB needed a proper legal framework for its activities. Hurd offered to send him details of the recent British legislation on wiretapping. The two men agreed that their agencies should cooperate. Hurd pressed Bakatin to reduce the number of Russian intelligence agents in London. Bakatin laughed. The British Security Service, he said, would not want all the Russian agents to go, lest they found themselves out of a job.

As 1991 drew to a close, representatives of Western intelligence agencies flocked to Moscow to meet their opposite numbers. In December Stella Rimington, then about to become Director General of the British Security Service, came to Moscow to call on Bakatin and Primakov. We had dinner in the KGB's guesthouse, a nineteenth-century mansion in the old business part of the town, the former residence of Beria's notorious deputy Avvakumov, who was shot not long after his master. KGB generals sat on one side of the table, including the man who had been 'handling' the British embassy in Moscow for the previous two decades. On the other side sat Stella Rimington, her deputy, an enthusiastic Russophile who surprised his hosts by quoting Pushkin and proposing a passionate toast in Russian, and myself. We complained about the KGB's harassment of the Embassy staff, and especially the way they burgled our people's flats and messed up their things in deliberately unpleasant ways. The general said his men were professionals. They did not do that sort of thing. It must be the fault of the new Russian criminals. I said that the same thing had happened when I was in Moscow in the 1960s. Now as then the KGB's 'professionals' were low-grade operatives. They vandalised our people's belongings from simple envy, and in order to undermine their morale. The general denied my accusations. But he gave me his telephone number and told me to ring if it happened again. For a time the harassment diminished. I was reminded irresistibly of the Christmas truce on the Western Front in 1914: muddy figures dragging themselves out of the trenches and stumbling across No Man's Land to embrace their enemies. That truce came to an abrupt end and the guns resumed their bombardment by the end of the day. I wondered whether the truce between the intelligence agencies would be all that much more durable. It wasn't. The battle resumed, though not at its previous intensity, as Primakov describes in his memoir of his time as head of the new Russian foreign intelligence service.

Four months later the Soviet Union collapsed and Bakatin was sacked. In his memoirs he commented sadly:

> I do not consider that the special services have yet ceased to be a threat to the citizen. There are no laws, no system of control, no change in the ideology to meet the requirements of a democratic state based on law. I did not succeed in bringing the matter to a conclusion. I hope someone else succeeds in doing so.

It was an accurate analysis. A few months later Jill and I went round the KGB's lugubrious museum. Our two young guides were still incensed by the destruction of Dzerzhinsky's statue on the square outside. They still believed in 'Chekism'. The purges in 1937, they thought, were 'a great tragedy, when we lost some of our best officers', rather than a crime which their predecessors had committed against the nation as a whole. They and other young KGB officers I met in later years still believed that the hounding of Sakharov, Solzhenitsyn, and the other dissidents was a state necessity. They could barely contain their hatred of Bakatin. After he departed, the number of secret policemen in Russia was still many times larger than in the West. In the new Russia, chaotic, pluralist, proto-democratic, the intelligence agencies lacked the clear ideological direction of their Tsarist and Communist predecessors. They and their organisations no longer gave the Russian state its peculiar character, and ordinary people were no longer so afraid of them. All this was an immense gain. But the secret policemen remained in place, in their offices, with their old contacts and their old files: available to any strong leader who wished to use their services.

Although Gorbachev continued to see his foreign friends on every possible occasion – at the Human Rights Conference in Moscow, at the Middle East

Conference in Madrid – the main international event that Autumn was the negotiation on debt with the countries of the G7, in which he had no role at all. Western creditor governments wanted to know when they would get their money back. They were in no mood to make concessions just because the Soviet Union was in the grip of a benign revolution. And they wanted to make it clear that, whatever happened to the Union, the Republics would get no new loans unless they accepted their share of responsibility for the Soviet debt. The negotiation took place over several days in October and November in the 'October' hotel where the agreement on Germany had been signed the year before. It focused on two issues: How was the debt to be divided between the Republics? and how was the responsibility for its repayment to be tied down?

The Western negotiators were the 'Deputy Finance Ministers' of the members of the Group of Seven, including Nigel Wicks, the British Treasury's senior official on international financial affairs. On the other side were the Finance Ministers and Central Bankers of the Soviet Republics. The Balts boycotted the meeting, though they were nervous that a settlement might be reached against their interests and behind their backs. Silaev, now formally Prime Minister of the Union (whatever that was now worth), led for the Union. Gaidar led for Russia, as Deputy Prime Minister for Economic Questions. The Ukrainian delegation was led by Prime Minister Fokin whose main aim was to ensure that he did nothing which could be used as evidence of a sell-out by his enemies in Kiev. The main aim of the Uzbeks was to ensure that their gold was not used to help settle the collective debt. The Central Bankers and Finance Ministers of some of the smaller Republics, whose function in the Soviet system had been almost entirely decorative, blinked and stumbled like moles as they emerged for the first time into the real world of international negotiation and international finance. Yavlinsky dissociated himself from the whole business. As so often, he preferred the role of the critical outsider who did not have to take responsibility when things went wrong.

The negotiations demonstrated the ignorance of the Republics about the realities of international economics, and their determination that they alone – not the 'Union' – should be the protagonists. The Soviet authorities as such had almost no word to say. The G7 Deputies, especially David Mulford, the Assistant Secretary from the US Treasury, pressed their case with brutal force. The republican representatives found themselves having to deal not with one another and with Moscow, with whom they could and regularly did sign documents which they later repudiated with impunity, but with the harsh facts of economics. It all ended with a reasonable fudge, largely brokered by the calm and skilful Wicks. By the time it was over it was clear that whatever else happened, economic power had slipped decisively from the centre to the Republics; and that for most of the Republics political considerations far outweighed economic ones. There was no longer any question that the former Soviet Union would evolve into the cooperative economic and monetary union for which the IMF, Yavlinsky and others still hoped. On the contrary, the exposure of republican officials to the outside world boosted their confidence, and taught them a number of useful lessons for the future. I told the British journalists in Moscow that the negotiations marked the practical engagement of the G7 in the Russian economy and the beginning of economic realism for Russia and the other Republics. As such it was an event as significant for East–West relations and for the world in general as the START and other arms control negotiations. It was an innocent hyperbole, but it did contain a germ of truth.

History took a further symbolic lurch forward at the beginning of November when Leningrad resumed its original name of St Petersburg. It was not the city's first change of name. At the beginning of the First World War the city was renamed 'Petrograd', because 'St Petersburg' sounded too Germanic. In fact Peter had originally taken the name from the perfectly neutral Dutch.

The Grand Duke Vladimir Kirillovich, the son of the last Tsar's brother, who was born in Finland in 1917, flew into the city for his very first visit to Russia in a small propeller-driven plane called *President Special*. He was greeted by Sobchak and his Deputy, Vladimir Putin. Putin stayed on with me while I waited for a British minister to arrive. He was a small man who found it hard to look you straight in the face. He waxed indignant about the Estonian parliament, whose anti-Russian posturing risked provoking a Russian backlash. He produced no more vivid an impression on me when I met him again on later visits to St Petersburg.

A religious service of rededication for the city took place the following evening in St Isaac's Cathedral. The church was packed to bursting. The service was conducted by Patriarch Aleksi. Vladimir Kirillovich stood in the place reserved for the Tsars: the first time a Romanov, or perhaps anyone, had stood there since 1917. For two hours he bore himself impassively, crossing himself gravely, and not twitching a muscle. His dumpy little Georgian wife, a Bagration princess, stood beside him with equal dignity.

The next morning we went to the renaming ceremony in the great square outside the Winter Palace, the scene of the armed scuffle which led to the overthrow of the Provisional Government in October 1917. It was bitterly cold, the square was half empty, and the people were listless. There was a military band, half of it dressed in eighteenth-century uniform. The midday gun roared to mark the moment for the change of name, and Sobchak spoke. He praised the Apostle Peter, whose intercession had at last allowed the name to be restored, and the Emperor Peter who first opened the window onto Europe. He bitterly attacked the seventy-four years of Communism. But he sensibly devoted a long passage to 'Leningrad', the name under which so many of the inhabitants fought and died during the Second World War. And he promised the crowd that food prices in the city's state shops would not go up – the only passage that gave rise to a cheer. As we left, parachutists carrying the Russian flag landed in the square, and stunt planes circled overhead – all kindly provided, the announcer said, by a *sponsor*, a new word to enter the hospitable Russian language, as a new tribe of 'businessmen' emerged to batten on the corpse of Communism.

As night fell, the battlements of the Peter Paul Fortress across the river were ringed with fire, and the two beacons by the Stock Exchange were aflame. There was a firework display: very tame to start with, but rising to an exhilarating crescendo. Great starbursts erupted over the Fortress, yachts and cutters sailed in and out of the Catherine-wheels on the river. A loudspeaker van blared out appropriate music: the finale to Beethoven's Ninth Symphony, and stirring choruses from the Russian operas. The people began at last to enjoy themselves, cheering, oohing and aahing in the good-tempered way of Russian crowds. The ceremonies ended with a Concert Ball in the elegant Tauride Palace which had once belonged to Potemkin. Embarrassed youths stood around, gawky in the uniforms of the eighteenth-century Imperial Army, and simpering girls delighted to be in crinolines. It was a crowded, colourful and grand affair. Ludmila Borisovna, Sobchak's wife, was there in her third outfit of the day.

But as we laid flowers on Falconetti's great monument to Peter, the Bronze Horseman, an elderly woman told me that the ceremonies had missed the point. She saw little to celebrate. She had spent two hours the previous day queuing for meat. By the time she reached the head of the queue there was no meat left. It was the first time she had left a queue in tears. She laid the blame squarely where it belonged: on the Communists and their seventy years of rule.

As the Autumn advanced another new word entered the language: *kolaps*, collapse. The Soviet Union was visibly falling apart, and people were beginning to speculate that Russia itself might disintegrate. Yeltsin had told John Major that he wanted to preserve the Union, and he changed his attitude only slowly. The coup was barely over before Yeltsin's spokesman said that any Republic that left the Soviet Union, apart from the Balts, would have to negotiate border changes. He had Kazakhstan and the Ukraine particularly in mind, because of the large numbers of Russians living there. Gavriil Popov spoke darkly on the television about Russia's territorial claims on other Republics. The Ukrainians were furious. Rutskoi and Sobchak flew urgently to Kiev on 27 August to calm them down.

Although Yeltsin had supported Baltic independence as a weapon against Gorbachev, he too was still under the illusion that the Balts wanted to remain at least in some kind of economic union of the fifteen. On 23 August, the day after the coup collapsed Ruutel, the President of Estonia, came to call on me unannounced. He wanted Britain to recognise Baltic independence immediately. That would make it harder for the extremists in the Russian minority, the army, and the KGB, to launch a provocation in the Baltic States. The present moment of confusion favoured the Balts. But if matters were delayed, even the Russians in Moscow would be tempted to change their minds over their previous support for Baltic independence. That afternoon Fyodorov, the Russian Deputy Foreign Minister, told me that although Russia recognised the Balts' 'sovereignty', they had not yet decided whether to recognise their 'independence', an equivocation which I challenged and condemned. I could not understand why the West did not recognise Baltic independence immediately and completely. The Foreign Office fiddled with a tortuous formula designed to ensure that we did not get ahead of the Americans. I had some ill-tempered exchanges on the telephone with London. Two days later the Latvians told David Manning in Riga that a Soviet military base had broadcast appeals to the Russian minority to take to the forests with their weapons. But we were still without instructions. The three Baltic prime ministers, Edgar Savisaar (Estonia), Ivars Godmanis (Latvia) and Gediminas Vagnorius (Lithuania), called on John Major during his visit on 1 September to express similar worries. They were determined on full economic as well as political independence, and were not prepared to enter into an economic union with one another, let alone with Russia.

On 6 September the short-lived State Council of the Soviet Union, set up the previous day and consisting of the Presidents of all the Republics, chaired by Gorbachev, took the formal decision to recognise the independence of all three Baltic States. Our own hesitation became irrelevant and faded from the memory. In mid-September Yeltsin summoned the European ambassadors to a meeting at the White House. We were addressed by Lennart Meri, the Estonian Foreign Minister (and later the

President of Estonia). He began with routine sentiments, in English, about human rights and Baltic independence. He then turned to Yeltsin, and said that he wanted to talk in Russian even though the language was forced on him and his people for fifty years. The Estonians had suffered from the totalitarian dictatorship of the Soviet Union; but so had the Russians. For all their hatred of the Russian system, the Estonians had never hated the Russians, whose language, literature, and culture they deeply admired. It was a moving gesture of reconciliation.

Although I believed that the Russians would withdraw from their empire peacefully, I continued to think that they would hang on to the natural frontier that they had fought for centuries to secure: the watershed of the North Caucasus, their barrier against a resurgent Turkey or Iran. But in November 1990 a 'Chechen National Congress' proclaimed the 'sovereignty' of Chechen-Ingushetia: the two tiny nations – ethnically almost indistinguishable – were still linked in a single Autonomous Republic with strictly limited local powers. A former air force general, Djokar Dudaev, one of the few Chechens to rise to high position in the Soviet armed forces, took over the Congress in June 1991, and exploited the continuing confusion in Moscow to expand Chechnya's room for independent manoeuvre. Vice President Rutskoi, a military veteran with severely underdeveloped political instincts, had his own recipe, drawn from his experience in Afghanistan. 'A *kishlak* [village] fires at us and kills someone,' he is said to have told a senior KGB officer, 'I send up a couple of planes and there is nothing left of the *kishlak*. After I've burned a couple of *kishlaks* they stop shooting.'[1] The Russian parliament issued an ultimatum. On 8 November Yeltsin declared a state of emergency in Chechnya at Rutskoi's prompting, and ordered the arrest of Dudaev. Gorbachev refused to allow Soviet forces, such as they now were, to cooperate in this operation. He was simply ignored. Six hundred Russian Interior Ministry troops were sent to Grozny, the capital. A few days later they were on their way home again with their tails between their legs: by bus, without their weapons, because their aircraft had been impounded by the Chechens. On 11 November the Russian parliament threw out Yeltsin's emergency decree.

Rutskoi was scornful of the democrats who talked about using 'political methods' to resolve the crisis. That was a recipe for doing nothing, he told me. When Yeltsin issued his decree, Dudaev had only 150 men under arms. A month later he had 35,000. Rutskoi himself would have dealt with Dudaev the way the West had dealt with Saddam Hussein.

As late as the Summer of 1994 Yeltsin still took the other view: 'Were we to apply pressure of force against Chechnya, the whole Caucasus would be in such turmoil and blood that no one would ever forgive us.' Four months later the Russians invaded Chechnya, with many of the disastrous results Yeltsin himself had predicted.

Meanwhile Gorbachev continued with his despairing efforts to cobble together a Union Treaty. Drafts of economic agreements, common fiscal systems, and unified military commands were put for signature to one meeting after another – in Moscow, in Alma Ata, in the discredited Soviet parliament. But all the meetings were boycotted by one or more of the Republics. Yeltsin's position became increasingly ambiguous. The Ukrainians were determined not to compromise their steady course towards full independence. At a meeting in Leipzig at the end of October I told Douglas Hurd and the German Foreign Minister, Hans Dietrich Genscher, that even at the best it would be possible to retain no more than a 'simulacrum' of the old Union.

My German listeners were not happy. But they drew the appropriate conclusions. In mid-November Chernyaev and Palazhchenko, Gorbachev's chief interpreter, complained to me that the Germans and the Americans had given the Union up for lost, and were encouraging the Republics on their road to separation and independence. This was a great mistake. The Union could still be preserved, thought Chernyaev. Gorbachev had once again threatened to resign if the other Republics did not accept his idea of a confederated state with an elected president, not a mere coordinating mechanism. The threat had worked. But it was probably the last time. If the negotiations now failed the consequences could be horrendous. Russia was going through a bad patch. But in a decade or two Russia would reassert itself as the dominant force in the huge geographical area which surrounded it. Yeltsin would have no choice but to assert Russia's position if it were challenged. If the Ukrainians were too provocative, Chernyaev said, Yeltsin would have to weigh in, with force if necessary. That was in no one's interest. Palazhchenko and Chernyaev understood that we had to accept the realities But the game was not yet played out. They appealed to the British to exercise their influence to prevent the Union from breaking up. I told them that we had previously thought that our interests could best be protected by the preservation of the Union. But we now believed that this was no longer a feasible objective and were reconsidering our whole policy.

The Ukraine was the key. A rump 'Union' without Ukraine made no sense at all. The relationship between Russia and Ukraine was fundamental to the future course of events in the former Soviet Union. None of the other relationships (including the relationship between Russia and Kazakhstan) mattered to anything like the same degree. People in the West did not understand the emotional charge involved on the Russian as well as on the Ukrainian side. Perfectly sensible Russians frothed at the mouth if it was suggested that Ukraine (from which they all traced their history) might go off on its own. I doubted that the Russians would simply acquiesce in Ukrainian independence, or that they had much understanding of Ukrainian sensibilities. The relationships were as combustible as those in Northern Ireland: but the consequences of an explosion would be far more serious. Our practical ability to influence the outcome was in any case very limited. Whether we liked it or not, the old Union was as dead as a doornail. The 'simulacrum of a Union' about which I had spoken in Leipzig might still emerge: but that convenient outcome was now unlikely. Our own interests were twofold. We wanted the constituent parts of the former Soviet Union to fulfil its international obligations, and to devise a reliable control over the military, especially the nuclear forces. We wanted to develop profitable political, economic, and security relationships with the successor states, of which Russia would be by far the most important, Ukraine second, Kazakhstan third, and the others a good way behind. So the question was not whether we recognised Ukrainian independence, but when and how. We should develop our practical relationship with Ukraine by every means. But we should go more slowly on formal recognition while the Russians had time to adapt to the new realities.

I put these cautious arguments to the Foreign Office in the middle of November. They were oversubtle and impractical, and they were almost immediately overtaken by events. They were also too pessimistic. Despite a good deal of friction over the next few years, the Ukrainians and the Russians handled their disputes comparatively sensibly

On 1 December the Ukrainians voted overwhelmingly for independence. Gorbachev issued a despairing appeal on television to the Republics to sign the Union Treaty. He predicted that the collapse of the Union would shatter personal, economic, scientific, and cultural links. It would provoke ethnic strife in the Baltic States. It could lead to bloodshed, even war. Even balanced Russians like Chernyaev and Sobchak agreed with him.

But Gorbachev's last illusions were soon swept away. On 8 December we gave a dinner for Michael Caine, the Chairman of Booker plc, who was in Moscow to promote his imaginative scheme for a Russian Booker Prize. The Russian guests were from the Moscow literary establishment. As they were leaving we happened to look at the teleprinter chattering away in the front hall. We were stunned to read that Yeltsin, Kravchuk, and their

Belorussian opposite number Shushkevich had met secretly in a hunting lodge at Belovezha on the border of Poland. They had announced that the Soviet Union was 'ceasing its existence as a subject of international law and a geopolitical reality' and would be replaced by a 'Commonwealth of Independent States'.

Despite its dramatic appearance, the new agreement was a natural consequence of the way in which power had flowed from the centre to the Republics since the August coup. What struck me most was that (despite a passing reference to 'Eurasia') its provisions were Slav- and Europe-oriented. Despite his close association with Yeltsin, Nazarbaev, the President of Kazakhstan, was not present at Belovezha. Yeltsin's subsequent attempt to pretend that his invitation had been lost in the post was unconvincing. The institutions of the new Commonwealth were to be in Minsk. That was almost as far West as it was possible to get without leaving the former Soviet Union altogether. The whole thing was a very far cry from the 'Union of Sovereign States' which Gorbachev and Chernyaev had been advocating so passionately only a few days earlier.

Kozyrev called the Western ambassadors in for an explanation. The Union, he said, had been falling apart and decisionmaking had broken down. 'The situation had become unbearable, and even threatened the integrity of the armed forces' (a menacing phrase which he did not explain). So the Slavs had been forced to set up a new Commonwealth, in which there would be no room for the old Union and its institutions. An honourable role might be found for Gorbachev if he went quietly.

Yeltsin claimed in the Russian parliament on 12 December that it had long been clear to him that the Union could no longer function. Since the putsch it had been in its death throes. There was never any question of the Ukrainians signing up to a Union Treaty: and no treaty was possible without them. The three Republics had acted to forestall chaos. The new Commonwealth would assume the international responsibilities of the Soviet Union, preserve the joint command over the 'common military-strategic space', and cooperate on foreign policy. There would be a 'common economic space': a single currency, a common budget policy, and a customs union. This was the 'simulacrum'. But it bore no relation to reality: the Ukrainians were as opposed as ever to anything which smacked of common or supranational institutions. Baburin, a hardline Communist, remarked sarcastically that the organisers of the August putsch had at least wanted to preserve their country: the organisers of the December putsch had destroyed it.

But this second coup was not to be reversed. Gorbachev demanded a

Union-wide referendum, and used inflammatory talk about the Russian minorities in the Baltics and Ukraine in a desperate attempt to regain some influence. But Sasha Motov, our average Muscovite, was delighted. At last somebody was doing something. The Slavs were standing together. Letting the Central Asians fall by the wayside was just fine.

The collapse of the Soviet Union coincided with the final disgrace of Konstantin Demakhin. He had always been unpopular with the British as well as the Russian staff of the embassy: I was seen as his uncritical protector. While we were on holiday in the summer, he drove the Rolls-Royce into a pothole and smashed the front axle, and he overstayed his leave in London. On my return David Logan told me that I would have to sack him. I called him in. I said that I would not sack him this time. But I had told the embassy administration that they could sack him without any further reference to me if he offended in future. He sulked for a few days until the excitement of the coup cheered him up. I thought all might be well. But in October *Literaturnaya Gazeta* published an interview in which he claimed to have quit the KGB after spying on the last seven British ambassadors, including me. My embassy colleagues told me that this time I really must sack him. I said that I could hardly sack him for falling out with the KGB: I wished the rest of the Russian staff would do the same. But I told him that it was not part of his duties to play public politics. He could have caused me considerable embarrassment in London ('Limp-wristed diplomat spied on by chauffeur'). He might at least have warned me that the interview was about to appear. He answered obscurely that he had done it because he was a 'Russian patriot'. I told him that he could continue to work for me until I finally left Moscow. But I would not be able to recommend him to my successor. He went into a decline, a sort of dazed nervous breakdown. He refused to speak to anyone. The Russian staff refused to speak to him, not least because his interviews on the KGB had broken the convention of silence on which they all depended. His driving became erratic and dangerous. I sent him to the doctor, and put him on two weeks' leave. The final straw occurred at the beginning of January when he nearly ran down Julie Bell. He offered to leave and I accepted his offer. He was in tears when he came to say goodbye. Jill and I felt guilty and almost equally sad.

Stunned by the Belovezha agreement, Western governments were anxious not to move prematurely. John Major sent Len Appleyard, the new Political Director in the Foreign Office, on a whistle-stop tour of Moscow, Kiev, and

Minsk to 'get a first-hand impression of what is going on in this country and seek assurances about human rights, nuclear weapons, and debt'. On Friday 13 December Appleyard and I called on Gorbachev in his office in the Kremlin for the very last time. Gubenko was hanging about in his outer office, looking cheerful but aimless. Aleksandr Yakovlev, Chernyaev, and Palazhchenko were with Gorbachev. He was in bouncing form, with his usual tan, bubbling with verbose and hectic charm. He launched into half an hour of self-justification. He had always stood for a Union State, not a Union of States (his alleged failure to distinguish between federation and confederation was one of the things that Lukyanov above all had held against him). All the problems which now so much troubled people – control of the armed forces, citizenship, frontiers – could be solved within a Union. He had secured agreement on this basic principle through the Novo-Ogarevo process. The Russians had been inclined to agree: Russia, for its own reason needed a Union as much as the other Republics did. But the Ukrainians had upset everything with their referendum. And once the result of the referendum was known, Yeltsin had exploited the new situation for his own ends. Gorbachev himself was a statesman, not a politician like the inexperienced populists who now ruled the roost (whom he called 'highwaymen', and 'hairy faces'). But he had to take account of reality and to look at the long-term consequences. The Minsk process was deeply mistaken. But it was not now to be reversed. So his task was to ensure that constitutional propriety was observed, and to restrain the opportunists. He was worried about nuclear weapons, minorities, Yugoslavia on a continental scale. Kravchuk had no idea how to manage his new army, and Gorbachev had sent two generals to Kiev to sort him out. As for Yeltsin, he had admitted that in ten years the Union would probably have been reconstituted.

This was not the behaviour of a man on the verge of resigning. On the contrary, he gave the firm impression that he believed that he still had a role. But Yakovlev looked more and more gloomy as he listened to his leader building castles in the air. Chernyaev took notes with deadpan determination. Gorbachev ended by sending his best wishes to Major. He was full of friendly remarks to me. Tony Bishop, the Foreign Office interpreter accompanying Appleyard, remarked that Gorbachev obviously felt the need for old friends. Gubenko was still hanging about in his outer office as we left. Isolation hung in the air.

In Kiev the Ukrainians were still highly suspicious of the Russians, and determined not to allow the new Commonwealth of Independent States to become an instrument of Russian imperial policy. The former opposition politician Pavlichko, who was now the Chairman of the Foreign Affairs Committee, was almost as suspicious of Yeltsin as he was of Gorbachev. Whatever the Minsk agreement said, Ukraine would have its own army, its own frontiers, and its own currency. It was not interested in a Slav Union: Ukraine was part of Europe, and that was all there was to it. Pavlichko, who had been at our dinner with Rukh in January 1990, remembered with pleasure Waldegrave's dinner toast to 'Ukrainian independence', and with rather less pleasure Mrs Thatcher's comparison between the Ukraine and California. Kravchuk confirmed Pavlichko's line. More than three hundred years had now passed since Khmelnitsky brought Ukraine under the Tsar. The empire was over, the Union was finished. The new Ukraine would be entirely independent. It would have its own army and its own foreign policy.

Minsk, which I had not visited before, was a much pleasanter city than I expected. The streets were clean and without potholes, and the architecture, though Stalinist, was tolerable. Belorussia suffered more than any other Soviet Republic from the war. One third of the population of nine million was killed, and all that was left of the prewar city was a few reconstructed blocks by the river: cobbled streets, flats for the intelligentsia, and restaurants. And Belorussia was much the worst affected by the Chernobyl disaster: most of its territory was exposed to the fallout, and agriculture had to be closed down in two whole regions.

On the huge square outside the massive parliament building (the largest and most useless square in Europe, the jolly Mr Shushkevich later remarked) a forlorn group of demonstrators was demanding the resignation of the government. Foreign Minister Kravchenko (or Krauchenka, as he called himself in Belorussian) – a sad-faced man, with an underdeveloped sense of humour – claimed that the three Presidents who met in Belovezha never had any intention of forming a purely Slav union. But he and everyone else we met was clearly in two minds about whether they wanted the Asiatic Republics in the new Commonwealth. What Krauchenka really yearned after was an association with Europe, which as far as he was concerned need by no means include Russia. At dinner Krauchenka paraded a number of 'little known facts', as he called them, to demonstrate the grandeur and continuity of Belorussian history, literature, and culture. We drank our toasts in a special Belorussian balsam the basis of which, he told us with a lugubrious air as if he was treating us to a special confidence, was bee shit.

In the first months of 1992 I went back to the Republics to see how they were coping with their new independence. In January I joined Douglas Hurd at

talks with Nazarbaev in Alma Ata. Nazarbaev was still bitter about the way
he had been left on one side when the three Slavs had signed their
agreement in Belovezha, and nervous about the prospects for newly
independent Kazakhstan. There was a risk of 'terrible' trouble if the new
Republics failed to get through their current transition quickly and
successfully. There was plenty of scope to reverse the move to democracy,
and set up the worst kind of dictatorship. But he believed that in the end
the members of the former Soviet Union – apart from Ukraine – would
come back to some kind of federation. It was a remarkable statement for a
man who was busily asserting his country's freedom. At dinner he loosened
up, with a charming twinkle in his eye and a dry and deadpan sense of
humour. When Hurd suggested he invite Mrs Thatcher as an economic
adviser, he said that it was already hard enough to prevent his existing
advisers from talking too much. He made Hurd carve the traditional
sheep's head. Hurd fulfilled the disagreeable duty with aplomb, and gave
the ears to his wife and to me, because (so Nazarbaev assured him) that
would ensure that we would do what he told us.

In March I flew to Baku in an RAF executive jet with Douglas Hogg, the
Minister of State in the Foreign Office. It was painted in camouflage
colours, and I hoped that the Azeris would not shoot it down in the belief
that the Armenians were about to bomb them. President Mutalibov had
just resigned: the Baku mob accused him of failing to act robustly after an
Armenian massacre of Azeris in Karabakh. We called on my old friend
Prime Minister Gasanov; the acting President Mamedov, who was almost
incoherent with emotion as he delivered a depressing historical tirade
against the Armenians; and on the representatives of the non-Communist
opposition in parliament who were more rational and measured. Everyone
was highly suspicious of Russian imperialist plots. All were preoccupied
with Nagorny Karabakh. The atmosphere was quite different from what it
had been on my previous visit. The Armenians were now proceeding from
victory to victory. The Azeris no longer ruled out negotiation. But they
were uneasily aware that they would be negotiating from weakness, and
that world opinion did not favour them. Even the 'opposition' seemed to
realise that if things got out of hand it would mean not only more
bloodshed in Karabakh, but a serious upheaval in Baku. The ousting of
Mutalibov might be only the beginning. Gasanov phoned me early the next
morning as I was listening to the BBC. The Armenians had attacked the
Azeri border town of Agdam, from which the Azeris had been supplying
their fighters in Nagorny Karabakh itself. The town was in flames, and piled
with dead. Gasan asked me to take the Minister to see for ourselves. I

refused. Instead I sent the embassy's political officer Tim Barrow, who was accompanying the party. When he eventually got there, Tim saw one building in flames, one corpse, and a lot of people leaving in panic. Gasanov was wrongly informed, panicking, or trying it on.

In Yerevan we were accommodated in the government guesthouse. It was very luxurious, and marginally less vulgar than usual. It was also extremely cold. The Azeri blockade had cut supplies of oil and gas to Armenia by 75 per cent, and we spent most of our stay in sweaters. I presented my credentials to President Ter-Petrosian – the first British ambassador to Armenia in 2,000 years or more, as far as any of us could tell. Hogg then had official talks with him. Ter-Petrosian was serious, concentrated, and open to the idea of negotiation over Nagorny Karabakh, an openness which six years later cost him his job. The members of the parliament whom we met next were less reasonable, especially when Hogg told them that there was no chance for an independent Nagorny Karabakh. My return to Moscow from Yerevan was a Russian – or rather Armenian – farce. When I was called to board the plane, a huge Ilyushin 86, it was still being unloaded from its inward flight. Flight mechanics and other interested parties were inspecting the front wheels with a worried air. I and three hundred other passengers stood around in the bitter cold waiting to be allowed to go aboard. Police were brought up to ensure that we did not riot. After half an hour or so my patience snapped and I stormed aboard. The others swarmed after me. We waited. One hour passed, then another. The Armenian passengers laid out huge spreads of food and got down to some serious drinking to while away the time. Then the captain, a large Armenian with a very depressed air, announced that the nose wheels had been changed. But the engineers could not get the jack off. Would all the male passengers go to the back of the plane to tip it down? Everyone tripped aft. The manoeuvre succeeded, the jack was removed, the plane tipped forward again, and we left three hours late.

At the end of April 1992 I visited Shevardnadze, now President of Georgia. Spring had come with a vengeance, the trees and flowers were out everywhere, and Tbilisi was looking at its most beautiful. But about half a mile of the Rustaveli Prospect, the city's main avenue, looked like Dresden in 1945: gaunt, burnt-out shells of buildings and bullet holes all over the walls. It was much more shocking than I had expected, a testimony to the extreme violence of the small civil war the previous year. Shevardnadze's office was in the building of the State Council – formerly the Institute of Marxism-Leninism. Despite his very real problems, he looked much more cheerful than in the months after his resignation. He obviously felt that he had a real role again.

On my way back to the residence for lunch the streets were cleared and I had a five-man motorbike escort. Smartly uniformed policemen saluted at each street corner. Shevardnadze's aide assured me that the President had given special orders for my presence to be marked with a splash, to demonstrate to the people that he still had the ability to bring in foreign support. No doubt he would also have preferred to avoid the political embarrassment which would follow if one of the first ambassadors to Georgia from a major power was assassinated on the streets of his capital city.

The Shevardnadzes invited us for dinner that evening. When we arrived at his old-fashioned and homely residence, situated securely inside the same guarded compound where we were staying, Shevardnadze was obviously in a foul mood. It emerged that Sigua, the Prime Minister, and Kitovani, the Minister of Defence, had failed to turn up. Over the table his mood improved. He reminisced about the events of the previous five years: the fiasco over the proposed ban on nuclear weapons at the Reykjavik Summit, when he was terrified that Gorbachev would sound off at the final press conference, and Gorbachev was equally terrified that he would be unable to control himself; the days of the putsch, when Nanuli packed a bag of warm clothes in case she was arrested; the boring times he had spent doing business with Reagan, who read from his briefs and was uninterested in the answers; and the amusing times he had spent at lunch with Reagan after business was over, listening to Reagan's inexhaustible anecdotes. The toasts succeeded one another, and Shevardnadze cheered up immensely. Just as were planning to leave for the airport, Sigua and Kitovani finally arrived. Sigua, a tall, neat man, with a clipped moustache and the manner of a member of the intelligentsia, was full of well-rounded sentences. Kitovani was a small, unmilitary-looking artist, not at all the man to lead the national guard into the mountains in defiance of Gamsakhurdia as he had done during the August coup, or to help to destroy the centre of Tbilisi as he had in December. He was almost incoherent. I assumed he had been drinking. More toasts were exchanged, Shevardnadze gave me a great big hug, and we left for the airport three-quarters of an hour late.

Successive British ambassadors had been banned by the Foreign Office's lawyers from going to the Baltic States, lest we seemed to be endorsing the Soviet occupation. But in April 1992 we visited independent Latvia to stay in Riga with our old friend Richard Samuel, the first British ambassador to Latvia for more than fifty years. His ambassadorial residence was the Riga Hotel, where he, his wife, two babies, an au pair girl, and a dog occupied two small suites. It was my first visit to the Baltic States since the 1960s. The barricades were still up around the parliament in the old city centre, concrete blocks cemented together across the narrow medieval streets: a more solid barrier than the ramshackle tangle which had surrounded the White House in Moscow during the August putsch. Although I was not on official business, I called on Jurkans, the Foreign Minister. A tall, good-looking man in his forties, a professor of English at the university, he received us in the large nineteenth-century villa which was currently his Ministry. A secretary busily scribbled notes. Halfway through our talk Jurkans took a call on his cellnet telephone: a technology still unavailable in Moscow, a sign of extreme modernity.

Jurkans challenged my view that the Russians had lost their imperial drive. At a recent conference Sobchak had ranted on at him for two hours and more. Shelov-Kovedyaev, the Russian Deputy Foreign Minister, a protégé of Galina Starovoitova and allegedly a liberal, had repeated the absurd proposition that the Balts had joined the Soviet Union voluntarily in 1940. There were still up to one hundred thousand Russian troops in Latvia, and the Russians were showing absolutely no sign of being willing to negotiate their departure. But Jurkans was almost equally critical of his own nationalists. The Latvians treated the Russians as occupiers and humiliated them in the streets. The proposed law on Latvian citizenship was discriminatory. Latvian nationalists were even reviving a claim to what was now Russian territory. They believed that international law and morality were on their side, and that the West would preserve them from the consequences of their intransigence. I said that the West was unlikely to do any such thing. Jurkans sadly agreed. His compatriots rejected his argument that Latvia would have to accommodate itself to the reality that it was condemned to live on good terms with its very large neighbour.

We drove back to Moscow through Estonia. The border between Latvia and Estonia was enthusiastically controlled by inexperienced young officials from both countries in brand-new uniforms: an assertion of statehood. On the frontier between Estonia and Russia at Narva two great fortresses glare at one another: the old Swedish fortress on one side of the river, and Ivangorod on the other. The Estonian frontier guards were deadly serious: two boys spent ten minutes looking at our passports. There was no one at all on the Russian side. But we immediately knew that we were back home: the roads were falling apart and the rubbish proliferated.

One of the greatest achievements of the Communist regime was to turn the Soviet Union from a country of illiterate peasants into a nation with one of the highest levels of technical education in the world. The brilliance and initiative of the Russian people were stifled by their narrow-minded and oppressive political system. But in the second half of the twentieth century the Soviet Union did indeed challenge America successfully in the most advanced fields of modern military technology. The Soviets built their own nuclear weapons, the best fighter aircraft of the 1950s, the most powerful rockets, the best tanks. They put the first satellite and the first man into space. All this produced a surge of unaccustomed self-confidence, a conviction that Russians were after all able to compete on equal terms with foreigners. In the 1950s and 1960s, even in the 1970s, there were few spoilsports in the Soviet Union to point out that these achievements were based on the ruthless impoverishment of the civilian sector, and that they could not be sustained. The mythical Radio Armenia, the endless source of Soviet political anecdotes, was wiser. 'Question: "What is the main difference between the dollar and the rouble?", Answer: "The dollar is backed by gold, and the rouble by tanks."' But most Russians felt an immense and uncomplicated pride in their country's technical achievements under the Soviet regime.

But by the 1980s it was becoming painfully clear that the Soviet system was no longer capable of sustaining these glittering achievements. We had a vivid insight into the Soviet Union's technological problems when Helen Sharman, Britain's first astronaut, came to Moscow to train for her flight on a Soviet space craft in 1991. We visited her at Star City in the forest about three quarters of an hour's drive from the centre of Moscow, where the training for the Soviet manned space programme was carried out. We clambered into the mock-up of the cramped launch module and the surprisingly spacious Mir space ship: stolid Soviet engineering, effective, reliable and easy to maintain, like a T-34 tank. General Leonov, the first man to walk in space and an enthusiastic amateur painter, led us round. Rather tactlessly in front of Helen, he told us what happens to the human body in the event of catastrophic decompression (each cell explodes and the body vaporises). Colonel Titov, the first man to spend more than a year in space, wanted to go back there but looked perfectly sane.

Star City had always been closed to foreigners and to most Soviet citizens as well. Now the troubles of the Soviet world outside affected even this protected environment. Four thousand people lived there. The shops were differentiated by rank: one for astronauts, another for trainees, another for the dependants of deceased astronauts, and another for the rest. Even in the elite shops the choice of goods was very limited. In the hardware department, full of plastic buckets of washing powder which by then was almost unobtainable in Moscow, Jill bought a ramshackle device apparently designed to plant potato seeds. The astronauts were the most privileged people in the Soviet Union. But even they were feeling the pinch.

The same air of shabby gentility lay over the launch site at Baikonur in Kazakhstan. On 18 May 1991 we flew down for the launch with Helen's parents, and were met at the airport by General Shumilin, who had worked at Baikonur for thirty years. The road from the airport was barren: flat sand, scrub, and a temperature that varied from minus 30 degrees in the Winter to plus 45 degrees in the shade in the Summer. Salt was seeping up through the ground: the result, said Shumilin, of the diversion of the Syr-Darya river to irrigate cotton production all over Central Asia. The town of Leninsk, where the people working on the cosmodrome lived, was surrounded by a wall of scruffy concrete panels. The guard post at the gate was unmanned and much of the wall was falling down, a gesture perhaps to the freedoms brought by Perestroika. In the centre of the town there was some carefully watered greenery; and a monument to the people who died in 1961 (fifty eight, Shumilin said – but some say it was as many as six hundred) including Marshal Nedelin, who had ordered a massive rocket to be fired before it was ready.

At the launch site there was an air of popular excitement: crowds, pop music, girls, children, generals everywhere. It was almost American, but not quite. The viewing platform and the facilities around it were entirely Russian: a ramshackle wooden construction, like the grandstand at a small provincial race-course. We were ushered into the room where Helen and her two Russian colleagues were putting on their space kit. They were segregated behind glass to protect them from infection. We waved and gestured. The three astronauts emerged onto a miniature parade ground, stood to attention in front of Colonel General Ivanov, the Chairman of the State Commission, and reported that they were ready to go. The rest of us were carefully segregated behind a cordon. But the cordon collapsed as the cosmonauts went forward to the battered school bus which was to take them to the launch site. We all rushed forward to kiss them, shake their hands, and wish them well. They drove off, together with our microbes. We were after all amongst Russians.

The rocket itself was about a mile away, lonely in the desert, steaming quietly to itself. On the television screens we could see Helen beaming happily from her couch in the capsule. Then the countdown, the launch, a silver-orange flame, and a ponderous, bone-shaking rumble – not a noise, but a physical and emotional sensation of immense power. The rocket disappeared smoothly into the clouds. The television screens went blank. Everyone heaved a sigh of relief when they flickered back a couple of minutes later, and Helen was still there. Shumilin gave Mrs Sharman a great hug and the business degenerated into a raucous lunch.

Afterwards we went to see the cottage where Gagarin had spent the night before his epic flight, and the one next door where Korolev, the 'Chief Designer' and father of Soviet rocket science, used to live. No one mentioned that Korolev's senior colleagues had been shot, and that he himself had had to be fished out of a concentration camp after the war when Stalin started to run out of German rocket experts. Nor did anyone mention the common theory that Gagarin was flying to collect more vodka when he crashed and killed himself.

For some years the Russians had been working on *Buran*, a Soviet space shuttle to match the Americans. The general in charge was much the most unhappy and nervous man we met that day. He refused to say how many shuttles were being built, when the next flight was to be, or what payload the vehicle could carry. He may still have been trying to keep some technical secrets, even in the age of Glasnost. More probably he was suffering from terminal depression. He must have known that *Buran* would never fly again, that the money had finally dried up, and that the glory days of the Soviet space age were over. It was not the end of the Russian space programme. The space station *Mir* had gone into orbit in 1987. It was still in orbit ten years later, long after its original designed date. In 1997 it suffered from a series of troubles, and unfavourable comparisons were made with the American space programmes. But the Americans too had had their disasters: *Apollo 13* and the explosion of *Challenger*. Even the most sophisticated programme is vulnerable to human error and the whims of fate, and the Russians were right to be proud of their achievements.

But now *Buran* stood huge and inert in the desert, a sad symbol of the end of a Russian dream of superiority.

Thus the Union finally fell apart. Its last days had gone by in a whirl. On 16 December 1991, Popov resigned as Mayor of Moscow and was replaced by the altogether more effective Luzhkov. On the same day the television showed the opening of the talks between Yeltsin and Baker. They went on for four hours, and took place in St Catherine's Hall in the Kremlin, where Gorbachev had met so many of his foreign friends. As a courtesy Baker also called on Gorbachev: but the conversation ran out of steam for lack of real substance. It could hardly have been more heavily symbolic of where power now lay.

By this time even Gorbachev was bowing to reality. At a six-hour meeting on 23 December he and Yeltsin negotiated the practical details of his departure – pension, car, dacha, bodyguard. But Gorbachev did not seem to realise, Kozyrev told me later, that if he departed elegantly, and kept quiet for a couple of months, he would resume the historic place he deserved in the esteem of the Russian people. Instead he was reacting 'hecticly', and arguing over every unnecessary detail. By then I had already drafted the telegram I would despatch when Gorbachev left – the telegram I had been composing in my head for over a year.

The finale came on Christmas Day. Gorbachev gave his resignation speech at 7 p.m. on the television. It was dignified, adequate, but no more. He told the viewers that he had known from his first days in office that the old system had to be changed from top to bottom. Despite the difficulties he had introduced democratic freedoms and economic reform. He was proud of his achievements. The country was now in crisis because the bureaucracy had resisted change. He had done what he could to preserve the Union. He did not agree with its dissolution. His views had not changed with the creation of the Commonwealth of Independent States, a decision which should have been put to the people. But he would do what he could to help the new arrangements succeed. He wished the people all the best. He did not mention Yeltsin at all. Immediately he had finished speaking, we looked out of our window. The Red Flag was coming down from the Kremlin for the last time.

The Gorbachevs came for a private dinner in April 1992 just before we left. They wanted to be on their own and we invited no one else. He was in bubbling and charming form. She was less stiff than before: relaxed and talkative, and she did not strain to impress. They addressed one another rather formally as 'Mikhail Sergeevich' and 'Raisa Maksimovna', as if they were already figures from history, as indeed they were. Raisa asked if we had provided an interpreter: I said that our Russian would serve well enough. Then our daughter Kate came in, and I translated inadequately. 'Mikhail Sergeevich, I told you we should have brought an interpreter,' fussed Raisa. And then we sat, just the four of us, snuggled up on the sofa and two armchairs in the Blue Room.

Gorbachev was already staging his return to the international stage, and was obviously exhilarated. He and Raisa had just got back from a trip to Tokyo and were off to America in another couple of days where he was to speak in Fulton. He had just read for the first time the full text of the speech which Churchill had delivered there more than forty years earlier, the 'Iron Curtain' speech which Russians maintained had launched the Cold War. Gorbachev had concluded that Churchill's arguments were much more sophisticated, and much less hostile to Russia, than the Russians had been led to believe.

Gorbachev said that his own two great achievements were to end the Cold War; and to make it possible for ordinary people in Russia to determine their own fate. He defended himself against the universal criticism that he was indecisive, and that this was at the root of his failure. Unconsciously echoing Hilaire Belloc ('Decisive action in the hour of need / Denotes the hero, but does not succeed'), he said that decisiveness of the wrong kind, and at a time of such profound change, would have led to bloodshed. He reminded me ruefully that Tsar Alexander I's first chief minister was the liberal reformer Speransky; but his last was the military despot Arakcheyev. Russian reform was neither easy nor certain. I found myself trying to comfort him. We in the West knew that he was responsible for lifting the fear of atomic annihilation from all of us, and for a fundamental change in the nature of Russian history. But even Moses was unable to bring his people into the Promised Land. Raisa commented tartly that after forty years in the desert the Israelites turned on Moses, and said they wished they had never left Egypt.

Gorbachev was now dictating his memoirs for two to three hours every day. He told us about the war. He remembered the Russian army retreating from Rostov as a disorderly rabble, leaving his village to be occupied by the Germans. His father was sent unarmed into his first hand-to-hand battle: he and his fellows had one rifle between two, and had to win their weapons on the battlefield. Raisa remembered her father having his head shaved, being put into uniform, and sent off to the front. He was brought back almost immediately. He was a skilled railway worker, so he was sent to build railways through the Siberian forest with the help of German prisoners, to transport the factories that were being evacuated from Western Russia and Ukraine. Life was very hard indeed. People supplemented their rations with berries and mushrooms from the forest. Even so, she saw people swelling up and dying from starvation. The German prisoners were the first to go. When she travelled round the villages on a motorbike in the Stavropol region while writing her sociology Ph.D. in the 1960s, she found that one in four households had only women in them, because so many men had been killed during the war.

Raisa told us what it had been like in Foros during the coup. Gorbachev had known something was wrong immediately he heard that a delegation was demanding to see him unannounced. When he discovered that his telephones were cut he told Raisa to expect the worst. He kept the visitors waiting for fifty minutes while she gathered their daughter and son-in-law for a family council. She was afraid that if something happened to Gorbachev the rest of the family might be eliminated as well. Nevertheless they all agreed that he had no choice but to reject whatever demands the visitors might make. He then went into his study with them, and she and the other two sat outside the door to await the outcome. The first to emerge was Varennikov, who strode out without looking at her. The others came up and offered their hands, which she refused. She was obviously, and not surprisingly, terrified throughout.

I remarked on the sequence in the BBC's film about the coup which showed Gorbachev, Yeltsin and Nazarbaev being eavesdropped on by the KGB. Raisa said bitterly: 'They listened to us for seventy years and they're listening to us still.'

Both had hard words about Yeltsin: his deliberate humiliation of Gorbachev in the Russian parliament on 25 August, the way they were bundled out of their official apartment as soon as Gorbachev had relinquished the presidency, the way the most loyal members of his bodyguard were being demoted or posted away from him (King Lear?). Gorbachev said he was determined, for good statesmanlike reasons, to avoid public recrimination. But he obviously found it a very great effort.

Liuda and Marina did their best to listen as they served dinner. Raisa could not believe that our house staff were Russian: Soviet embassies, she said, had Soviet servants only. Gorbachev laughed: the question of domestic staff in embassies was a complicated one. He laughed again when I reminded him that in May 1989, at the time of our mutual expulsions, he and I had had our troubles on just that score. Afterwards Liuda and Marina told us they were delighted at the chance of meeting Gorbachev. It was he after all who had given them the freedom to talk and the freedom to travel.

Gorbachev nevertheless suffered from the intense dislike, and in many cases the contempt, of his fellow countrymen while he was still in power and for years afterwards. The reactionaries regarded him as a traitor for giving up Stalin's empire in Eastern Europe, and for causing the collapse of the Communist Party and the disintegration of the Soviet Union. The radical liberals accused him of remaining an unreconstructed Communist to the last. Those in the middle said that he never had a viable strategy, and that in the end he lacked the courage either to take a reforming grip on the economy or to stand up to the hard men in the Party, the military and the KGB. Ordinary people blamed him for the collapse of the economic system and for the poverty which came with it, although both had begun before he came to power.

But Gorbachev eased Russia into a profound historical transition. He broke with the discredited Soviet system and took the first steps towards transforming it into something more democratic and more efficient. He took the crucial initiatives which brought about the end of the Cold War. A different Soviet leadership might have tried to resist the pressure of history, and that would have made the task much harder, much bloodier, and much more dangerous for all of us. Gorbachev's own people owed him a debt they were reluctant to recognise. Losing an empire was painful; but not as painful as fighting a nuclear war.

Of course Gorbachev made mistakes. He was acutely aware of what had happened to Khrushchev, a far less radical reformer. He feared – rightly as it turned out – that he too might wake up one day to discover that he had been taken ill, lost his job, and become a non-person. So he ducked and weaved and economised with the truth and cajoled and bullied and harangued. He compromised right up to the limit with the men who had the guns and tapped the telephones. But in the Spring of 1991 he turned away from the bloody path into which the reactionaries were leading him. When they tried to reassert themselves in August, they failed. It was Gorbachev who had made it possible for the 'little people' as well as the leaders – in the cities, in the army and in the KGB itself – to think for themselves about politics. The instruments on which the plotters relied came to pieces in their hands. Thereafter Gorbachev's historical task was done, and it was left to his successor to carry Russia on to the next stage.

If Gorbachev had then withdrawn from public life, as de Gaulle did in 1953, he might have retained the respect of the people as an elder statesman. Alas, he was unable to keep his mouth shut. Every time he spoke in public he involuntarily reminded his listeners why they had become so impatient with him in the first place. His final humiliation was his gallant but futile presidential campaign of 1996, when he received less than one per cent of the vote. The death of Raisa Maksimovna in 1999 was a personal catastrophe for him. But ironically it marked a turning point in the popular attitude to him as ordinary Russians sympathised with his grief. His seventieth birthday at the beginning of March 2001 was covered widely and sympathetically in the national press and on television. By contrast his old rival Yeltsin had passed his own seventieth birthday a month earlier, ill and in hospital yet again, a lonely and almost ignored figure from the past. But Gorbachev remained the same – charming, ebullient, unpompous – speechifying and dancing until past midnight at his birthday party in a Moscow hotel, surrounded by colleagues from the Perestroika years, friends, his daughter and his two granddaughters. The last Secretary General of the Communist Party of the Soviet Union was not only a major historical figure. He was also a genuinely nice man.

10

Arguing about the Economy

In capitalist society variety, quality and volume of production are controlled by the market. Can we not use this instrument in our Socialist economy?

Reader's letter to Pravda, 23 August 1964

The first week of January 1992 was bitterly cold and miserable. Lynda Chalker, the Minister of State for Overseas Development, came to St Petersburg to observe the delivery of British emergency aid. After inspecting a consignment of British grain at the docks we looked in on a modern suburban supermarket: an attractive, clean, relatively well-constructed building. There was a long queue of people – mostly women of course – waiting outside in minus twelve degrees and a biting wind. Mrs Chalker said who she was and why she was there. One woman weighed into her straightaway: none of the foreign aid was reaching ordinary people – it was all being siphoned off and resold by the crooks. Most of the others supported her. But one elderly woman, friendly and motherly, told me that the crowd was exaggerating. Not everyone in Russia was a crook. No one in particular could be blamed. Humanitarian aid was all very well, but it was only the most temporary of solutions. She told me her story. She grew up near Pskov under German occupation. When the Germans started to retreat, they rounded up the young people and set them to digging anti-tank ditches. Her mother hid her brother in the barn, and sent her instead. She spent six months in a German camp. She was twelve years old at the time. Now all she wanted was peace and quiet. I gave her an inadequate hug and wished her well.

Inside the shop, the shelves were bare. One girl struggled to sell rations of vegetable oil to another long queue. Although she could not cope, the other assistants stood around doing nothing. A thickset middle-aged man came up to us and said aggressively that Gorbachev, Yeltsin, and Sobchak had betrayed the people. Things were better during Brezhnev's time. It was

all the fault of the Yids, who were planning to take over the world. Zhirinovsky was the man the country needed. Two women asked if we could get
the manager to open two or three more selling points. The manager, a
worried looking woman in her thirties, began to look even more worried:
was she about to suffer the fury of a Russian *bunt*? I shepherded Mrs
Chalker out of the shop.

How had the Soviet economy managed to come to such a pass? All but the
most sceptical had convinced themselves that the Soviet economy was the
second most powerful in the world, and assumed that this was at least in
part due to the merits of the Soviet system. Nehru, Nkrumah, and the other
leaders of the Third World looked at Western capitalism and its record of
interwar failure, and concluded that the Soviet economic model – forced
industrialisation under state control – was the key to the development of
their backward countries. In the 1970s the capitalist countries of the West
were reeling under the oil shock. Despite their glittering economic
performance of the 1950s and 1960s, they began to believe the Soviet claim
that the Communist system was after all destined to triumph in economic
competition, just as Marx had predicted. It was the Threat in a new guise.

But even in 1961, when Nkrumah made his first visit to the Soviet Union,
the Soviet economy was already in serious trouble. Stalin's economic
system was crude but – apart from the human cost – fairly effective in a
country which was in the early stages of mass industrialisation. The
planners set high targets for a few key materials – steel, coal, electricity;
divided the product among the various industries making tanks, tractors
and so on; and ensured growth simply by adding a suitable percentage
increase to the previous year's target. Artificial production 'indicators' were
devised to help the planners monitor the fulfilment of the plan. Factory
managers were encouraged to meet their targets by a combination of sticks
and carrots, including from time to time the death penalty for 'sabotage'.
The same penalty was used to discourage private enterprise, which was
reclassified as 'speculation'. Prices were kept down by administrative fiat.
Excessive demand was squeezed out of the system by sending the *deman-
deurs* to the camps. For many years the Soviet economy (as measured by the
index numbers for coal, iron, steel, electricity and so on) grew as fast or
faster than any other. The Soviet 'agricultural revolution' was a bloody
failure from the start. There were and are those who argued that the ends
justified the exceptionally brutal means adopted.

The system did indeed deliver massive industrial expansion, though not
as massive as its apologists claimed. In 1987 the journal *Novy Mir* published

an article by Khanin and Seliunin which argued that Soviet economic growth between 1928 and 1986 was only six- or seven-fold, instead of the ninety-fold increase claimed by the official statistics.[1] The system succeeding in generating a military technology which overcame the Germans and was for a while able to compete with the Americans. But it was not an economic system in any normal meaning of the word. Soviet 'money' was not real money, but a mere accounting device. In the local museum in Murmansk there is a collection of Russian banknotes which reflects the political and economic history of Russia itself. There are Tsarist notes from the time of Peter the Great, notes and bonds issued by the innumerable warring groupings during the Civil War (White notes bearing a crowned double headed-eagle until the Tsar's death, an uncrowned eagle thereafter), notes issued by the British intervention forces in 1919, a billion rouble note from the period of war communism, another issued in 1920 by briefly independent Armenia, one from the Emirate of Bukhara in Arab script, one issued by the secret police for the concentration camps. Pozhidaev, the museum's enthusiastic director, pointed out that once Stalin began his forced revolution in industry and agriculture Soviet banknotes had no economic backing: they were 'political' notes, not economic ones. So when the Germans tried to undermine the Soviet economy by flooding the place with false notes during the occupation, their plan failed. The rouble survived unscathed, because it was meaningless anyway.

Just as the money was not money, so the Soviet 'banks' were not banks. They were mere accounting offices for the state. They charged a derisory interest rate, and their 'loans' to industry were by no means always repaid. It was the investment in scientific and technical training, and the diversion of resources on a grossly wasteful scale to programmes of the highest priority, which enabled the Soviets to score their spectacular successes in space and in advanced fields of military technology. A conservative estimate is that towards the end more than 30 per cent of the economic activity of the Soviet Union was devoted directly or indirectly to defence. Some respected Russian economists later put the figure at 50 per cent or more.[2]

By the early 1960s the Soviet leaders knew that the economy was stagnant. Ambitious and hugely expensive investment projects lay unfinished for years, sometimes for decades. Shoddy goods, which even the long-suffering Soviet consumer refused to buy, piled up in the warehouses. Agriculture lurched from one crisis to another. Concealed unemployment was on the increase. Advanced technology created by the Soviet Union's brilliant scientists and technicians languished on the drawing boards because there was no effective mechanism to bring it into production.

Official statistics claimed that growth continued, even if the tempos were reduced. But in 1964 a young economist from Novosibirsk, Abel Aganbegyan, told his professional colleagues that the official figures were false, and advised his listeners to use the figures put out by the CIA instead. It was increasingly difficult to conceal the reality from foreign businesspeople, who could see for themselves the gap between Soviet achievements in space and the gross waste and incompetence in the Soviet factories which they visited. The economy worked as well as it did only because of the lubrication provided by the all-embracing system of *blat*; because of the emergence of an underclass of *tolkachi* – fixers and middlemen who could provide the connection between supply and demand that the central planners were unable to encompass; and above all because of the heroic efforts of managers in the factories and the farms, driven as they were by a mixture of dedication, ambition, ruthlessness, and a well-grounded fear of the consequences of failure which in Stalin's day could be literally fatal.

Khrushchev understood that something needed to be done. At first he tried the traditional solutions – mounting political campaigns, punishing scapegoats, and fiddling with the administrative system. He grumbled about *izhdivenchestvo* – the dependency culture which encouraged people to do nothing until they had received orders and funds from above. But each new 'reform' simply produced new problems. In the early 1960s Khrushchev permitted a more fundamental debate. Soviet economists were divided. Some thought that a version of the old central planning machinery could be made to work if it were computerised. Others believed that this was impossible in principle: even the most powerful computer could never capture and process the volume of information needed to replicate the complexity of a living economy. Instead they timidly began to advocate solutions which bordered on the heretical. Professor Liberman worked out ways of replicating market forces by simulating more realistic interest rates, and by introducing a carefully controlled notion of 'profit'. But no one dared to argue that the reintroduction of private property would be by far the best means of encouraging economic actors to behave rationally. At the height of the debate in late 1964, the British ambassador in Moscow told the Foreign Office that 'for all the talk of profit, [it is not] in the least likely that the Soviet Government will ever allow individual citizens to amass private wealth and put it to work: they shoot the few who try.' Years later I met an entrepreneur in Rostov on Don who had himself been part of the underground economy at this time. For him the men who were shot – Roifman, Shakerman, and others (some of whose 'crimes' were committed even before Khrushchev passed the relevant law) – were genuine martyrs in the sacred cause of free enterprise.

Nevertheless in 1965 Prime Minister Kosygin did make a systematic attempt at economic reform. The attempt was stifled by bureaucratic resistance and Brezhnev's desire for an easy life. In 1970 Andrei Sakharov warned Brezhnev that 'dislocation and stagnation' in the economy would continue to grow unless something was done about the 'anti-democratic norms of public life' set up by Stalin and never wholly abandoned.[3]

In 1974, Baibakov, the Chairman of the State Planning Committee, Gosplan, warned that the economy was in serious trouble. Morale declined among the Party's own officials as they realised the extent and nature of the crisis. Among ordinary people discontent grew, Gorbachev remembers, as the volume and variety of goods in the shops declined.[4] Yeltsin, then First Party Secretary, told the people of Sverdlovsk in 1981 that food rationing would continue: families could expect no more than one kilo of meat products per person on holiday occasions, that is, on May Day and Revolution Day. In per capita consumption the Soviet Union was, by the late 1980s, in seventy-seventh place in the world. Forty-four per cent of Soviet pensioners received less than the official subsistence minimum.[5] In 1989 Gorbachev's Health Minister Chazov revealed that one in four Soviet hospitals had no drains and one in six no running water; that tens of thousands of medical workers received wages below the poverty level; and that the USSR spent less on health care than any other developed country.[6] The Soviet economic and welfare systems had failed long before Gorbachev started to tinker with them. These distressing facts were forgotten in later years, when ordinary people understandably, and Communist and nationalist politicians for their own reasons, began to blame Gorbachev and then Yeltsin for the sufferings which came upon so many Russians in the 1990s.

Gorbachev had seen the growing crisis even before he arrived in Moscow in 1978 to work in the central organs of the Party. But the reality at the centre was even worse than he had expected. Defence and the defence industrial sector, he found, had acquired absolute priority in the Party's decisionmaking. Everything in the Soviet system was subordinated to the attempt to maintain strategic parity with the United States, to extend the Soviet Union's political influence beyond Europe, and to police the Soviet empire in Eastern Europe. Brezhnev may have accepted that the economy would not improve until the system was reformed. But in his mind, and that of Ustinov, the Politburo member responsible for the defence industry, even food production had a lower priority. Quite how great the burden was the rest of the Politburo had little means of knowing: they were refused the facts on the grounds of 'national security'.

Gorbachev allowed the debate to resume where it had been broken off by Brezhnev. The men of the 1960s – the *shestidesyatniki* – who had been involved in the earlier debate began to redeploy their ideas in public. They now accepted that tinkering would not do. There was no alternative to far-reaching change. But the *shestidesyatniki* were gradualists. Change would have to take place slowly and deliberately, and in the light of developing experience. 'Socialism' – whatever they meant by that – would have to be preserved. They were not yet prepared to argue that 'Socialism' itself was the cause of the problem. The obstacles to any change were indeed formidable. Millions of bureaucrats in the Party, in government, and in industry, had a vested interest in leaving things as they were. Soviet managers had little relevant experience, and were shy of taking responsibility. Their workers would fear the decline in living standards which would be the inevitable, if transient, result of a real reform. Not even the leading 'reformers' had a solid grasp of what was needed.

Even before I arrived in Moscow, I set out to know all the economists I could find. Abalkin, the Head of the Institute of Economics, was quiet, thoughtful, and lugubrious, as if – like Eeyore – everyone had just forgotten his birthday. When he visited London in early 1988 he told me that the Japanese were so successful compared with the Soviet Union because their society was feudal and collectivist, whereas Russians were Christians who valued the individual above all: still a surprising sentiment in the mouth of a Communist official. Bogomolov, in charge of the Institute for the Economy of World Socialism, had a more sanguine nature. His institute was in the forefront of new thinking on political as well as economic matters: it was his colleague Dashichev who warned the Politburo in April 1989 that German reunification was inevitable. Bogomolov became increasingly bitter as the *shestidesyatniki* were replaced under Yeltsin by Gaidar and the young Turks. Aganbegyan came to London in November 1987. He tried to explain at a private lunch how Soviet prices were to be liberated piecemeal and over a period. He was unconvincing both in theory and practice, and left his listeners with the distinct impression that he had no practical grasp of the business. He later fell out with Gorbachev over the crisis in Armenia, and became a successful operator in the post-Soviet economy. Petrakov, the Deputy Director of the Central Economic-Mathematical Institute, whom I met in 1990, talked plausibly about the need to cut the deficit, to control the money supply, and to reduce inflation. The most orthodox Western economist could not have faulted him. But in and out of office he, and others like him, slid away from the main question: how were these desirable aims to be achieved in practice? They spoke fluently and intelligently of the need for change. But they never got to grips with the radical practical measures without which change was impossible. That was only partly their fault. Their ideas could only have been implemented if they had been forcefully backed by the political leadership. And this was something Gorbachev was never willing to do.

Change was equally impossible without a far-reaching overhaul of the banking and monetary system. Unlike their colleagues in the industrial and planning bureaucracies, some Soviet bankers had an inkling of how real economies worked because of their unavoidable dealings with financial and commercial organisations in capitalist countries. Not long after I arrived in Moscow, I called on Garetovsky, the Chairman of the Soviet State Bank I had first met in London. His main aim was to get a law on banking regulation onto the statute book. He was pessimistic about the prospects. Nobody in the Soviet Union, he said, apart for himself and a handful of colleagues in the State Bank, had any conception of what a real banking system involved. This was not too harsh a judgement. When the Governor of the Bank of England told a seminar of Soviet 'bankers' in Moscow at the end of 1990 that the interest on personal loans in Britain was over 25 per cent, one of them gasped: 'But that is usury.' In March 1992 I met a banker in Siberia who told me that it was her 'sacred duty' to provide credits to firms in trouble. She could not see why firms needed a financial plan now that there was no longer an All-Union Finance Ministry to submit it to. 'Bankers' like these were backed by the bureaucrats, politicians, factory managers, and ideologists. Together they emasculated Garetovsky's draft law and robbed it of its provisions for a proper regulatory role for the State Bank, for instruments of fiscal and interest rate policy, and for a clear definition of the functions of the new investment banks which Perestroika was meant to encourage

In the Summer of 1989, Garetovsky was replaced by the infinitely more cunning Gerashchenko, the son of a former State Bank Chairman, who had served in the Soviet banks in London, Beirut, and Germany. He too believed that the State Bank should be independent, able to control the money supply, to influence interest rates by open market operations, and to force the lending banks to foreclose on bad debtors by imposing a reserve ratio requirement on them. He grumbled that the government lacked the will to impose tough measures even if it understood what was needed. But despite his command of the subject, I found him fatalistic, coy, and less convincing than his predecessor. He understood the problem but seemed to have little commitment to the search for a solution.

At first Gorbachev tried the old-fashioned Soviet remedies: more work, more discipline, more science and technology, and less vodka. But his new advisers rapidly convinced him that the old remedies were hopelessly inadequate. Abalkin, Bogomolov, Aganbegyan and the rest argued that the enterprise managers must be freed from central tutelage and exposed to financial disciplines instead. Only then would they become aware of the needs of the customer and pay some attention to the constraints imposed by real money. Gorbachev backed them in a series of attacks on the state bureaucracy. The Enterprise Law of 1987, the Law on Cooperatives of May 1988, and the provisions for joint ventures with foreign companies, marked real progress. The West reacted with disproportionate enthusiasm to what looked like the precursors of a far reaching and genuine reform. But the limited remedies of the *shestidesyatniki* did not work either. Normal economic incentives could not function in an economy which had no banking system, no taxation system, no price system, no private property, and no real money. They could not function in a country where economic imperatives were easily and routinely overridden by Party and state bureaucrats pursuing political, institutional, and personal aims. And they could not function amongst a people permeated by the politics of envy and the principle 'We pretend to work and they pretend to pay us.' The new measures fatally undermined the old economic system: something desirable in itself. But they put nothing solid in its place.

Instead there began to emerge the first manifestations of what was later to be called 'bandit capitalism' or 'grabbitisation'. In April 1989 there was a bizarre ceremony on the great square in front of the main building of Moscow University, a huge Stalin skyscraper on the Lenin Hills (now once again the Sparrow Hills) which dominates the city. The ceremony marked the signature of a joint venture agreement between a British company and a cooperative set up under the new legislation by the Komsomol (the Communist Youth organisation) to manufacture hot air balloons in the Soviet Union. There were long speeches by the organisers, a police band, a parade of vintage cars with jazz bands aboard, teams of tiny drum majorettes countermarching across the square, all blue and drenched by blinding freezing rain. Later there was a reception in the Praga, one of Moscow's smartest restaurants. This was my first encounter with the Perestroika phenomenon of the ex-Party businessman: bright young men who were getting very rich by moving into 'business' and taking Party funds with them. The smartest people had already made the transition by the time the Party was banned in August 1991.

Abalkin was the first of the *shestidesyatniki* to achieve high office. In the Autumn of 1989 Gorbachev made him Deputy Prime Minister for Economic Reform. Two months after his appointment he gave a lengthy interview to *Ogonek*, serious, glum, and decent as always. He had been back to his academic institute to tell his former colleagues how he was getting on in government. After describing the mess the economy was in, and people's unwillingness to give the government even a year's respite to sort things out, he concluded: 'I know of no occasion in history when a government has found itself in such a position.' But his deputy answered: 'Leonid Ivanovich, I can offer you a historical analogy: Germany in 1932.' 'God forbid,' was all he could say in reply.

Abalkin put together a far-reaching economic package. This contained potentially revolutionary draft laws on property, on land, on taxation, on the trade unions, and on the banking system. And it was backed by an economic programme for 1990 designed to reduce the budget deficit, cut back on the gross waste in the investment programme, bring the money supply under control, and put more goods in the shops. These proposals were a good deal more sophisticated and carefully elaborated than their predecessors. But they aroused hostility on all sides. The confused and increasingly conservative deputies in the Soviet parliament still clung to the comfortable certainties of 'Socialism': 'keep hold of nurse for fear of worse.' Alarmed by growing shortages and pressure from disgruntled consumers, they clung to what they knew best: instructions from the centre for enterprises to produce what was needed rather than what was profitable. Abalkin was unable to persuade them to accept even the traditional stand-by of tight budgets – increased taxes on beer, wine, and tobacco to mop up excess savings and squeeze inflation. At a conference of economists in the middle of November 1989 he was viciously attacked by conservatives – much to his own surprise, since he had assumed that it was the radical liberals who cared least for his policies. Prime Minister Ryzhkov gave him no political support in the parliament. And Gorbachev – typically and in the end fatally – kept out of the public debate almost entirely.

Petrakov was the next to move into government. Gorbachev appointed him his economic adviser at the beginning of 1990. By then the full extent of the Soviet economic crisis could no longer be hidden even from those with no desire to see. A public debate on the economy took off; and the forces of reaction began to gather as the conservatives became increasingly convinced that Gorbachev was leading the country into the abyss. In March Gorbachev told his newly created 'Presidential Council' that he would shortly make proposals to accelerate the move to a real market economy.

His speech had evidently been drafted by Petrakov, who called on me to explain the proposals. The new package, he said, would provide for a moderate price reform. But its central theme would be the demonopolisation of the economy, the break-up of the mammoth organisations such as Aeroflot, the dismantling of the ministerial bureaucracy, 'the biggest monopoly of all', and legislation to encourage leaseholding, shareholding, and small private and family businesses. It was a grandiose wish-list, but Petrakov was unclear about how it was to be put into effect. He implied that it would be done through a series of Presidential decrees, rather than through laws which would have to be debated, and perhaps fatally emasculated, by the Soviet parliament. But he could not explain to me how his activities fitted in with those of Abalkin; or with those of Prime Minister Ryzhkov, who was still mesmerised by the principles of Marxist-Leninism. Both the organisation and the responsibilities were now hopelessly confused.

Even the inadequate official statistics showed how fast the economy was now deteriorating. I had persuaded the Foreign Office to pay for 'visiting fellows' to spend a few weeks or months at the embassy, experts on the Soviet economy to supplement our amateur efforts. The first was Professor Alec Nove, perhaps the wisest of all. He documented the facts of decline in a gloomy paper which he wrote at the end of 1989. I told the Foreign Office in the New Year that economic pressures could combine with headlong political change to bring Soviet Communism to an end quite soon.

But Gorbachev's new economic advisers seemed at last to have convinced him that Perestroika would not work without modern instruments of macroeconomic management. He appeared to be putting his new Presidential authority behind the cause of economic reform. If, I said hopefully, the Petrakov package worked and the government were able to pursue a coherent macroeconomic policy, to stem inflation, to create a viable currency, and to stem the trend towards regional autarky, the country might by the end of 1990 reach what Abalkin called the 'critical mass', the point at which economic change would become self-generating despite the opposition of the bureaucrats. It was not a very accurate prediction.

Douglas Hurd called on Gorbachev on 10 April 1990, shortly after he had launched Petrakov's package. As so often, Gorbachev managed to be both plausible and unconvincing. Beaming confidently, he said that the Presidential Council was about to consider his plan for radical and accelerated economic reform. The economy was dead in the water. The old system had been destroyed, but the new one was not in place. He was now determined to create a 'full-blooded market' with far-reaching measures on prices, banking, shareholding. Everyone complained he did not act. Then they rejected his ideas because of the pain they would cause. He was, he said cheerfully, like Nazreddin of Bukhara (a Muslim folk hero who was a favourite of Gorbachev at the time). The crowd criticised him for riding his poor donkey in the heat; but when he got off, and hoisted the donkey onto his own shoulders, they laughed and said, 'There's one donkey carrying another.' Now he and his colleagues had eighteen months to put things right. If they failed, they would have to leave. He asked for massive aid from the West: $2 billion in untied interest-free credit straightaway, and another $15–20 billion thereafter in credits, goods, and knowhow – figures similar to those he later put to me at our night-time meeting after the coup.

None of Gorbachev's brave words was translated into reality. The Presidential Council rejected Petrakov's plan almost entirely. Ryzhkov began to construct an alternative, which Bogomolov told me would be 'a death sentence for the government'. It would lead to higher prices and more unemployment. It contained none of the structural measures which Gorbachev had promised: no privatisation, no measures to break the monopoly of the ministries, no independent central bank, no progressive taxation of profits, no provision of goods and services to private agriculture, no genuine freedom for enterprises or workable concept of private property. The system of state orders – that is, the monopoly of the Plan – was barely dented. Thanks to the obstruction of the bureaucrats the government would get the worst of both worlds.

Ryzhkov presented his watered-down ideas to the Soviet parliament on 24 May. They failed to pass. The deputies were angered by his simultaneous proposal to increase prices, including the price of bread, that trigger of revolutions. Gorbachev's longer-term prediction to Douglas Hurd was right. Within eighteen months, almost to the day, he lost his job.

After the defeat of the Petrakov package, the public argument about economic reform resumed and became increasingly disorderly. The idea took root that what the Soviet economy needed was a massive injection of Western money, a rerun of the Marshall Plan that had put the economies of Western Europe back on their feet after 1945. Even inside the Soviet government, many people opposed credits on the ground of national prestige, or on the more rational ground that very large credits could provide the excuse to postpone necessary change, as they had done in Poland in the 1970s. Outside the government the feeling was if anything stronger, not only on economic grounds, but also on the political grounds that it would be quite wrong to help the Communists out of their difficulties. Elefthery, the worldly and intelligent Abbot of the Lavra (monastery) in Kiev, put the argument to me with particular force: instead of giving large loans to the USSR, which would simply be wasted, the West should send three hundred businessmen to show the Russians how to run their country. I commented that Mrs Thatcher would agree. He said Mrs Thatcher was a very wise woman.

Inside the Soviet Union one rival plan succeeded another, and none was adopted. In late July 1990 Abalkin told me that the government was working on yet another reform plan. A package of laws would be presented to the Soviet parliament in September. These would create proper mechanisms for banking, taxation, and monetary policy, for the privatisation of large enterprises and the breaking up of ministerial empires. They would come into force on 1 January, and would be accompanied by price rises. Abalkin welcomed the helpful statements which the European Community and the G7 had recently made at their Summits in Dublin and Houston. Western management expertise and training, support for small enterprises, capital investment for long-term projects would all be useful. Short-term credit for consumer goods would be politically convenient. But in an uncharacteristic burst of emotion, Abalkin went on to say that the West should not treat the Soviet Union as if it were merely another East European, still less a Third World country. One could give 'aid' to Hungary. But the Soviet Union was and would remain a great power. Political and economic conditions were unacceptable. Gorbachev did not need the West to tell him that market reform was essential, and he would push ahead whether the West supported him or not.

Throughout that Summer rival groups of economists beavered away on their various schemes. Although Abalkin was already at work, Gorbachev agreed with Yeltsin in July that Shatalin, Petrakov, Yavlinsky and others should put together joint proposals. They came up with a Five Hundred Days Plan for radical (if somewhat fantastical) therapy to the Soviet economic system. Prime Minister Ryzhkov countered with another Plan of his own. For his own political reasons Yeltsin backed Shatalin. So initially did Gorbachev. But faced with opposition from his conservative Prime Minister, and true to his instinct for seeking the middle ground even where it did not exist, he commissioned Aganbegyan to produce a compromise between Ryzhkov's Plan and Shatalin's: an attempt to mate a hedgehog and a snake, as Yeltsin sarcastically remarked. On the streets Yuri Afanasiev and his supporters demanded the adoption of the Shatalin Plan and the resignation of the Ryzhkov government.

By now Yeltsin was using the economic issue as a potent weapon in his campaign to isolate and emasculate Gorbachev whatever the practical cost.

In September 1990 he told Douglas Hurd that Ryzhkov's proposals for reform had no future. They had been advanced too often, and rejected too often. Ryzhkov would have to go – and soon. Gorbachev was still trying to protect him. If he was not careful, Gorbachev would be dragged down as well. But if economic reform were not based on a single central bank, on a single currency and a single monetary policy, the Union itself would break up. Yeltsin emphatically did not want that, but he continued to distance himself from the existing mechanisms of the Union where it suited him. Most of the existing Union Ministries, he told Hurd, would have to go. The Union should be responsible only for transport, the KGB, defence, and foreign affairs. Even in this context, he pointedly told Hurd who did not rise to the hint, Russia was already in a position to sign independent treaties with foreign countries. Everything now on Russian territory – raw materials, most of the Soviet Union's defence industries, factories, public buildings including 'our Kremlin', as he called it with stolid menace – belonged to Russia, not to the Union. That evening at dinner, Boris Fyodorov, Yeltsin's Finance Minister, loyally informed us that Yeltsin had not read the Five Hundred Days Plan which he was backing so enthusiastically. Gorbachev, by contrast, had read every word twice.

All this was theory. The practice was even more intractable. One of the largest black holes in the Soviet economy was the system of agriculture. In the West Yeltsin was being portrayed as the champion of private farming, in pleasing contrast to Gorbachev, the died-in-the-wool collectivist. Kulik, the Russian Minister of Agriculture, told his British colleague John Gummer that the Russian government would give every Russian citizen the right to a private plot. People now working on the big farms could set up on their own, and some of the ten million people who had left the land for the towns would be attracted back. There would be no restrictions on the further buying and selling of land. So far, so good, though as usual the awkward details were quite unclear.

The practical difficulties of even these modest proposals were illustrated when Gummer visited the 'Vladimir Ilyich' collective farm close by the country house outside Moscow where Vladimir Ilyich Lenin died. Saksenberg, the farm chairman who had worked there for thirty years, was a tiny man with an engaging twinkle. He had studied animal husbandry at university, travelled abroad, and admired Western agricultural methods. He bombarded us with statistics: the farm had 1,600 hectares and 700 workers, 900 cattle, and a large number of chickens. Gummer asked why he did not rear pigs as well. He laughed: 'And me a Jew?' Saksenberg was quite clear that he was not going to give up his land to any new breed of 'farmers'. None of his own people wanted to leave, and he needed all the land he had to run a profitable enterprise. In a genuine market economy, most of the collectives would be unable to compete. He certainly would not advise a foreigner to put any commercial money into the 'Vladimir Ilyich' collective farm.

Saksenberg was not an aberration and certainly not a fool. Eighteen months later another chairman from a farm near Kostroma said much the same thing. He was roaring drunk – he had just come from his mother-in-law's funeral – but he was none the less lucid for that. He was deeply opposed to private farming. His farm was profitable, and all his workers benefited, not least because he was developing small industry in the farm buildings (he turned to the local priest, who confirmed that he was telling the truth). There was no infrastructure for private farming. The Russian law which allowed private farms could be reversed at any moment, like all other Russian laws. He would neither give away land from his collective farm, nor would he take land himself.

Farm managers like him and Saksenberg – intelligent and practical men according to their lights – went on sabotaging agricultural reform for years. Farm workers feared to strike out on their own for perfectly sensible practical reasons. This, rather than Kulik's windy schemes, was the reality of Russian agriculture with which the genuine reformers would eventually have to cope.

The industrial economy was breaking down as well. In February 1991 Jill and I went to Stalingrad (renamed Volgograd after Stalin was debunked) on the thirty-eighth anniversary of the German surrender. We landed at Gumrak, the last airfield in German hands as the defences collapsed, in weather bitterly and appropriately cold. Here we were met by Albert Orlov, the Head of the Foreign Economic Relations Department of the Volgograd Region Executive Council. Albert, a stocky and cheerful fellow, the descendant of Cossacks, started life as a farmer. It emerged fairly soon that he had once been the Chairman of the Volgograd Executive Council: what he called 'the Governor'. But he had lost his job when the Party leadership was thrown out a year earlier as a result of the tomato scandal. He evaded any discussion of these exciting events, but claimed that he was in any case happy enough, since he now had more time to enjoy with his grand-children.

Albert took us to see local politicians and journalists, the museum of the battle and the grandiose memorial to the defenders on the Mamaev Kurgan, the hill in the centre of the city round which much of the fighting had swirled. But the key objective of our visit was the Tractor Factory. This was set up during the first Five Year Plan on the very shores of the Volga with the assistance of American engineers. When war began it shifted to the production of T34 tanks, which were still rolling off the production lines as the Germans burst into the city in the late Summer of 1942. The factory saw bitter fighting, and had become a symbol of Soviet success in war and peace about which children were taught from their earliest years. Now it was in deep trouble. The director, Budko, showed us the two assembly lines: one for domestic sales, one for export, both very messy indeed, components lying around in muddled piles and dirt everywhere. Because the state planning system had broken down, Budko's suppliers were not fulfilling their contracts. Krasny Oktyabr, the factory next door, no longer provided sheet steel because their own raw material – scrap metal – was being sold abroad by profiteers. His former customers in Eastern Europe would no longer buy his obsolete tractors. He would welcome the freedom to manage, if that was what reform meant, provided the government disciplined his errant suppliers. He had tried to diversify. He now produced ice cream freezers and kitchen utensils, as well as tractors. But this was chicken feed. He could barely pay his workers: a quarter of a million souls together with their families. He provided them with works canteens, a piggery and a sausage factory. He bartered with local collective farms for dairy products and poultry to sell in the company shops, which also sold imported clothes, washing machines, sewing machines and videos. He could not escape his responsibilities towards these people.

Budko and his colleagues, the 'Red Directors' of Soviet industry, were pilloried by their critics for their opposition to genuine market reform. At the end of 1990 thousands of them attended a conference in Moscow. They demanded that the old system be restored. It had at least worked after a fashion. These men were no more stupid than the best bosses in the collective farms. They were trapped in an old system in the last stages of decay, loaded with responsibility for their people, and with no access to funds for the massive restructuring their factories needed if they were to survive. Western economists said that it would be better if the factories simply went under. A short sharp crisis would be less painful even in the comparatively short term. From a theoretical point of view they may well have been right. But it was not reasonable to expect the men on the spot or their employees to see it the same way.

In the third week of September 1990, Gorbachev put his new plan – a souped-up version of the Ryzhkov Plan (or a watered-down version of

Shatalin's) – to the Soviet parliament. Once again he failed to secure their agreement. Outside parliament, opposition was heating up. Both the economic conservatives and the economic radicals were weighing in. Managers of large metallurgical plants told Gorbachev that they would need government subsidies even under a market system. Shcherbakov, at that time the Chairman of the State Committee for Labour and Social Affairs, claimed that the Shatalin proposals would put forty million people out of work. *Pravda* asked, 'What are we going to eat this winter?' and 'Will the Communist Party survive?' People left the Party in accelerating numbers. Gorbachev's response was atavistic, a bow towards the reactionaries: he called for increased vigilance, more activity by the KGB against economic crime, and the reintroduction of vigilante patrols on the streets. In the Russian parliament a few days later, to the cheers of his supporters, Yeltsin accused Gorbachev of bad faith and violently attacked his attempt to find a middle ground between the various schemes of economic reform. Russia would now have to go it alone. I thought he was bluffing. How could 'Russia' implement such a unilateral declaration of independence in practice? Would the Russians take over the Soviet customs posts at Moscow airport? How would they actually exercise control over the Soviet enterprises on Russian territory which came under Soviet ministries? These reasonable questions missed the point: Yeltsin was not primarily interested in the details of reform. He was out to win.

Thus assailed by Russian patriots, radical economists, and conservative Unionists, Gorbachev's efforts to reform the economy sputtered and went out. His plan was published in the press: respectable but vague proposals for a federal banking system, market pricing, greater freedom for enterprises, support for small farmers, a clear role for foreign business. He promised a series of Presidential decrees. But his ideas pleased no one. Petrakov and Shatalin attacked them publicly, even though they were still acting as his advisers. He lost his nerve, and sent his plan off to a parliamentary committee. From now on his main preoccupation was to fend off the conservative backlash. The time for reform was over. For the next nine months the economy was in the hands of his Finance Minister, soon to become his Prime Minister, Pavlov. The practical consequences of dithering between the sclerotic and unviable command system and a genuine market economy began to make themselves felt in everyday life. Goods disappeared from the shops. Local authorities organised food rationing in Moscow and the provinces. As normal distribution broke down, factories and government departments handed out food packages to their employees. Just outside the lavatory in the Ministry of Finance – the least attractive of the lavatories I saw in Moscow in one of the least attractive ministries, which is saying a lot – officials dished out food and dairy products to the employees.

Actual distress began to increase amongst ordinary people. And it was at this point that Pavlov introduced an economically illiterate plan to stabilise the currency by withdrawing large-denomination banknotes. The savings banks were swamped by hysterical pensioners striving to exchange their banknotes before the expiration of an impossibly short deadline. Olga Trifonova's maid was in tears, her life's savings wiped out. The Central Post Office was overwhelmed with people sending money orders to themselves – and paying for them with 50 and 100 rouble notes. When the money order forms ran out, they went to the railway stations, and bought expensive railway tickets for everywhere. Almost the sole result of this measure was to convince the population that the government was once again robbing them of their savings. Gorbachev's credibility was undermined yet further.

In the Summer of 1991, Yavlinsky and Graham Allison, a Harvard academic, elaborated and tried to sell the idea of a Grand Bargain, another version of the Marshall Plan. The West would put up massive credits – Jeffrey Sachs, the Harvard economist, had suggested as much as $300 billion – in parallel with a Soviet programme of radical economic change. I myself agreed with those who thought that there was no point in pouring massive credits into a system which was incapable of using them. We should instead get the Soviets into the international financial organisations. We should provide them with management training and practical economic education. We would thus bring them up against the realities of banking, finance, taxation, commercial legislation, and the workings of small and medium business of which, for obvious reasons, they were almost wholly ignorant. On the whole this was the policy which the British government followed over the next few years.

Gorbachev found it hard to understand why the friends in the West for whom he had done so much – withdrawing from Eastern Europe, agreeing to German reunification, backing action in the Gulf – were unwilling to grant even a fraction of the aid that put Western Europe back on its feet after the Second World War, or of the vast sums that they spent on the Gulf War. But he was unable to shift those who argued that Western financial assistance would be wasted as long as the Soviet political and economic systems remained essentially unreformed. As a second best, but one with real political symbolism, the idea began to take root that Gorbachev should attend at least part of the G7 Economic Summit in London in July 1991. We, the French, the Germans, and the Italians were in favour. The Americans were dubious, and the Japanese were opposed because of their dispute with the Soviet Union over the Kurile Islands, which the Soviet Union had annexed from Japan at the end of the war. After a good deal of pointless dithering an invitation was issued at the very last moment.

The Soviet government continued to manufacture an optimism which was no longer justified by the facts. A month before the Summit, Laptiev admitted to me that the economy was still in a power dive. But at least, he claimed, the government was now hauling back on the joy-stick, and the plane would soon flatten out. Primakov, now a member of Gorbachev's Presidential Council, said that Gorbachev understood that he would not get huge credits at the Summit. But Primakov – no doubt speaking for Gorbachev – still hankered for a bargain, whereby the West would in its own interest, but without strings, bail out the Soviet Union with massive and urgent grants up front. I told him that we intended to keep control of any money we dished out. We were certainly not going to give it to the old-fashioned ministerial baronies who would merely use it to reinforce the old structures. Delors, the President of the European Commission, called on Gorbachev a few days later. Prime Minister Pavlov was there too. In his usual cynical way he explained the old-fashioned 'Anti-Crisis Programme' which had now become government policy and which Gorbachev was to bring to London as evidence of his commitment to serious economic change. Gorbachev spoke grandly about his plans. He would arrive in London with the Union Treaty under his belt. He would propose a partnership to bring the Soviet Union into the world economy. He was taken aback when Delors told him that present Soviet economic policy had no credibility abroad.

All this faced the leaders of the G7 with an unpleasant dilemma. They could have a broad political discussion with Gorbachev. That might serve his immediate purposes but would not help him or anyone else in the longer run. Or they could bring him up sharp against the economic facts of life. That could lead to a sensible programme of economic discussion, advice, and eventually assistance. But it would be hard for Gorbachev to present back home as a success. To avoid a fiasco, John Major sent Nigel Wicks of the Treasury, who was preparing the London Summit, to explain the realities to Gorbachev and to sort out some of the tactics with him. We called on him on 1 July. He had Chernyaev and Primakov with him. He looked well, listened with great attention, and spoke with unusual deliberation. Wicks explained how Economic Summits worked: frankness, intimacy, no long speeches, no attempts to bounce people into commitments they might later regret. Hence the lengthy preparation by the 'Sherpas', senior officials from the participating countries. Gorbachev broke in with a sarcastic grin: would there be anything left for the national leaders to do by the time the Sherpas had finished? Wicks reassured him, and went on to say that there would be no money on the table in London. Gorbachev would need to convince his Western colleagues that his Union Treaty would hold, and that he had an economic reform programme that he could actually put into effect. Gorbachev explained that he needed a success in London. What could he expect to come back with? The first moves towards bringing the Soviet Union into the world economy, a move towards partnership (not yet membership) in the international financial institutions in Washington, and the beginning of a serious dialogue on economic affairs, answered Wicks.

Shcherbakov was now Deputy Prime Minister responsible for economic policy. We met him in the old Gosplan building opposite the Moskva Hotel: an unfortunate symbol (after 1993 it became the seat of the new Russian parliament, a better symbol). Wicks told him outright that Pavlov's Anti-Crisis Programme was not credible. This brought out all the old-fashioned administrative-command economist in him. How did Wicks know that the plan was no good, since he hadn't seen it? A whole lot of second-rate people who had lost their jobs in the entourage of the President (he probably meant Yavlinsky) were travelling the world rubbishing the plan for reasons of personal ambition and pique. It was an appallingly atavistic performance, but an education for Wicks. Wicks was somewhat reassured when Abalkin – sober, realistic, gloomy, as ever – later insisted that the Russians would have to help themselves before the rest of the world could help them.

Gorbachev and his colleagues ignored these careful and unambiguous warnings. Primakov came to London in advance to lobby his master's case. On British television he peddled the line that the Soviet Union would collapse into chaos if the West did not provide material assistance immediately, a forlorn and very ill-judged attempt to blackmail the G7 leaders by turning their own public opinion against them. Wicks nobbled Primakov to reiterate that Gorbachev could expect no money, and not even formal membership of the International Monetary Fund, only some newfangled 'associate status', a mechanism to articulate the future relationship between the Soviet Union and the G7. Primakov got gloomier and gloomier, and warned that Gorbachev would be extremely disappointed at being offered so little. It was surprising that such an old fox did not understand that neither Gorbachev nor the Seven could afford a failure: they would have to present even bricks without straw as a success. If his intervention had any effect at all, it was to draw unnecessary – and in Soviet domestic terms damaging – attention to the gap between Gorbachev's expectations and his achievement.

When Gorbachev himself arrived in London on 16 July 1991, he was full of beans as usual. Raisa looked grey and badly run-down: I guessed that she had been acting as the emotional shock absorber for her husband. Primakov, Shcherbakov, Medvedev, and Chernyaev were among those who also got off the plane. Yavlinsky refused to come at the last minute, apparently because Gorbachev had finally decided against the 'Grand Bargain' in favour of Pavlov's Programme. Gorbachev met his G7 peers the following afternoon. He got neither the money for which he had asked, nor an explicit 'mechanism': only good advice and the prospect of a closer relationship with the International Monetary Fund and the World Bank. At the subsequent press conference he had the wit to claim that the meeting itself was the germ of a continuing relationship with the G7. He concluded disarmingly: 'I was told to discipline myself' (perhaps a reference to Wicks's earlier injunction to be brief) 'and I tried to discipline myself; but I spoke too long as usual.'

The meeting between Gorbachev and the G7 was widely and justly criticised for its lack of substance. I nevertheless believed that it had at least launched a process of adult education on how to modernise and transform a command economy. Neither Gorbachev nor his Western mentors knew what this would involve. None had convincing answers. All needed to learn. But provided that there was no serious trouble in the Baltics or elsewhere (a big if), the process would probably lead inexorably to the creation of a permanent relationship of economic cooperation, with the Soviet Union as a full and equal participant. It might even lead – perhaps quite soon – to the provision of real financial assistance by the West. If so, Gorbachev would have achieved his major objectives.

As Gorbachev left the next day, he whispered to me: 'Stay in touch with Chernyaev on the follow-up.' Primakov and Shcherbakov had already suggested separately, and with an even greater air of conspiracy, that I should stay in touch with them. It said little for the clarity of the hierarchy: another example, I thought, of the organisational void which surrounded Gorbachev. Now that the rigid structures of the Party – the General Secretaryship, the Politburo, and the Central Committee Secretariat – had crumbled, the Soviet government had become a tribal, or at best a medieval, system in which every one competed almost on equal terms for the ear of the chief. Perhaps, I thought, this organisational and political chaos had a useful side-effect for Gorbachev. It made it harder for anyone to build up an organisational base from which to challenge his authority. The coup which followed five weeks later rather undermined the credibility of this judgement. I later consoled myself with the thought that the coup failed amongst other reasons because the Soviet machine was indeed no longer capable of executing the will of its erstwhile masters.

The collapse of the hardline coup increased the pressure on the West. Some people, mostly outside government, saw no reason to bail out the defeated Communist enemy. Governments still saw no point in pouring money into the decaying system of centralised planning. Faced with recession and unemployment at home, they were also unwilling to appear to be subsidising Soviet jobs at the expense of their own people. Norman Lamont, the British Chancellor of the Exchequer, had visited Moscow in July as a first step towards creating the 'continuing relationship' between the G7 and the Soviet governments which Gorbachev had been promised in London. He was fascinated by what he found. Now, as Autumn began, he was followed by a swarm of Western advisers – from the international financial institutions, from national governments, from think-tanks, and increasingly from accountancies and management consultancies. Even the well-intentioned aroused resentment among the Russians. They flew in, stayed in the growing number of Western-style hotels while the country outside was apparently collapsing into near starvation and chaos, dispensed their views without reference to local reality or sensibilities. Before they had had time to learn better, they flew out again, 'Saying [like Hilaire Belloc's doctors] as they took their fees, "There is no cure for this disease".' The Western experts knew some of the answers: but did not appreciate the full complexity of the questions. The Russians were only too well aware of the questions; but were floundering about for the answers.

In September the World Economic Forum met in the Metropole Hotel in Moscow. The main speaker was Jeff Sachs, the young Harvard professor who had had great success with his stabilisation plan for Poland and later became an adviser to the Gaidar government. He argued for rouble convertibility within six months. Only thus would Russia attract foreign investment. The foreigners gave him an ovation. I said it was more complicated than that. Russia would not attract foreign investment unless it provided political stability, clear economic policy, and a reliable framework of commercial law and ethics: a far harder task than the application of a single panacea. I reminded Sachs that the American imposition of sterling convertibility on Britain as a condition of their postwar loan had been disastrous. Yet Britain had had the basic institutions of a capitalist economy intact. Worse disasters could occur in the Soviet Union if convertibility were introduced in the absence of the fundamental structures of the market. Sachs looked at me sadly: another effete and economically illiterate diplomat who had gone native and failed to understand the situation.

Fundamental institutional change and a macroeconomic shock were both needed. In the real world the problems of timing and sequence were unmanageable. So both were eventually attempted together. The results were messy. Yeltsin's government made the rouble partially convertible. An essential process was launched. But for years the new Russia had only limited success in attracting foreign direct investment. So perhaps both Sachs and I were right.

By now Gorbachev had finally lost the initiative to Yeltsin and the Russian government, and it had ceased to matter what he thought about the economy. In mid-October 1991 I called on Yegor Gaidar – then still the Director of the Institute for Economic Policy. After Gorbachev, Shevard-nadze, and Yeltsin, Gaidar was the most potent catalyst for change and the most significant figure in the revolutionary years 1988–92. It was a spectacular performance for someone who had hitherto spent the whole of his brief career – he was thirty-five years old at the time – in the academic world or on the fringes of journalism. Like the three older men – practised politicians all – he was later much vilified by his own people. He came from the heart of the Soviet establishment. His grandfather was a hero of the Civil War and a popular writer, who was killed fighting as a partisan against the Germans in 1941. His father, also a writer, was a senior officer in the Soviet navy. Gaidar himself was born three weeks after Khrushchev denounced Stalin in 1956. He was thus able to grow up and study economics in an atmosphere that was already somewhat more open to intellectual enquiry. He was a man of exceptional determination and courage, clearminded, straightforward, and with a self-deprecating sense of humour. He was well aware of his weaknesses as a public politician; but as he told the press, his odd appearance and nervous splutter did not in themselves disqualify him from being serious. His economic ideas were firmly held, lucid, and practical. Because of his youth, he carried little of the intellectual baggage of Marxism, and little of the political and psycho-logical baggage of the years of fear and stagnation. He combined a slightly hectic manner with remarkable coolness. He had learned his staccato English from books: his pronunciation was distinctly idiosyncratic, even though his grammar was normally impeccable. Now he told me that Yeltsin was determined to reform banking, agriculture, and the military industrial complex. Subsidies would be removed, and unprofitable enterprises wound up. Yeltsin would announce a new Russian government of professionals at the end of the month. Gaidar added with surprising force that economic reform could only succeed if Russia put its own interests first. Too much had been sacrificed to trying to keep the Union in being. If the other Republics were willing to cooperate with Russia, well and good. If not, Russia would make its own way. This was the exact opposite of what the IMF was advising at the time.

There is a photograph of Gaidar and the other young reforming economists in his team, taken in the 1980s before they were burdened with responsibility. They all have mops of hair like the Beatles. Ten years later many of them were already going bald.

Yeltsin announced his reforms to the Russian parliament on Monday 28 October 1991, a historic date. They would, he said, be decisive and unpopular. Whether or not Yeltsin had bothered to read or understand the original Five Hundred Days plan, his presentation – written for him by Gaidar – was very far-reaching. The tax system would be reformed. Prices would be liberalised before the end of the year. Living standards would fall, as an essential preliminary to any improvement. But they would rise again in a year. Russia would join other Republics in an economic and monetary union only if there were a single currency and a single central bank. The Russian parliament approved Yeltsin's reforms in principle. It gave him special powers to override the local and central bureaucracies. I was still suspicious. Did Yeltsin have the intellectual and political capacity to carry his radical ideas forward? Could he retain popular support? Would he be tempted to fall back on more authoritarian means? But for the first time he appeared to be moving beyond words to deeds. And that was a significant change.

At the end of October I visited the Russian Trade and Commodity Exchange in Moscow's old Post Office building. This was the largest of a number of exchanges that had sprung up around the country to trade in the wholesale goods, machinery, and raw materials that were now no longer being conveyed to those who needed them by the creaky mechanisms of the state plan. Even on the pavement outside one could feel the excitement. Inside the place was seething. The floor of the hall was crowded with brokers, and round the edge were little stalls where girls wrestled with computers. An infinite variety of goods was being traded: from one hundred thousand tons of oil to seven subscriptions in Vladivostok for an American business weekly. The Chairman, Konstantin Borovoi, who showed me round was still boasting about the contribution the Exchange had made to Yeltsin's victory two months earlier. They were amongst the first to support the White House publicly, and it was they who provided the great tricolour which was carried in the funeral procession. Borovoi introduced me to some of the brokers, all under thirty: a shifty young woman from the Komsomol, an enthusiastic and poverty-stricken ex-engineer who needed the money for a decent flat and a car, and an aggressive, slightly older man in a leather jacket. All preached the virtues of free enterprise with great fire. A real market seemed to be emerging behind the facade of the collapsing official economy.

Yeltsin's new government took office on 8 November. Burbulis was the First Deputy Prime Minister: a former lecturer in Marxist philosophy in Yeltsin's home town, one of his closest associates at the time, a man curiously twisted both physically and intellectually, a man who always conversed as if every word from either of us carried a complex meaning far beyond what appeared on the surface. Gaidar and Shokhin, who had been Shevardnadze's economic adviser in the Foreign Ministry, were the two Vice Premiers, the first responsible for economic reform, and the second for social policy, including unemployment.

Konstantin Kagalovsky, an awkward, bearlike economist in his thirties with a nervous tic who had been working on the Yeltsin plan, called on me to set out the thinking behind it. The first thing was to free prices, reform the tax and banking systems, and get the money supply under control. The next stage, said Kagalovsky, was to privatise as rapidly as possible. About half of the enterprises already freed were 'privatised' only in name: their managers had simply changed the labels on the doors calling themselves, for example, 'concerns' instead of ministries (a process of 'badge engineering'). Most of the managers were Communists: where else could you find competent people? Many of those who were not Communists were crooks – but competent crooks. This was an inevitable stage on the road to the market, though not of course something one could say in public. There were no quick savings in the military sector. The soldiers had to be paid and housed, and much of the expenditure would have to be borne by Russia as the Union broke up. I said that this would have to be carefully explained. Western politicians were expecting big and early cuts in military expenditure as part of the price of giving aid. Kagalovsky turned out to be wrong. The Gaidar government slashed expenditure on procurement and other military purposes by some 70 per cent early in 1992, and it was not restored. Military salaries were cut by the simple expedient of delaying payment. The military nevertheless failed to mutiny. The West never gave Gaidar the credit he deserved for this decisive act, which was as much in the interests of the West as it was of Russia itself. The Russian military did not, of course, appreciate the logic, not least because none of Yeltsin's governments ever took the coherent and determined action needed to reduce, reform and re-equip the Russian armed forces so that they could meet the country's security requirements in the post-Cold War world.

The *shestidesyatniki* felt themselves superseded, and were critical. Petrakov told me that Gaidar was an economic journalist, not a real economist. No serious work had been done to back up the rhetoric of reform. Yeltsin had been wrong to announce price rises with no plan and no date for implementation. The townspeople were already stripping the shops bare, and the countrypeople would withhold their goods until the prices had gone up. Gerashchenko at the Soviet State Bank was sure that the country was on the verge of hyperinflation. All the presses in Western and Eastern Europe would be too few to print the paper notes that would be needed. He particularly opposed the idea of breaking up the currency union: the Russian government would discover that their negotiating position was weaker than they thought.

Despite his reputation as a young reformer, Yavlinsky was also critical. He believed that the Russian reforms were ill-prepared, and that they would not succeed. Like the International Monetary Fund, he preferred an Economic and Monetary Union of all the former Soviet Republics.

Even where they were justified, these were the criticisms of people who did not bear the responsibility of having to choose between action and inaction.

As the moment for the reforms drew nearer, Yeltsin warned the public on television that there would be hardship during the coming Winter. The economy continued to implode and the Western press scented disaster. On the eve of the European Summit in Maastricht in December 1991 the European ambassadors in Moscow were asked by Brussels for a collective judgement. My colleagues and I agreed that – despite scare stories in the Soviet and foreign press – there was no hunger nor even a serious lack of food. There could be pockets of genuine hardship: but no nation-wide famine. But the uncertainty meant that consumers were hoarding, farmers were holding their produce off the market, and the mafia was profiting. It was a crisis of distribution, not supply. These were things that only the Russians themselves could deal with. We were uneasily aware that this comparatively complacent analysis could be wrong. We remembered the early 1930s, when Western observers were bamboozled into believing that there was no famine in Ukraine.

Perhaps we were wise to hedge our bets. For Gaidar the December of 1991 was 'one of the worst of my memories. The gloomy queues, without even the usual quarrels and rows. The virgin emptiness of the shops. The women rushing about in search of even the least attractive food … The general expectation of catastrophe.'[7] Whether or not the ambassadors' analysis was correct, political and emotional pressure made it impossible for Western governments to remain inactive. Much of the popular emotion sprang from a generous desire to help. Some of the pressure came from editors in Western capitals, who demanded that their Moscow correspondents (who shared our scepticism) should provide photographs of babies starving in the streets. In Germany, where people had particular cause to be grateful for the recent evolution of Soviet policy, it became an electoral issue. Horst Teltschik, Kohl's adviser, arrived with a huge team to discuss the supply of humanitarian aid. The German Defence Ministry proposed that the Luftwaffe should deliver emergency rations. Western ambassadors joked that the last such winter airlift, the one that failed, was the airlift to Stalingrad in 1942. In January and May 1992 the Americans organised two grandiose and wholly useless conferences on humanitarian aid to Russia, the first in Washington and the second in Lisbon. Bizarrely, the Russians themselves were not invited.

For the Russians the politics were painful and hard to handle. Voronin, the Soviet Deputy Prime Minister in charge of organising food aid, told me that he and his fellow countrymen genuinely appreciated the upsurge of fellow-feeling in the West. But they felt desperately humiliated at the prospect of accepting food from their former enemies, and worried that Western governments would take the opportunity to play politics. They wanted us to deal with the central authorities, not with the Republics, the cities, and the people on the spot. I said that we thought that talk of an emergency had been exaggerated. We wanted to show solidarity with Gorbachev. We did not want to get mixed up in the local politics. But we really did want to be sure that the assistance got through to the people who needed it.

The Western donors set up a tight system of control, with monitors at the ports and in the distribution system to ensure that the food aid was not creamed off by the villains. One ironic consequence was that Nigel Shakespeare, the Assistant Military Attaché expelled in 1989, was allowed back as a monitor. The Russians put up with surprising grace with a tutelage that was both humiliating and mildly insulting. Needless to say, much of the aid still fell into the wrong hands.

Gaidar liberalised prices in Russia on 2 January 1992 and launched a revolution in the Russian economy. Immediately he was in the maelstrom.

'It felt like being under the pressure of a fire hose; you had not only to keep on your feet, but to keep a clear head and to go not in the direction in which circumstances were pushing you, but in the direction you had chosen for yourself. And all the time, day and night, the most worrying thing was the question of bread.' On the very same day I got entangled in an absurd row about British beef. A year earlier the Russians had imposed a ban on British beef because of worries about Mad Cow Disease. They had sustained their ban although the European Commission allowed British beef to circulate freely throughout the Community. We wanted to send beef to the Russians; and we wanted a written assurance that the stuff would be allowed in when it arrived. Deputy Prime Minister Shokhin told me that the Russians were hardly in a position to impose stricter standards than the Commission. But he needed to persuade the Russian veterinary experts. Unfortunately they were out of action. They were still reeling after their New Year celebrations. Some had not even recovered from the shock of working on 7 November, which they had been used to celebrate as the anniversary of the Revolution.

Nevertheless Shokhin signed the necessary document, and the storm broke. A huge Antonov aeroplane flew into Sheremetievo from Stansted with £250,000 worth of British beef on board. The Russian vets wanted evidence that none of it had come from farms with Mad Cow Disease. The frozen beef remained at the airport, getting slowly warmer. Ministers in London grew increasingly hysterical: they feared that they would be flayed by the British farmers, the British press and the British Prime Minister. A Soviet minister threatened to get the army to move the beef into Moscow. The Russian vets threatened to resign if they were overruled. The Foreign Office told me that British ministers wanted me to ring Yeltsin. I said that it would be politically almost impossible for him to overrule his vets, and refused to act without a specific instruction from the Foreign Secretary or the Prime Minister. One bright official in London suggested that the Prime Minister might withdraw his proposal that Yeltsin should join the forth-coming special UN Security Council meeting if the Russians did not come up to scratch. I heard no more of this brilliant formula for shooting ourselves in the foot. Tempers rose. London blamed the Russians, the Russians blamed London, and both blamed the embassy. I told the Foreign Office that many Russians (and I myself, though I did not say so) thought that the whole thing was a cynical operation by the British to force Russian hands over the beef ban, unload a whole lot of surplus beef, and gain political credit for aiding the Russian people in their hour of need.

In the end it was Gaidar, taking time off from far more important things, who brokered the deal with his usual good sense. The Russian vets agreed that the plane should go to Murmansk because (they said) there were no cattle that far North to catch the disease. It arrived there and was duly turned into sausages to the dismay of the local housewives, who would have preferred to turn it into steaks. It was only later that I remembered Klimentiuk, the Secretary of the Murmansk City Council, boasting to us three years earlier that that dairy yields in Murmansk were the largest in the Soviet Union.

Gaidar never complained of the distraction, then or later. But I did not feel very proud that we had found it necessary to burden him with our trivial affairs at such a difficult moment.

But 'humanitarian aid' was a side-show. The real challenge was to transform the whole economy. On 5 December Gaidar had invited the G7 ambassadors to call to receive a message from Yeltsin. Some of my colleagues wondered whether they should ask for instructions before calling on the mere Deputy Prime Minister of a state which was not yet internationally recognised. I said firmly that I did not need instructions. I would certainly see Gaidar. He might well have something interesting to say. The others thought again, and followed. So we met Gaidar the next day in the old Central Committee building on Staraya Ploshchad. Yeltsin was asking for a stabilisation fund of $4–5 billion to back his economic reforms. This would stabilise the Russian budget at the cost of a price increase of 200 per cent and a wage increase of 100 per cent. The rouble would settle at 20 = $1. Without a stabilisation fund inflation would run out of control, and food prices could increase twenty or thirty times. If the fund was not in place by April the government would not survive beyond June. It was not a bad prediction. The fund was not forthcoming; by the middle of 1992 inflation was beginning to run amok; and at the end of the year Gaidar was forced to resign.

Anders Aslund, a Swedish economist very experienced in Russian affairs, was advising the Gaidar team. He called on me with John Odling-Smee of the International Monetary Fund. They drew a sharp distinction between this new request for money and the ones that Gorbachev had made earlier in the year. In their view Gaidar knew what he was doing. His plan was not wholly coherent. But in the present chaos it was not possible to finish and implement a plan in the orderly way we might adopt in the West. The simplistic, dramatic approach might be the only one that could generate enough political steam to crash through the chaos.

My American colleague Bob Strauss and I agreed. The argument that there was no point in throwing money into a black hole was no longer justified. There was now a genuine reform programme, of the kind the West had demanded as a condition for its assistance. The money was peanuts compared with what we had spent on the Gulf War. And the stakes were much higher. Neither of us was sanguine that Western finance ministries would suddenly become generous, and Bob doubted that the US Congress would produce much money in an election year. But we agreed to try to shift our governments.

Douglas Hurd was due again in Moscow. On 11 January I telegraphed to say that he would be arriving at another crucial moment in Russia's history, though the drama this time was more complex, and slower burning. Gaidar's price liberalisation was a full-blooded move towards economic reform. It was also a leap in the dark. Neither Yeltsin, nor Gaidar, nor anyone else could predict how Russian producers and consumers would react, nor how long their patience would last. This might be the last best chance for economic reform and hence political stability in Russia. If Gaidar were swept away we could soon find ourselves back with voodoo economics, and an authoritarian leadership trying to divert popular discontent against a foreign (Ukrainian? Western?) enemy. The G7 should therefore commit itself to finance a stabilisation fund, and press the International Monetary Fund to admit Russia in the very shortest time. An early announcement would be a political shot in the arm for the reformers. But it would need to be followed by real money quite quickly. Despite the difficulties the British government, which still held the chair of the G7, should take the lead. There was no course of policy towards Russia which did not carry a risk. We were looking for the lesser evil.

I showed my telegram to Gaidar so that he would know exactly what arguments I was putting forward. I urged him and Yeltsin to explain three things coolly and in detail to their Western interlocutors. They should say that the situation was serious; the Russians had launched the reforms for which the West had pressed; it was now time for the West to fulfil its side of the bargain. Gaidar was sniffy about the offer to push Russian membership of the International Monetary Fund: the Fund's advice so far had been less than brilliant. I told him that membership was not to be sneered at. The Russians would do themselves a good turn if they pressed for the earliest possible entry.

On seeing my telegram a friend in the Treasury rang to warn me that for domestic political reasons Western governments could not or would not produce the money. We would have to settle for getting the Russians into the International Monetary Fund as quickly as possible. Yeltsin could help by lobbying Western leaders more effectively. A proper International Monetary Fund programme would call forth the money. A definitive answer to my telegram arrived later. It said that the Russians should pay their debts before they could expect new money. Feeling guilty that I had been too supine over the G7 negotiations the previous Autumn, I sent a sarcastic comment to Rod Lyne, now back in the Foreign Office. The orthodox bankers, I pointed out, had found themselves unable to ignore the debtors in Latin America. Did they really think that it would be easier to ignore a bankrupt Russia? Rod said that my ideas were catching ministers' imagination. Policy was moving glacially forward. Yeltsin's forthcoming visit to London was concentrating minds. The G7 Finance Ministers met in Washington on the eve of his visit. But although Norman Lamont spoke out in favour of the stabilisation fund, his colleagues were cautious.

Yeltsin visited London on the last day of January on his way to New York for the special session of the United Nations. It was his first voyage to the West as President of an independent Russia. During the Prime Minister's preparatory briefing session, everybody spoke up for Russia. Hurd said that British policy had reached a turning point: it was our partners who were lagging. Lamont said that we should take the plunge, and support the systemic change that was now occurring in Russia. It was exciting rhetoric. The concrete proposals put forward by the Whitehall officials were distinctly less exciting. There was old language about the International Monetary Fund, a bare hint that the G7 just might be prevailed upon to add its mite, and a modest promise of highly conditional export credits.

The next day Yeltsin arrived in Downing Street, looking healthier than in Moscow: his eyes less hooded, his complexion less yellow. He listened gravely and impassively. From time to time a slow smile would spread over his face, especially if he was faced by an awkward question. He expounded his reforms at ponderous length. Gorbachev, he said, was afraid to take unpopular measures and never even began to understand the need for privatisation. Now time had run out, and he himself had acted. He had liberalised prices. Privatisation would come next. The government had survived its first month. But the price changes would take a year to work through. People on fixed incomes were already in difficulty. The patience of ordinary people was not unlimited. Major managed to stem the flow long enough to underline our desire to help. Yeltsin thanked him with a touch of irony. He understood that the West had its own economic problems, and would find it hard to put the money together. But if the Russian reform failed, dictatorship would return, and the West would once again have to spend hundreds of billions of dollars on defence. That was why help was needed now.

There was a brief discussion of military matters. Yeltsin was expected to talk in Washington about further measures of arms control, and the British were worried that he would take the opportunity to call in public for the British and French to cut their nuclear arsenals. The Prime Minister explained to him that our armed forces now numbered less than one quarter of a million. Our nuclear deterrent was only a very little one. Did Yeltsin really think it was necessary to raise the matter in public? Yeltsin – evidently thunderstruck by the thought that any serious power could have such a very small army – magnanimously assured the Prime Minister that he would take care not to exaggerate the importance of the independent British deterrent.

In the next weeks the British government continued to take the lead, pressing for early Russian membership of the International Monetary Fund, supporting the idea of a stabilisation fund, and looking at the idea of bridging finance for Russia from the G7. Our partners continued to drag their feet: the Japanese because of the Kuriles, and the Americans because of worries about voting rights in the International Monetary Fund and the unpopularity of giving money to foreigners during an election year. The American attitude was of course the key. By the end of February opinion in Congress seemed to be moving towards support for Russia. Even the US Treasury was coming round. Influential Americans – the former Chairman of the Federal Reserve, Paul Volcker, and Gerry Corrigan, the Chairman of the New York Federal Reserve Bank – were acting as Yeltsin's personal advisers. Bob Strauss visited Washington to drum up support for Russia in the US Congress and elsewhere. His efforts received a great boost when Richard Nixon published a Memorandum attacking the US administration for its inertia, and warning that if nothing was done the question in the 1990s would be 'Who lost Russia?', just as the question in the 1950s was 'Who lost China?'

But for the time being the main issue was Russian membership of the International Monetary Fund. By now we had won the Russians' trust, and they asked us to sponsor their application. David Peretz, our Executive Director at the International Monetary Fund, came to Moscow to see Gaidar and work out a common line. Gaidar's office in the old Central Committee building on Staraya Ploshchad had previously been used by Suslov and other ideological chiefs of the Communist Party. Its walls were covered with paintings of industrial scenes from the 1930s, in depressing Lowry colours. One of Gaidar's aides remarked that the paintings were a reminder of where the economy was coming from and the depths to which it had now sunk. From now on things could only get better. We discussed tactics and the best way to handle the Fund and the Americans. It was an eerie thing to be conspiring with the Russians in what had once been the powerhouse of the world Communist movement.

At the end of March Nigel Wicks came to report progress. Gaidar was cool, lucid, and determined. He was grateful for our efforts. I asked what he thought were the chances for his programme. He said that all would depend on the balance of power after the parliament met in April. If the government survived, and if Yeltsin was not stripped of his emergency powers, then a compromise was possible. Meanwhile it would be a great help if the West could promise in public to back his programme with real money, and emphasise that none of the alternatives being proposed by the nationalists would work. Whatever he did, the nationalists would accuse him of selling his country to the West and dancing to the music of the IMF. But he needed to be able to counter the whispering among potential supporters that the West would provide only words, not deeds.

In the end we successfully negotiated the Russians into the Fund. Gaidar and his colleagues came to lunch on May Day to celebrate our common victory over the forces of darkness in the US Treasury, the Japanese Finance Ministry, and the International Financial Institutions. It was a very jolly affair. Gaidar was as confident and equable as always. His companions spoke and looked like American lawyers, self-evidently the new generation, although I assumed that the elemental Russian lurked somewhere under the skin. Gaidar made a generous speech praising the British for being the first to give unequivocal support to the new Russian reforms. He and his colleagues were all equally generous about the older generation of economists who had prepared the way: Bogomolov, Abalkin, Aganbegyan.

I had however prudently noted in my diary that 'such is the perversity of politics I suppose it is just possible that the opposition can present [the success] in a negative light.' So indeed it proved. The Russian parliament met in the middle of April. Khasbulatov, who had turned against Yeltsin after their common defence of the White House, forced through a resolution instructing Yeltsin to abandon his emergency powers and form a new government. Yeltsin wavered. Khasbulatov expressed his 'profound contempt' in an Italian newspaper for Gaidar and his people, whom he called 'little worms'. Gaidar and his team offered their resignations. A thoroughly bamboozled parliament adopted a chaotic compromise resolution, broadly backing the economic reforms. Gaidar remained in office. But the reform process was robbed of some of its initial steam. Gaidar watered down his timetable for reform, and gave the Fund and the G7 renewed excuse for caution.

Jeff Sachs called on me to discuss how the West could help. We disagreed again, this time about the difficulty of running down the defence industry.

In the Siberian closed cities hundreds of thousands of people had no other source of employment. Sachs thought that the people there could simply be paid to do nothing for five years. They would soon devise new and profitable forms of economic activity. I wondered whether it would be that easy. The workers might be too apathetic to go for something new. The political and social consequences could be horrendous. What worked in the derelict steel towns of Britain, surrounded as they were with the opportunities available in a highly sophisticated and flexible economic system, would not work in one-company towns hundreds of miles from anywhere in a country whose misdeveloped economy was falling apart. Sachs scoffed at the figure of forty million potential unemployed which was being bandied about both in Russia and the West. He thought that fourteen million would be the absolute maximum, and he turned out to be right. But we did agree that Gaidar now needed to turn his mind to structural policy, to concentrate on modernising the energy sector, converting the defence industry, transforming the food industry, and setting up a viable social welfare safety net.

Sachs thought that the West could help best by associating Russia more formally with the G7 Economic Summit mechanisms. This was indeed the thrust of the very last policy telegram which I sent from Moscow at the beginning of May 1992. By then the preparations for the G7 Summit meeting in Munich in July were already well under way. The previous year the G7 decided, as they were bound to decide, at the last minute and after a wrangle with the Americans and the Japanese, to invite Gorbachev to London. In 1992 they repeated the charade, and Yeltsin too was invited only at the last minute. It was a humiliating way of dealing with a man whom we were hailing as a partner. I argued that the encouragement of the Russian economic reform would be the main issue the G7 faced at Munich. Gaidar and Yeltsin understood well enough that economic success depended on a robust macroeconomic reform, and on rapid structural change in agriculture, energy, defence and welfare. But they faced intense political and practical difficulties. Neither we nor they would be able to walk away from reality. There would be delicate judgements to make as Russian reactionary industrialists and the Russian people tried to make the Russian government abandon the pure milk of the Fund programme. In any case the Washington institutions could not carry the burden on their own. We therefore needed to devise some more intimate and durable relationship between Russia and the G7, an arrangement suitably tailored to the needs of a superpower fallen on hard times. I did not attempt to argue that Russia could join the G7 as a full member. But the dialogue with Russia was now engaged. I did not see even the Japanese, let alone the Italians who would be the hosts in the following year, breaking the pattern once the Russian leader had met his peers two years running. The intense economic discussion launched at the Summit in London between Russian officials and their G7 counterparts at all levels was an essential part of the educational process through which the Russians had to pass if their economic reforms were to succeed. Russia's membership of the G7 should be formalised.

It was not to be for another five years. Yeltsin was invited to attend the last day of the Munich Summit in 1992, but only to talk about grand political matters. And there was no more talk of a stabilisation fund: the finance ministers had prevailed over their colleagues from the foreign ministries in the G7 capitals. A figure of $24 billion was incorporated in the final communiqué at Munich 'for political reasons'. It was the usual mixture of double-counting, export credits, and 'aid' which would in the nature of things mostly end up in the bank accounts of Western consultants. Whatever short-term purpose this figuring served – and Yeltsin too found it a useful political expedient – Russians soon came to see it as a confidence trick, fairy gold with no real value. Yeltsin's enemies used it as proof that he and his young reformers were not only willing to sell out to the West, but gullible as well.

Though it not easy to strike the balance of the argument, the West's response to Russia's economic crisis in the last part of 1991 still looks inadequate. Gorbachev was right to point out that a coalition which had spent $100 billion on a short sharp victory in the Gulf could afford the comparatively small sums for which he was asking. But Father Elefthery of the Kiev Lavra was equally right to argue that there was little point in pouring large sums of money into an economic system in collapse as long as those directly responsible were unable to make up their mind what they wanted to do. The analogy of the Marshall Plan was much bandied about at the time. But it was a false analogy. The Marshall Plan was designed to save Europe from the threat of Communism. It was directed at countries which already had all the human skills and institutions they needed to make a market economy work. Once their cities, their factories, their railways and their docks were rebuilt, economic recovery began to come quickly. But economic reform in Russia required a historically unprecedented change not so much in the physical infrastructure – the Russians had plenty of that, although by now it was distinctly decrepit – but in the minds and the institutions of men.

The G7 debt negotiation in the Autumn of 1991 was a particularly unimaginative response. A determination to recover our money, and the offer of a dollop of expensive advice, was not really the best way of helping the Soviet Union to make the difficult transition. Experience in Latin America in the 1980s, and indeed in Russia after the crisis of 1998, undermines the negotiators' argument that a country which defaults on its debts, or even asks for a rescheduling, disqualifies itself for good from participation in the world economy. Coming from the creditors themselves, this judgement looks a mite self-serving. But at the time no one came up with a more imaginative alternative, let alone one which would find its way through the thicket of objections in the G7 capitals.

But things should have changed when Yeltsin and Gaidar showed that they were determined to push through a genuinely radical reform on just the lines that the West had advocated. The economic objections to a generous Western response became less convincing by the day. The disreputable argument that Western voters would not allow their governments to subsidise Russia while unemployment was rising at home was never tested. Elected politicians are always less able than they claim to interpret the public mood. Determined Western leaders could have tapped into the general sympathy for Russia and put together a genuine stabilisation scheme which would have mitigated the pain of transition and relieved much of the distress which ordinary Russians were to suffer over the next few years. It can be argued that money given at the beginning of 1992 would have found its way into corrupt pockets. But the mechanisms of corruption were not yet in place, and Western aid at the right moment might well have helped turn the corner. It is another of the 'ifs' of history.

Gaidar's own judgement is balanced; but the bitterness shows. No Western leader, he wrote, not even John Major, was willing to undertake the responsibility of organising adequate measures of support:

> During the critical months from January to April 1992, even a few hundred million dollars of freely convertible currency reserves would have allowed us substantially to extend our freedom of economic manoeuvre, but even these sums were not available to us. By the time the bureaucratic procedures were at last complete, the stabilisation programme was already disintegrating before our eyes.

This is hard on John Major. He was highly effective in dealing with foreigners. He could negotiate toughly while leaving no bruised feelings, a skill which served him well in Europe and on Ireland. He took full advantage of Britain's ephemeral special relationship with Russia after the August putsch to press Russia's case with his Western colleagues. But he was not able to overcome their inertia, scepticism, and lack of imagination. Though it was not the British government's fault this time, I was irresistibly reminded of what Lytton Strachey wrote about the preparations to relieve General Gordon at Khartoum. 'The ponderous machinery took so long to set itself in motion; the great wheels, once started, revolved with such a laborious, such a painful deliberation, that at last their work was accomplished – surely, firmly, completely, in the best English manner, and too late.'[8]

11

Towards a Radiant Future?

ON 19 March 1917, the *Petrograd Bulletin* brought out an extra edition to report the abdication of Tsar Nicholas II. It carried the massive headline:

НОВАЯ ВЕЛИКАЯ ЖИЗНЬ ИДЕТЪ, РУССКІЕ ЛЮДИ!

Eighty years later, I bought a battered copy of the *Bulletin* on the banks of the Volga at Uglich, where the young Tsarevich Dmitri had been slaughtered, allegedly on the orders of Boris Godunov. I showed the headline – RUSSIAN PEOPLE, A GREAT NEW LIFE IS ON ITS WAY! – to the elderly man who had sold me the paper, a man with the look of a former member of the intelligentsia fallen on hard times. He laughed ruefully. So did the peasant woman selling Russian dolls next to him. For them, another promise of hopeful change was already turning sour.

In the decade after Yeltsin came to power in Russia there were two Presidential elections, three parliamentary elections, a national referendum, numerous local elections, a brief civil war, two bloody conflicts in Chechnya, and an unexpected change in the country's leadership. *The Economist* chose to call this 'phoney democracy', though the proceedings were no more rough and ready than those in modern India.

But the economic question was closest to the core of the problem. Gaidar's radical reform was deliberately intended to sweep the old system away in its entirety, and substitute the mechanisms of the modern liberal market. His liberation of prices had precisely the textbook effect. Goods flowed into the shops, a surprising number of people seemed to be able to afford them, and the queues vanished. Ordinary people paid the price.

Economic change offered the enterprising and the unscrupulous great opportunities to enrich themselves at their country's expense. Even in the last days of the Soviet Union, before Gaidar changed the rules of the game, figures from the past – Komsomol leaders in Moscow and Leningrad, ex-ministers from the Gorbachev government, generals and former Party Secretaries from the provinces – reinvented themselves as 'businessmen' and went into what were euphemistically called 'the commercial structures'. Many of them used their personal links from the old days and exploited the ambiguities which surrounded the fate of the former Party funds. Some of the new businessmen set up 'banks' which lent money on easy terms to friends and cronies. Others traded in raw materials and scrap metal, the detritus of the old system as it flew apart, or set up pyramid schemes which robbed millions of people of their savings. The most powerful cultivated the clique around Yeltsin himself: judicious payments to the right people could get you an immensely lucrative tax exemption on the import of sports goods, cigarettes, and other profitable consumer goods. All were helped by the government's flawed macroeconomic policies which allowed speculators to enrich themselves in the financial markets. Not only the locals profited. Russia became a popular 'emerging market' for many foreigners whose aims, methods, and morality were often equally suspect.

By such means the rich – perhaps 5 per cent of the population – got disgracefully richer. The poor and the elderly got poorer. The immediate side-effects of change were runaway inflation, the destruction of savings, the stagnation of industry and agriculture as subsidies were withdrawn, social distress and a widespread increase in poverty. The payment of wages and pensions in the remaining sectors of the state economy and in the bureaucracy was delayed, often for months at a time. Alcoholism and street crime increased, and male life expectancy tumbled. In the past beggars had been swept off the streets by the police, and if necessary sent to the camps to get them permanently out of the way. Now they became a fixed part of the urban landscape.

Every Winter the Communists waited hopefully for the call: once again they would overthrow a corrupt and incompetent bourgeois government, as they had done in October 1917. Observers wondered why there was no explosion. Why did the tattered military not mutiny? Why did the ordinary people not do as they had done so often before, and descend into the streets to burn, loot, and kill? But the *bunt* never happened and the Communists were disappointed.

Statistics, poll results, and anecdotal evidence abounded. Many people used them to promote a picture of Russian decay which was sometimes wildly exaggerated. It was not easy to judge the extent of the distress among the newly unemployed, the old, the single parents, the disabled. Official figures appeared to show that the Russian economy declined by as much as 40 per cent between 1990 and 1995, though the basis of comparison was unclear and the statistics took insufficient account of the rapid growth of the grey economy.

With all its many faults, the Soviet welfare system had given the people the feeling that they would be properly looked after from the cradle to the grave. To a significant extent, this sense of security was an illusion. By the time the Soviet Union collapsed, according to official statistics, over a third of the population were living below the official subsistence level.

They lived on nostalgia instead. In defiance of the facts, if such they were, people doggedly continued to believe throughout the 1990s that it was Gorbachev, Yeltsin, and Gaidar who had destroyed their living standards. Stalin, they maintained, had regularly reduced the price of food. Brezhnev had kept prices stable and low. People forgot that the cheap goods were rarely for sale to ordinary people: they went out of the back of the shop to those with connections and the money to pay a premium for scarce goods. The truth of what people really felt in those years was different, more bitter, more cynical, more resigned. It can be reconstructed from the political jokes of the day.[1] But the popular image of the Soviet past was understandable as a way of compensating for the humiliation of collapse. The Communists were bound to try to exploit it, and the government was bound to take it into account.

Russia's size continued to pose almost insoluble problems. As the country got poorer, arrangements designed to encourage people to live in the remote regions of Siberia and the North began to disintegrate. Transport costs ratcheted upwards. Heating systems broke down. Whole cities began to freeze in places where the winter temperatures could fall to minus forty degrees centigrade. Huge enterprises ground to a halt as the demand for their products disappeared. Pay differentials were no longer attractive. Those who could, left for the rich pickings of the new economy in Western and Central Russia to join the four-fifths of the population who already lived there.

But many could not leave. They remained in cities of up to a million people, often dependent on one no longer viable industry; or in tiny settlements far from most of the trappings of modern civilisation. However hopeless these places might be from a purely economic point of view, no Russian government could afford to ignore them. Pensions and salaries had to be paid, even if nothing of value was being produced. Every Autumn supplies of food and fuel had to be got together, at government expense, to enable people to get through the harsh Northern Winter. Nonchalant Western advisers told the Russian government that these things would sort themselves out as market disciplines began to bite. People would get on their bikes and seek employment elsewhere. Local enterprises, exposed to 'hard budget constraints', would turn to producing quality goods that the customer actually wanted. This was perfectly unrealistic. The burdens which nature and Stalinist misdevelopment imposed on the Russian economy would take many decades to sort out. Some would always remain intractable.

Ordinary people devised a variety of survival strategies. They tilled their tiny plots of land, they took second jobs, they set up small businesses, and as Russians had always done they helped one another out through their networks of family and friends. By the Spring of 1992 the peasants in the little villages around Moscow – charming but rickety wooden houses, standpipes or wells in the streets in the absence of piped water, the occasional battered church – were working their private plots with hoes and spades. It was like the grainy photos of peasant life in the nineteenth century, except that the peasants now wore tracksuits instead of folk costumes. Some were using home-made cultivators – small petrol engines precariously lashed to scrawny frames. Some were even ploughing with horses, the first working horses we had ever seen in Russia. Chickens, sheep, and goats scrambled around the village streets. In places the villagers had taken land into cultivation which had been abandoned by the collective. The oppressive state was no longer in a position to satisfy their basic needs, and they had no choice but to use the initiative which had been so brutally suppressed by Stalin.

And in a very significant new departure, non-governmental bodies mushroomed to supplement or even replace the functions of the failing welfare state. In Soviet times independent organisations were thought to threaten the political monopoly of the Party, and they had been banned. In the new Russia organisations sprang up to help the poor, the homeless, the single mothers, the orphans, the alcoholics and the disabled, who had been looked after inadequately by the socialist state, and who had been largely abandoned in the new Russia. In towns and cities throughout the country, people combined to alleviate the distress they saw around them. Many were ex-Communists – some were still Party members – who had performed similar functions in the past, decent people who knew how to manage the local reality. Western advisers gave them patronising and often ignorant and inappropriate advice. The Russians reacted at first with enthusiasm, then with resentment, and finally with discrimination as they learned to accept the advice which made sense, and politely ignore the advice which did not. Some of the largest charities were notoriously corrupt devices for exploiting new opportunities for enrichment. But others filled a real need and functioned with increasing efficiency. They were among the vital first shoots of something the Soviet Union had lacked: a genuine civil society.

Despite the hardships, life began after a few years to take a modest turn for the better for a surprisingly large number of people. The economy began to lurch forward. Small business had been illegal in the Soviet Union. It was not easy in the new Russia either: it was discouraged by economic instability and by the depredations of corrupt officials. But as the old sources of more or less guaranteed income began to dry up ('They pretend to pay us, and we pretend to work') a substantial and increasing number of people moved into petty manufacturing and the service industries. In the mid-nineties Jill and I attended a party to launch a 'Small Business Incubator' in Nizhny Novgorod – an organisation devoted to aiding the very smallest start-up companies with legal advice, technical assistance, and petty loans. Almost all the budding entrepreneurs were women. I asked one of them why this was. She looked at me stonily and asked, 'And what do you know about Russian men?' As the Soviet industrial system collapsed, the men had gone fishing or taken to drink. It was the women who had – as so often in the past – had to improvise new ways of raising money to keep their families together. Traumas like these occurred with the collapse of heavy industry in Britain. But this was *The Full Monty* on a continental scale.

By now the grey economy was said to be growing at a rate of 10 per cent a year, and to account for nearly half of the economic activity in the country. This was not reflected in the official statistics, since the new entrepreneurs preferred not to reveal their earnings to the tax collector and the local protection gangs.

The party appeared to come to an end when the Russian stock market collapsed and the rouble crashed in August 1998. The crash was triggered by the Asian flu, the sharp decline in oil prices, and by corruption, mismanagement, and cronyism worse than those in Asia. Imports dried up. The government froze its foreign debt. Most of the 'banks' were revealed in all their raddled and fraudulent nakedness. Western governments and Western bankers were incensed at the Russian default, and predicted that Russia would be a pariah in world markets for years to come. The rest of us felt scant sympathy for foreign speculators who up until a couple of months earlier had been earning up to 180 per cent on Russian Treasury bonds.

Moscow was particularly hard hit. The smart restaurants, each more bizarrely decorated than the next, fell empty as their patrons – businessmen, bandits, and their elegant whores – found they could no longer afford the absurd prices demanded. More respectable people, the new middle class of financial professionals, journalists, and small entrepreneurs, suffered particularly. They had not been in a position to strip the assets of Russia's few viable companies or exploit monopolies granted to them by an increasingly corrupt Kremlin. Their savings were wiped out.

But contrary to gloomy expectation, the crash did not cause an economic meltdown. What happened in Moscow did not in any case much affect the millions of people eking out their existence in the provinces. To the delight of the theorists of liberal reform, the economy started to respond to the stimulus of a low exchange rate rather quickly. Russian manufacturing industry was able to start exporting again at competitive prices. Local businesses, especially in the food industry, began to produce Russian goods – to Russian taste – to replace the consumer goods that were no longer being imported.

According to official figures, the economy began to grow at a rate of 7 per cent during much of 2000 – for the first time for very many years. It continued more modestly the following year. Consumer spending rose substantially. So – significantly – did domestic investment. The government was at last collecting its taxes, and the federal budget went into surplus for the first time. High oil prices meant that the current account was in healthy surplus.

This new prosperity appeared to give the lie to those who said that economic reform in Russia was doomed. But it was precarious. It was too dependent on high oil prices. It was not accompanied by any serious reconstruction of industry. The courts and the bureaucracy remained incompetent and corrupt. The system was still littered with banks that were incapable of providing the services which normal banks are supposed to provide, and the central bank was doing nothing about it. The practice of capitalism in Russia (it was much too early to talk about genuine capitalist institutions) was still riddled with confusion, corruption, and crime.

Change was reflected not only in the vulgar behaviour of the *nouveaux riches*, but in the very look of the country's capital. Moscow became a boom city. Driven by its energetic mayor Luzhkov, and financed as only he knew how, the place was transformed. Monuments which had been allowed to decay under the Communists were restored to their previous glory. Many had been deliberately destroyed by Stalin and Khrushchev. They were rebuilt from scratch: the massive and ugly Cathedral of Christ the Saviour, built to celebrate the victory over Napoleon, blown up in 1931 by Stalin and replaced by an open-air swimming pool; the tiny Kazan Cathedral on Red Square, built in 1625 to celebrate Russia's liberation from the Poles; and many others. Moscow was once again dominated by the ancient cupolas and fiery crosses of which Pushkin had written nearly two hundred years earlier. The eternal potholes in Moscow's roads were filled in, the ring road widened and a new one begun. Hotels and offices sprang up all over Moscow until it looked like a perpetual construction site. So – in a city where it had been almost impossible to get a decent meal – did Japanese, French, Italian, Indian restaurants, many of them financed by gangsters seeking to park their money. Shops were full of the consumer goods that Muscovites had hitherto seen only in films from the West. Outside the city ugly brick-built villas – their owners called them 'dachas' or 'kottedzhi' (an American, not a British usage), but they bore no resemblance to the elegant wooden constructions of the past – began to proliferate like diseased mushrooms. They too were a convenient way for sharp businessmen and corrupt officials to park their money. Moscow at last began to rival the more sophisticated capitals of Europe.

People would tell you that things were very different outside Moscow. But things were changing in the provinces as well. Jill and I returned in the Summer of the year 2000 to the Party hotel in Vologda where we had stayed on the eve of the putsch. It was now called the Spasskaya – 'The Hotel of the Saviour' – in honour of the new Orthodoxy. The bathrooms had been given what Russians call a 'Euroremont'. The service and food in the restaurant were vastly improved. And the city itself was booming. The admonition over the central market, so typical of Soviet days – 'TAKE CARE WHEN USING GAS!' – was still there, in metal letters three metres high. But the authorities were making a determined effort to restore the churches and the local Kremlin. The monastery, used successively as a prison, an orphanage, and a military base, had been handed back to the monks. The elegant wooden town houses were being discreetly restored as offices by businessmen who valued their central location. The ball-bearing factory was exporting at a profit. So was the revived dairy industry, which before the First World War sent butter to Paris. The central street of Vologda, dreary in 1991, was now full of attractive little restaurants and small private shops selling electronic goods, clothes, and a wide variety of foodstuffs. Much of the produce was Russian – bread, butter, sausage, meat, vegetables. The prices were reasonable, people were buying, and the staff were clean, well dressed, and courteous.

These signs of relative prosperity were not confined to the regional capital. A couple of hours drive from Vologda lies the tiny, jewel-like monastery of Ferapontovo. The Bolsheviks shot the Mother Superior after the October Revolution. But the monastery buildings survived, with their austerely beautiful frescoes painted in the fifteenth century by Dionisy and his two sons (in thirty-five days, the locals proudly tell you: eat your heart out, Michelangelo). In the adjoining village of five hundred inhabitants there were now three little shops, one private, one run by a company from Vologda, and one apparently by the local authorities. All were selling oranges and bananas, fruits almost unknown to Soviet man. To a Westerner, these sights might seem trivial. To anyone who had lived in the old Soviet Union, they signified a new revolution.

Things looked less good as you got further North towards the river towns – Kargopol, Totma, Veliki Ustiug – which lay along the trade route from Muscovy to Western Europe. That early trade had brought prosperity and an efflorescence of religious art and building. But the prosperity began to fail after Peter the Great redirected the trade routes through his new capital of St Petersburg. And things got much worse in the twentieth century. Stalin's policemen drove the independent peasants into the new collective farms, a serfdom they had never experienced before. The policemen destroyed ancient churches and used the monasteries as transit stations for prisoners on their way to the Gulag. The prisoners, ill-fed and ill-clothed, died in their tens of thousands in the murderous logging camps in the surrounding forest. When the camps were dispersed in the 1950s, Khrushchev resumed the destruction of churches, and herded the peasants out of their collectives and into huge and heavily subsidised state farms. Many former prisoners and their guards stayed on in the Northern forests to which they had become grimly accustomed. Kargopol – headquarters of one of the islands of the Gulag archipelago – still has four times its former population.

The timber trade, the state farms, and lavish subsidies gave these small towns a modest standard of living in the last decades of Communism. By the beginning of the new century their few industries had run down. Forestry was almost the only activity to provide a lucrative job. The men had reverted to traditional pursuits: hunting, fishing, and the building of wooden houses – often now for rich clients down in Moscow. The women complained that drunkenness was even more widespread than before, that drug abuse was growing, and that any youngster with initiative left for the big cities and never returned. The local bureaucrats were modestly corrupt, as they had always been. But there was not much serious crime in Kargopol, and it was too poor to sustain its own mafia.

Indeed little was happening in Kargopol any more. The airport had been closed down, the only hotel was no more than a doss-house for travelling bureaucrats, and there were only two battered nightspots for the young, who otherwise spent the long summer evenings mooning around the streets, eyeing one another in a gloomy Northern parody of the Mediterranean *corso*. Starved of other excitements, people still remembered the time in 1991 when a yeti appeared in a nearby military camp and then disappeared, no one knew whither, after receiving full coverage on national TV. You could see why the youngsters were leaving.

And yet even Kargopol was not entirely without hope. Some bedraggled shops were scattered around. A pharmacy, a small food shop, and a radio shop camped out in tiny rooms inside the 'hotel' itself. They were rather better stocked than they would have been in Soviet times, though they did not begin to compare with Vologda. There was a small and very efficient tourist agency, and a small community of local artists and craftsmen. The bell-ringer in the main church had recently won the All-Russian competition for bell-ringing. In 1999 only two people in the town were on the internet. A year later there were twenty-five. The locals placed great store by the new road which was being built across Northern Sweden and Finland, through the Kargopol region, and on to the Urals. This, they hoped, would at last open the place properly to the outside world.

Outside the towns even this hope seemed denied. When the Soviet Union collapsed, the local state farms were 'privatised' and were now called Joint Stock Companies. This meant little in practice. They were mostly run by the same people, and such prosperity as some of them still enjoyed depended on the energy and business connections of the chairman, as it did even in Soviet times. But large-scale agriculture was dying. The huge fields had not yet reverted to forest. But the cattle herds had dropped by two-thirds in a decade. The great barns and cowhouses built in the 1960s and 1970s were sagging and collapsing. Private farming had not prospered either. Independent-minded peasants had attempted to take advantage of the new laws which Gorbachev introduced to encourage private agriculture. None of these 'farmers' was left. They had all succumbed to the lack of infrastructure and agricultural credit, and the hostility of the authorities, the state farms, and their own neighbours.

With admirable if dour cheerfulness, the people carved their small allotments out of the broad fields on the outskirts of every town and village, even in their centres. These little plots were looked after with loving care. The soil was combed and brushed and wholly clear of weeds. Each plant was protected by its own plastic cover. In Britain you would assume that the gardeners were preparing for the village flower show. Up there in the North it was a matter of life and death to grow and store your supplies before the

Winter descended once more. People survived, as they had always done. But the agricultural economy of the North was reverting to its preindustrial state.

Outside the villages people had more scope to exercise the traditional Russian skill of survival through *blat*, by working around the edge of law. The sleeping car attendant on the train back from Kargopol earned 1,500 roubles a month, and her husband 3,000. (Comparisons based on exchange rate calculations are of course meaningless. But a Samsung ghettoblaster cost 1,300 roubles in Vologda, which gives some idea of what these sums were worth.) Unlike many others she had no access to a private plot for food. But she could live. She was even able to help out her widowed daughter, whose pension was only 400 roubles a month. I told this story to a Russian friend a few days later. He roared with laughter. A sleeping car attendant would net far more than 1,500 a month. She would charge for delivering parcels all along her route, a much more reliable arrangement than the post; and for all sorts of other small services as well. She was, in fact, at the innocuous bottom end of the system of corruption which pervaded the whole Russian railway system. The top end, to judge by the regularity with which regional rail bosses got assassinated, was often literally a matter of life and death.

In later years Russians and foreigners argued passionately about Gaidar's shock therapy. Had he been right to force the pace of economic reform? Could the more stately approach advocated by Gorbachev, Bogomolov and many others have mitigated the distress which economic change brought to the Russian people? The radicals among Gaidar's colleagues and their foreign advisers argued that the reforms had stumbled because they had not been far-reaching enough. Greater political will and more consistent support from the President, these 'market Bolsheviks' believed, could have forced through the reforms at such a rate that the forces of reaction would never have recovered their balance and much distress would have been avoided.

The arguments do not entirely convince. Yeltsin did fail to provide consistent support to his young reformers, or to protect them from their detractors. But the young reformers themselves were politically inept, and never realised the importance of explaining their policies in terms that ordinary people could understand and support. They had no effective strategy for tackling the obstacles posed by the lack of market institutions and the rule of law. Neither they nor their foreign advisers can escape responsibility for the failure of their policies to deliver the rapid results they had predicted.

Yet even that is not the whole story. Reform was inescapable, and the distress it brought with it was an inevitable consequence of the collapse of the tottering Soviet regime. No group of mortal men, however intelligent, well-meaning, competent and far-sighted, could have devised and implemented a policy that would cope simultaneously with all the economic, institutional, and social challenges which Russia faced. Gaidar chose to go for the most rapid economic reform he could get through the political system. A slower tempo might well, as he argued, merely have protracted the distress. A faster tempo was almost certainly politically impossible.

The economy may have been the key to Russia's future. But – as in other countries – the solution of economic problems was always hostage to politics. Politics in Yeltsin's Russia was raw, corrupt, and occasionally violent. And unlike Gorbachev, Yeltsin showed comparatively little aversion to the shedding of blood.

The first bloody confrontation came in 1993, triggered by a crude struggle for power between the Duma and the President. The Duma was led by Vice President Rutskoi, and the Speaker, Ruslan Khasbulatov, both Yeltsin's allies during the 1991 coup. They were demagogic, irresponsible, and deliberately offensive to the President, whom they tried unsuccessfully to impeach in the Spring of 1993. In the Autumn they used armed bully boys to storm the offices of the Mayor of Moscow next to the White House. An armed mob marched to the television studios at Ostankino and opened fire. Inside the White House there were calls to hang Yeltsin and his associates. After a failed attempt at mediation by Patriarch Aleksi, Yeltsin persuaded a very reluctant army to send its tanks against the White House on 4 October 1993. Several hundred people were killed in the fighting.

Western governments backed Yeltsin with little question: at the end of the day, a government has to govern. But many Russians believed that the crisis could have been resolved earlier if Yeltsin had shown more political skill. Some thought that he had provoked it deliberately in order to get rid of his parliamentary enemies and open the way for new elections. Few forgave him for spilling blood in Russia's capital.

In the elections which followed that December, the democrats did badly and the Communists did well. But the most sensational result was the showing of Zhirinovsky's inaptly named 'Liberal Democratic Party of Russia'. Zhirinovsky's crude national rhetoric, his barely disguised anti-Semitism, and his lively performance on television appealed to an electorate disgusted with the events in Moscow and bored with the fare they were offered by reformists and Communists alike. Russian liberals and

Russia's foreign well-wishers panicked. Those who did not wish Russia well remained convinced that nothing in Russia had changed, and predicted that the country was on the verge of a fascist dictatorship. It took many months before either noticed that the parliamentary performance of Zhirinovsky and his people was surprisingly meek. They regularly voted with the government, their convictions reinforced, so it was said, by liberal subsidies from the Kremlin's war chest.

Yeltsin took advantage of the parliamentary election to slip through a new constitution modelled on the French, which greatly tilted the balance of power in favour of the President. Many were convinced that the constitution had not received the number of popular votes needed to bring it into law. No doubt there was electoral fraud. But an experienced electoral observer from Northern Ireland commented to me that he had noticed nothing that he did not regularly see at election time in his own home province.

In December 1994 violence broke out again, this time in Chechnya. The origins of this war – in the shadow of important elections in Russia itself – were murky. The suspicious believed that the explanation lay primarily not in unrest in the region, but in corrupt business links and in Russian domestic politics. The first war ended in a Russian defeat: one of the few Russian successes was the killing, in an elegant technical operation, of Dudaev, the Chechen leader. A peace was brokered by General Lebed. It gave the Chechens reasonable terms, which would have led them to independence if they had played their hands sensibly. Lebed's patriotism was questioned by some former liberals who should have supported him. But the Russian people welcomed the ending of the bloodshed, and for a while Lebed became an almost credible national politician.

The war was renewed in the Summer of 1999. By then political authority had all but collapsed within Chechnya, and a series of terrorist outrages gave the Russians the excuse to intervene once more. The government argued that Chechnya was legally part of the Russian Federation. They had the right and indeed the duty to prevent secession. It was the same argument that the French used to justify their bloody war in Algeria. But unlike the French, the Russians believed that they also faced a serious threat in their recalcitrant province from terrorism and Islamic fundamentalism. Foreign governments could not dispute these arguments of principle. But they thoroughly disliked the Russian methods of dealing with the Chechen problem in practice. These were crude, brutal, and incompetent. Indiscriminate bombing and shelling resulted in large numbers of civilian deaths. Many Russians thought the foreign criticism unfair. They reminded their critics that France's war in Algeria cost perhaps up to a million dead. They muttered about the bombing of Iraq and Serbia. And they pointed out that the Americans dropped four times as many bombs on Cambodia in the early 1970s as they had done on Japan in the whole of the Second World War.

Yeltsin fell due for re-election to the Presidency in the Summer of 1996. By then the electorate could see for themselves that he was becoming ever more erratic, spent ever more time resting or sick, and was surrounded by an ever more blatantly corrupt and divided court. For many it was an uncomfortable reminder of the last years of Brezhnev and the 'rule' of the gerontocrats which followed his death. Meanwhile the country appeared to be falling apart. Regional governors became ever more arrogant towards the central government. The new capitalists were little interested in the finer points of commercial ethics. They evaded their taxes, violated the rights of their shareholders, stripped their companies' assets and hid the proceeds in Switzerland, and if necessary used Kalashnikovs to collect their debts. The rest of the country noticed. By the beginning of 1996 Yeltsin's popularity ratings had fallen to less than 5 per cent.

Fearful that he might lose the 1996 election, Yeltsin and his backers brandished the Communist bogey. Some of his entourage suggested that it would be safer – in the name of 'anti-Communism' – to cancel the election altogether. Anatoli Chubais, Gaidar's highly competent lieutenant in the early days, had become an arch political operator. He delivered the election to Yeltsin by a ruthless manipulation of the press, the economy, and the political system. His message was simple. Yeltsin's rule might be muddled, corrupt, and incompetent; but it was a lot better than a Communist comeback.

The threat was exaggerated. With the disappearance of the ineffective Polozkov, the Russian Communist Party was now led by Gannadi Ziuganov, a former teacher from Orel in the 'Red Belt' south of Moscow. Ziuganov was skilful enough to hold his divided and backward-looking party together and to remain at its head. He was clever enough to pose as an orthodox Communist patriot to his followers, and as a modern man of reason to liberals and Western businessmen. But he had neither the charisma nor the conviction to take his party forward. His electoral programme called for a limited return to state intervention. It would not have worked, though it would have further delayed the building of a healthy political and economic system in Russia.

But the truth was that the Communist threat had already ceased to exist in any of the previously accepted senses of the word. There were of course still plenty of Communists and ex-Communists at the top of the Yeltsin regime, including Yeltsin himself. These people were not stupid, and many of them embraced the new ways to the best of their ability. But they had got to the top through the Communist system of *nomenklatura*, designed to ensure that the ambitious could make their careers only in subservience to the state. By the late 1980s that system was breaking down. A new generation could now make their way in the world by their own efforts and talents. Where all had been stagnant, the faces at the top – in the provinces as well as in Moscow – now changed with bewildering rapidity as ambitious men and women shouldered their way forward in a crude and unedifying struggle for power and riches.

Against this turbulent background the Russian Communist Party seemed increasingly irrelevant. Ziuganov had enough skill to hold his fractious followers together. The Party did not split between its extremist and its social democratic wings, as many had expected. But Ziuganov relapsed increasingly into a muttered and incoherent mixture of orthodoxy and old-fashioned Russian nationalism which convinced few voters outside the elderly and provincial Party faithful who still yearned for the old days. He did surprisingly well in the Presidential election of 1996, forcing Yeltsin into a second round of voting. But when you talked to them, it was clear that he and his people had lost the will to victory. They did not expect to win, and did not even seem to care very much. The Communists went on getting votes. But Communism as a menacing force in Russia was finished.

In 1998 Yeltsin sacked his Prime Minister, Chernomyrdin. Chernomyrdin had served for five stolid years but was acquiring irritating presidential ambitions. For more than a year Yeltsin experimented with one Prime Minister after another. The longest lived was Yevgeny Primakov, who was imposed on Yeltsin by the Duma on a promise to bring stability, pay wages and pensions, and restore the good name of Russia in the world. He had some success, but he made three cardinal errors. He started to pursue corruption uncomfortably close to Yeltsin's associates. He was insufficiently zealous in warding off the growing pressure in the parliament to impeach his boss. And he too began to be talked of as a potential president.

By now Yeltsin was interested not in policy, but in finding a successor who would guarantee him and his family immunity from harassment once he left office. He sacked Primakov in May 1999, and after one more unsatisfactory experiment appointed Vladimir Putin as his last Prime Minister in August. On New Year's Eve 1999 he pulled off one of the most spectacular political coups of his career. He announced on television that he would stand down six months before his term formally came to an end. He apologised to the Russian people for his failures. And he named Putin as Acting President, and as his designated successor. An election at the end of March 2000 confirmed Putin in office with just over 50 per cent of the votes. His opponent was, as usual, the Communist Ziuganov.

If Gorbachev was the Moses who led the Soviet people out of Egypt, Yeltsin was his Aaron, though the new Russia over which he presided was by no means flowing with milk and honey. Although the two men were of an age, and although they both rose through the Communist Party machine from great poverty to the highest position in the state, they could hardly have been more different. Yeltsin was a big man, a ponderous man, a man with hugely effective political instincts. He lacked Gorbachev's spontaneity, openness, intellectual curiosity and quickness of wit. In his political style he was a bull, where Gorbachev was an eel. There was a gambling streak in him which was foreign to Gorbachev. Gorbachev was a brilliant pupil, who won his way from the village school to Moscow University, and started his Party career with every advantage. Yeltsin stayed in the provinces for his education and for much of his political career. He was a natural outsider where Gorbachev always wanted to be an insider. Yeltsin ran against the system and gained the hearts of all those who hated it.

Yeltsin was nevertheless in many ways a much more traditional Russian leader than his predecessor. This at first did him no harm with the voters, many of whom still hankered after the uncomfortable but uncomplicated days of undisputed central authority. His manipulation of court intrigue in the Kremlin was a throwback to the claustrophobic politics of the Politburo and the Tsars. Gorbachev was surrounded by colleagues who were considerable political figures in their own right. Yeltsin made sure that even the most competent of his associates were dependent on his favour, and he had no compunction about sacrificing them if he thought they were getting above their station. Yeltsin's nickname 'Tsar Boris' was only half an irony.

At first Russian liberals and Western intellectuals believed, on no obvious evidence, that Yeltsin was more committed to democracy than Gorbachev, that he would be able to push through the liberal economic reforms which Gorbachev had failed to implement. As Yeltsin settled into supreme power after 1991, he did indeed seem to have decided that the path of reform would prevail and that it would secure his place in history, though it was his gambling instinct and his imperious will, rather than mere intellectual conviction, which led him to put his full authority behind Gaidar's programme of radical economic reform. Apart from Chechnya, he managed the continuing retreat from Empire in reasonably good order.

My own prejudices against Yeltsin were fed by the whispering campaign against him. I disliked what I saw as his lack of charm, his bullying manner, the poverty of his ideas, his relentless destructive opposition to Gorbachev. The first volume of his memoirs, which I read in June 1990, gave an initial sense of his courage and willpower. By the time I paid my last call on him in May 1992 I was largely won over. He was businesslike, relaxed, and cheerful, able to handle complex issues without notes. He had, I thought, grown considerably in stature since becoming undisputed President of a real country, the new Russia. But many remained suspicious. A fierce and bearded 'investigative journalist' from *Moskovsky Komsomolets* warned me that Yeltsin was a drunken autocrat, open to every manipulation by his entourage, and capable of every abuse of power. When I demurred, the journalist accused me of being seduced by the charm that power exercises. Perhaps he was right. It is the professional deformation of bureaucrats to put the best light on the actions of the man at the top.

But Yeltsin too was a transitional figure, unable to satisfy all the hopes that had been placed in him. His commitment to democracy and to the rule of law was not a matter of intellectual conviction, as it was with Gorbachev. He showed little understanding or interest for the details of economic reform. His manipulation of the constitution and his tolerance of corruption even in his close entourage did nothing to encourage the estab-lishment of an orderly political and economic system, the *Rechtsstaat* which Russia had never had. In an irresistible image, Leon Aron thus describes Yeltsin in his last years of power: 'In the Russian political firmament, Yeltsin looked more and more like a black hole: a giant star exerting enormous gravitational pull on everything around it, but coming to the end of its life, depleted of fuel and incapable of projecting light.'[2]

And yet after wrenching the flame of reform from Gorbachev's failing grasp, Yeltsin did indeed run with it for the vital next lap. Despite the corruption and confusion of his last years, he managed to keep the spark of reform alight. He turned out after all to be a kind of guarantor of a sort of democracy in the making.

With the arrival of Vladimir Putin, Russia's second elected President, the Russian and the foreign press fell into an orgy of fevered speculation: Who was Putin? Did it matter that he had spent the first twenty-five years of his professional life in the KGB? Were the hard men about to take over again?

Putin came straight from the more modest levels of the old *nomen-klatura*. After studying law, he joined the KGB, but after many years service only reached the rank of colonel – at an age when his two predecessors, Gorbachev and Yeltsin, had already begun to make their mark on national politics. After a stint as Deputy Mayor of St Petersburg, he was brought to Moscow to work in the Kremlin administration, and his career was launched. But even as Prime Minister and then as President he seemed inscrutable, a shadow from the secret world. When you looked more closely, there always seemed to be less to Putin than met the eye.

But Putin rapidly became by far the dominant Russian political figure of his day. He was as popular as Yeltsin in his prime. After the years of humiliating corruption and confusion, Russians had began to look for a new man, someone to give them order, someone honest, someone sober, someone who understood how Russia worked. They were not looking for a new dictator, as foreigners feared. They sought a real leader for a time of crisis or national decline, as the British sought a Churchill in 1940 or a Thatcher in 1979. It was a legitimate enough aspiration, and Putin seemed the man to meet it.

Putin was quick to tell the Russian people just how badly off they were. If Russia grew at 8 per cent a year for fifteen years, he said, it could attain a standard of living similar to that of Portugal today. Russia, he said, needed free political parties, a free press and a free, though properly regulated, market economy. Russia must of course stand up for itself. But its place in the world was inevitably diminished and the Empire was dead. Russia's future lay in close cooperation with all its neighbours, but especially with the Europeans and of course with America.

Ordinary people, such as my namesakes the Novgorod Braithwaites, found Putin baffling at first. But the hard truths seemed to filter through. Russians appeared increasingly to accept that theirs was indeed a poor country, and that its natural resources – expensive to extract and transport – were not the advantage that they had always thought. Such realism could only help generate the political will needed if Russia was to get out of its economic and political mess.

All this was just what Yeltsin's critics had been demanding. They found it hard to believe their ears. Did Putin understand what he was saying? Did he mean it? Could he deliver?

Putin's record in his first two years was not unimpressive. He moved quickly to restore an air of authority to the government. He reined in the regional governors, and cut the 'oligarchs' down to size. He dismayed liberals by reining in the press as well, though he fell well short of a real crackdown. He began to get some important economic and legal reforms through a complaisant Duma. He presided over a more lively economy. In the Autumn of 2001 he held a 'Civic Forum' to encourage non-govern-mental organisations: suspicious liberals surmised, no doubt unfairly, that he was trying to stifle the new civil society with kindness. He showed a deft hand in the conduct of Russia's foreign relations. He strengthened links with Russia's neighbours in the Far East. He nudged closer to the Europeans. Rather to everyone's surprise, he had by the middle of 2001 begun to get Russia back onto reasonable terms with the new American Administration as well. The process was reinforced as the two governments discovered a common interest in combating terrorism in the aftermath of the attacks on New York and Washington in September 2001.

Despite the apparent clarity and forcefulness of his public statements, Putin's dominance was not, of course, complete. He had to juggle with contradictory advice from three different bits of his entourage. The still influential remnants of Yeltsin's 'family' struggled to retain shreds of their former power. An apparently influential group of liberal economists pushed for Russia to become a properly functioning part of the world economy. And Russia's Security Council, under the influence of Putin's former colleagues from the KGB, stood up for domestic discipline, Russian greatness and a strong military. These groupings sometimes seemed to be more interested in frustrating their rivals than in the constructive promotion of genuine policy. As so often in Russia, there was a gap between words and deeds.

It was of course depressing to observe the secret policemen preening themselves again, bearers of the 'Chekist philosophy' against which poor Bakatin had fought so hard and so unsuccessfully. But Putin launched no assault on Russia's fledgling democracy. Ordinary people welcomed the stability which, under Putin, seemed to have replaced the roller-coaster politics of the previous decade. Even his critics among the Moscow liberal intelligentsia began to come round to him, comforting themselves with the thought that, almost regardless of its President, the country would continue to move in the right direction, towards greater prosperity without abandoning the democratic gains it had made under his two predecessors.

Gorbachev had set himself the objective of unleashing the frustrated energy and initiative of the Soviet people. This was an ambitious, but not an unattainable goal. Ivan and Pavel Kharitonenko and many of their fellow countrymen, the sons and grandsons of serfs, had shown at the end of the nineteenth century that Russians, too, could shed their servility and generate an impressive capacity for enterprise.

But the old merchant-capitalists cared as much for the respect of their fellow countrymen as for acquiring yachts and villas in the South of France.

They built genuine productive enterprises in the real economy. They were often extravagantly open-handed in their entertainment and their way of life. But they also put a great deal of money into charity and the arts. They returned to society a respectable part of what they took from it. For the most part they obeyed the law, respected the institutions, and abided by the rules. They were close to being real capitalists, as the Western world understood the concept.

The same could not be said of most of their successors a hundred years later. Post-Soviet businessmen were operating in a country where public life and public morals had been corrupted beyond measure by the disasters which had fallen on it since the beginning of the First World War. Greed, a normal driving force in commercial affairs, ran out of control in the last years of the Soviet Union and the first years of the new Russia. People saw, for the first time in their lives, a golden opportunity to enrich themselves. Optimists drew a parallel between the robber barons of the late twentieth century in Russia and their American predecessors at the end of the nineteenth century. Realists pointed out that the robber barons in America were brought to heel because in America the rule of law was effective. The Rockefellers were tamed by the anti-trust law. In Russia the rule of law barely existed, and there were no effective legal instruments to curb the barons.

Change would not happen through the passage of new laws in a society where a corrupt and weak government had little power and few incentives to enforce them. Lectures from foreigners about the need for good corporate governance could do little to help. Real change would happen only as a part of the wider cultural revolution on which Russia had embarked, when a substantial proportion of the 'New Russians' concluded that life without enforceable rules was becoming too unprofitable or too dangerous, and that it would be better for them and their families to enjoy their wealth lawfully, in peace and quiet. By the turn of the new century, some of the former bandits were trying to buy themselves a better public image as good corporate citizens because, as one of them put it, simply making money eventually became boring. He and his fellows wanted to enjoy their wealth peacefully in a modern and civilised country; and they wanted to be able to answer with a reasonably good conscience their grandchildren's questions about what they had done during the Great Capitalist Revolution. Even if it was no more than hypocrisy, what La Rochefoucauld called the homage of vice to virtue, it was a first step in the right direction.

Alongside the bandits – sometimes in alliance with them – educated Russians went into the new capitalist professions as bankers, accountants, consultants. This growing middle class found that they could at last afford things taken for granted by their opposite numbers in the West: decent bathrooms in their cramped apartments, a good education for their children, a car, the occasional holiday abroad. Russians travelled abroad in rapidly increasing numbers: from half a million in 1991 to nearly twenty million five years later. These were by no means only the rich 'New Russians' and their families. Middle-class mothers took their children round the museums of Europe. Working-class people from Siberia visited their British sons- and daughters-in-law. The old policy of closing the frontiers to keep the Russian people from contamination by the outside world had been a recipe for economic stagnation. Now it had perforce been abandoned. Despite the financial crash in 1998, the new middle class proved more durable and resilient than many people had expected. By the year 2001 the official statistics were claiming that more than a third of the population of Russia belonged to it.

One group of people still nursed a particular grief. The intelligentsia lamented that the old Russian culture was dying, submerged in a flood of cheap American imports. At the end of 1997 Daniel Granin, a distinguished representative of the old Leningrad liberal intelligentsia, wrote sadly that the two-hundred-year-old history of the Russian intelligentsia was coming to an end. In every difficulty the Russian intelligentsia had preserved the moral categories of honour, charity, conscientious work, decency and honesty. But the 'democratic' politicians for whom the intelligentsia had demonstrated in 1989 no longer needed them: they needed bankers instead. The intelligentsia no longer led the way, because it had lost both its way and its function. Was it really true that Russia faced the fate of other capitalist countries, where there was no intelligentsia, merely a collection of intellectuals? Granin feared the worst. [3]

With the new pluralism, the role of the intelligentsia as the moral voice of the nation and the only source of alternative political opinion was bound to decline. The heavily subsidised scientific and cultural establishment of the Soviet Union was sore hit by the widespread withdrawal of funds which took place under Yeltsin. But after a dispiriting decline, music, the theatre and the cinema began to flourish once again. Russian singers conquered the opera houses of the world. Audiences flooded back to the theatre, to see avant-garde productions which would have been banned in the Soviet time. The old state publishing houses collapsed, and officially approved authors could no longer count on print-runs of tens or hundreds of thousands. But small commercial publishing houses began to pop up all over the country. Do-it-yourself books on the law, on foreign languages, on business methods, poured off the presses. In the last year of the Soviet Union some 1,500 new titles were published annually. By the end of the 1990s the number had increased to 12,000. Pornography and thrillers proliferated. But so did a widening range of classical and modern literature. The bustling bookshops were crowded with buyers. Competent and ingenious authors, no longer the conscience of the nation, began to produce a literature of high quality but only moderate seriousness. The new middle class fell on it with enthusiasm. Russian culture was acquiring new life without losing all the old pungency.

Russians naturally saw little constructive purpose in endless and unrelenting self-flagellation. Yet the more thoughtful among them suffered from an uneasy feeling that there was much in Russian history of which they could not be proud, from a sense that in most measurable ways Western societies had been more successful than Russia, from the fear that, as the American scholar-diplomat George Kennan once put it, 'the term "Russia" does not really signify a national society destined to know power and majesty, but only a vast unconquerable expanse of misery, poverty, inefficiency, and mud.'[4] Pushkin put it in an extreme form: 'Of course I despise my country from top to toe,' though he added, unsurprisingly, 'but I am irritated when a foreigner feels the same.'[5]

Successive Russian regimes tried to construct a state ideology to offset these unhelpful obsessions. Count Benkendorf, the Tsarist secret policeman, castigated the philosopher Chaadaev for his gloomy analysis of Russia's past: 'Russia's past was worthy of respect; her present is nothing if not splendid; as for her future, it is beyond the reach of even the boldest imagination. That, my dear fellow, is how one should understand and write about Russian history.'[6] Stalin spread the word that all the most significant devices of the industrial age had been invented in Russia.

Not surprisingly, the disasters and humiliations which the collapse of the Soviet Union heaped on the Russian people generated their own kind of fevered nationalism as an antidote. Old myths about the peculiar nature of the Russian destiny and the Russian soul found a new lease of life. The Messianism of the Russian Communists had been the mirror image of the Messianism of Dostoevsky and his fellows. Pallid versions of these old debates re-emerged in the new Russia. Yeltsin set up a committee which produced a new version of the 'Russian National Idea'. It was no more convincing than Benkendorf's. But at least Russia was never gripped by the aggressive nationalism which overtook Germany after the humiliation of defeat in the First World War. Despite widespread fears abroad, neither

Pamyat nor Zhirinovsky and those who thought like them gave the tone to politics in the new Russia.

This Russian particularism was nevertheless a damaging barrier to change. It helped to protect Russians from a sense of responsibility for what had happened in their country, for the massive injustices, the arbitrariness of power, and for the failure – and it was a failure of the Russians themselves, which they could not reasonably blame on others – to create the institutions and the laws which would have kept injustice in check. The myth of Russian uniqueness, the promise that Russia was destined to show the light to less fortunate peoples, was a soothing but irrelevant guide to Russia's future.

All Russians believed that their country should remain 'One and Indivisible'. Despite much talk at the time, it was never likely that Russia itself would break up after the Soviet collapse. But Russia's size and geography – of which Russians remained so proud – still imposed almost insoluble problems of national security. Russia had the longest frontier in the world, and more neighbours than any other. In shape it resembled a tadpole. The brains, heart, and stomach were in Europe. The Siberian tail, fleshless and extended, was potentially at the mercy of any enemy who cared to snip it off. Russia no longer faced a military threat to the West, though Russian generals contemplating the enlargement of NATO were not convinced of that. But no Russian general could ignore the possibility that one day, perhaps far distant, the Chinese would eventually decide to reorganise things at their end of the continent. Even some of Russia's smaller neighbours posed the threat of political instability, or as sources of drugs, crime, and terrorism. Imperial powers used to deal with such problems by raiding and then occupying the turbulent territories beyond the *limes*. The Russians no longer had the strength or the will to do that. But they would certainly need, and perhaps eventually create, a modern military force to manage these problems, with a competent nuclear component if only to deter China. For the foreseeable future Russia's Southern and Eastern frontiers would not resemble the peaceful border which now divided those old enemies, France and Germany.

When the Soviet Union collapsed, Westerners fell into unjustified optimism, just as they did after the Tsar was overthrown in 1917. Russians would, they hoped, soon become prosperous liberal democrats just like the rest of us. Western feelings of goodwill towards Russia were widespread and genuine. But when the facile optimism was disappointed, Western euphoria faded, and Russophobia returned. It fed, and was fed by, old-fashioned Russian nationalism, laced by resentment at what Russians saw as Western triumphalism at the outcome of the Cold War. Both sides seemed uncomfortable at the absence of a clear enemy and the loss of the simple certainties of confrontation.

The new Russophobia was not the paranoia of the Cold War, which had derived from a real threat. It was much more like the settled paranoia of the nineteenth century, the paranoia of *The Times* of 1829. Western governments struggled to maintain a balance. The new Russophobia was expressed not by governments, but in the statements of out-of-office politicians, the publications of academic experts, the sensational writings of journalists, and the products of the entertainment industry. It was fuelled by those who argued that the Russian Orthodox civilisation was doomed to remain apart from the civilisation of the West. The outpouring of films and novels in which the villainous KGB officer was replaced by the villainous Russian mafioso was deeply wounding to ordinary Russians. Modern communications gave them access to what was said about their country by foreigners and nourished their xenophobia.

Why was Russophobia so vigorously alive and well at the beginning of the new century? Russia was a very large country, a close neighbour right on the flank of Europe, an ex-empire with a history of repressive government. And Russia was still theoretically capable of blowing us all to pieces. All this seemed rather menacing. But it was hardly sufficient to account for the storm of criticism and even abuse with which Russia was continually assailed.

Much that the Russians were doing at the turn of the century, in Chechnya and at home, could legitimately be criticised. But foreign criticism of Russia sometimes lacked measure, and fell into emotional self-indulgence. Many Russians concluded that the West was judging them by double standards, or that the West's criticism was driven by sentiment, by its own domestic politics, or by some sinister plot to exploit and undermine their country. So they simply shut their ears, convinced that the West did not after all have anything useful to offer them.

In the decade after the fall of the Soviet Union, a debate took place of almost childlike simplicity. Who Lost Russia? Was the ineptness or worse of the Clinton Administration to blame? Was it the arrogant and impractical narrow-mindedness of the World Bank and the International Monetary Fund? Was it the innate incompetence and depravity of the Russians themselves? In Russia there was a similar debate. Was the degradation of a once great country the result of Gorbachev's treachery? The erratic drunkenness of Yeltsin? The misguided, perhaps the corrupt, enthusiasms of his young reformers? The machinations of the CIA?

There was of course incompetence on both sides. Foreign as well as Russian villains, con-men, fraudulent consultants, battened on the corpse of the Soviet Union and got rich. There were moments when Russia looked as though it might lurch into a Latin American morass of social injustice, rotten government, and criminalised business. Some Westerners, especially in Washington, began to argue that it didn't much matter who had lost Russia, since Russia was finished anyway. The declining birth-rate, the fall in life expectancy, the return of old diseases like tuberculosis and the spread of new ones like AIDS; the increase in violent crime and corruption; the failure to build viable institutions of civil society and government; the inability to adapt to the requirements of modern industry and agriculture; the decay of the military – all these meant that Russia was doomed to irrelevance or worse.

Democracy and the free market are a matter of deep-rooted culture. The difficulties and reverses faced by Russian reform had plenty of precedents in the history of other countries. The struggle for power and riches which broke out in Russia in the 1990s resembled the rough and ready division of property in England after the Norman Conquest and the Dissolution of the Monasteries, a process equally accompanied by cynical corruption and outright violence. Securely rooted in the English tradition of freedom under the law, it took the Americans three generations and a bloody civil war to clarify the issue of states' rights, one of the central points of the constitution they had written for themselves. It took another three or four generations for them to establish a secure franchise for all their citizens of whatever race, sex or colour.

Under Gorbachev and Yeltsin the Russians started from a much less promising base. Within a decade, despite the confusion and the distress, the skulduggery and the setbacks, Russia was a pluralistic society. Its frontiers were open. The press and the broadcast media were free by the standards of the past, though still in thrall to financial or political power. The political police had been curbed, though not sufficiently. The political process was corrupt and heavily personalised. The party system was undeveloped. The electoral process was graceless. But it was unlike anything that had happened in Russia before. All in all, it was not such a bad beginning for the new Russian democracy.

How soon, if at all, Russia would enjoy a finished democracy or a genuine civil society nevertheless remained a question much discussed among Russians and foreigners alike. The intellectually lazy took the easy route. Because Russia had always had an empire, they argued, Russians would always be driven by imperial instincts. Because Russia had always been an autocracy, democracy could never flourish there and the Russians would always demand a strong leader backed by an oppressive police. Because the Russian economy had always been dominated by the state, Russians would never be capable of orderly free enterprise. Because Russians had always been emotional, warm-hearted, patient, disorderly, drunken and mendacious, they would always remain so. That was after all the 'Russian national character'.

In fact modern history is littered with examples of countries making quite sharp changes of course. In the past two centuries France, Germany, and Spain abandoned authoritarian forms of government and turned to democracy. In the twentieth century the landborne and seaborne empires of Central and Western Europe were dismantled. The West Europeans devised institutions which stood a reasonable chance of ending the bloody wars which had torn them apart for centuries. Countries of the Far East, which until the second half of the twentieth century were despised for their innate inability to adopt the disciplines of market economics, turned out to be surprisingly good at competing with their Western mentors. History and geography may have placed Russia at some distance from the liberal European tradition, but there are no secure grounds for thinking that Russia is uniquely incapable of overcoming its past.

My Russian friends seemed to believe that an ambassador shares the astrologer's gift of foretelling the future and used to ask me what would happen to their country. I told them that I did not know. But I thought that over three generations of bumpy progress, seventy years of cultural revolution punctuated by political and economic crisis, Russia could reasonably hope to achieve a recognisably liberal political and economic system. It would be a Russian system, differing in important ways from the American or even the European model of democracy. But if Russia was to become prosperous, comfortable, and respected by its neighbours, its future political and economic arrangements would have to be largely based on the same principles which have worked elsewhere. The 'Russian Way' was a myth.

My friends had been brought up on a diet of Communist promises that a Radiant Future lay just round the next corner but one. They were not best pleased at having to contemplate yet again the bitter fact that they themselves would not see the end of the road. But most of them knew that the only practical response to Russia's troubles was a kind of guarded optimism, and an acceptance that it was for the Russian people – for the underlings, not the bosses – to take responsibility for their own fate at last. Despite their intense unhappiness with the way things seemed to be turning out in the present, successive opinion polls showed that a majority of Russians saw no point in returning to the past, and believed that in future things would take a turn for the better, if only for their grand-children.

As for the rest of us, we would for very many years to come need patience, steady nerves, and a firm grasp of the wise advice which George Kennan formulated half a century ago when Stalin was still alive and kicking:

> When Soviet power has run its course, or when its personalities and spirit begin to change (for the ultimate outcome could be one or the other) let us not hover nervously over the people who come after, applying litmus papers daily to their political complexions to find out whether they answer to our concept of 'democrats'.
>
> Give them time; let them be Russians; let them work out their internal problems in their own manner. The ways by which people advance towards dignity and enlightenment in government are things that constitute the deepest and most intimate processes of national life. There is nothing less understandable to foreigners, nothing in which foreign influence can do less good.[7]

Notes and Comments

Prologue

Epigraph from George Buchanan, *My Mission to Russia* (London, 1923), vol. 2, p. 247.

1 It was in fact the fourth revolution Russia underwent in the twentieth century. The first was the revolution of 1905, which ushered in a period of constitutional monarchy. The second was the revolution in February 1917 which overthrew the Tsar. The third was the Bolshevik coup d'état in October 1917.

1 The View across the River

Epigraph from Aleksandr Pushkin, *Eugene Onegin*, 7, xxxvi, tr. Oliver Elton (London, 1937).

1 'The Devil, having nothing else to do / Went off to tempt my Lady Pettigrue. / My lady, tempted by a private whim, / To his extreme annoyance, tempted him.' (Hilaire Belloc)
2 *Stolitsa i Usadba* [Town and Country], no. 32, 1915, pp. 4–9. This also contains photographs of the estate.
3 The incident of the naval officer's suicide is described by Bruce Lockhart in *Memoirs of a British Agent* (repr. London, 1937). The account does not convince, but leaves open the possibility that the suicide took place that night, but not in the Kharitonenko House.

4 The prototype of the *Ilya Muromets* first flew in 1913, only four years after Bleriot made his precarious hop across the English Channel. It was designed by a 23-year-old engineer, Ivan Sikorski, who later made his name as a designer of helicopters. The *Ilya Muromets* was not much smaller that the RAF's *Lancaster* bomber and carried a crew of at least four. It operated successfully on the Eastern Front throughout the First World War, and only two aircraft were lost to enemy action. There is a full-sized replica of the *Ilya Muromets* at the spectacular museum of Russian aviation history at Monino outside Moscow. See Harry Woodman, *Ilya Muromets* (Berkhamsted, 2000).

2 The Russians are Coming

1 Sigmund von Herberstein, *Description of Moscow and Muscovy 1557*, ed. B. Picard (London, 1989).

2 Turbervile's homesick doggerel and the instructions of the Muscovy Company to their representative in Moscow come from Richard Hakluyt's *Voyages*, vol. 1 (Everyman edn, London, 1967).

3 Catherine the Great's theory of autocracy is quoted by Tibor Szamuely in *The Russian Tradition* (London, 1988).

4 Pushkin's remark about the nature of the Russian *bunt* comes in *Kapitanskaya Dochka* (*The Captain's Daughter*), in *Works* (Leningrad, 1978), vol. 6, p. 349. *Bunt* is usually translated as 'mutiny' or 'rebellion'. The first implies a military context. The second implies some organisation and geographical extent. A *bunt* is elemental and mindless, as Pushkin says. 'Violent backlash' may give the right idea (a thought for which I am indebted to Strobe Talbott).

5 Benkendorf's cynical view of the law is quoted by Richard Pipes, *Russia under the Old Regime* (London, 1974).

6 Kzhizhanich's advocacy of closed frontiers is quoted by Szamuely in *The Russian Tradition*, p. 83.

7 Patriarch Tikhon's commination of the Bolsheviks is quoted by Richard Pipes in *Russia under the Bolshevik Regime* (London, 1994).

8 Kostomarov's remarks on mendacity in the time of Boris Godunov come in *Russkaya Istoriya v Zhizneopisaniyakh ee Glavnykh Deyatelei* [Russian History through the Lives of its Main Protagonists] (repr. Moscow 1990–2).

9 Hakluyt, *Voyages*, vol. 1, p. 390.

10 Teddy Roosevelt's pained remarks about Russian mendacity are quoted

by George Kennan in *Russia and the West under Lenin and Stalin* (London, 1961).

11 Vladimir Gusev was the television critic who saw Pushkin as the last of the saints. He is quoted by C. Nepomnyashchny, *Abram Tertz and the Poetics of Crime* (New Haven and London, 1995).

12 Che Ka (ЧК) are the initials for the Russian phrase 'Extraordinary Committee', a mild title for a murderous organisation. The Cheka set out their objective of exterminating the bourgeoisie in their house magazine *Krasny Terror* [Red Terror] in November 1918: quoted in Frederic Zuckermann, *The Tsarist Secret Police* (London, 1996).

13 Peter the Great's remark about Russia emerging into the light is quoted by V. P. Potemkin, *Istoriya Diplomatii* [History of Diplomacy] (Moscow, 1941), p. 270.

14 The general who feared the 'overgrown power of Russia' was John Mitchell, whose *Thoughts on Tactics and Military Organisation together with an Enquiry into the Power and Position of Russia* was published in London in 1838. He is quoted in Paul Dibb, *The Soviet Union: The Incomplete Superpower* (London, 1988).

15 The voices of those who were sceptical about the Russian threat come from J. H. Gleason, *The Genesis of Russophobia in Great Britain* (Cambridge, Mass., 1950).

16 The acronym 'MAD' was coined by Robert McNamara, the US Secretary of Defense at the time. The phrase was half ironic. The reality was terrifying.

17 Lawrence Freedman, *Kennedy's Wars* (London, 2000), p. 180. Presidents Eisenhower and Kennedy were equally sceptical of the arguments used by their military.

18 Geoffrey Hosking, *Russia and the Russians* (London, 2001), p. 515.

19 In America it has been possible for many years to write serious history, based on official documents, on matters such as the official analysis of the Soviet threat, the evolution of deterrence theory, and the Western military response. By contrast, the British obsession with official secrecy – 'secrecy useful and secrecy useless', as Custine would have called it – left British historians with meagre fare until the Major government decided in 1992 to declassify Cabinet documents on nuclear military affairs and assessments of the Soviet threat by the Joint Intelligence Committee. Although they still have access only to documents at least thirty years old, British historians are beginning to take full advantage of the opportunities now available to them. In *The Hidden Hand* (London, 2001), Richard J. Aldrich describes the difficulties that historians of intelligence matters face even when governments are willing to release a selection of relevant

documents. Peter Hennessy's *The Secret State* (London, 2002) casts a riveting light on the way in which, in the decades immediately after the Second World War, successive British Prime Ministers, advised by dedicated officials and military officers, took decisions potentially affecting the life and death of the whole nation without even informing all their Cabinet colleagues. In the circumstances of the day, this reticence was inescapable. But it is a sad comment on the way in which democracy, too, was distorted by the Cold War.

20 Leon Aron, *Boris Yeltsin: A Revolutionary Life* (London, 2000), p. 147.

21 Report by the Joint Intelligence Committee of 15 Dec. 1969, *Documents on British Policy Overseas*, series III, vol. 1, (London, 1997), p. 200

22 Anne Hessing Cahn, *Killing Détente* (University Park, Pa., 1998), p. 124.

23 Ibid., p. 169.

24 Frances Fitzgerald, *Way Out There in the Blue* (New York, 2000), p. 150, quotes both Jones and the article by Gray and Payne in *Foreign Affairs*.

25 John Newhouse, *The Nuclear Age* (London, 1989), p. 289.

26 M. R. Beschloss and S. Talbott comment: 'Americans who voted for Reagan in 1980 had little idea that on this issue they were electing a radical, a heretic, an idealist, a romantic, a nuclear abolitionist', *At the Highest Levels* (London, 1993), p. 113.

27 In an admirable display of openness, the CIA published at the end of 1999 a selection of intelligence assessments covering the period 1988 to 1991, and organised an academic conference to discuss the material. Not surprisingly the CIA's analytical record is mixed. Neither the CIA nor the American national interest appears to have suffered from this bit of Glasnost. But it is hard to imagine their British opposite numbers following suit. The assessment referred to above, NIE-11-89, is in B. J. Fischer (ed.), *At Cold War's End* (Washington DC, 1999, p. 227). Fischer's introduction is an admirably succinct and balanced account of the period 1989–91 and the evolving attitudes of the American intelligence analysts.

28 Fischer, *At Cold War's End*, p. xii.

29 Cahn, *Killing Détente*, pp. 1–2

30 These and other remarks by Mrs Thatcher come from her memoirs, *The Downing Street Years* (London, 1995).

31 Ibid., p. 480.

32 *Demokratizatsia* – 'democratisation' – is not, of course, the same thing as democracy: it is the process by which you move away from authoritarianism. Glasnost – 'openness' – is not the same as freedom of speech, though by 1989 the Soviet press was beginning to lose sight of the

distinction between freedom and anarchy. Perestroika – 'reconstruction' – implied rightly enough that Gorbachev's aim was to reform not overthrow the Soviet system. Many Western sceptics sneered at all three slogans, which they regarded as a smokescreen behind which Gorbachev intended to revive the old Communist dream of universality.

3 The Flight of the Bumble Bee

1 Beschloss and Talbott, *At the Highest Levels*, p. 48.

2 The Windsor menu is recorded in I. Korchilov, *Translating History* (London, 1997), p. 224.

3 A. Chernyaev, *Shest' Let s Gorbachevym* [Six Years with Gorbachev], (Moscow, 1993), p. 289.

4 Kryuchkov's memoirs (*Lchnoe Delo* [Personal File], Moscow, 1996) are not necessarily reliable, but give a fascinating picture of the secret police mentality. They contain moments of unconscious humour, as when he complains that those who jailed him after the August 1991 putsch refused to let him see his lawyer.

6 Beschloss and Talbott, *At the Highest Levels*, p. 356.

4 Democracy Comes to the Soviet Union

1 Aron, *Boris Yeltsin*, p. 264n.

2 M. S. Gorbachev, *Zhizn' i Reformy* [Life and Reforms] (Moscow, 1995), p. 279.

3 Ryzhkov's appraisal of his 1989 government team comes in his disappointing and self-regarding memoir *Perestroika: Istoriya Predatelstv* [Perestroika: A Story of Betrayal] (Moscow, 1992).

4 Beschloss and Talbott, *At the Highest Levels*, p. 84.

5 Ibid., p. 92.

5 The Ashes of Victory

Epigraph from Witte, Memoirs, quoted by Paul Dibb, The Soviet Union: The Incomplete Superpower (London, 1988), p. 194.

1 The ceremony with the flags at Borodino is portrayed in Ozerov's fascinating series of films about the war on the Eastern front made over more than twenty years from the late 1960s. The films are a lavish

reconstruction of events, employing huge numbers of men and machines, and altogether last about as long as *The Ring of the Nibelungs*. Although the series is made from the point of view of the Soviet armed forces, it is reasonably accurate and casts a fascinating historiographical light on attitudes towards Stalin's wartime role. I have no independent confirmation of the story of the banners.

2 The figures for Soviet war casualties given by respectable sources vary between twenty million and twenty-seven million. Those given here come from Martin Gilbert, *Second World War* (London, 1989). John Keegan in *The Second World War* (London, 1989) says that over four million German servicemen died. Nearly six hundred thousand German civilians were killed by bombing. Over a million German civilians died in the forced expulsions from the East at the end of the war.

3 The story about the defecting Soviet frigate is on pp. 268–70 of *The Threat* by Andrew Cockburn (New York, 1983). Cockburn gives many examples of the inadequacy of Soviet equipment. Needless to say, his views were not accepted by Western defence establishments at the time.

4 Zhukov's lament for his ignorance comes from his memoirs and is quoted in H. Shukman (ed.), *Stalin's Generals* (London, 1997), p. 397.

5 Custine visited Russia briefly in 1839. His *La Russie en 1839* has been a handbook on Russia for foreigners ever since. Russians ruefully recognise the accuracy of many of Custine's sharp comments though they rightly point out that his wholly negative picture is unfairly one-sided.

6 E. Shevardnadze, *The Future Belongs to Freedom* (London, 1991), p. 132.

7 Ibid., p. 134.

8 John Major's remarks were later published verbatim by the Russian Foreign Ministry.

9 Chernyaev, *Shest' Let s Gorbachevym*, p. 299

10 Thatcher, *The Downing Street Years*, p. 794.

11 Quoted in Fischer, *At Cold War's End*, p. xii.

12 Shevardnadze was particularly angry about the way the Soviet generals had misled him about the purpose of the sophisticated radar system in Krasnoyarsk, which the Americans believed was part of a new anti-ballistic missile system, banned under their 1973 treaty with the Soviets.

13 One account of Western attempts to get to the bottom of the Soviet biological warfare programme is in Mark Urban, *UK Eyes Alpha* (London, 1996), p. 129ff.

14 G. D. G. Murrell, *Russia's Transition to Democracy* (Brighton, 1997), p. 61.

15 Shevardnadze's sensible remarks about the nature of national greatness are quoted in *Literaturnaya Gazeta*, 18 April 1990.

16 Pavel Palazhchenko, *My Years with Gorbachev and Shevardnadze* (University Park, Pa., 1997), p. 182.

17 The figures for the size of Russian divisions in 1998 were given by General Kvashnin, Chief of Staff, to *Argumenty i Fakty* on 23 June 1998.

6 Fraying at the Edges

Epigraph: The Ukrainian deputies' remarks were recorded in *The Economist*, 7 May 1994.

1 Dostoevsky's belief in the Russians' peculiar ability to promote the brotherhood of mankind can be found spread throughout his works. This one comes from his speech at the dedication of the first statue to Pushkin in 1880.

2 Gorbachev's remarks on the openness of the Russian nation were broadcast in February 1991, and are recorded by Boldin, his executive assistant who joined the coup against him, in his rancorous memoir *Ten Years that Shook the Kremlin* (New York, 1994).

3 The Western scholar who predicted the break-up of the Soviet empire was Hélène Carrère d'Encausse, in *L'empire éclaté* (Paris, 1978).

4 John Baddeley's very readable *The Russian Conquest of the Caucasus* was published in London in 1906.

5 Sobchak's judgement on the Tbilisi massacre is in the first volume of his memoirs, *Khozhdenie vo Vlast'* [The Road to Power] (Moscow, 1991), p. 93.

6 Beschloss and Talbott, *At the Highest Levels*, p. 95.

7 Tolstoy's story *Hadji Murat* was one of his last works. It is set in 1851. Some of Yeltsin's people regretted not advising him to reread it before embarking on his own attempt to conquer the Chechens. The passage quoted comes from chapter 17.

8 Huntington, *The Clash of Civilisations* (New York, 1996), p. 51. Huntington's other thesis – that Orthodox Christianity is doomed to remain in conflict with 'Western Christianity' – is no more likely to prove correct than our grandparents' similar belief about the relationship between Protestant and Catholic Christianity.

7 The Lurch to the Right

1 A. Brown, *The Gorbachev Factor* (Oxford, 1996), pp. 105–6.

2 Chernyaev, *Shest' Let s Gorbachevym*, p. 336.

3 Polls conducted by the well-regarded VTsIOM showed that Gorbachev remained the most popular politician in the Soviet Union until May 1990, when he was overtaken by Yeltsin (see Brown, *The Gorbachev Factor*).

4 Chernyaev, *Shest' Let s Gorbachevym*, p. 337.

8 Diary of a Coup

Epigraph from A. Lukyanov, *Perevorot Mnimy̆ i Nastoyashchy* [The Fake Coup and the Real Coup] (Moscow, 1993).

1 A garbled version of the story of Major's message to Yeltsin is contained in Urban, *UK Eyes Alpha*, p. 190. The incident was also referred to in television programmes about the Secret Intelligence Service in 1993.

2 Linda Colley gives a breakdown of North American support for and against the Revolution in *Britons* (New Haven, 1992), p. 137.

3 Percy Cradock, the chairman of the British Joint Intelligence Committe at the time, describes London's reactions to the coup in *In Pursuit of British Interests* (London, 1997). The background to Bush's warning is in Jack Matlock's *Autopsy of an Empire* (New York, 1995). Both he and Chernyaev describe how Matlock conveyed the message to Gorbachev, who dismissed it. The two accounts coincide except in minor details. The CIA's analysis of the prospects for a coup is described by the then head of the Agency, Robert Gates, in *From the Shadows* (New York, 1996).

4 Congress's views on the fragility of intelligence are contained in the supplement to *Defense for a New Era: Lessons of the Persian Gulf War*, House Armed Services Committee, August 1993, quoted by Mark Urban, *UK Eyes Alpha*.

9 The Rubble of the Dictatorship

1 Rutskoi's views about the best way to pacify Chechens, and Yeltsin's rejection of the use of force there, are quoted in C. Gall and T. de Waal, *Chechnya: A Small Victorious War* (London, 1997), p. 97.

10 Arguing about the Economy

1 Brown, *The Gorbachev Factor*, p. 135.

2 The higher estimate of Soviet defence expenditure is taken from

Vladimir Mau's *The Political History of Economic Reform in Russia, 1985–1994* (London, 1996), p. 5.

3 Sakharov's warning to Brezhnev is taken from *The Awakening of the Soviet Union*, Geoffrey Hosking's 1988 Reith Lectures.

4 Gorbachev, *Zhizni i Reformy*, pp. 327ff.

5 Aron, *Boris Yeltsin*, pp. 90, 281–4, 295.

6 *Izvestia*, 11 July 1989.

7 Gaidar's views come from his memoir of the period *Dni Porazhenii i Pobed* [Days of Defeat and Victory] (Moscow, 1996).

8 Lytton Strachey's account of the British preparations to rescue General Gordon comes from *Eminent Victorians* (London, 1984), p. 247.

11 Towards a Radiant Future?

1 These jokes are recorded in *Istoriya SSSR v Anekdotakh 1917–1992* [A History of the USSR in Jokes, 1917–1922], (Moscow, 1991). The book is a hilarious revelation of what the Soviet people thought, year by year, about the Soviet reality.

2 Aron, *Boris Yeltsin*, p. 572.

3 Granin's article 'The Russian intelligentsia departs' appeared in *Izvestia*, 5 November 1997.

4 George Kennan's comment about Russian mud comes from a paper which he wrote in 1994 called 'Russia – seven years later', annexed to his *Memoirs 1925–1950* (Boston, 1967), p. 505.

5 Pushkin's disobliging remark about his own country comes in a letter of 27 May 1826 to Prince Vyazemsky.

6 Beckendorf's vision of the sweep of Russian history is quoted by Peter Squire in *The Third Department* (Cambridge, 1968), p. 232.

7 Kennan's remarkable prediction about Russia after Communism was made in an article 'America and the Russian future', which was published in *Foreign Affairs*, April 1951. It was drawn to my attention by Vladimir Sobell. I am most grateful to him and to George Kennan for giving permission to use the extract.

Bibliography

The number of books which have been written about Russia is beyond count. The events surrounding the collapse of the Soviet Union have received particular attention at the hands of academics, economists and journalists. Most of the protagonists have written their own accounts – politicians, diplomats, officials, intelligence chiefs from almost all the countries involved, including Russia, America, Germany, and Britain. What follows is merely a selection of the literature, on which I drew in preparing this book.

Istoriya SSSR v Anekdotakh, 1917–1922 (A history of the USSR in jokes, 1917–1922), Moscow, 1991.

Kto yest kto v Rossii [Who's Who in Russia], Moscow, 1993.

Stolitsa i Usadba [Town & Country], 1915, no 32.

Albats, Y., *KGB: State within a State*, London, 1995.

Aldrich, R. J., *The Hidden Hand*, London, 2001.

Aron, L., *Boris Yeltsin: A Revolutionary Life*, London, 2000.

Aslund, A., *How Russia Became a Market Economy*, Washington DC, 1995.

Baddeley, J. B., *The Russian Conquest of the Caucasus*, London, 1906.

Baedeker, K., *Baedeker's Russia 1914*, repr. London, 1971.

Bakatin, V. V., *Izbavlenie ot KGB* [Getting Rid of the KGB], Moscow, 1992.

Baring, M., *The Mainsprings of Russia*, London, 1914.

Baron, S. H. (ed), *The Travels of Olearius in Seventeenth-Century Russia*, Stanford, 1967.

Belloc, H., *Complete Verse*, London, 1991.

Bennett, G. and Hamilton, K. (eds), *Documents on British Policy Overseas*, series III, vol. 1: *Britain and the Soviet Union, 1968–1972*, London, 1997.

Berdyaev, N. A., *Istoria i Smysl Russkogo Kommunizma* [The Roots and Meaning of Russian Communism], Moscow, 1990.

Berton, K. and Freeman, J., *The British Embassy Moscow: The Kharitonenko Mansion*, London, 1991.

Beschloss, M. R. and Talbott, S., *At the Highest Levels*, London, 1993.

Billington, J., *The Icon and the Axe*, New York, 1970.

Blasi, J., Kroumova, M. and Kruse, D., *Kremlin Capitalism*, Ithaca, N.Y., 1997.

Boldin, V., *Ten Years that Shook the Kremlin*, New York, 1994.

Brown, A., *The Gorbachev Factor*, Oxford, 1996.

Brown, A. (ed.), *The Soviet Union: A Biographical Dictionary*, New York, 1990.

Brown, A., Kaser, M. and Smith, G. S. (eds), *The Cambridge Encyclopedia of Russia and the Former Soviet Union*, Cambridge, 1994.

Brumfield, W. C., *Gold in Azure*, Boston, 1983.

Buchanan, G., *My Mission to Russia*, London, 1923.

Cahn, A. H., *Killing Détente*, University Park, Pa., 1998.

Carrère d'Encausse, H., *L'Empire éclaté*, Paris, 1978.

Cockburn, A., *The Threat*, New York, 1983.

Colley, L., *Britons*, London, 1992.

Conquest, R., *The Great Terror*, London, 1968.

Conquest, R., *The Harvest of Sorrow*, London, 1988.

Cradock, P., *In Pursuit of British Interests*, London, 1997.

Custine, Marquis de, *Journey for our Time* tr. from *La Russie en 1839*, London, 1980.

Davies, R.W. (ed.), *From Tsarism to the New Economic Policy*, London, 1990.

Dibb, P., *The Soviet Union: The Incomplete Superpower*, London, 1988.

Dunlop, J. B., *The Rise of Russia and the Fall of the Soviet Empire*, Princeton, 1993.

Edmonds, R., *Pushkin: The Man and his Age*, London, 1994.

English, R., *Russia and the Idea of the West*, New York, 2000.

Figes, O., *A People's Tragedy*, London, 1996.

Fischer, B. B. (ed.), *At Cold War's End*, Washington DC, 1999.

Fitzgerald, F., *Way Out There in the Blue*, New York, 2000.

Freedman, L., *Kennedy's Wars*, London, 2000.

Freeland, C., *Sale of the Century*, New York, 2000.

Gaddis, J. L., *We Now Know*, Oxford, 1997.

Gall, C. and de Waal, T., *Chechnya: A Small Victorious War*, London, 1997.

Garton Ash, T., *The File*, London, 1998.

Gates, R., *From the Shadows*, New York, 1966.

Gerschenkron, A., *Europe in the Russian Mirror*, Cambridge, 1970.

Gilbert, M., *Second World War*, London, 1989.

Gleason, J. H., *The Genesis of Russophobia in Great Britain*, Cambridge, Mass., 1950.

Goldmann, M., *Lost Opportunity*, New York, 1994.

Gorbachev, M. S., *The August Coup*, London, 1991.

Gorbachev, M. S., *Zhizn' i Reformy* [Life and Reforms], Moscow, 1995.

Gregory, P. R., *Before Command*, Princeton, 1994.

Grey, I., *Ivan and the Unification of Russia*, London, 1973.

Grossman, V. S., *Zhizn' i Sudba* [Life and Fate], 1988.

Grossman, V. S., *Vse techet* [Forever Flowing], Evanston, Ill., 1997.

Hakluyt, R., *Voyages*, vol. 1, London, 1967.

Hennessy, P., *The Secret State*, London, 2002.

Herberstein, S. von, *Description of Moscow and Muscovy 1557*, London, 1989.

Hertz, N., *Russian Business Relationships*, London, 1997.

Hosking, G., *The Awakening of the Soviet Union* (Reith Lectures), London, 1988.

Hosking, G., *Russia and the Russians*, London, 2001.

Howe, G., *Conflict of Loyalty*, London, 1995.

Huntington, S., *The Clash of Civilizations*, New York, 1996.

Johnson, J., *A Fistful of Rubles*, Ithaca, N.Y., 2000.

Kagarlitsky, B., *The Thinking Reed*, London, 1988.

Kennan, G. F., *Russia and the West under Lenin and Stalin*, London, 1961.

Kennan, G. F., *Memoirs, 1925–1950*, Boston, 1967.

Kennedy, P., *The Rise and Fall of the Great Powers*, London, 1988.

Kiessler, R. and Elbe, F., *Ein runder Tisch mit scharfen Ecken* [A Round Table with Sharp Edges], Bonn, 1993.

Korchilov, I., *Translating History*, London, 1997.

Korzhakov, A., *Yeltsin: Rasvet i Zakat* [Yeltsin: Dawn and Dusk], Moscow, 1997.

Kostomarov, N. I., *Russkaya Istoriya v Zhizneopisaniyakh ee Glavnykh Deyatelei* [Russian History through the Lives of its Main Actors], repr. of 1874 edn, 3 vols, Moscow, 1990–2.

Kozyrev, A., *Preobrazhenie* [Transformation], Moscow, 1995.

Kryuchkov, V., *Lichnoe Delo* [Personal File], Moscow, 1996.

Layard, R. and Parker, J., *The Coming Russian Boom*, London, 1996.

Lebed, A. I., *Za Derzhavu Obidno* [Farewell to Greatness], Moscow, 1995.

Ledeneva, A., *Russia's Economy of Favours*, Cambridge, 1998.

Lewin, M., *Stalinism and the Seeds of Soviet Reform*, repr. of 1974 edn, London, 1991.

Lieven, A., *Chechnya: Tombstone of Russian Power*, London, 1999.

Lieven, D., *Empire*, London, 2000.

Lloyd, J., *Rebirth of a Nation*, London, 1998.

Lockhart, B., *Memoirs of a British Agent*, London, 1937.

Lukyanov, A., *Perevorot Mnimy I Perevorot Nastoyashchy* [The Pretended Coup and the Real One], Moscow, 1993.

Malia, M., *Russia under Western Eyes*, London, 1999.

Matlock, J., *Autopsy on an Empire*, New York, 1995.

Mau, V., *The Political History of Economic Reform in Russia, 1985–1994*, London, 1996.

Medvedev, Z., *Soviet Agriculture*, London, 1987.

Merrifield, C., *Night of Stone*, London, 2000.

Milosz, C., *The Captive Mind*, London, 1953.

Morrison, J., *Boris Yeltsin*, London, 1991.

Murrell, G. D. G., *Russia's Transition to Democracy*, Brighton, 1997.

Nepomnyashchny, C., *Abram Tertz and the Poetics of Crime*, New Haven, 1995.

Nesterov, M. V., *Vospominaniya* [Memoirs], Moscow, 1985.

Neumann, I. B., *Russia and the Idea of Europe*, London, 1996.

Newhouse, J., *The Nuclear Age*, London, 1989.

Nove, A., *The Soviet Economy*, London, 1961.

Nove, A., *Stalinism and After*, London, 1975.

Nove, A., *Glasnost in Action*, London, 1989.

Owen, T. C., *The Corporation under Russian Law, 1800–1917*, Cambridge, 1991.

Owen, T. C., *Russian Corporate Capitalism from Peter the Great to Perestroika*, Oxford, 1995.

Palazhchenko, P., *My Years with Gorbachev and Shevardnadze*, University Park, Pa., 1997.

Pipes, R., *Russia under the Old Regime*, London, 1974.

Pipes, R., *Russia under the Bolshevik Regime*, London, 1994.

Potemkin, V. P., *Istoriya Diplomatii* [History of Diplomacy], Moscow, 1941.

Pryce-Jones, D., *The War that Never Was*, London, 1995.

Pushkin, A., *Works*, Leningrad, 1978.

Putin, V., *S Pervogo Litsa* [First Person Singular], Moscow, 2000.

Razgon, L., *Nepridumannoe* [Nothing but the Truth], Moscow, 1989.

Riasonovsky, N. V., *A History of Russia*, 2nd edn, Oxford, 1969.

Richards, D. J. and Cockrell, C. R. S., *Russian Views of Pushkin*, Oxford, 1976.

Rieber, A. J., *Merchants and Entrepreneurs in Imperial Russia*, Chapel Hill, N.C., 1982.

Roxburgh, A., *The Second Russian Revolution*, London, 1991.

Ryzhkov, N. I., *Perestroika: Istoriya Predatelstv* [Perestroika: A Story of Betrayal], Moscow, 1992.

Sakwa, R., *Gorbachev and his Reforms, 1985–1990*, London, 1990.

Semler, H. B., *Discovering Moscow*, Wellingborough, 1989.

Shapiro, L., *Russian Studies*, London, 1986.

Shevarnadze, E., *The Future Belongs to Freedom*, London, 1991.

Shevtsova, L., *Yeltsin's Russia: Myths and Reality*, Washington DC, 1999.

Shukman, H. (ed.), *Stalin's Generals*, London, 1993.

Sinyavskyi, A. (Tertz, A.), *Progulki s Pushkinym* [Strolls with Pushkin], Paris, 1989.

Sobchak, A., *Khozhdenie vo Vlast* [The Road to Power], Moscow, 1991.

Solzhenitsyn, A., *Arkhipelag Gulag* [*Gulag Archipelago*], Paris, 1973.

Squire, P. S., *The Third Department: The Political Police in the Russia of Nicholas I*, Cambridge, 1968.

Steele, J., *Eternal Russia*, London, 1994.

Strachey, L., *Eminent Victorians*, London, 1984.

Szamuely, T., *The Russian Tradition*, London, 1974.

Szporluk, R., *Ukraine: A Brief History*, Detroit, 1982.

Thatcher, M., *The Downing Street Years*, London, 1995.

Trenin, D., *The End of Eurasia*, Washington DC, 2001.

Urban, M., *UK Eyes Alpha*, London, 1996.

Utechin, S. V., *Everyman's Concise Encyclopaedia of Russia*, London, 1961.

Vaksberg, A., *The Soviet Mafia*, London, 1991.

Volkogonov, D. A., *Triumf i Tragediya* [Triumph and Tragedy], Moscow, 1990.

Woodman, H., *Ilya Muromets, Type Veh*, Berkhamsted, 2000.

Yakovlev, A. N., *Predislovie, Obval, Posleslovie* [Foreword. Collapse. Afterword.], Moscow, 1992.

Yeltsin, B. N., *Against the Grain*, London, 1990.

Yeltsin, B. N., *The View from the Kremlin*, London, 1994.

Yergin, D. and Gustafson, T., *Russia 2010*, New York, 1991.

Zhirinovsky, V., *Posledni Brosok na Yug* [Last Lunge to the South], Moscow, 1993.

Zuckerman, F. S., *The Tsarist Secret Police*, London, 1996.

Index

Acknowledgements

Russians often ask how I became interested in their country. The answer goes back to my earliest childhood. Anna Collingwood, the wife of my father's fellow conductor at Sadler's Wells Opera, was Russian. Her formidable personality imprinted itself on her family, her way of life, and all her many friends. Some of it rubbed off on me as well.

Professor Boyanus taught me my first words of Russian in 1950. My education continued under my teachers in Cambridge, Peter and Natasha Squire, Lucian Lewitter, and the late Nikolai Andreyev. The Foreign Office then sent me off first to study with Arthur Birse, Churchill's mild-mannered interpreter during many of the great wartime conferences with Stalin; and then to Poland, Moscow, and All Souls College in Oxford, where I spent a further year boning up on Russian history. Deutsche Bank enabled me to return regularly to Russia for a decade after I ceased to be Ambassador there. I am most grateful to all of these for helping me to get to know a fascinating country and its people.

I am also grateful to those who helped more directly in the preparation of this book with their comments, suggestions, and corrections on the manuscript: Michael Alexander, Duncan Allan, Archie Brown, Julie Chechet, Anatoli Chernyaev, Julian Cooper, Geoffrey Hosking, Strobe Talbott, and Dmitri Trenin. Kathy Berton Murrell was immensely helpful in researching the history of the Kharitonenko mansion and making her encyclopaedic knowledge of Moscow and its surroundings generously available.

I could not have functioned in Moscow without my colleagues in the Embassy. Some of them figure in this book, but they are, alas, too numerous to thank individually.

Amongst our many friends in Moscow Jill and I owe particular gratitude for endless hospitality and advice to Yura and Lena Senokosov, and to Marina and the late Sasha Chudakov.

Errors of fact and judgement are my own.